ECONOMIC PHILOSOPHY OF MAHATMA GANDHI

GANDHIAN STUDIES AND PEACE RESEARCH SERIES

1. Gandhian Model of Development and World Peace— **R.P. Misra** (Ed.)
2. Conflict Resolution Through Non-Violence: Role of the Universities—Volume I : Science and Ethics—**K.D. Gangrade** and **R.P. Misra** (Eds.)
3. Conflict Resolution Through Non-Violence: Role of the Universities—Volume II : Development without Destruction— **K.D. Gangrade** and **R.P. Misra**
4. The Social Philosophy of Mahatma Gandhi— **K.S. Bharathi**
5. Gandhian Humanism— **Mohit Chakrabarty**
6. Gandhian Holistic Economics— **Shashi Prabha Sharma**
7. Gandhian Spiritualism : A Quest for the Essence of Excellence— **Mohit Chakrabarty**
8. Gandhian Perspective on Population and Development— **A.K. Sharma**
9. Thoughts of Gandhi and Vinoba: A Comparative Study— **K.S. Bharathi**
10. Economic Philosophy of Mahatma Gandhi— **Shanti Swarup Gupta**

About the Author

Dr. S.S. Gupta (1929-2018) is M.A., Ph.D., D. Litt. He retired as Principal of D.S. Post-Graduate College, Aligarh after 37 years of distinguished service. He has been a good student, a popular teacher and recognised as an able administrator. He held important offices as member of the Executive Council of the Agra University: Director, Principal's Workshop: Secretary, Principal's Association: Member, Zonal Advisory Committee, Life Insurance Corporation of India (Kanpur Zone), Founder Member, Lion's Club. Aligarh, etc. In all these capacities he made bold experiments and got rich experiences. His family background gave him discipline, simplicity, fearlessness and boldness, courage of conviction and love for Indian culture. Dr. Gupta, therefore, writes with conviction. He has a prolific pen. He has always broken new grounds and given new dimension. His important works are: *Economic Philosophy of Mahatma Gandhi, Socio-Politico-Economic set-up in Valmiki Ramayan, Varna-Vyavastha, Castes and Scheduled Castes, Integrated Development Plan for India: Goal, Tools and Strategies. A Draft Plan of the Indian Education. Planning for Academic Excellence, Socio-Economic Survey of College Students, Utilization fo Electricity in the Village*, and dozens of articles. Nobel prize winner, Prof. Gunnar Myrdal and other authors have made use of Dr. Gupta's writings.

GANDHIAN STUDIES AND PEACE RESEARCH SERIES—10

ECONOMIC PHILOSOPHY OF MAHATMA GANDHI

SHANTI SWARUP GUPTA
Vice-Chancellor
Agra Univeristy, Agra

CONCEPT PUBLISHING COMPANY PVT. LTD.
NEW DELHI-110059

ISBN: 978-81-7022-548-5

Edition 2023

Published and Printed by

Concept Since 1974

Concept Publishing Company Pvt. Ltd.
A/15-16, Commercial Block, Mohan Garden,
New Delhi-110059 (India)
T: 91-11-41101460
E: publishing@conceptpub.com, *W*: www.conceptpub.com

PREFACE

Was there ever a man like Gandhi who lived, worked and mesmerized people of India, nay of the World? If a man like Gandhi lived upto January 31, 1948, is he dead now? Gandhi stood for a way of life—Socio-Politico-Economic. What was that life? Is this way of life practicable? Is it good? Is it for India alone or for each country of the World, big or small, strong or weak, rich or poor? such questions continue coming.

India became free in 1947 with a promise that its leaders who were trusted, tested and trained in Gandhian way of life will soon succeed in removing unemployment, poverty, illiteracy and scarcity of essential things of life and succeed in creating a new socio-politico climate. But what has happened in the last half a century. The ambitions of people have been awakened beyond reasonable limits. Unemployment is not less, may be more. Uneven distribution of wealth has increased. We have failed to provide necessities of life like pure drinking water, sanitary conditions, even a small hut to live in, primary education, etc., to the bulk of people and on the other hand, a few lucky ones have multiplied their wealth beyond all reasonable limits. Moreover, life has really become unsafe with ever rising graph of murders, kidnapping, land grabbing and violence—caste, class and religious. It appears mafia people have taken over the command. It has become difficult to find out patriotic people with the result that states after states are becoming centres of anti-national activities. The economic, social and political life are crossing the danger marks. We are likely to be drowned in the rising water of debt, both internal and international. The utility of GATT and other international agreements is debatable. So, the million dollar question is; what can be the alternative?

This forced me to revive my old love. The present work is an outcome of this love.

It has been the rare good luck of persons of my age-group that from our childhood we have seen Gandhi being at the helm of affairs, controlling and directing the destinies of millions of his countrymen, sometimes in politics, and sometimes in economics, but always, step by step, taking us nearer to the much coveted goal of human happiness. For anybody to come under the spell of the greatest man of the century was but natural. So I was no exception to it. I also started revering him and loving him. But this reverence and love was based, I must admit, not on a deep reading and understanding of his philosophy of life. It was due to Gandhi's hypnotic personality. He was considered a hero, a symbol of India's freedom, a first rate humanist and, to crown it all, a saint. But then came the fateful 1947. The partition of the country followed by the unbounded flow of innocent blood left me, like my many countrymen, shocked, bewildered and frustrated. Since such bloodshed breeds anger, so I too was angry. I started asking to myself: Is Gandhi right? Are his teachings doing any good to us or like those of Buddha are they making us impotent and cowards? In that atmosphere of heat and hate a feeling grew within me that I must condemn Gandhi and all that for which he stood. But this condemnation, unlike that of my friends, I decided, should find a basis in scientific and logical reasoning and should flow from a study and analysis of Gandhian ideals. Consequently my reading of Gandhi started. I got a definite direction in 1950, soon after I entered the teaching profession, when I was called upon to supervise a thesis on "The Economic Ideas of Mahatma Gandhi" for the M.A. Degree. Since then my study of Gandhi has continued, sometimes with vigour and sometimes leisurely with the only exception of the three years when I was busy with my Ph.D. work. However, I must admit that the purpose for which these studies had started was thrown, I do not know when, in the wilderness and an inner conviction grew within me that what the frail man of India was saying was neither disjointed, nor nonsense lacking in practicability, nor mere illogical thinking based on half-knowledge. It was a complete, well-knit and logical treatise, which due to shortage of time, and incapacity of the receivers, was given, bit by bit, through utterances and writings and demonstrated through actions. The present work is, therefore, nothing but a modest attempt at collecting, systematising and presenting Gandhi's writings in a manner, which may look logical, coherent and a complete whole.

With time and reading of Gandhi, a feeling took me over that Gandhi was a phenomenon in himself. It is impossible for a single individual to understand and interpret him fully. For this in the words of a great economist, "A Trimurti" is required: A German to collect all necessary and unnecessary data, an Englishman to sort it out and systematise it and a French to write it.

To me, Gandhi represents a beautiful synthesis of the best of the East and the West—He challenges the much advertised slogan, "East is East and West is West and never the twain shall meet". The East represents spiritualism and the West materialism. A dynamic happy combination of both will alone lead the bleeding humanity to permanent happiness and real progress. Today's progress which is nothing but advancement of material comforts at the expense of 'real happiness' is no progress at all. It is stained, as many will readily agree, with the blood of the millions all over the world. Gandhi called a halt to such a progress and indicated the path towards real progress.

Gandhi, like Adam Smith, believed in homogeneity of class interests. He even went a step further and said that there cannot be a clash between nations, if they stick to their just interests. He also believed that life is one and it is wrong to break it, under the plea of specialisation, into water-tight compartments of economics, politics and religion, so he came forward with an integrated plan, socio-politico-economic to revitalise life as a whole.

My well wishers and friends, even at the cost of inconvenience, continued to help me in completing this work which leisurely went on for several decades. To thank them and thereby easily forget their debt is not in my culture. To remember in silence is real thanks giving.

S.S. GUPTA

CONTENTS

1

Biographic Sketch

In order to know Gandhi's economic thinking in the correct perspective, it is essential to have a brief peep into his life and know his mental and psychological make up and how it developed with the passage of time.

For authenticity sake, this brief study is based on the Autobiography of Gandhi and eight volumes of Tendulkar on Mahatma. Further, only important aspects have been selected.

Mohan Dass Karam Chand Gandhi, the saint politician of India, was really a great man. People wondered whether such a man ever walked on earth in twentieth century. Naturally, therefore, the question arises: How Gandhi became such a great man? The question becomes more intriguing when we find that Gandhi, as a child and also as a young man, was a most ordinary one—lean and thin with a weak constitution, shy, coward, always afraid of ghosts, snakes and evil spirits, having weak personality, easily dominated by friends, financially weak, not a brilliant student, not known for sharp intellect, given to carnal pleasures, etc. How such an ordinary man could transform himself into a saint, a Messiah for billions, a thinker, a man with foot on earth, a great fighter and a heroic patriot.

Gandhi's father, Karamchand Gandhi, alias Kaba Gandhi, was a member of Rajasthanik Court where he settled disputes between the chiefs and their fellow clansmen. He became Prime-Minister of Rajkot, a princely state in Gujarat. He married four times, three wives died in quick succession. The forth wife, Putlibai, mother of M.K. Gandhi, bore three sons and one daughter. Youngest of the children was M.K. Gandhi. Gandhi was born on 2nd October 1869—twelve years after the war of independence.

Kaba Gandhi, the father of Mohan Dass was religious, fearless, brave, truthful, generous, practical minded, able administrator, loyal to ruler, ill-tempered and given to carnal pleasures. He had no ambitions to accumulate riches and so left very little for his children. Gandhi's mother, Putlibai, was a saintly lady given to prayers, fasting and visits to temples, she was strong willed, having strong commensense and a sharp intellect.

If genes theory is to be believed then Gandhi must have inherited these parental qualities. It is another thing that some of them might have lied dormant in the early period of life and might have sprouted later on getting the right climate.

How Gandhi could change his personality, how could he transform himself from an ordinary human-being to an extraordinary saintly person, needs a close look. A humble effort has been made in the following lines.

From Fear, Shyness and Cowardice to Fearlessness and Boldness

In childhood Gandhi had fear of ghosts, spirits and serpants.

Gandhi, at the age of 18 years, sailed for England on 4th September, 1887. He had difficulty in communicating in English. So, he could not befriend co-passengers, most of whom were foreigners. He could not even muster courage to enquire which food was vegetarian. His fear was so great that he preferred to take his daily food in his cabin.

While in England, he joined a vegetarian society and was elected to the Executive Committee. However, he could not muster courage to express himself in those meetings. Once he tried to write his thoughts and read them. His nervousness was so great that he could not read his paper.

At Ventnor, the daughter of his landlord, as common practice, took Gandhi to a lovely hill. The fear of falling made it difficult for him to climb to the top and more painful to climb down. The young lady taunted Gandhi althrough.

At Bombay, after return from England, Gandhi took his first case. It was a small case and he had made good preperations. When he got up to cross-examine the plaintiff's witnesses, courage left him and he could not utter a single word.

A small matter concerning Ranasaheb of Porbandar was lying with the Political Agent. This gentleman, in England, was fairly friendly with Gandhi. His brother, who was the secretary and adviser to Ranasaheb forced Gandhi to go to this Political Agent and put a word. The Agent refused to hear him and showed him the door. Gandhi pocketed the insult with pain and had not the courage to protest.

In Africa, Gandhi was travelling from Durban to Pretoria. When the train reached Maritzburg, the capital of Nepal, in spite of valid first class ticket, Gandhi, duc to colour prejudice, was forcibly taken down with the help of a police constable because the whiteman could not tolerate a coloured man in the compartment. The train steamed away. Gandhi had not the courage even to ask for his luggage from the Railway authorities and take out his over-coat. He passed the whole night shivering. But this was the turning point of his life.

Gandhi had to travel from Charlestown to Johnnesburg in a stage coach. First, he was not allowed to sit inside the coach to which he was entitled. In the way the leader of the coach insulted Gandhi further and asked him to sit on foot-board because he wanted to come out from inside to smoke. Gandhi refused and the man belaboured him. On the intervention of white passengers he was saved. This shook Gandhi, "My heart was beating fast within my breast, and I was wondering whether I should ever reach my destination alive".

At Transvaal, Indians were deprived of all their rights. They could not even walk on footpaths and remain out of their houses after 9 p.m. Gandhi used to go for long walks through President street to an open plain. One day, one of the policeman, outside the house of President Kruger, without warning, pushed and kicked Gandhi. A friend, Mr. Goates, saved him and reprimended constable. Gandhi did not thought it worth while to take the case to court.

A reading of Gandhi's Autobiography gives the impression that faith in God and conscious efforts to gradually go from religious culture to spirituality – know thy-self, helped Gandhi to transform his personality.

Mohan had a religious background. Both his parents had a religious culture. Most probably, Gandhi inherited this religious culture.

To overcome the fear of ghots, spirits and serpants, Gandhi's nurse, Ranbha, suggested, as a remedly, the repetition of Ramanama. This must have laid down thc devotion to Lord Rama which continued till last.

A cousin forced Gandhi to remember by heart Rama Raksha-mantra and recite it daily. This must have strengthened religious foundation and devotion to Rama.

Father, while ill, listened to the *Ramayana*. A great devotee of Rama—Ladha Maharaj of Bileshvar was the reader. He had a melodious voice. It was said that Ladha Maharaj had cured himself of leprosy not by any medicine but by the regular repetition of *Ramayana* and applying *bilva* leaves which had been cast away after being offered to the image of lord Mahadeva. Gandhi, who was thirteen then, was enraptured by his readings. That laid the foundation of his deep devotion to the *Ramayana* and Lord Rama.

A friend, whom Gandhi wanted to reform, tried to misguide him. Gandhi was persuaded to take meat and visit brothel. His weakness for carnal desire was a contributing factor. But Gandhi was saved. "I went into the jaws of sin, but God in his infinite mercy protected me against myself. I was almost struck blind and dumb in this den of vice. I sat near the woman on her bed, but I was tongue tied. She naturally lost patience with me, and showed me the door, with abuses and insults... But I have ever since given thanks to God for having saved me". This, and such other incidents, with religious background, must have enhanced Gandhi's faith in God and religion.

Gandhi, learnt religious tolerance from childhood. His parents had equal respect for all branches and sects of Hindu religion—Rama, Shiva, Jain, etc. They visited their temples and invited their saints. A reading of *Manusmriti* (Laws of Manu), a book which he got from his father's collection, did not impress him and inclined him towards atheism.

Gandhi's father had Muslim and Parsi friends. They often talked to him about their own faith and he would listen to them always with respect and often with interest. Gandhi being a nurse to his father had a chance to be present at these talks. Naturally he got influenced and this inculcated in him a toleration for all faiths.

A Gujarati didactic stanza—return good for evil-gripped Gandhi's mind and heart.

Towards the end of second year in England, Gandhi met two theosophists. They talked about *Gita*. Since then Gandhi took a fancy for *Gita*, "The book struck me as one of priceless... I regard it today as the book for excellence. It became a book of daily reading".

Introduction with Madam Blavatsky and Mrs. Besant created an interest in theosophy but it also stimulated a desire to read books on

Hinduism and disabused the nation fostered by the missionaries that Hinduism was rife with superstitions. A friend suggested Gandhi to read *Bible*. He purchased one and read it.

Gandhi, through experience realised "Supplication, workship, prayers are no superstition, they are acts more real then the acts of eating, drinking, sitting or walking... I have not the slightest doubt that prayer is an unfailing means of cleansing the heart of passions. But it must be combined with the utmost humility."

Gandhi was introduced to one Raychand or Rajchandra. He had a phenomenal memory. He had a wide knowledge of scriptures and a burning passion for self-realization. Gandhi was deeply influenced by him but was not prepared to take him as his *Guru*. However, he always sought his advice at the time of spiritual crises. Probably his intimacy with Raychand made Gandhi to go from religion to spirituality, i.e., self-realization and self-correction.

Gandhi decided to go to Africa. On ship he developed friendship with the captain of the ship. At Zanzibar, captain took him for an outing on shore. He was taken to a Negro women's quarter. He was even shown a room. Gandhi feels that only God saved him. This was the third trial of its kind. The incident increased Gandhi's faith in God.

Gandhi read religious books of different religions and came in contact with religious people. Some people tried to get Gandhi converted to their religion as they felt that it is the only way to salvation. Gandhi was not convinced and he did not see any reason to give up his own religion. His guide and philospher, Raychand Bhai's one sentence influenced him. The sentence was: "On a dispassionate view of the question I am convinced that no other religion has the subtle and profound thought of Hinduism, its vision of the soul, or its charity". By this time, Gandhi had learnt to follow the inner-voice.

Gandhi's childhood fears, became a thing of past because of his religious culture, spirituality, i.e., trying to know himself and remove his defects, follow inner-voice, prayer, fasting, social service and unflinching faith in God and His mercy. All this transformed his personality. The boldness and fearlessness inherited by parents helped him.

Gandhi's initial shyness forced him to remain silent, be brief, think and use measured language. This gradually became a virtue. But this shyness disappeared because of the impact of religion, spirituality and deep desire to reform others and do good to others.

Gandhi's cowardice gradually became a thing of the past. This transformation was partly because his experiences, specially at Maritzburg where he had to spent whole night shivering; journey from Charlestown to Johannesburg where he faced humiliation at the hands of the leader of the coach and Transvaal because of coloured prejudices and discriminating laws and partly due to his onword march on the path of spirituality.

From Carnal Desires to Self-control

Gandhi has this to say about his father, Kaba Gandhi; "To a certain extent he might have been given to carnal pleasures. For he married for the fourth time when he was over fourty". It may, therefore, be presumed that Gandhi had also this weakness through inheritance.

Gandhi was betrothed thrice because two of the girls chosen had died. The third betrothel took place when he was seven years old. Therefore, marriage could be solemnized only with the third. This marriage took place when Gandhi was 13 years old.

Gandhi was passionately fond of his wife. "Even at school I used to think of her, and the thought of nightfall and our subsequent meeting was ever haunting me . . . I used to keep her awake till late in the night . . . If with this devouring passion their had not been in me a burning attachment to duty, I should either have fallen a prey to disease and premature death, or have sunk into a burden some existence . . . I was very anxious to teach her, but lustful love left me no time".

Gandhi, inspite of this lust and passion was deeply devoted to her wife and could not think of quenching his thurst at any other place. So, when his friend took him to brothel, not once but several times, he came out clean. "God, in his infinite mercy protected me against myself". Similarly, Gandhi was saved by God when the captain of the ship took him to a Negro women or when attending a vegetarian conference, he took undue liberties from the land-lady.

Father of Gandhi was ill. He, as a devoit son, was nursing him. He was 16 years old. While messaging the leggs of father in night, Gandhi's mind hovered about the bedroom. And as soon as the work was over, he ran to his bed-room. The same thing happened the night his father passed away. He retired at 10.30 p.m. Within 5 to 6 minutes, the father breathed his last. Gandhi called it his shame. He wrote, ". . . if animal passion had not blinded me, I should have been spared the torture of seperation from my father during his last moments".

Gandhi decided, with a view to put his friend at ease, to cultivate accomplishment befitting a polished society. He tried to become an English gentleman. So, he got new clothes at the Army and Navy stores and an evening suit in fashionable Bond Street. He also purchased a chimney—pot hat. He learnt the art of tying tie to look fashionable. He started using brush to keep his hair in position. He joined dancing classes. He purchased a violin and started learning it. This infatuation to become an English gentleman hardly lasted three month.

Gandhi could control his carnal desires partly because of his natural instincts, partly by his efforts and mainly because of the mercy of the Almighty. For example, he could never develop a taste for meat. The pressure of his friend, and a keen desire to become physically strong, which, he was given to understand, meat eating will help, persuaded him to take to meat. But his inborn trait for truth which was strengthened by the story of Harish Chandra, prevented him to give false excuses to his mother of not taking food at home, the day he took meat outside. The fear that when the parents will come to know that he take meat, they will be deeply shocked, was the contributing factor. So, Gandhi resolved not to eat meat. Becharji Swami, who was a Jain monk and a family advisor, took three vows from Gandhi before granting him permission to go to England. One of them was not to touch meat. This vow worked as an armour in England. Then, Gandhi saw that people in England. who were mainly meat eaters, are leaving it and forming vegetarian societies. This strengthened him in his resolve not to take meat. Similarly, habit of smoking, due to paucity of funds, led to first picking up stumps of cigarettes thrown away by his uncle—not a respectable thing, and then to theft. The situation was not satisfactory and in utter disgust, he decided to commit suicide. "I realized that it was not an easy to commit suicide as to contemplate it. The thought of suicide ultimately resulted in his bidding good bye to the habit of smoking".

Shyness of Gandhi, devotion to wife, faith in God and his mercy repeatedly saved Gandhi from the sin of having sexual enjoyment with any other lady except his wife. But then, Gandhi's reading of books on the benefits of vegetarianism and his experiment on diet enabled him to gradually acquire self-control. With diet control, he gradually acquired other methods of self-control.

Later on, Gandhi came to know of *Brahamachary*, i.e. self-control in word, thought and action. The increasing love in persuing the life of a *Brahamachari* and the visible effect of it, made his a better man and a saint.

From Economy via Self-sufficiency to Simplicity

Gandhi was not from an affluent family. As a student probably he was not getting any pocket money. So, when he wanted to smoke cigarettes, he had to resort to stealing from servant's pocket.

As a habit from childhood, Gandhi kept accounts of every penny that he spent and calculated his expenses. Every evening he used to strike balance. In England, soon he started self-introspection and cutting down his expenses. So, he decided to leave the family with whom he was living as paying guest and rent out, first, two room set and thereafter single room; started walking to save fares, etc. It reduced his expenses to half.

Back home, Gandhi tried to be a lawyer. He failed to argue even a small case due to his nervousness and had to return the fee money. He was almost a briefless lawyer. So he walked to High Court and back. This took 45 minute on one side. This saved him money and also from illness. Soon, it became a habit.

Gandhi, through public work and self-introspection. "Learnt the principle of never having more money at one's disposal than necessary".[1] From this, economy in expenses was a natural corollary.

The need to economise forced Gandhi to cut down expenses in South Africa. He started washing his own clothes and ironing them. In the beginning he was ridiculed by the other Barristers. He could not make them appreciate "The beauty of self help".[2] In the same way he freed him-self from slavery to the barber mainly because white barber refused to cut the hairs of Gandhi due to colour prejudice.[3]

Thus seed for self-help and simplicity was sown.

Gandhi insisted on travelling in a third class compartment of Railways for economy sake but primarily to know the condition of third class travelling which was awesome.

In 1903 Theosophist friends wanted Gandhi to tell them something about Hindu religion. So Gandhi started memorising *Gita* and share it with friends. Thus, "*Gita* became an infallible guide of conduct. It became my dictionary of daily reference. I turned to this dictionary of conduct for a ready solution of my troubles and trials, words like *Aparigraha* (non-possession) and *Samabhava* (equability) gripped me . . . How was one to divest oneself of all possession? Was not the body itself possession enough? . . . I could not follow him unless I gave up all I had. . . I understood the *Gita* teaching of non-possession to mean that those who desired salvation should act like the trustee who, though having control over great possessions, regards not an iota of them as his own. It became clear to me as day light that non-possession and equability presupposed a change of heart, a change of attitude . . .".[4]

With the growing simplicity of life, dislike for medicines steadily increased. To get himself relieved of headaches, Gandhi dropped the morning breakfast. The headache disappeared. This led him to conclude that "I was eating more then I needed".[5]

The Phoenix settlement strengthened love for self-help and simplicity.

Gandhi stopped taking tea in 1908. He gave up salt and pulses.

Vegetarianism

Gandhi was vegetarian since birth. After passing High School in 1887, a family friend, Mavji Dave, sold the idea of going to England for a barristers course. Gandhi wanted to be a medico. Family members were opposed to the idea. Ultimately, due to intervention of Becharji Swami, a Jain monk and a family adviser, Gandhi was permitted to go to England after taking three vows – not to touch wine, woman and meat.[6]

Gandhi tried to search out a vegetarian restaurant at London. By chance he saw Salt's Plec for vegetarianism. It impressed him. Thus, the restriction of a vow was replaced by a choice. Gandhi read a number of books, the most important ones being,

(i) Howard William, The Ethics of Diet.
(ii) Dr. Anna Kingsfords, The Perfect Way in Diet.

The result of reading all this massive literature was that dietic experiments came to take an important place in Gandhi's life.

Gandhi joined a vegetarian Society in England and was elected as a member of the Executive Committee. As a result of his experiments, he –

(a) Stopped taking sweets and condiment,
(b) Gave up tea and coffee; and
(c) Gave up starchy food

These experiments were first mainly from the point of view of economy and hygiene, but later on in Africa they were taken with a religious aspect.

Gandhi started a Vegetarian Club but soon it came to an end.

Gandhi took a vow of *Brahmacharya* in 1906. He realised that control of the palate is the first essential in the observance of the vow. His experiment showed him:

(i) Milk diet makes the *Brahmacharya's* vow difficult;
(ii) Fresh fruit and nuts are ideal food;
(iii) Fasting is important for *Brahmacharya* and *Satyagrahi*;
(iv) Gandhi limited the articles of his daily diet to five and took a vow never to eat after dark; and
(v) With what to eat and what not to eat, the quantity should also be reduced to the minimum.

From Truth to Greater Truth

Gandhi was wrongly penalised by the principal of his school under the impression that he has spoken a lie. This pained him. He realised that "a man of truth must also be a man of care".[7]

Gandhi's father was a lover of his clan, truthful, brave and generous.[8] Gandhi inherited these virtues. So even at formative years of his life, he did not resort to untruth. Gandhi records that upto the age of 12 years "I do not remember having ever told a lie".[9] The play, Harishchandra, captured Gandhi's heart. He acted like Harishchandra." Why should not all be truthful like Harishchandra ? was the question I asked myself day and night".[10]

The will to become strong and daring templed Gandhi to take meat. After the feast of meat with his friend outside eating at home was impossible. So, Gandhi had to speak a lie to his mother. This was too much for Gandhi." I abjured meat out of the purity of my desire not to lie to my parents".[11]

Gandhi was a very shy person. He could not speak in the Executive Committee of the Vegetarian Society of England. He failed to even read his speech. He could not speak on the eve of his departure for U.K. To it Gandhi wrote, "I must say that beyond occasionally exposing me to laughter my constitutional shyness has been no disadvantage whatsoever... Its greatest benefit has been that it has taught me the economy of words... experience has taught me that silence is part of the spiritual discipline of a votary of truth. Proneness to exaggerate, to suppress or modify the truth, wittingly or unwittingly, is a natural weakness of man, and silence is necessary in order to surmount it. . . My shyness...has helped me in my discernment of truth."[12]

Gandhi, like the other Indian youths, indulged in an untruth when he posed as a bachelor for companion sake of English girls. But he could not keep up with this untruth for long. So, he wrote a letter and told truth.

In the first public speech in his life in Pretoria, Gandhi pleaded for "observe truthfullness in business".[13]

Gandhi was enrolled as an advocate at Natal. He was asked by the court to remove his turbam which he did. This was not liked by friends. Gandhi wrote, "But all my life through, the very insistence on truth has taught me to appreciate the beauty of compromise. . . But truth is hard as adamant and tender as a blossom".[14]

Natal Govt. sought to impose an annual tax of £25 in 1894 on the indentured Indians. A fierce campaign was organised. Some labour lost their lives and over ten thousand suffered imprisonment. "Truth triumphed in the end. The suffering of the Indians were the expression of that truth".[15]

Insistance on truth forced Gandhi to tell the client to accept a mistake in accounts which was deducted later. Senior councel was not in favour. Gandhi was allowed to accept it. Judge favoured Gandhi because of his truthfulness. In another case, Gandhi found out that the client has spoken a lie as he broke down in witness box. Gandhi appealed for the dismissal of the case. In another case, his friend Rustumji was caught. He was involved in smuggling. He consulted Gandhi. They decided to accept the fault and pay the penalty. Thus, Gandhi proved that truthfulness pay even in legal matters.

From Meat-eating, via Vegetarianism and Self-realization, to Non-violent Non-cooperation (Satyagrah)

The concept of non-violent non-cooperation (*Satyagrah*) was not the result of some well thought out scheme but it evolved gradually. It was the ultimate outcome of family background, experiments on vegetarianism, consistent efforts of self-realization and events as they developed.

Family Background

Gandhi's parents were highly religious. His mother was a sainty lady. She would not think of taking her meals without her daily prayers. Going to Haveli—the Vaishnava temple—was one of her daily duties. She would take the hardest vows and keep them without flinching. And his father had that bind of religious culture which frequent visits to temples and listening to religious discourses provides.[16] He read *Gita* and repeated its verses. Jain monks frequently visited him. Thus, a super-religious atmosphere prevailed in the family. Naturally, Gandhi had a deep impression of this religious atmosphere and culture of the family. Gandhi was deeply devoted to his parents. And in those days Jainism was strong in Gujarat and its influence was felt every where and at all occasions. This gives a clear picture of Gandhi's psychological and mental make up as a child.

Meat-eating

Gandhi, in spite of the advice of mother, elder brother and wife, developed friendship with a class fellow of his elder brother. He had an idea to reform him. This friend convinced Gandhi that meet-eating is necessary to be strong and also for driving out Englishmen from India who are meat-eaters. So, Gandhi took goats meat. He did not relish it. Further, "I had a very bad night after-words. A horrible nightmare haunted me. Every time I dropped off to sleep it would seem as though a live goat were bleating inside me . . .".[17]

Whenever Gandhi took meat thinking it to be a necessity, he could not take food at home and had to lie to his mother. This was too much for a devoted and loyal son. So, he said to himself,

"Though it is essential to eat meat—yet deceiving and lying to one's father and mother is worse than not eating meat. In their life time, therefore, meat-eating, must be out of the question".[18] This also convinced Gandhi that" A reformer can not afford to have close intimacy with him whom he seeks to reform".[19]

Self-Realization

Gandhi was a God-fearing man. Since his childhood he started reading scriptures. Rambha, the maid servant, suggested repetition of Rama nam to overcome fear of Ghosts and spirits. A cousin taught Rama-Raksha. Father gave the taste of *Ramayana*. Gandhi heard *Bhagavat* on every Ekadashi. He read *Manusmriti* which was in his father's collections. Two theosophist friends persuaded him to read *Gita* with them. Thereafter, several books of different religions were read, main being:

(i) Sir Edwin—*The light of Asia*
(ii) Madame Blavatsky—*Key to Theosophy*
(iii) *Bible*
(iv) Carlyle—*Heroes and Hero-worship*
(v) Miss. Besent—*How I became a Theosophist*

Rajchandrabhai impressed Gandhi very much but he could not think of making him his religious *Guru*. He was the real seeker of truth. He wanted to see God face to face.

On his way to Natal the Captain and he became friends. The boat stopped at Mombasa. Captain took Gandhi to a negro women's quarter. It was a grace of God that "When the Captain called me I came out just as I had gone in".[20] Earlier also, a friend took Gandhi to a brothel. The bill had already been paid. "I went into the jaws of sin, but God in His infinite mercy protected me against myself. I was all most struck blind and dumb in this den of vice. I sat near the women on her bed, but I was tongue tied. She naturally lost paitence with me and showed me the door with abuses and insults".[21] In four similar incidents God came to Gandhi's rescue.

In England Gandhi discovered the futility of mere religious knowledge. He realised "Supplication, worship, prayer are no superstition; they are acts more real than the acts of eating, drinking, sitting or walking. It is no exaggeration to say that they alone are real.

all else is unreal".[22] In his life he realised how God saves a man.

Comparative study of religious woke in Gandhi a desire for self-realization. He felt that God can be realised only through service. Gandhi's wrote:

"Here (in Pretoria) it was that the religious spirit within me became a living force..."[23]

"I had long since taught myself to follow the inner voice. I delighted in submitting to it. To act against it would be difficult and painful to me".[24]

Christian believed that we all are sinners. Our attempts alone will not help. Jesus can only save us. So throw sins on Jesus. This did not convince Gandhi. He thought of leading a sinless life. He insisted on Self-purification. Gandhi thought:

1. Knowledge of religion is not sufficient,
2. Prayer, worship, etc are important to realise God,
3. God in His mercy saves man,
4. Self-realization is important. For this one should follow inner voice.

Events As They Enrolled

Events so developed that willy-nilly Gandhi marched on the path of non-violence. Some instances are given below:

1. Abdulla Sheth requested Gandhi to go to Pretoria in connection with a case. The case was against Sheth Tyeb Haji Khan Muhammed who was a near relative of Abdulla Sheth. A first class seat was booked and Gandhi left Durban for Pretoria. The train reached Mortizburg, the capital of Natal, at about 9.00 p.m. A white passenger came and he through two officials, asked Gandhi to go to a van compartment. Gandhi said he had a valid ticket. In spite of this, Gandhi was pushed out and luggage kept at platform. Gandhi spent all night in waiting room. He ultimately decided that "it would be cowardice to run back to India without fulfilling my obligation... I shall try if possible to root out the disease and suffer herdships in the process".[25] Thus one step towards non-violence was took.

2. Gandhi travelled from Charletown to Johannesburg in a stage-coach. With great difficulty, inspite of a valid ticket, Gandhi was allowed to travel in the coach. Gandhi, as a last resort, was given a seat on the coach box where white leader used to sit. He pocketed

this insult. After some time leader wanted to sit where Gandhi was seated. He asked him to sit on the foot-board. The insult was more than what Gandhi could bear. Resistance was met with box on the ear. Effects were made to drop him. Co-passengers came to his rescue.

From Johannesburg Gandhi again travelled in first class to Pretoria. Again the history would have been repeated had the white copassengers not intervened in favour of Gandhi.

These hardships were the second step in the direction of non-violence.

3. When the case was concluded, Gandhi decided to go back to India. The very day the papers revealed the introduction of a Bill which was to deprive Indians of their right to elect members of the Natal Legislative Assembly. Gandhi was told that elders were ignorant and the youngers, educated at Africa, are under the influence of white clergy-men. This opened the eyes of Gandhi. It was decided to oppose this Bill. Gandhi was detained. "Thus God laid the first step of my life in South Africa and sowed the seed of the fight for national self-respect".[26] Volunteers were enrolled. A telegram was dispatched to the Speaker of the Assembly to postpone discussion on the Bill. Speaker postponed it for two days. The petition was drawn and sent to the Speaker, Press etc. It got wide publicity. But the Bill was passed. But it infused a new life in the community. A monster petition was submitted to Lord Ripon, Secretary of State for the colonies. Press supported the Indian demands. Thus Gandhi was drawn to public service and he settled down at Natal. It was the third step in the direction of non-violence.

To continue the opposition of the Act, Natal Indian Congress was found on the 22nd May, 1894. Subscription were raised. Meetings were held to train up people to start thinking and speaking on important matters of public importance. Efforts were made to ventilate the grievances and stimulate thought amongst the young Indians and to propogate so that others may hear and appreciate India's point of view.

4. The condition of indentured Indians was miserable. In 1894, The Natal Government wanted to impose a tax of £25 per family on the indentured Indians who were invited to help white people to cultivate sugarcane. These Indians, after their term of five year, were released from bondage. They settled down at Natal and grew vegetables, Mango and entered trade. This shocked white-men. The

first suggestion was to forcibly repatriate Indians. The second suggestion was to impose an annual tax of £25. Natal Indian Congress organised a fierce compaign against this tax. Viceroy reduced the proposed tax from £25 to £3. "Unflinching faith, great patience and incessant efforts" and insistance on truth brought them success.

5. Gandhi was called back to Africa in 1897. His boat was not allowed to enter the harbours for 23 days under the hope that Gandhi alongwith other Indians will go back. When Gandhi landed, he was spotted and attacked. Stones, brickbats, rotten eggs etc., were herald at him. He was boxed and kicked. He fainted. Mrs. Alexander, wife of the Police Superintendent saved her. Mr. Chamberlain, the then Secretary of States for Colonies cabled asking the Natal Government to prosecute Gandhi's assailant. Gandhi refused to prosecute anybody. He felt that the truth will come out and then people will feel sorry on what they had done. Exactly this happened. Lynching utlimately proved to be a blessing.

6. "Events were so shaping themselves in Johannesburg as to make the self-purification on my part a preliminary as it were to *Satyagraha*... The principle called *Satyagraha* came into being before that name was invented".[27] In Gujarat, it was called 'Passive resistance'. Gandhi offered a nominal prize through Indians Opinion to the readers who made the best suggestion. Manjan Lal Gandhi coined the word *Sadagraha* and won the prize. Gandhi later named it *Satyagraha*.

7. Kasturbabai, started getting haemorrhage. When relief was not coming, Gandhi suggested her to give up salt and pulses. She refused and said that even Gandhi can not give it up when advised. So, Gandhi decided to give up both for one year. She was shocked. This was called Domestic Satyagraha.

8. Raj Kumar Shukla, an agriculturist, acquainted Gandhi in 1916 the woes of Champaran indigo cultivators (a District Head-quater of Bihar). Here the tenant was bound by law to plant three out of every twenty part of his land with indigo for his landlord. Gandhi decided to take up their case. Planters and the Commissioner threatened Gandhi and served with a notice to return. He declined. Thus, he was face to face with *Ahimsa*. He started taking evidence of people and reject which he doubted. This massive evidence was submitted to government and given wide publicity. The Trikathia System was abolished and thus a century old exploitation ended. For disobeying court orders, Gandhi was also prosecuted.

The case was later withdrawn.

9. Shrimati Anasuyabai, sister of mill owner, Shri Ambalal Sarabhai, acquainted Gandhi of the condition of mill workers in Ahmedabad. Gandhi suggested arbitration. Mill owners refused. So, Gandhi advised workers to go on strike. The strike went on for 21 days. Gandhi had to resort to fast to boost up morale and unity of workers. Ultimately a settlement was reached.

10. There was crop failure at Khodic district. The cultivators wanted the revenue assessment for the year suspended. Petitions were sent. Government refussed to hear. So, Gandhi advised the Patiedars to resort to *Satyagraha*. Ultimately the Government agreed if well-to-do cultivators pay the land revenue. Rowlatt bill was passed. Gandhiji, inspite of a very low health, decided to oppose it call of a *hartal* was given. It started on 6th April, 1919. Gandhi called it, 'A Himalayan Mis-calculation" and withdrew it as people were not sufficiently prepared.

These instances increasingly show that Gandhi took to non-violent non-operation as the incidents after incidents unrolled before his and he had no other alternative.

Summing Up

This brief narration will convince anybody that *Satyagraha*, i.e., insistance on truth or non-violent non-cooperation technique to get justice without hard feelings between adversaries is possible only when the soul-force of the Satyagrahi is of high order. For this, vegetarianism and control of palate are the first pre-requisite. Brahamacharya, insistance on truth, religion for self-purification, faith in God. etc., are other necessities.

To Bread-Labour

Gandhi belonged to an upper middle class family and had domestic servants. He stole copper from servants pocket. From here he walked a long distance to self-sufficiency and dignity of labour.

The need to economise laid foundation for self-sufficiency. First he started walking long distances. This proved a boon in disguise. It saved him from illness. Second, he shifted to one room house. Third, he started cooking at home. Later on, he simplified food. Reading of scriptures of different religions revealed to him the greater nececessity of practising religion through prayers, worship, fasting, etc. This opened the royal road of self-realistion and self-purification.

Mr. Polak came to see off Gandhi at station. He gave Ruskins 'Unto This Last'. Gandhi liked it immensely. He even translated it into Gujarati, entitling it *Sarvodaya*. It restrengthened Gandhiji on transforming his life. It taught his the beauty of Bread-Labour.

Ruskin's book, when translated into action, first gave Phoenix Settlement in 1904 in Africa and thereafter *Satyagraha Ashram* in 1915 with 25 men and women. It was later shifted to a place near Sabermati Central Jail with 40 inmates.

Today, these Ashrams, which were centres of political activity and new experiments, are in a poor state of health but they helped Gandhi in evolving his philosphy, may be political, social or economic.

From Loyalty to British Empire to Quit India

Probably, loyalty to rulers was in blood of Gandhi. Gandhi's grandfather, Uttam Chand Gandhi, was a Diwan of princely state of Porbandar. Intrigues compelled him to leave Porbandar and to seek refuge in Junagadh. There he saluted the Nabab with the left hand because the right hand was already pledged to Porbandar.

Gandhi, to begin with, was a loyalist to British Empire to the core. He himself admitted, "Hardly ever have I known anybody to cherish such loyalty as I did to the British constitution. I can see now that my love of truth was at the root of loyalty. . . I believed that the British rule was on the hole beneficial to the ruled".[28] So, in spite of his bitter experiences he struck to his loyalty to British Empire. Following cases can be cited as illustrations.

During his stay at Africa, Gandhi faced several humiliations and launched several agitations yet his loyalty to British empire persisted. For example, at Durban Court, he was asked to take off his turban to humiliate colour barrister.

At Maritzburg, the capital of Natal, at night, he was forcibly moved from first class compartment in spite of a valid ticket.

While travelling in a stage-coach from Charlestown to Johannesburg, inspite of a ticket for the coach, Gandhi was forced to sit on coach-box and thereafter an footboard. He was also beaten to drill fear and complex.

The condition of Indians in the Transvaal and the Orange Free State was worse. They could work only as waiters or menial callings. They had to pay a Toll Tax of £ 3 as fee for entering into the Transvaal. They could not walk on public footpaths and could not move out of doors after 9.00 p.m. One day a police-man pushed and kicked Gandhi.

Indian Franchise Bill was introduced to deprive Indians in Natal of their legal rights. Gandhi was persuaded to stay back and fight for national self-respect.

When Natal Government sought to impose a tax of 25 in 1894 on the Indentured Indians, and due to fierce campaign it was reduced to £3.

On return to Durban in 1897, Gandhi was forced to wait for 23 days on boat under one pretext or the other and was later attacked by white people for the simple crime of organising colour people.

Mr. Chamberlain gave a cold shoulder to the Indian deputation who demanded a seperate Department for Asiatics to control return to Transvaal.

Indians were treated like untouchables and were forced to live outside town in South Aftrica. In Johannesburg there was a location where the Indians had property rights. Municipality wanted to disposses the settlers. Gandhi fought cases. He won and the municipality had to pay compensation. But at the time of Black Plague, hardly any relief or help was provided either by the municipality or the government.

In spite of all this, Gandhi's loyalty to British Empire persisted. When the Boer war was declared Gandhi's personal sympathies were all with the Boers but inspite of this he said "My loyalty to the British rule drove me to participation with the British in the war".[29]

Zulu rebellion broke out in Natal against the atrocities of the rulers. Gandhi offered to serve British by working in Ambulance corp. He said "I saw that there was nothing to justify the name of rebellion...At any rate my heart was with the Zulus" and yet he "believed that the British Empire existed for the welfare of the world. A genuine sense of loyalty prevented me from even wishing ill to the Empire".

The First World War broke out. "I felt that Indians residing in England ought to do their bit in the War. . .[30] A number of objections. . . We were slaves and they were masters. I felt then that it was more the fault of Individual British official than of the British system, and that we could convert them by love". "I thought that England's need should not be turned into our opportunity".[31] So Gandhi offered to help in recruitment of soldiers.

But at last, a turning point came. Gandhi said "But of, having lost my faith in the system, I refuse to cooperate with the British Government today".[32]

It was Champaran experience which started changing heart of Gandhi. He realised that the British system is not good. "That day in Champaran was an unforgettable event in my life of a red letter day for the peasant and for me".[33]

The Kheda Satyagraha, which was started to get the revenue assessment for the year suspended due to wide-spread crops failure, convinced Gandhi that British Government is not fair.

Gandhi wrote a long letter to Viceroy for not attending a conference meant for recruitment in First War. "I love the English nation and I wish to evoke in Indian the loyalty of Englishmen".[34] But "Performance of duty automatically confers a corresponding right".[35] Gandhi found it missing. He wrote, "disappointment of hope means disillusion"[36] and at last Gandhi got disillusioned.

Face to Face with Untouchability

Studies of scriptures revealed Gandhi that *Varnas* were not castes. In *Varna*, there was no concept of higher and lower and the question of untouchability never arose. In early vedic period, people lived in clans and lead a nomad life. These clans attacked each other and took mainly ladies and some strong young men as prisoners. They were known as *Daas* or *Daasi*. With passage of time, they got absorbed in the clan. At that time there was neither the institution of marriage nor of a family. Later on, when techniques of cultivation were discovered these clan started settling down in what was later called villages. From the beginning, there was a division of work which was the basis of *Varna*. *Veda* says that all are born *Shudras*. Then hymn says that from different parts of super-man different Varnas were born. Another hymn says that from the different parts of super-man, Sun, Moon and Stars were born. This simply means that the Veda is describing the creation of universe, how and when life came on earth and its different stages of progress. Therefore, to conclude hastely from the utterances or writings of Gandhi that he believed in Varna-Vyavastha, i.e., caste system, on the basis of birth, is doing the greatest injustice to him. He believed in Varna-Vyavastha which was not caste system. Even Manu, the much maligned social scientist, only tried to codify Varna-Vyavastha so that different rules and practices prevalent in different parts of the country then may have an uniformity and the society may get better organised. Here again, the concept of caste-system was not there. It came much later, when due to progress of the society, a stage was reached when Varna, i.e., the devision of the society on the basis of broad division of work, could not hold good. Several new professions cropped up and so Varna-Vyavastha gave way and degenerated into castes and later on, in sub-castes.

Caste-system in modern India is considered a symbol of discrimination, social injustice and dividing society in an hierarchical order and so bad and condemnable. How a believer in Truth, Non-violence, Dignity of labour, etc., could subscribe to this stinking system?

Gandhi faced humiliation, discrimination, physical and emotional torture in South Africa due to a similar caste-system known by a different name, i.e., white versus non-whites. A man who fought against this caste-system could certaining not be its advocator. The following instances taken from his *Autobiography*, etc., will reveal the truth.

Before the instance of humiliation of Gandhi are described, one more fact deserves mentioning. In India, the Indian Constitution refers to Scheduled Castes, Scheduled Tribes and Backward Classes. However, it does not give, nor any subsequent Government publication provides, the exact number of Scheduled Castes or the number of Scheduled Tribes or number of Backward Classes of whole of India. It is also a pity that the number and names of these Scheduled Castes, which are untouchables, are also not mentioned. This gives an erronious impression that all Scheduled Castes are untouchables.

G.O. No. 1432/26-3-86-11(v.s.) Dated 10.7.1986 informs us that U.P. has 66 Scheduled Castes, 5 Scheduled Tribes and 21 Backward Classes. Out of these 66 Scheduled Castes mainly two—*Valmiki* and *Dom* are untouchables.

In Africa, Gandhi tested untouchability as practiced by white rulers. Here are some important and widely known instances :

1. At Durban Court, the white magistrate asked Gandhi, a black barrister, to take off his turban. This was height of humiliation for a

self-respecting man.

2. All Indians were called *Coolies* or *Samis*.

3. At Mortizburg, inspite of a first class ticket, Gandhi was forcibly removed from the compartment as white co-passengers refused to travel with a black. He spent all night on the platform shivering and thinking of his plight.

4. From Charlestown to Johannesburg, Gandhi had to travel in a stage coach. Inspite of a ticket, he was forced to sit on coachbox. Later on, he was beaten for not agreeing to sit on the foot-board. Probably such physical torture is hardly given by upper castes in India to their Scheduled Caste brotherens.

5. In the Orange Free State, Indians were deprived of all their rights by a special law enacted in 1888. They could not come out of their houses after 9.00 p.m. and they could not walk on footpaths. Gandhi got a letter authorising him to walk in night. Yet he was pushed and kicked by a constable.

6. On his return to Africa in 1897, Gandhi along with other Indian passengers, was not allowed to land for 23 days under the pretext that they might have brought plague to Africa. Thereafter, he was attacked and humiliated on his way to his home, for the fault of being a black and trying to organise Indians. Probably such treatment was rarely given to untouchables in this country.

7. A leper met Gandhi and sought his help. Gandhi offered him shelter and dressed his wounds. Later, he started attending patients for two hours a day in a small hospital. Probably, even the scheduled caste people will not be willing to serve a leper brother.

8. In Natal, a charge was made against the Indians that they are slovenly in their habits and do not keep the house and surroundings clean. Gandhi tried to educate his countrymen. He played an active role when plague was reported in Durban.

9. Just as in India, untouchables are relegated to remote quarters of a town or a village, similarly in Africa, Indians were given *coolie* locations or *Ghettoes*. There was a criminal negligence of the municipality. Luckily, plague broke out in one of the gold mines and not in the *coolie* locations. Gandhi plunged in the relief work. Later, municipality wanted to evict Indians and burn the Ghettoes. Gandhi fought legal cases and got the municipality to pay compensation. Thus, he fought for "untouchables", both Indians and other blacks in Africa.

10. Gandhi returned to India in 1901 and attended Congress

Session at Calcutta. There he observed uncleanliness. He took a broom and cleaned a latrine.

Gandhi opened the chapter of Harijan welfare work in India in 1920, to be more correct in 1896. Plague brokeout in Bombay. Gandhi offered his services to sanitation department. A committee was formed. Gandhi insisted on visiting latrines of each house. He made suggestions. He also visited the localities of depressed classes and was widely shocked when told that they had no latrines. He observed that his suggestions were more readily agreed by the depressed classes than the upper castes.

At 12.40 in the night, August 1, 1920, Lokamanya Tilak passed away. Gandhi reached Bombay. The funeral procession included people of all religions and all castes. Tilak was a Brahmin and some of his relatives desired that only Brahmins should lift the bier. Gandhi was prevented to lift one end of the bier. Gandhi stood up for a moment and said, "Public man know no caste." He bent down again and lifted one end of the bier.

The Congress was held at Nagpur on December 26, 1920 under the Presidentship of Vijayaraghavachari. In this congress, for the first time Gandhi moved a resolution on removal of untouchability which was passed. From then Gandhi never saw backward.

Gandhi established an Ashram on May 25, 1915 which was known as "Satyagraha Ashram". Hardly a few months had passed that Gandhi was put to a test. Amrit Lal Thakkar wrote a letter to Gandhi asking him whether an untouchable family will be welcomed in the Ashram. All the inmates of the Ashram agreed to accept the family. This created a series of problems. First, the man in charge of water-lift started looking at the Ashramites as if they were all untouchables. The strict discipline of *Satyagrahis* ultimately put to shame the man. Secondly, the monetry help was stopped. But God proved kinder. An unknown Sheth donated Rs. 13,000. This shook, as Gandhiji observed, the untouchability to its foundations.

Gandhi was arrested on May 4, 1930 for salt satyagraha. He was released on January 25, 1931. He left for England to attend Round Table Conference on September 15, 1931. Gandhi demanded adult suffrage and suggested indirect elections through village Panchayats. He opposed seperate electorate for depressed classes. On his return to India, Gandhi resumed the civil disobedience movement. He was arrested on January 4, 1932 and put in the Yeraveda Jail. It was followed by issuing four ordinances supressing civil liberty. Ruthless supression started. During the first four months there were 80,000 arrests even when people were leaderless. Then came the news that the Government has decided to give communal award. Gandhi gave a notice to the British Government that he proposes to go on a "fast unto death" if this is done. But the Government announced the provisional scheme of minority representation commonly called the communal award of August 17, 1932.

Gandhi started his 'fast upto death' on September 20, 1932. This shook India. Dr. Ambedkar called it a "Political Stunt". Gandhi said, "My fast I want to throw in the scales of justice, and to wakes up caste Hindus from their slumber, and if they are roused to a sense of duty, it will have served its purpose". The fast had the desired results. The caste Hindus fraternized with the untouchables and mixed freely in thousands of meetings. Soon, a large number of temples were thrown open to the untouchables. A meeting of leaders was held in which efforts were made to find out a solution. Dr. Ambedkar changed his attitude. A pact was drafted in which both wings of the depressed classes—one owning allegience to Dr. Ambedkar and the other to Dr. M.C. Rajesh . . . were willing parties. The caste Hindus, including, Malaviya were also party to it. This pact was sent to London for the cabinets acceptance. The cabinet accepted it. Meanwhile, Gandhi's health had entered the danger zone. At last Gandhi broke his fast on September 26, 1932.

Throughout India, Untouchability Abolition Week was observed from September 27, 1932 to October 2, 1932.

Gandhi was not allowed to carry out his work on untouchability from jail, but later on, in Novemeber 1932, he was allowed to carry on his work. So, Gandhi appealed his countrymen to intensify campaign against untouchability. Naturally, the question that started agitating the public mind was whether civil disobedience is more important or the erradication of untouchability. Meanwhile, Gandhi gave out his intention to again go on fast if caste Hindu do not open the doors of temples for untouchables.

Government allowed Ranga Ayer to introduce Untouchability Abolition Bill on January 23, 1933 but did not permit Dr. Subbarayans to introduce Temples Entry Bill.

Gandhi got a call from within to go on fast. So, he declared his 21 days fast from May 8, 1933 to May 29, 1933. This was mainly to arouse his countrymen against the evil of untouchability. He was released on May 8. 1933.

Gandhi participated, inspite of his weakness, in the inter caste marriage of his son, Devdas with Laxmi, daughter of C. Rajagopalachari.

Gandhi disbanded 18 years old Satyagraha Ashram, commonly known as Sabarmati Ashram and offered it to the government, as Gandhi had decided not to pay revenue dues. All the 33 Ashramites decided to march from the Ashram to Ras on 31st of July 1933.

Gandhi was again arrested on August 1, 1933 and taken to first Sabarmati jail and then to Yerveda jail on the charge of active incitements to continuance and intensification of civil disobedience. He was released on August 4, 1933 with orders not to leave Pune city. Gandhi made it clear that he will not obey the orders. So, he was again arrested, tried and imprisoned for one year. Gandhi was also refused the permission to continue Harijan work from jail. Gandhi, therefore, decided to go on hunger strike if not permitted to continue Harijan work. Government allowed him the facilities. Gandhi thought that facilities were insufficient and so commenced a fast upto death on August 16, 1933. On August 23, 1933, he entered the danger zone and so was released unconditionaly. It was with this background that Gandhi decided that for the remaining imprisonment period he will do only Harijan work.

Gandhi started his nine months Harijan Tour on November 7, 1933 with the sole purpose of awakening Hindu masses to the necessity to give up untouchability. In these nine months, i.e., November 7, 1933 to August 2, 1934, he travelled 12500 miles by car, train and on foot and collected more than 8 lakh rupees for the Harijan cause. He visited Wardha, Nagpur, Katol, Amraoti (Berar), Raipur, Anantpur, Jubbulpore, Mandla, Delhi, Bezwada, Masulipatanam, Madras, Guntur, Cocanada, Ellore, Rajahmundry, Vizagapatanam, Badanval, Bangalore, Malabar, Guruvayur, Badagava, Calicut, Kottayam, Alleppey, Trivandrum, Nagercoial, Tinnevelly, Madurai, Muzaffarpur, Darbhanga, Madhubani, Bhagalpur, Saharsa, Monghyre, Patna, Rupsi, Deoghar, Jassidi, Ranchi, Jhorsaguda, Puri, Harikrishnapur, Chandapur, Balianta, Cuttack and Banaras

Some quotable sentences from his speeches and writings are worth mentioning here.

1. At the meeting at Selu, Gandhi observed :

"It has been my firm belief for the last fifty years that there is

> no place in Hindusim for untouchability as we are observing it today...I should consider the sacrifice of my life as none to great for the sacred cause of the removal of this curse of untouchability. And, I have not a shadow of a doubt in my mind that if untouchability is not removed by root and branch, then Hinduism is bound to perish, for no religion can ever nurture itself on the degradation of its Votaries".[37]

2. At Amraoti, Gandhi said, "I would ask you to trust me when I say that there is no political motive behind my Harijan work. The political consequences of the removal of untouchability have no attraction for me."[38]

3. "For me, the money you give is a token of your identification with the Harijan cause." "Mere money will not avail; I must have your heart also with your money".[39]

4. "Harijan service is a religious obligation. There is no room in it for cunning. It has to be absolutely truthful and non-violent. It can be accompanished only by sacrifice and penance."[40]

5. "It can be demonstrated that by our shoddy treatment of Harijans we not only lose spiritually, but also materially".[41]

6. "If we approached this question with any political motive, we should fail to serve Harijans and we world damage Hinduism".[42]

7. "Temples are meant for sinners, where they can wash their sins. What is the use of temples to a liberated sinless soul, who sees God everywhere ? If you believe that Harijans are in their present plight as a result of their past sins, you must concede that they have the first right of worship in temples. God has been described by all the scriptures of the world as a protector and saviour of the sinner".[43]

8. "If you consider Harijans untouchables because they perform services, what mother has not done such service for her children ? It is the height of injustice to consider Harijans, who are the most useful servant of society as untouchables and outcastes".[44]

9. "We shall dig our own grave if we do not purge ourselves of this curse of untouchability...Let us awake to the sense of this sin and save, before it is too late, ourselves and our religion from going to prediction".[45]

10. I have not hesitated to say that if untouchability lives, Hinduism dies".[46]

11. To Harijans Gandhi gave his usual advice of self-improvement : "You should wash your children everyday, and so

should you wash yourselves. In the morning you should have what I call internal wash, that is to say, the first thing you should do on getting up is to take to Ramanam and pray to God that you should pass the day in scaredness, so that no wrong word may pass your lips and no wrong act may be done by you. Then you should give yourselves an external wash".[47]

When Gandhi was told that Harijans of the locality have given up eating beef, he said :

"I would like you to be able to say the same thing about drink. What is the use of paying for some coloured water which makes us so mad that we forget to distinction between mother, wife and sister".[48]

12."If this untouchability is not removed root and branch from Hinduism, Hinduism is bound to perish. I would not have untouchability removed by force or show of force or compulsion of any kind whatsoever. Removal of untouchability is not a matter of law or of compulsion, but it is a matter of change of heart, perfect purification on the part of millions of Hindus".[49]

12. It is totally wrong to believe that when Harijans are economically lifted, all their woes will be over".[50]

13. "I share the belief with the whole world, civilized and uncivilized, that calamities such as the Bihar one (Earthquake) come to mankind as chastisement for their sins. I regard untouchability as such a grave sin as to warrant divine chastisement ..."[51]

Gandhi's utterances on the earthquake brought a sharp rejoinder from Rabindra Nath Tagore. He said, "I am compelled to utter a truism in asserting that physical catastrophies have their inevitables and exclusive origin in certain combination of physical facts". To this, Gandhi wrote in Harijan of February 16, 1934.

"To me, the earthquake was no caprice of God, nor a result of a meeting of mere blind forces. We do not know the laws of God nor their working. Knowledge of the tallest scientist or the specialist is like a particle of dust...I believe literally that not a leaf moves but by His will. Every breath I take depends upon His sufferance.

"He and His laws are one. The law is God... I do believe with Gurudev in the exorableness of the universal law in the working of which God himself never interferes. So, God is the Law. But I submit that we do not know the law or all the laws fully, and what appears to us as catastrophes are so only, because we do not know the universal laws sufficiently.

"Visitations like droughts, floods, earthquakes and the like, though they seem to have only physical origins, are to me, somehow connected with man's, morals...I have the faith that our own sins have more force to ruin the structure than any mere physical phenomenon. There is an indissoluble marriage between matter and spirit".[52]

14. "Awake, arise and realize the sin which you have inherited and harboured. Purify Hinduism, or it and we perish".[53]

The narration of Gandhi's tour to awaken Hindu society will be incomplete without the mention of one instance, amongst dozens, to show his magic. Gandhi wrote in *Harijan* about a touching scene of January 13, 1934 of Badagara.

"I had finished my speaking and was selling the presents received when gently walked up to the platform Kaumudi, a girl sixteen years old. She took out one bangle and asked me if I would give my autograph. I was preparing to give it. When off came the other bangle. She had only one on each hand. I said, "You need not give me both. I shall give you the autograph for one bangle only."

"She replied by taking off her golden necklace . . . Her hands automatically went to her ears and out came her jwelled ear-rings amid the ringing cheers of the public... I reminded Kaumudi that she was not to have the ornaments replaced. She resolutely asserted to the condition. Gandhi asked her several questions. The last one was, "But when you get married...Your husband will, perhaps, not like to see you without any ornament. What will you do then ?" Kaumudi said, "I will select a husband who will not compel me to wear ornament." Gandhi wrote that she kept her promise to the last.[54]

On the initiative of Gandhi, All India Village Industries Association was born on December 14, 1934 at Wardha. Gandhi wrote in *Harijan* dated November 16, 1934.

"The idea of forming the Association took definite shape during the Harijan tour as early as when I entered Malabar. A casual talk with a Khadi worker showed to me how necessary it was to have a body that would make an honest attempt to return to the villages what has been cruelly and thoughtlessly snatched away from them by the city dwellers. The hardest hit among the villagers are the Harijans. They have but a limited choice of the industries that are open to the villagers in general. Therefore, when their industries slip away from their hands, they become like the beasts of burden with their lot is Cast".[55]

This shows that Gandhi came to know that the craftsmen in

villages were mainly Harijans (i.e. Scheduled Castes, Scheduled Tribes and Backward Classes). So, to improve their economic condition and provide them work at their homes, he thought out the idea of revival of village industries. No greater service to Harijans could be contemplated. Incidently, this revolution should show what type of harmonious and good relations existed in India between caste Hindus and Depressed Classes and whether untouchability was a myth or a reality.

At Nasik, on October 13, 1955, on the initiative of Dr. Ambedker, Depressed Class Conference adopted a resolution recommending a complete serverance of the Depressed Classes from the Hindu fold. At this 800 Harijan youths burnt Manusmriti. Gandhi, thereupon through his articles in Harijan, interviews and speeches clearly stated that conversion of innocent and ingnorant Harijans to different faiths – christianity, Islam etc. is not justified.

Gandhi, wrote, "The present caste system is the very antithesis of Varnashram".[56]

Gandhi went on insisting that temples be opened to Harijans. He congratulated Travancore ruler for throwing open all state temples to Harijans in 1936.

Gandhi came out with the idea that "the ideal *bhangi* – would be a Brahmin par excellence – A *Bhangi* does for society what a mother does for her baby – The Brahmin's duty is to look after the sanitation of the soul – the Brahmin generally does not live up to his duty".[57]

In the Executive Committee of Harijan Sewak Sangh in September, 1935 a resolution was passed saying, "Resolved the efforts be made for the cordination of the activities of the Charkha, Gram Udyog and Harijan Sevak Sangh."[58]

Gandhi, in 1939, said, "For there is only one Varna today – all of us are shudras – ."[59]

Gandhi habitually started living in *Bhangi's* quarters. Explaining the reason for this decision, Gandhi wrote in *Harijan* of March 31, 1948, "I have for some time being saying that we must all be *bhangis* or untouchables. But it has worried me that I have not accorded the statement with corresponding action. It may not be possible to establish complete accordance with the wish. But it ought to be done so far as possible". So, Gandhi started living in *Bhangi* colonies.

Untouchables started agitation against Gandhi. But he kept cool. In 1946, several questions were posed; viz.,

What is going to be the place of the untouchable as a minority ? Gandhi said that they are not a minority. Harijans are a minority, if Brahmins, Ksatriyas and Vaishyas are a minority.,

Gandhi welcomed the idea of inter-caste marriages between Harijans and upper-castes.

On the initiative of Gandhi Sheth Shablal of Ahmedabad formerly dedicated Satish Kunj at Panchgari for the use of poor, including Harijans.

In 1947, Gandhi opined. "I would rejoice to think that we had a mehtar girl of stout heart, in corruptible and of crystal like purity to be our first President".

REFERENCES

1. Gandhi, M.K., *Autobiography*, p. 109
2. Ibid, p. 155
3. Ibid, p. 155
4. Ibid, p. 195
5. Ibid, p. 198
6. Ibid, p. 28
7. Ibid, p. 12
8. Ibid, p. 1
9. Ibid, p. 5
10. Ibid, p. 6
11. Ibid, p. 17
12. Ibid, p. 45
13. Ibid, p. 91
14. Ibid, p. 107
15. Ibid, p. 114
16. Ibid, p. 4
17. Ibid, p. 16
18. Ibid, p. 17
19. Ibid, p. 14
20. Ibid, p. 75
21. Ibid, p. 17
22. Ibid, p. 51
23. Ibid, p. 95
24. Ibid, p. 98
25. Ibid, p. 81
26. Ibid, p. 100
27. Ibid, p. 235
28. Ibid, p. 124
29. Ibid, p. 156
30. Ibid, p. 255
31. Ibid, p. 256
32. Ibid, p. 25

33. Ibid, p. 304
34. Ibid, p. 331
35. Ibid, p. 330
36. Ibid, p. 330
37. Tendulker, D.G., Mahatma , Vol, III, p. 267
38. Ibid, p. 276
39. Ibid, p. 273
40. Ibid, p. 275
41. Ibid, p. 275
42. Ibid, p. 276
43. Ibid, p. 282
44. Ibid, p. 283
45. Ibid, p. 287
46. Ibid, p. 288
47. Ibid, p. 292
48. Ibid, p. 282
49. Ibid, p. 295
50. Ibid, p. 298
51. Ibid, p. 305
52. Ibid, pp. 305-09
53. Ibid, p. 332
54. Ibid, pp. 296-98
55. Ibid, p. 3
56. Ibid, p. 51
57. Ibid, p. 128
58. Ibid, p. 48
59. Ibid, p. 117

2

Why All's Not Well with the World

A study of the History of Economic Thought clearly shows that since the very beginning man has been in search of answers to two questions, viz., 'what is wrong with our present world?' and 'what should be done to improve matters?' Take, for example, the fore runners of economic science, the Mercantilists. They looked around and found out that for human happiness it was essential that a nation should have ever increasing stocks of gold and silver, because that represented strength. So, a philosophy of restrictions and emphasis on exports followed. A trial of this philosophy for a century or so showed that the nations and the world at large could not be happier than what they had been.

As a reaction, a new philosophy, in the form of physiocracy, grew which advised peoples to seek for solace in mother nature and asked people to revert back to agriculture. The people, in search of happiness, followed that philosophy but matters remained where they were.

Then came the Master, Adam Smith. He laid down the foundations of what is today known as Classical Economics or *laissez-faire* Economics or Capitalistic Economics. The spell of the Master tempted people to believe that industrialization, free play of forces, private ownership and the minimum interference by the Government, would improve matters. For some time the countries which followed this advice seemed to prosper. It was felt that the key to happiness and a passport to heaven had been found out.

Next came a succession of giant followers, such as Ricardo, Malthus, Mill and Marshall, to name only a few, to broaden the path laid by the Master and smoothern it out by trying to solve a few knotty problems left-solved or not solved properly. But, alas! The mass of people in general and the thinkers in particular again started asking the age-old question 'Are we happier than before?' The answer was certainly not in the affirmative.

The revolt was started by Sismondi who disagreed with the Classical School on the aims and methods of economic study and criticised the growing use of machines. St. Simon was also no believer. He wanted to build an Industrial Society and reorganize the Government. Fedric list, for the first time, raised the slogan against the much repeated theory of Free Trade of Adam Smith and convincingly pleaded the case of Protective Trade. Robert Owen was also dissatisfied with the then prevailing society and was anxious to build up a new society on the basis of cooperation. P.J. Proudhan, J.K. Rodbertus and, to crown them all, Karl Marx, the father of Socialism, gave the greatest jolt to the capitalist world. Under these growing criticisms, the classical doctrines could not hold the fort for long and were substantially modified by Marshall, Keynes, Schumpeter and others.

However, it is to be noted here that all the economists of the West, whether the followers of the classical school and its critics, or the propounders and followers of socialism of different shades and colours, wanted material advancement of men, because they thought that human happiness and material progress go together. Hence, the emphasis on industrialization, large scale production, growing automation, ever increasing wants etc., is visible in all the existing systems. The only difference between socialist thinkers and classical school economists, it can safely be said, centres round the problem of distribution and ownership of means of production.

When the two so called rival systems were preparing themselves for a fight the first Armageddon came as a bolt from the blue. The people were shocked by its destructive and calamitous effects, which it produced on the world. The people, however, led themselves into the delusion that it was a mere accident, an event occurring due to the careless handling of mutual differences among various countries. A world organization sprang up to decide and settle international issues by negotiations. A period of peace followed. Prosperity and progress appeared to march hand-in-hand.

But the reign of peace was suddenly thrown out of gear. The world organization seemed to crumble down. Destruction seemed to pervade all walks of life. Life was no more a pleasure-ride. Countries no longer seemed to march towards prosperity of the masses, the welfare of the common man. Everything was in turmoil. This was the beginning of the Second World War. It left men with intelligence gaping, thinking, brooding and retrospecting. Something fundamentally wrong seemed to be there in the thoughts, actions and behaviour of the politicians, economists and philosophers. It appeared that either the aims or the methods, or both were wrong. A review to find out the fault seemed essential. The result of all this thinking and brooding was the establishment of the United Nations with all its allied agencies. Yet the goal—human happiness, peace and prosperity—appears to be as distant as it used to be and the clouds of a third world war are gathering which rain in local form sometimes in Korea, sometimes in Cuba, sometimes in Vietnam, sometimes in Indo-China or on Indo-Pakistan borders and sometimes in different parts of South Africa and Europe. Though material comforts are increasing but with them are also increasing tensions, diseases, anxiety and unhappiness. The world has ceased to be a place worth living with so much misery all around.

This brief review of the Western economic thought reveals that no one in the accident has so far been able to answer the basic questions adequately. All the experiments made in the garb of different 'isms' have failed to deliver the goods to the commoner. It will, therefore, be worthwhile to turn Eastward and try to search out the answers to the two important questions in the outpourings of oriental thinkers, philosophers and men of action. Gandhi lived with us and was well-versed in the way of life and thought of both the East and the West. He is, therefore, ideally suited to be able to answer these knotty questions. So let us turn to what he has to say in answer to these questions.

Gandhi, the Mahatma of India, earnestly believed that there is not much to choose between capitalism and communism. The malady is not merely confined, as the western economists wish us to believe, to the ownership of means or the distribution of the produce. It is more deep-rooted. He was of the opinion that the present day unrest is due mainly to our laying too much emphasis on matter and material comforts to the complete neglect of moral values. He argued with us, on the basis of his vast experience and great learning, that our misfortunes were due to three factors:

1. Ever Increasing Wants,
2. Growing Use of Complicated Machines, and

3. Methods of Distribution.

It will be worthwhile to analyse these factors from the Gandhian point of view in some detail.

I
EVER INCREASING WANTS

Gandhi is of the opinion that the first important factor responsible for driving the world away from peace, happiness and real prosperity is the idea that multiplicity of wants, even beyond a minimum, and happiness are directly related. The people trained in the western ideology seem to differ from him. It is, therefore, worthwhile to find out the truth.

The aim of consumption, we are told by an economist, is to get maximum satisfaction, i.e. happiness. But what is happiness? Does it mean that the person who consumes greater number of goods is necessarily a happy man? An economist, trained in the western ideology, will say, 'Yes' but a Gandhi, or a Ruskin would say 'No'. Ruskin feels that true happiness lies in providing the body with the essential things of life and helping others also in getting them. He once wrote, ".....that man is the richest, who having perfected the functions of his life to the utmost, has also the widest helpful influence, both personal and by means of his possessions, over the lives of others."[1] Gandhi also feels that happiness relates not merely to bodily and material needs but also to all those innumerable items that go to enrich and ennoble life and raise it above the level of mere physical existence. He once observed:

> "The itch to own things for the mere pride of possession is the disease of petty, vulgar minds. 'I do not know how it is', said a very rich man in my hearing, 'but when I am in London, I want to be in the country and when I am in the country I want to be in London.' He was not wanting to escape from London or the country but from himself. He had sold himself to his great possessions and was bankrupt. In the words of a great teacher, 'his hands were full but his soul was empty, and an empty soul makes an empty world.' There was wisdom as well as wit in that saying of the Volobbs that 'he who was born first has the greatest number of clothes.' It is not bad rule for the pilgrimage

of this world to travel light and leave the luggage to those who take a pride in its abundance."[2]

It will not be out of place to mention here that similarity of ideas exists between Gandhi and Prof. J.K. Mehta of the Allahabad University. Prof. Mehta argues with his counterparts of the west that there is a difference between 'pleasure' and 'happiness'. Westerners tell us that wants are unlimited and men cannot satisfy all of them. Hence, to maximise his satisfaction, i.e. utility, he selects only the most urgently needed wants. But how is this urgency to be found ? Prof. Mehta tells us that want is felt as the most intense which causes the maximum amount of pain. And the intensity of pain is equal to the pleasure that its removal can give. The pain of a want is felt in proportion to the memory of the pleasure obtained on a previous occasion by the removal of a similar want. It is the utility obtained in the past by the satisfaction of such a want that measures the intensity of the pain caused by its presence now. It is thus the expected utility that determines the painfulness of a want and this painfulness determines its intensity or urgency.'[3] So when we talk of maximisation of utility, it simply means minimisation of pain because utility consists merely in the removal of pain. But pain cannot be minimised to a zero because economists tell us that wants are not only unlimited but they recur. Prof Mehta, therefore, concludes that modern economists simply want to maximise pleasure by maximising wants i.e. by minimising pain. But this pleasure or removal of pain can be compared with the pleasure that a man gets when his headache subsides after taking an aspirin tablet. The Westerners do not want to consider a situation of happiness where the headache may not occur, and so the question of taking aspirin may not arise. Thus, Prof. Mehta points out the fallacy of the thinking of modern economists and tells us that "maximum happiness" and not "maximum pleasure" should be our aim. This is possible only when there is a state of complete "wantlessness" because pain and pleasure are associated with wants. He, therefore, defines economics as "a science that studies human behaviour as an attempt to reach the State of Wantlessness."[4]

The Hindu saints, from the very beginning, have been of the opinion that 'Happiness' does not lie in enjoying physical comforts because physical goods, like the body, are short-lived. Hence, all the physical things give enjoyment to the body only temporarily. To quote *Gita*, a book very dear to Gandhi:

> "As enjoyments born of contacts (with external objects), have a beginning and an end, they become the cause of unhappiness. The wise man, O Kaunteya ! does not find happiness in them."[5]

Not only is the enjoyment of physical things short-lived, but there is also no limit to the desire for such things. Gandhi has explained it in these beautiful words:

> "The human mind is like a restless bird, the more it gets, the more it wants and still remains unsatisfied."[6]

The *Kathopanishad*[7] agrees with this view-point.

The Indian view-point is that 'happiness' has very little to do with the consumption of worldly things. Happiness depends upon the mental state of a person. It is a matter of common experience that a man, who is fabulously rich, generally remains worried, both mentally and physically, and by no stretch of imagination, can he be called a happy man. On the other hand, a person, not living in luxury, or even in comfort, is found to be happy and well contented. The example of millions of Indian villagers can be cited in proof thereof. Again, when one helps someone with money or other worldly things, judged by the economists' stand-point, he must grow unhappy but all of us know that this is far from the truth. Hence, it can safely be concluded that beyond a limit, the multiplication of wants and their satisfaction do not promote happiness and certainly not in the same proportion.

It will be useful to reproduce here at some length, extracts from the speech of Mahatma Gandhi which he delivered under the auspices of the Economic Society of the Muir Central College, Allahabad on December 22, 1916:

> "Before I take to the field of my experience and experiment it is perhaps best to have a mutual understanding about the title of this evening's address: 'Does Economic Progress clash with Real Progress?' By economic progress, we mean moral progress, which again, is the same thing as progress of the permanent element in us. The subject may, therefore, be stated thus: Does not moral progress increase in the same proportion

as the material progress?... No one has ever suggested that grinding pauperism can lead to anything else than moral degradation."

"Every human being has a right to live and, therefore, to find the wherewithal to feed himself and where necessary to clothe and house himself. But for this very simple performance we need no assistance from economists and their laws... The only statement that has to be examined is, whether it can be laid down as a law of universal application that material advancement means moral advancement."

"Now let us take a few illustrations. Rome suffered a moral fall when it attained high material affluence. So did Egypt and so, perhaps, most countries of which we have any historical record. The descendants and kinsmen of the royal and divine Krishna too fell when they were rolling in riches."

"... But Jesus answereth... Children, how hard is it for them that trust in riches to enter into the kingdom of God. It is easier for a camel to go through the eye of a needle than for a rich man to enter into the kingdom of God."

"I should not have laboured my point as I have done. I do not believe that in so far as we have made the modern materialistic craze our goal, in so far we are going down the hill in the path of progress. Hence the ancient ideal has been limitation of activities promoting wealth."

"Here is what Wallace, the great scientist, has said as his deliberate judgement: 'In the earliest records which have come down to us from the past, we find ample indications that general ethical conceptions, the accepted standard of morality, and the conduct resulting from these were in no degree inferior to those which prevail today.' In a series of chapters he then proceeds to examine the position of the English nation under the advance in wealth it has made. He says, 'This rapid growth of wealth and increase of our power over nature put too great a strain upon our crude civilization and our superficial Christianity, and it was accompanied by various forms of social immorality almost as amazing as unprecedented."

"He then shows how factories have risen on the corpses of men, women and children, how as the country has rapidly advanced in riches it has gone down in morality. He shows this by dealing with insanitation, life-destroying trades,

> adulteration, bribery and gambling. He shows how with advance in wealth, justice has become immoral, how deaths from alcoholism, and suicide have increased, how the average of premature births and congenital defects have increased, and how prostitution has become an institution. He concludes his examination by these pregnant remarks: 'The proceedings of the divorce courts show other aspects of the result of wealth and leisure, while a friend who had been a good deal in London society assured me that, both in country houses and in London, various kinds of orgies were occasionally to be met with, which would hardly have been surpassed in the Rome of the most dissolute Emperors. Of war, too, I need say nothing. It has always been more or less chronic since the rise of the Roman Empire. But there is now undoubtedly a disinclination for war among all civilised peoples. Yet the vast burden of armaments taken together with the most pious declarations in favour of peace, must be held to show an almost total absence of morality as a guiding principle among the governing classes."[8]

One thing more is to be noted here. A person by having an aim in life and working wholeheartedly for it, is compelled to select his wants which may be helpful in the fulfilment of the object. Take the case of a scientist busy with his research work. The work alone gives him happiness though he neglects his worldly comforts, sometimes even his food. Gandhi's life is an illuminating example of it. For uniting India and winning political freedom, Gandhi sacrificed many worldly comforts and subordinated his wants to this one aim and still remained happy. So, will it be wrong to conclude that the aim in life and devotion to this aim automatically reduce wants (as only those wants are satisfied which promote the cause) and promote happiness.

The disciples of Marx want to do away with private ownership and Gandhi seems to echo their voice but with the ostensible difference that whereas in the former case, the emphasis is on denial by force, in the latter on renunciation. The Hindu way of thinking is based on the idea of renunciation and Gandhi, like the ancient Hindu saints, believed that absolute non-possession, which is the corollary of absolute love, means total renunciation. This would demand that man should have no house, no clothing and no stock of food for the morrow, and depend on God for his daily bread. The body too is a possession and man should learn to use it for the purpose of service so long as it exists, so much so that service and not bread, becomes the stuff of life."[9] "Non-possession thus means non-dependence on material things. It implies total abolition of private property in all kinds of belonging, a view more radical than that of extreme communists."[10]

Absolute non-possession is an abstraction and is unattainable in its fulness. In the words of Gandhi:

> "To possess nothing is, at first, not like taking your clothes of your body but like taking your flesh off your bones."[11]
> "But if we strive for it, we shall be able to go further in realization of a scale of equality on earth than by any other method."[12]

Gandhi admits that a certain degree of comfort, physical and cultural, is essential for the moral and spiritual advancement. But the satisfaction of these needs must not go beyond a certain level, otherwise it will degenerate into physical and intellectual voluptuousness."[13]

The aim should be not the multiplicity of material wants but their restrictions consistent with comfort. One should not choose to think of getting what he can. On the other hand, he should decline to receive what others cannot get.[14]

Gandhi's critics, as Acharya Vinoba writes in the *Harijan*, also cavil at the ideal of poverty which is inconsistent with the materialistic outlook of capitalism and marxism. But the vow of non-possession, it should be remembered, is the ideal of voluntary poverty, the poverty of divine meekness that is capable of inheriting the earth, the poverty that enriches, ennobles and elevates. It is not the involuntary, demoralising poverty of destitution, the poverty of despair and inertia.[15]

Gandhi's own long dedicated life had been a model of non-possession.

Gandhi is not alone in thinking that nothing belongs to man, not even his corporal frame. Jesus also once said, "Provide neither gold, nor silver, nor brass in your purses nor scrip for your journey, neither two coats, neither shoes, nor yet staves; for the workman is worthy of his meat".[16] "It is easier for a camel to go through the eye of a needle than for a rich man to enter into the kingdom of God."[17]

The expression 'Standard of Living' as used by the economists is vague. It is a relative term and differs from place to place, person to person and time to time[18]. It is for this reason that it is qualified with two more words 'High' or 'Low'.

The two words, 'High' and 'Low' are also not appropriately used. 'High' or 'Low' indicates gradation, the quality. If we make the multiplicity of material wants artificially created as our standard of judging things, then only these terms have any significance. But if we choose happiness as our standard, this terminology will convey no sense. It is not necessary that the standard of an American labourer consuming more things (of an inferior quality) may always be of a higher order than that of an Indian using lesser things but of a higher quality. We can, therefore, call the standard of the American worker, at the most, a 'complex standard' and that of the Indian as a 'simple standard.'[19]

Not only is the term 'Standard of Living' vague and the two words 'High' and 'Low' inappropriately used but also the love for material progress i.e. 'complex standard' is leading the world towards chaos. An economist opines that the multiplication of wants leads to greater happiness. But in the same breath he reveals that normally no country can be self-sufficient in the production of all the commodities demanded by its citizens, as wants are unlimited and the resources of a country are limited. But then how to satisfy these ever-growing wants? As a solution he suggests that let there be specialisation. Every country will produce only those commodities which it can produce cheapest and will exchange its surplus produce with the commodities required by it and produced by other countries. He draws a rosy picture of the advantages of this specialization and international trade. But perhaps he forgets that this specialisation has the seeds of standardisation of the product and of mass production which will, after some time, create the problem of securing markets to dispose off the surplus produce and purchase raw materials. This will give birth to exploitation of one country by the other, to imperialism, colonialism and world wars.

One may argue that resources are limited and so, if production is suitably organized, the question of over-production resulting in imperialism and world wars will not arise. But the basic question is: who will properly organize production of all the countries of the world? Till an effective world Government interested in the welfare of all, irrespective of caste, colour, religion, state etc., is established, this problem of over-production in a country cannot be effectively solved. The history of the countries bear a testimony to it.

But this is not all. With the establishment of mass production, machines will be harnessed and the independent craftsman will be forced to leave his shop and take shelter under the shed of the factory, as he will be unable to stand the competition with the factory. He will be thrown to the mercy of the owner of the machines. Society will be divided into two groups, the exploiters and the exploited, who will start fighting each other for their gains. Hatred, violence, jealousy and rivalry will spread. The whole country will turn into a hell.

Multiplication of wants creates another chaotic condition. It makes a few rich persons consume more things at the cost of the majority of people that consists of the poor. As the factors of production are limited in a country, they can produce only a limited number of things. Hence, in a capitalistic set-up, only such things are produced as bring greatest amount of profit to the capitalist, irrespective of their utility and disutility. For example, in India there is an acute food shortage these days. We are forced to import foodgrains in order to keep away famine knocking at our doors. But to our greatest misfortune, more and more land is being transferred to the production of spices, oil-seeds, sugarcane, tobacco, cotton, etc., as they bring more profits to the farmers in comparison to the production of foodgrains. Similarly, grapes can be grown to prepare wine even though millions might be starving. And when wants increase—and wants of the rich only, who have the means to satisfy them and can effectively increase them, more and more factors of production are transferred to satisfy these ever-increasing new wants of a few rich and lesser and lesser things, which are consumed by the poor, are produced. This, naturally multiplies misery manifold. Probably for this reason, Mahatma Gandhi once wrote:

> "Our ignorance or negligence of the Divine Law, which gives man from day-to-day his daily bread and no more, has given rise to inequalities with all the miseries attendant upon them. The rich have a surplus share of things which they do not need and which are, therefore, neglected and wasted, while millions are starved to death for want of sustenance. If each retained

> possession only of what he needed, no one would be in want, and all would live in contentment. As it is, the rich are discontented no less then the poor."[20]

This love for high standard of living is making people crazy and the shrewd businessman through his powerful propaganda machinery is able to exploit and befool them. Take the case of a piece of clothing, a Bush-shirt. There is hardly any extra advantage in wearing a Bush-shirt over an ordinary shirt. But then how did Bush-shirt come into fashion? It was the producer, who, with his powerful propaganda machinery, made the consumer, who is trying to seek happiness by multiplying his wants, feel that the use of Bush-shirt will bring him more happiness, as it adds to his present large stock of wants. Look at the vegetable ghee. It came into existence and was able to oust pure ghee, not simply because it is slightly cheaper than pure ghee, but also because the consumer was assured by the producer that it can be matched with pure ghee in every way.

Thus Gandhi seems to argue with his friends trained in the glittering materialistic atmosphere of the West that multiplication of wants, beyond a limit, does not tend to human happiness, rather it retards it. Prof. J.K. Metha, the noted Indian Economist, holds almost identical views in regard to the concepts of happiness and pleasure as two different things. He holds that when the Westerners use the word happiness, they actually mean pleasure which is based on the removal of pain, which recurs at short intervals Gandhi argues that sunce physical things are short-lived, the pleasure derived out of them can never be permanent and so the question of complete satiety does not arise. Gandhi seems to enquire why one gets inner happiness when one donates one's physical belongings to some one else, if happiness is to come only by increasing the stock of physical belongings. He quotes scriptures of different religions to prove his point and hints at that by advocating the abolition of private property, the communists and socialists are also leading towards the ultimate goal, i.e. absolute non-possession. Gandhi philosophically challenges the correctness of the use of the terms 'Standard of Living' and 'High' and 'Low' and proceeds to point out in a convincing way, which even the western economists admit unreservedly, that this love for multiplicity of wants has released greater calamities on the people in the form of exploitation of one man by another, of one country by another, imperialism, world wars, jealousy, hatred, ill-will, production of luxury goods at the cost of necessities badly needed by the majority and introduction of foolish fashions and vulgar tastes.

II
GROWING USE OF MACHINES*

Gandhi's opposition to machines can be analysed under two broad divisions. First, he saw and disliked the mad craze for technological advancement in the West and analysed the evil consequences that followed. In this respect, his opposition to machines was of a general type. Secondly, Gandhi was basically a man of the East, deeply influenced by the philosophy and mode of life of the Hindus and was keen to preserve it, as, according to him, it was the only way to salvation. As such he opposed the slavish imitation of the Western way of life in India, a way of life that can well be described as the 'machine civilization'. In this respect his opposition to machines was particular; and in spite of the evolution in his ideas – his opposition to machines was total in 1908 but not so from 1928 onward – it continued. It will be worthwhile to study Gandhi's views on machines under these two division.

General Opposition

In Europe and America, speedy mechanisation and technological developments were thought to be a necessity because, though these countries had abundant capital, they suffered from the scarcity of labour. But even in the West, the machine has outlived its utility by being carried beyond legitimate limits. It has even grown into a menace and source of tragedy. In the latter half of 1955, a public opinion-poll in Detroit, the city of wheels, showed that, second only to the danger from U.S.S.R., it was automation that was causing people most concern. The American Federal Society of Labour also observed that the technical developments engendered a whole host of fears in the minds of the workers-fear of change, fear of technology itself, fear of displacement, fear of unemployment, fear of machines, fear of science in general. Gandhi was, therefore, right in

* Gandhi never used the word 'technology' but obviously he meant it.

opposing the use of machines beyond a certain limit. His objections were based on international, sociological and economic grounds.

International Grounds

The materialistic interpretation of History provided by Karl Marx appeared to be an intelligent approach. World Wars have confirmed it. People seem to have accepted it. At least the Great Mahatma of India appears to be in perfect conformity with the view of Marx[21] though the methods to secure world prosperity suggested by both are poles apart. Marx was of the view that the uncontrolled mass production by the capitalists is the root cause of the miseries of the present-day world. In the pre-historic period, when there were no machines, one produced only what one could consume. As such, the head of a clan could not exploit his fellow beings as he could not gain anything out of them. Life was simple and peaceful. But man started exploiting Nature. He wanted to conquer it. So he invented 'tools', small tools, in order to increase his productive capacity. It became profitable to have slaves who could produce more with the help of 'tools' than they could consume. Thereby, man began to exploit other's labour for the accumulation of personal wealth. The story of kings, feudal lords and Zamindars is a story which amply testifies to it. The 'tools' thus laid the foundations of exploitation of man by man. Soon society got split up into two groups of 'haves' and 'have-nots' because the poor, independent craftsman could not stand in competition with the mill owners, using better types of machines, and was forced to become a worker in the mighty mill. This gave birth, within the country, to class conflict, hatred, jealousy and ever-growing exploitation. Gandhi wrote, "If a spinning mill is put up in every Taluka it will result in nationalising the exploitation of the many by the few".[22] Elaborating the point he wrote "If an enterprising baker puts up cheap bakeries in our village so as to replace household kitchens, the whole nation, I hope, will rise against such an enterprise".[23]

The wheel of industrial progress moved on. Less complicated machines were replaced by more complicated and bigger ones. Larger production, greater exploitation, more accumulation of wealth became possible. The inventions of better means of communication and quicker transport radically reduced the size of the world. This gave an opportunity to the capitalist, who was exploiting his countrymen so far, to expand his field of activity. The growing factories, the ever increasing production found a way into other countries. International markets were created, where manufactured goods were dumped and raw materials were purchased. It is well known that English, French, Dutch and Portuguese traders, soon after Industrial Revolution had started in their respective countries, established trade relations with almost all the backward countries such as India, Ceylon, Burma, Indonesia, Malaya, China etc. Thus, the wealth of industrially backward countries was systematically sipped in by a few more industrially advanced countries. It is apt to quote here from D.G. Tendulkar:

> "A series of inventions in the industrial field found Britain ripe for industrial revolution in 1770. To make it success, she needed an expanding market and cash capital which prostrate India meekly provided. The East India Company looted Bengal to fill its coffers. India's ruinous condition was demonstrated by a famine in Bengal in 1770 in which 10 million people died. Yet land revenue was increased and rigorously collected. By 1813, the Company's monopoly of the Indian Trade had been terminated and a new policy of exploitation began. It was designed to expand the India's production of raw materials for the benefits of British Industry. In the name of free trade, British products were allowed free entry into the country while tariffs were raised high against Indian goods entering England. In 1787, the exports of Dacca muslin to England amounted to three million rupees; in 1817 they ceased altogether. By 1850, the India who for centuries had exported cotton goods to the whole world was importing one fourth of Britain's cotton textile exports."[24]

But this was not the end of exploitation. Soon competition between the industrially advanced countries started. Therefore, it became necessary for the manufacturing countries to have political power over other countries, in order to control their markets. Thereby, Imperialism grew, colonies sprang up and misery increased. A few were fed at the cost of the millions. The map of the world was changed. The story of fights between English, French and Dutch in India, resulting in the ultimate subjugation of the vast country, has its own tale to tell. And this was not with India alone. The same story was repeated in almost all the industrially backward countries. Gandhi was aware of this and so he asked his people to burn the foreign cloth. Mr. Andrews got greatly disturbed at it and he wrote a letter in 'loving language'. Gandhi justifying his action replied: "Love of foreign cloth has brought foreign domination, pauperism and what is worst, shame to many a home ... weavers of Kathiawad having found their calling gone, became sweepers for the Bombay Municipality."[25] Again, "God forbid that India should ever take to industrialism after the manner of the West. The economic imperialism of a single tiny island kingdom (England) is today keeping the world in chains."[26]

The story of the exploitation did not end here. It went on. Some newly industrialised countries, like Germany and Japan, could not afford to be silent spectators. They wanted markets and raw materials for their won factories. But by the time they came on the scene, all industrially backward countries had already been appropriated by the fortunate ones, and new markets could not be created. The only way left for these countries was to have control over the world markets by increasing their political power and by annihilating the political power of their rivals. The First World War was fought for this reason but it could not settle the issue. No permanent solution could be found. Hence, not long afterwards the Second World War was fought. After enormous destruction of man and material, the war came to an end. But the rivalries and jealousies between various industrialised countries, as well as backward countries continued and are mouting day by day. It is feared that a Third World War with still greater power of destruction and annihilation will come, unless something positive is done to prevent the rivalries and jealousies. It was for this reason that Gandhi said:

> "What is the cause of the present chaos? It is exploitation, I will not say, of the weaker nations by the stronger, but of sister nations by sister nations. And my fundamental objection to machinery rests of the fact that it is machinery that has enabled these nations to exploit others."[27]

The progress of the Industrial Revolution increased the rivalries and jealousies between different groups—rich and poor, capitalist and labourer, employed and unemployed—within the country, as well as among different countries. The thinkers, therefore, were trying to find out a solution. One solution came from Karl Marx in the form of Communism, the other was advocated by England in the shape of mixed economy, and the third has been advanced by the established U.N.O. in the form of negotiations and financial and technical help to the industrially backward countries so that they may be able to establish new industries.

Let us examine here results of these new experiments.

The Marxist thesis, which was practised with certain modifications in U.S.S.R., aimed at achieving equality, prosperity and peace by liquidating the power of the industrialist to exploit his countrymen. Hence, all the means of production were nationalised and were harnessed in the interest of the people by the State. Production and Distribution were no longer left to the sweet will of the individual but were ensured food, work and living accommodation to every one. This definitely cheeked exploitation within the country to a great extent. But to say that it has stopped exploitation of one country by another is wrong. What incited Russia to help the Chinese Communist Party in their domestic warfare? Why is she spreading her hand towards the backward Eastern countries of the world? It is not true to say that Russia wanted to help the backward nations in industrialising them, or to spread her ideology, or to sale down the differences of incomes. Was it not because Russia wanted to keep her own furnaces burning? Had it not been so, Russia would not have treated Hungary as she did. No justice loving nation would have done that. And whatever doubts might have been there the younger brother — Red China has perfectly washed them away. Subjugation of Tibet, forceful occupation of Indian Territory, character assassination of Prime Minister Nehru, troubles in South Viet-Nam etc., prove it.

It will not be too much to point out here that the Marxist thesis as practised in a few countries, by pinning its faith in automation, has not been helpful in checking imperialism and colonialism but has only changed its form. To add to misfortune, it has developed several new vices into the bargain.

In a communist State, freedom of consumption and occupation is greatly curtailed. One is made to consume what the State decides to produce and distribute. Similarly one is to serve wherever posted by the State as all work is in the hands of the State.

The human individuality is not allowed to grow freely in a communist society. The idea that the State is supreme while man is subordinate to it, leads to too much regimentation of life. Mass slaughter of animals in Russia when New Economic Policy was launched, brute methods of 'purifying' the partymen, 'Labour Camps' etc., are only a few of the shocking examples that bear out the above statement.

Production is carried on according to the social requirements and hence factors of production are directed where they are required and not where necessarily they are the most efficient.

The commodity price is always determined by the supply of and demand for it. In a communist society, the correct valuation of goods is not possible, as the demand for and supply of a commodity is predetermined. Moreover, in the case of perfect Monopsony and Monopoly, prices cannot be determined correctly even though there may be an artificial sale or purchase.[28]

It is no secret that even the ownership of production and distribution apparatus by the state could not produce sufficient goods for the hungry population of U.S.S.R. and the whole system crumpled like a house of cards. The mighty Russia is no more there. This is the visible evil of ever increasing use of machines even when they are state owned.

The other system introduced by the believers in private ownership is of *Mixed Economy*.[29] It will not be harsh to say that this system has also failed to wipe off *all the socio-economic evils of the capitalistic society*, viz. *class struggle, exploitation, accumulation of wealth in the hands of a few*, imperialism, *wars and the like evils, as it only touches the fringe of the problems and does not get down to the root*.

The U.N.O. is failing not because it lacks authority to press its decisions. The cause of its failure is that every effective member of U.N.O. wants to use this machinery for the purpose of keeping the power driven wheels of his country revolving. Moreover, the U.N.O.'s scheme of helping backward nations by setting up new industries will not meet with any success as it ignores the consequences which will follow when these countries will be industrialised and, therefore, will no longer remain markets for the present industrially advanced countries and they themselves be in search of markets of dispose off their surplus goods. The coming up of China, India and other countries on the Industrial Map of the world has already started posing new problems. Gandhi aptly remarked:

> "God forbid that India should ever take to industrialism after the manner of the West. The economic imperialism of a single tiny island kingdom (England) is today keeping the world in chains. If the entire nation of 300 millions took to similar economic exploitation, it would strip the world bare like locusts.[30]

Again in 1931, Gandhi could say:

> "The future of industrialization is dark. England has got successful competitors in America, France, Japan and Germany. It has competitors in the handful of mills in India, even so there will be an awakening in South Africa with its vastly rich resources—natural, mineral and human. The mighty English look quite pigmies before the mighty races of Africa... and in the course of a few years the Western nations may cease to find in Africa a dumping ground for their wares..."[31]

Hence it can be concluded that the recent reforms will not be able to stop the present day ills or coming evils introduced by machines and mass production.

Sociological Ground

The psychological effect of machinery on the worker as well as its sociological effect on society is difficult to calculate as it is not easy to give it a statistical formulation. Yet it is desirable to have some idea about it.

With the introduction of machine, slowly but surely, the average man's power to judge, decide and act for himself decreases. How many youths are there in this country who know what subjects will pay them best dividends; what type of jobs are best suited for them and what is the aim of their life? How many workers are there, who know what is their real worth? Whether they should take part in a labour strike? How can they be better workers? How many consumers are there who are able to select things for their consumption without being swayed by fashion, advertisement, etc? It was for this reason that Gandhi said:

> "In modern times it is beneath human dignity to lose one's individuality and become a cog in the machine. I want every individual to become a full blooded and full developed member of society."[32]

Prof. Karl Mannheim in his "Man and Society" has also expressed similar sentiments:

> "The fact that in a functionally rationalised society the thinking out of a complex series of actions is confined to a few organizers, assures these men a key position in the society. A few people can see things more and more clearly over an ever widening field, while the average man's capacity for rational judgement steadily declines, once he haa turned over to the organizer the responsibility for making decisions."[33]

The machine has deprived the workers of the sense of achievement and joy in their work. Had it not been so, the necessity of giving incentive to workers for improving their efficiency might not have been felt; the economists might have not thought of a new concept of Human capital; the workers would not have thought of organising themselves into strong trade unions and stage a fight for their rights. Probably, some one may say that trade unions are formed out of the economic needs of the workers. But has one ever heard of a trade union of painters, sculptors, writers etc., howsoever poor may be the remuneration for their work? The joy of the work counteracts economic loss in their case. But it is not so in the case of a factory worker. The realist in Gandhi could observe this when he came in contact with workers. He was pained and expressed his views in these words:

> "I am afraid, by working with machines we have become machines ourselves, having lost all sense of art and handwork."[34]

Gandhi is not alone in observing this painful development. Earnest Hund has also remarked: "We are witnessing an extra-ordinary development of power which lends to turn craftsmen into clogs in a soulless mechanism. Whereas in former days the artisan had pride in the creative element in his work, which he, very often, carried on in *his own house or workshop*, he has now become a *mere cipher* in a factory, perhaps not even known by a *name but a number*." Karl Marx, who was by no means a machine baiter, has also said: 'The work of the proletariat has lost all individual character, and consequently, all charm for the workman'.

Machinery undermines health and shortens life. The operation of a machine creates a great noise which adversely affects the nervous system of the worker and shortens his life. The use of machine has also been the cause of filth and immoral surroundings in the industrial towns. Thousands and thousands of workers, who due to the temptation of better wages, flock round the mighty factory, vomiting fire, gas and filth, catch the germs of it and pay heavily for it. What is still left is completed by the over-crowded pigeon-holes in which workers generally reside without getting the facilities of proper sunlight, air, water, lavatory and drainage system. Gandhi was aware of this,[35] and so he wanted to take back the industry to villages.[36] His talk of decentralisation and emphasis on *Charkha*, which is a symbol of decentralisation, will bear it. He, being a realist, knew that no malady can be permanently cured if the root is not tackled. He will, therefore, not agree to the half-hearted measures such as construction of a few 'Model House' for the factory workers: opening of a few clubs and places of recreation; fitting the man-killing factory with apparatus like cooling plants etc.

The impact of machinery had an adverse effect on our social life too. It snatched the work from the happy craftsman and made him a tool in the hands of machine owners. Society got divided into two rival groups of 'haves' and 'have-nots'. Hatred, jealousy, group rivalry, coupled with the sobbing of unemployed, half-clad, half-fed people multiplied. Society degenerated into a hell. Is it not a great social cost? These social costs, which man has to pay to keep the wheel of machinery going should also be added to the cost of produce. Hobson has rightly remarked:

> "Businessman is right for his standpoint in measuring by reduced amount of cost and increased amount of utilities, disregarding the human significance of these terms. But the economist, unless he accepts the post of an intellectual servant

> of capitalism, has no right to adopt this scale of values as well as this method of valuation. His rightful role is that of assessing cost and utility, production and contribution towards a desirable human life or a desirable society."

It is this realisation which made Gandhi talk about duties and not rights, of homogeneity of class interest, love, non-violence, a new production pattern, and restrictive use of machines.

Gandhi came to know of another important social evil of growing use of more and more complicated machines. He realised that machine 'enforces leisure' when people do not know what to do with it. This causes physical and mental upsetting. Gandhi was asked by a friend, "You have no regard to the question of leisure". To this Gandhi replied, "I am trying to deal with people who do not know what to do with their enforced leisure. It is the enforced idleness that has made them like so many lifeless machines."[37]

Dr. Donald D. Greaves agrees, "Technology has mastered the art of saving time, but not the art of spending it, and idleness causes trouble – mental trouble. We are getting patients now who are bored, restless, depressed and apathetic because they do not know how to rest."[38] So, on the one hand the employed get more and more leisure and they do not know how to use it and relax, while on the other, the unemployed live in tension and misery. The result is that the paradise of automation – America – has the largest number of problem children and persons suffering with blood pressure, heart diseases and mental troubles. It was for this reason that Gandhi wanted people to utilise their leisure time in some craft which will relieve tensions, improve health, give the joy of creation and add to income.[39]

Economic Ground

Use of machine leads to centralisation of production which has seeds of periodical slumps and booms. These slumps and booms which are known as Trade Cycles, shake the whole economic structure and are causes of failure of firms, uneven distribution of wealth, scarcity and abundance of commodities, rise or fall in the level of unemployment etc.

Gandhi felt that Trade Cycles are mainly the result of mass localised production which has disturbed the equilibrium of supply and demand. In his own words:

> "Granting for the moment that the machine may supply all the needs of humanity, still it would concentrate production in particular areas, so that you would have to go in round about way to regulate distribution, whereas if there is production and distribution both in the respective areas where things are required, it is automatically regulated, and there is less chance for fraud, none for speculation."[40]

> Again: "Distribution can be equalized when production is localised, in other words when the distribution is simultaneous with production. Distribution will never be equal so long as you want to tap other markets of the world dispose of your goods...."[41]

Gandhi is not alone in holding this view. The view that a round about system of production is responsible for recurring booms and depressions is held by others also. "That the period of production is often unalterably determined for a long time in the future, once the time consuming process has been started, is of great significance for the theory of business cycle. The inherent difficulties of the cycle cannot well be explained without reference to those rigidities which are due to the fact that time consuming process cannot be easily interrupted and that the factors of production cannot be shifted at will from earlier to later stages of production or *vice versa*. Once time-consuming processes have got in underway, there is a strong presumption that they will have to be continued and that they are, therefore, not very sensitive to adverse price changes. If the business cycle theory has to explain why the adjustment of the economic system to irregular changes does not come about smoothly and continuously, then it is obvious that technological rigidities which determine that length of the period of production are of great importance."[42] Lord Keyne's theory of Trade Cycle also agrees with it. According to this theory, when due to some reasons, the Marginal Efficiency of Capital becomes higher than the rate of interest, investment increases and a period of boom comes.[43] But if Marginal Efficiency of Capital becomes lower than the rate of interest, new investment is stopped. Fall in investment results in the fall of employment and income and a period of depression starts.[44] Thus, booms and slumps are occasioned mainly due to the inability of the investor to calculate demand and supply accurately because of the mechanised mass production. Hence, logically concluding, mass production with the help of modern machines is not in the interest of the country. A Huxley has said: "At present the management of large scale production is in the hands of irresponsible individuals seeking profit – it is the uncoordinated activity of large scale production that leads to periodical crisis and depression which inflicts such untold hardships upon the working masses of industrialised countries. Small scale production carried on by individuals, who run the instruments with which they personally work, is not subject to periodical slumps."

A communist claims that there can be no booms and slumps in his country, in spite of the use of machines and large scale production. Even if we agree to it, we will have also to concede that it is achieved at a much higher price as it robs a person of his freedom of consumption, occupation and production. Moreover, it does not permit the development of a man's personality according to his own wishes. Gandhi could never vote for such a regimented life simply to retain machines. He remarked:

> "Centralisation as a system is inconsistent with non-violent structure of society."[45]

Moreover, Gandhi was the prince among individualists and certainly he would never agree to any curtailment of individual liberty or individualism. Democrats will also agree with him.

While judging the well-being of a nation, our consideration of it should proceed on the lines on which purchasing power is distributed among the people. Economists tell us that the more even distribution of the purchasing power bring greater amount of satisfaction and happiness. Therefore, the method of production should be such as may ensure greatest possible even distribution of the purchasing power, i.e. wealth.

Large scale production with the help of machines requires considerable amount of accumulated capital to begin the work. The foundation of the large scale mechanised production, therefore, is based upon the accumulation of wealth and it results also in uneven distribution of wealth. It is for this reason that in all industrialised democratic countries, Governments frame their tax policies on the progressive system so that they may be able to reduce the disparity of incomes to some extent. Death duties are one such example. It can, therefore, be easily concluded that mechanised large scale production creates the problem of distribution and generally leads to uneven distribution of wealth. Gandhi, therefore wrote:

> "Today, machinery merely helps a few to ride on the back of millions. The impetus behind it all is not the philanthropy to save labour, but greed."[46]

Again:

> "We should not substitute lifeless machines for the living machines...Today, it is used to pour wealth in the pockets of the chosen few. Little attention is paid to crores of people from whom the machine snatches away their bread."[47]

With uneven distribution of wealth is tagged another important problem. The spread of automation will have the effect of conferring very great advantages upon big businessmen in a highly competitive world. Consequently the trend towards the growth of large concerns will receive a powerful stimulus.

These large and powerful enterprises will, for all practical purposes, be controlled by a handful of technicians, engineers and managers. This may pose a new problem. The whole economic, social and political structure will becomes too much dependent on the top executives of automatic concerns. Democracy will, in reality, be thrown to the wind.

For this reason, Mahatma of India was afraid of industrialisation. In his own words: "Industrialism is, I am afraid, going to be a curse for mankind."[48] Again, "We shall need a Nadir Shah to find out other worlds to exploit, that we shall have to pitch ourselves against the naval and military power of Britain, Japan and America, of Russia and Italy."[49] Gandhi was definite that machines will bring more troubles than success. "I have heard many of our countrymen say that we will gain American wealth but avoid its method. I venture to suggest that such an attempt, if it were made, is foredoomed to failure. We cannot be wise, temperate and furious in a moment."[50] Mr. Pollock agrees with Gandhi, "It seems clear, too that automation will be an important factor in rapidly strengthening the position of the big concerns as against the medium sized and smaller business" and "encourage concentration of economic power and financial control over the production and distribution of goods and services".[51] Again, "The small number of engineers with the ultimate control of these automatic factories could hold society upto ransom, the ransom being control of man's consumption and habits in the interest of machines...It will lead to the creation of a class of people who may be termed as working class aristocrats." Again, "Those who belong to this class think alikc on fundamental questions. They have the pride and exclusive feelings of a ruling class whose members have to solve similar problems and overcome similar difficulties. They are linked by the knowledge that they hold great power in their hands and that both from an intellectual and material point of view, they are superior to the vast of population. This new social class controls (directly or indirectly) all the mass media of influencing public opinion...The resulting attitude of mind to both material and spiritual matters coincides with the authoritarian tendencies in all phases of management... Such a class structure would be a very insecure foundation for a free society. The great power of minority coupled with the ignorance and weakness of the majority might well lead to the establishment of an authoritarian in place of a democratic form of Government."[52]

Large scale production leads to specialisation and concentration of factories in particular areas. In the present days when clouds of war are hovering over every country and can burst out at any moment, this concentration of factories, which is unavoidable in the large scale production, is not desirable as it can be an easy target of bombing and can throw the whole economic life of the country completely out of gear. Gandhi was voicing the views of most of the modern economists when he remarked:

> "Concentration of production and infinitum can only lead to unemployment. You may say that workers thrown out of work by the introduction of improved machinery will find occupation in other jobs. But in an organised country, where there are only fixed and limited avenues of employment, where the worker has become highly skilled in the use of one particular kind of machinery, this is hardly possible."[53]

> "Machines will only help in making all the thirty-five crores of people unemployed."[54]

> "Every such machinery (Power wheels for the grinding of corn) puts thousands of hand *Chakkis* out of work, and takes away employment from thousands of housewives and artisans who make these *Chakkis*. Moreover, the process is ineffective and spreads to every village industry."[55]

To this, the economist, trained in the classical school may not agree. He most emphatically may argue that with the installation of a new machine, cost of production of the commodity will go down. With the cost lowered, consumers will be able to save some money which otherwise they were spending on this commodity. They will spend the money thus saved on the purchase of other commodities and, therefore, the demand for other commodities will increase. With the rise in demand for other commodities production will have a tendency to expand, giving rise to further employment. Even in this particular industry where a machine was installed, fall in cost will induce new buyers to include this commodity in their budget. The demand will increase which will mean recruitment of more persons to run the added machines. Thus the total employment will increase. It is only in the transitional period that the level of employment may go down with the introduction of machinery.

The reading of classical economists regarding increase in employment with the use of machine was correct at the time when industrial revolution had just begun. This was the stage when reduction in costs was achieved by the external economies of large scale production. But now a stage has been reached when economies are not achieved by large scale production but by the introduction of newly invented machines which require lesser persons to run them. It is the 'Labour saving Devices' under the internal economies which are the cause of reduction of costs.[56] But in the present age, use of more and more machines is becoming the cause of growing unemployment. The touch-stone of cold statistics will convince an impartial person of the truth of this statement.[57]

Commenting on this, Dr. Ghate observed: "The Table 2.1 shows that in most of these countries there is a tendency for the proportion of industrial workers per 1000 of the total occupied population to decline."[58]

It is also not correct to say that any decrease in the cost of production will always increase demand. Demand depends upon the income propensity to consume and propensity to save. If any of these factors are reduced, with the introduction of machinery, demand will not increase. Generally, it is seen that with the installation of machines, a few persons are thrown out of employment and the wages of the labourers do not increase so as to compensate the loss of total incomes of people turned out the factory. Income, instead of increasing, decreases. The same is true of propensity to consume and propensity to save. Thus, even when cost of production has gone down, it is not necessary that demand will always increase. And if demand does not increase, level of employment cannot rise.

TABLE 2.1

Country and year to which the figure relates	Total population gainfully employed (in lakhs)	Total population occupied in industry (in lakhs)	% of the industrial population to total working population
U.S.A.			
1910	328	107.	27.9%
1920	416	128	30.8%
1930	488	141	28.9%
England and Wales			
1911	162	699	42.1%
1921	172	55	32.3%
1931	189	60	31.7%
Germany			
1925	320	122	35.1%
1933	323	117	36.2%
Japan			
1920	273	53	19.4%
1930	292	53	18.1%
Canada			
1921	32	8	23.8%
1931	39	7	17.3%
India			
1921	1460	167	11.0%
1931	1540	153	10.5%
1941	1700	163	9.6%

Probably, some one may say that even if it may not be possible to increase the demand for the produce within the country, it will not be very difficult to push the sales abroad and raise the demand for the produce. But this argument lacks force. If it is possible for you to capture foreign markets and export unemployment, is it not equally possible for other countries to capture your home market ? And if one can protect home market with the help of import duties, quota system, exchange control, etc., other countries can also be sufficiently wise to do the same. Wherein then lies the advantage?

To conclude, we can say that on the question of machinery, the classical writers were unanimous, though unanimity is not quite absolute. Ricardo in the third edition of his 'Principles' added a chapter on machinery in which he admitted that he was mistaken in the belief the machines after a short period always proved favourable to the interest of the workers. He recognised that the workers might suffer. Sismondi does not deny that theoretically in the long-run, machines are useful but when he applies the touchstone of reality he differs. "Every new product must in the long-run give rise to some fresh consumption. But let us examine things as they really are. The immediate effect of machinery is to throw some of the workers out of employment, to increase the competition of others, and so to lower the wages of all . . . No one will deny the advantage of substituting a machine for a man, provided that man can obtain employment elsewhere.[59]

Sismondi makes another remark which is no less just. What disgusted him was not merely that workmen should be driven out by machinery, but that the workers who were retained had a limited share of the benefits which they produced.[60] "The earnings of an entrepreneur sometimes represent nothing but the spoilation of the workmen. A profit is made not because the industry produces much more than it costs, but because it fails to give to the workman sufficient compensation for his toil. Such an industry is a social evil."[61]

Sismondi, speaking in the vein of Marx, tells us that industries have spilt society into two classes whose interests are divergent. "The intermediate classes have all disappeared, the small proprietor and the peasant farmer of the plain, the master craftsman, the small manufacturer and the village tradesman, all have failed to withstand the competition of those who control great industries. Society no longer has any room save for the great capitalist and his hirelings."[62]

Someone may argue that technological development in U.S.A. has not increased unemployment and even if unemployment increases, it will be short-lived. Mr. Pollack has taken great pains to explode this myth. He says that though "in 1955 the redundant workers (as a result of automation) did find new jobs, but that does not mean that their successors in later years will always be equally fortunate. If there were a slowing down of a cessation of the continued expansion of the economy, it is indeed doubtful if even the combined efforts of Government, industry and organised labour could stem the flood of technological unemployment unless all three agree to make planned and fundamental changes in the entire structure of American Economy."[63] The truth of Pollock's views can be demonstrated by the fact that War, which is a boom for full-employment, could not bring full employment in a highly industrialised and technologically advanced country like U.S.A. Jather and Beri writing in the Indian Economist were very correct when they remarked, "A permanent margin of unemployment among industrial workers is a feature of economic system called into existence by the industrial revolution in Western countries. Palliatives as unemployment insurance, allowance of relief funds etc., do not touch the fundamental cause of unemployment."

The Economist, trained in communist ideology, may say that all this stone throwing has been in vain. There is so much of starvation, poverty, sweating and overwork that it is preposterous to entertain the fear of unemployment with the introduction of machines. We, by raising the standard, shortening the hours of work and increasing the number of shifts, can easily meet the challenge of the machines.

Alas! The first country who tried to give practical shape to Marxism, could not stand for long and collapsed because of the inherent contradiction of the system.

Standard of living is a vague term. It carries no meaning by itself. Moreover, one can understand the multiplicity of material goods only to a certain limit. One car or even two are understandable but a queue of a dozen cars for a family is meaningless. Again, you may go on raising the standard of living but even then it will not be possible to check unemployment. In India, between 1911 and 1936, the number of factories increased from 2700 to 9300 yet during these years, the percentage of industrially occupied people to the total of working population fell down from 11 to 9.6.[64] And this is true of every country of the world. Thanks to technology, we require proportionately fewer men to produce additional wealth. Even in the home of communism—U.S.S.R., the efforts to raise the standard of living accompanied by a rise in industrial employment has proved a misnomer. Dr. Lokanathan commenting on the effect of industrialization on employment in the U.S.S.R. pointed out that "between 1928 and 1934, about 18 million workers were transferred to urban employment and yet the percentage of rural population remained 73.5 per cent, showing that the pace of industrialisation had just kept pace with the natural increase in population. All that industrialisation achieved was to maintain this increase in population without a decline in their standard of living but rather with some increase in it."[65]

People talk of reducing hours of work and, thereby raising volume of employment ? But how much can it be reduced ? Every reduction in hours of work beyond a certain limit, where efficiency will cease to increase, will mean an increase in cost. And no country in the world can afford the continuous rise in prices. Consumers will revolt against such a policy and producers will be forced to stop production and their profits will dwindle away. The reduction in hours of work is no solution for maintaining or increasing the volume of unemployment.

From The Indian Point of View[66]

Gandhi was very much influenced by the Indian way of thinking, life and value-system. He wanted to preserve them as he was convinced of their utility for India, and for the matter of that, for the whole of Asia, and he believed that the blind use of machines and technological development will destroy that value-system. So, he consistently opposed the growing use of machines[67] and for this very reason he opposed England or the Western or even the European Civilization. Here is a fairly long extract from *Hind Swaraj*.

"Reader : You have denounced railways, lawyers and doctors. I can see that you will discard all machinery. What, then, is civilization?

"Editor : The answer to this question is not difficult. I believe that the civilization India has evolved is not to be beaten in the world. It is a charge against India that her people are so uncivilized, ignorant and stupid, that it is not possible to induce them to adopt any change. It is a charge really against our merit. What we have tested and found true on the anvil of experience, we have not changed. Many thrust their advice upon India and she remains steady. This is her beauty, it is the sheet-anchor of our hope.

"Civilization is that mode of conduct which points out to man the path of duty, Performance of duty and observance of morality are convertible terms. To observe morality is to attain mastry over our mind and our passion. So doing, we know ourselves. The Gujarati equivalent for civilization means 'Good Conduct.'

"If this definition be correct, then India as so many writers have shown, has nothing to learn from anybody else and this is as it should be : (we notice that the mind is a restless bird; the more it gets the more it wants, and still more unbridled it become). Our ancestors, therefore, set a limit to our indulgences. They say that happiness was largely a cultural condition...We have had no system of life-corroding competition. Each followed his own occupation or trade and charged a regulation wage. It was not that we did not know how to invent machinery, but our forefathers knew that, if we set our hearts after such things, we would become slaves and lose our moral fibre. They, therefore, after due deliberation decided that we should only do what we could with our hand and feet. They further reasoned that large cities were a snare and a useless encumbrance. They were, therefore, satisfied with small villages. They say that kings and their swords were inferior to the sword of ethics and they, therefore, held the sovereign of the earth to be inferior to the *rishis* and *fakirs*...

...Now you see what I consider to be real civilization. The tendency of the Indian Civilization is to elevate the moral being, that of the Western Civilization is to propagate immorality. The latter is Godless, the former is based on belief in God. So understanding and so believing, it behaves every lover of India to cling to the old Indian Civilization even as a child clings to the mother's breast."[68]

It is obvious from the above extract that Gandhi felt convinced that civilization means "good conduct with the entire weight on performance of duty and observance of morality."[69] The performance implied proper use of hands and feet and the process led to the limitation of indulgences, reduction of wants and simplification of life. All these ideas formed a whole pattern of thought, beliefs, attitude and action which placed Indian civilization in sharp opposition to what Gandhi sometimes called the Western, at other times, the European, but what was in reality the modern civilization clustered round material values."[70]

The Hindu values, it is obvious, centred in 'renunciation and nonpossession.' In other words, the 'ideal' pattern of Hindu values was never forsaken by Gandhi. It was woven round 'wantlessness'. How could technology and machines, geared to the production of goods for the satisfaction of wants, which created more wants—joint wants, derived wants, the infinite hyperbole of wants—be consonant with the pattern of Indian norms. How could such norms square, for that matter, with economics, grounded as it was on wants and their satisfaction ? If absolute liberation of the soul from the body be the utter sum of existence, then Gandhi and with him every Hindu who was aware of his ancestry, would raise the eternal query; 'Why this craze for machinery?' 'Why machine civilization at all?' Other problems such as machines helping a few to ride on the back of millions, the concentration of power and wealth, of justice for the labourer as man, securing attractive conditions of life for him and giving him security of employment, etc., would be subsidiary. These letters, in Gandhi's opinion, ultimately hinged upon non-possession, *aparigraha*, wantlessness, subordination of body and bodily wants to the need of the soul's liberation from its physical encasement, which was the end."[71]

Gandhi made slight modification in his stand against machines. He realised that people are not yet prepared for the supreme renunciation Hindu values demanded. Non-violence, truth, simplicity, non-possession and bread-labour have not yet become the bread of masses. So, a sense of limit grew in him. Gandhi of 1924 started thinking that the State controlled factories of power driven machinery will control the profit, produce for the benefit of humanity, love taking the place of greed as the motive. In his own words: "I am socialist enough to say that such factories (viz. factory for making Singer Sewing Machines) should be nationalised or State controllect. They ought only to be working under the most attractive and ideal conditions, not for profit, but for the benefit of humanity, love taking the place of greed as the motive."[72]

This was a compromise. Non-possession in the context of human history has been an individual value, and at best, one ideal value for the elite group, known as the *Brahmin* caste, to be perpetually practised by it. Others practised it, but the Brahmin was the specialist. Gandhi would institutionalise it in the State that would own and not possess it for greed or profit.[73] To this extent he was a socialist but with the difference that his socialism did not grow out of industrial civilization, technological values, class conflicts, or according to the operations of the laws of dialectics.

It will be wrong to think that his compromise means a sacrifice of the basic i.e. the ideal position. In Gandhi's own words:

> "Ideally, however, I would rule out all machinery, even as I would reject this very body, which is not helpful to salvation and seek the absolute liberation of the soul. Form that point of view, I would reject all machinery, but machinery will remain because like the body, they are inevitable. The body itself as I told you, is the purest piece of mechanism, but if it is hindrance to the highest flights of the soul, it has to be rejected."[74]

Thus the Gandhian conclusion in regard to machines and technology is logical if one accepts the postulate,

that "(a) India has a separate norm of values with the hidden assumption that values determine conduct, that (b) she has a separate principle of social organisation which would be disturbed, and even destroyed by large scale use of machinery for greed and profit, that (c) a proper use would presuppose certain requisite attitudes, some traditional and others not, but all working in alliance, and also that (d) a type of State would won and control large machines, if they were indispensable for defined purposes. Otherwise the machines to be used would be of special type suitable for removing the drudgery of handicraft and improving its quality. They would operate in the general context of decentralised economy in close alliance with agriculture. Gandhi would thus remove the stings of capitalism and socialism alike."[75]

To sum up, Gandhi's opposition to machines and mass

production was neither total nor motivated out of selfishness or ignorance. It was based on correct reading of the situation. He came to know that it lays the seeds of exploitation within the country as well as outside the country; it breeds violence, class-conflict and misery; it provides unwanted leisure to few by robbing it from majority, it gives unemployment, booms and slumps, uneven distribution of wealth, wars and imperialism; it makes a few to ride on millions; it demands a huge social cost by uprooting innocent people from their homes and villages, spoiling their health and intelligence and depriving them of joy in their work and even in life. Even the western economists and thinkers agree with Gandhi. However, they do not want to go to the roots of the malady and want to rejuvenate life by giving temporary boosters which, in course of time, bring more disaster, confusion and chaos. Gandhi did not agree with them. Half-hearted measures never satisfied him.

III
METHODS OF DISTRIBUTION

Mahatma Gandhi was of the opinion that the third factor responsible for disturbing the equilibrium of the world peace and which is mainly an outcome of the first two, was to be found in the existing method of distribution of the produce among the various factors of production. In the present era, the share of a factor of production is calculated on the basis of demand for and supply of that factor. We are, therefore, told by the economist that a factor of production cannot get more than its marginal productivity, i.e. its utility to the employer.

Gandhi was probably not well acquainted with the modern theories of economics and as such he could not have debated, like some scholars, with the help of mathematical tools, that if all the factors of production are paid according to their marginal productivity, will some residue be left which shall be grabbed by the employer as his super-profits? Leaving aside this important but somewhat technical question for the economists, Gandhi appears to pose another question. He seems to enquire whether the productivity of a poor labourer is so low as not to enable him to have even his bare necessities of life? And whether the productivity of a capitalist is so high as to enable him to have all the amenities of life and even then leave a surplus? What made the productivity of the two so different? Is this difference, if at all it exists, not due to the starving conditions of one factor which has reduced his working capacity? If it is so, and there is every possibility of its being correct, we are not doing full justice by paying factors according to their existing working capacities. It we wish to stick to this old theory, Gandhi seems to suggest us, that we should first feed the unfed or semi-fed factors properly and thereafter measure their productivity. In Gandhi's own words:

> "The contrast between the rich and the poor today is a painful sight. The poor villagers are exploited by the foreign Government and also by their own countrymen – the city dwellers. They produce the food and go hungry. They produce milk and their children have to go without it. It is disgraceful. Everyone must have a balanced diet, a decent house to live in, facilities for the education of one's children and adequate medical relief."[76]

Gandhi being a humanitarian, objected to the theory of paying factors according to their productivity – even when it may be possible to measure it correctly and accepting the wrongful contention that the productivity of different factors is so different as to enable one to live in luxury and refuse the other the chances of satisfying the bare necessities of life. He, like Keynes, appears to argue that acceptance of this theory will result in uneven distribution of wealth which, besides creating many social problems, will also reduce the propensity to consume and propensity to invest, which in its own turn, will adversely affect the level of employment and income. Moreover, because of this uneven distribution of wealth, limited factors of production, governed by profit motive, shall flow in those productive channels which may not promote maximum social welfare. We have already experienced in India that because of this uneven distribution of wealth, land was switched over to the production of cash crops from food crops, even though the people were dying of hunger and food was imported from abroad. This was because the few fortunately placed capitalists could compel, by way of paying better prices to the farmers, to convert their lands from food production to cash crops production. Naturally, all this will lead to many complicated socio-economic problems such as scarcity in the midst of plenty, unemployment, falling level of incomes, poverty associated with its natural evils, class conflict, personal jealousies, etc. It is for this reason that now greater and greater attention is being paid to this problem, the importance of which was almost negligible in the days of Adam Smith.

It is these three factors—greater and greater use of machines; ever-increasing wants and method of distribution which, according to Gandhi, are responsible for the present day economic, political and social unrest. He, therefore, came out with a new thesis, which of course, he never gave us in the form of a well-knit theory but which he developed over a period of time.

REFERENCES

1. Ruskin. *Unto This Last.*
2. D.G. Tendulkar, *Mahatma*, Vol. IV
3. J.K. Mehta, *Advanced Economic Theory*, 1948, p. 6-7.
4. Ibid, p 9.
5. B.G. Tilak, *Gita-Rahasya*, p 978.
6. *Hind Swaraj.*
7. *Kathopanishad*, Chapter I, p 26.
8. D.G. Tendulkar, *Mahatma*, Vol. I, pp 236-42.
9. *Yervada Mandir*, pp 38-39, vide G.P. Dhawan, *The Political Philosophy of Mahatma Gandhi*, p 93.
10. Ibid, p 40-44.
11. Ibid, p 40-44.
12. N.K. Bose, *Studies in Gandhism*, p. 201 and also in *Mahatma Gandhi* edited by Dr. S Radhakrishnan, p 56.
13. *Harijan*, August 29, 1936, p. 226; G.P. Dhawan, *The Political Philosophy of Mahatma Gandhi*, p 94 and R.D. Gillespie, *Psychological Effects of War on Citizen and Soldiers*, p 100 and 240.
14. G.P. Dhawan, *The Political Philosophy of Mahatma Gandhi*, p 94.
15. Vinoba; *Harijan*, May 16, 1936.
16. *Matthew* X, 9-10.
17. *Matthew* XIX, 24.
18. The standard of living of an American Mill-hand, who owns a radio and a car, may be low judging from the American standard, but it may be very high looking from an Indian or Chinese standard. Again, the standard of living which is termed as very low by the average American or Englishman might be considered very high by his own grand-father if he were to see it now.
19. J.C. Kumarappa, *Economy of Peace.*
20. *Yervada Mandir*, p 34.
21. Gandhi had read *Das Capital* of Karl Marx and he was well versed with the communist literature. Writing in *Harijan* of December 10, 1930, Gandhi observed, "All your literature that I have studied..."
    Also see *Young India*, November 15, 1928; *Young India*, March 25, 1931; *Harijan*, December 10, 1938.
22. *Young India*, June 26, 1924.

23. *Young India*, July 17, 1924; *Harijan*, May 16, 1936. Gandhi was a believer in the unity and homogeneity of life. Neither he divided it in water-tight compartments nor did he believe that just interests of classes clash with each other. He, therefore, came forward with his theory like that of Adam Smith and others. of homogeneity of class interests and suggested a realistic way to achieve the aim. For details, see Chapter VI.
24. Tendulkar, *Mahatma*, Vol. I, p. 1. Gandhi, one of the greatest humanist the world has produced, could not be a silent spectator to this exploitation of one country by another. He, therefore, put forth his ideas on mass production and international trade to minimise this exploitation. See Chapters V, VI and VII.
25. *Young India*, September 1, 1921, p. 318.
26. *Harijan*, January 28, 1939.
27. *Young India*, October 12, 1931. p. 318
28. Pigou, A.G., *Socialism vs Capitalism*
29. In this system the nationalised industries and privately owned and managed industries exist and work side by side. All the key and basic industries are nationalised in the interest of the country. But still sufficient sphere is left for private capital. Sometimes even the private sector is controlled and regulated by the State with the help of price fixation, wages fixation, etc.
30. *Harijan*, January 28, 1939. Also see *Young India*, November 12, 1931.
31. *Young India*, November 12, 1931.
32. *Hind Swaraj*, 1938, p.148; *Young India*, November 13, 1924, August 13, 1925.
33. M.L. Dantwala, *Gandhism Reconsidered*, p. 43.
34. D.G. Tendulkar, *Mahatma*, Vol. IV, pp. 238-39.
35. *Harijan*, July 7, 1936. "I was taken to the huts of the workers in the Kolar Gold Fields the other day. I could not help remarking that the huts were not fit for human habitation. With the mining company declaring fat dividends of 30 to 40 per cent, it seemed to be cruel to me that those who earned the profits for them were housed in those dismal hovels." Also see *Harijan*, June 16, 1946 when he pleaded for houses for labourers on hills.
36. *Harijan*, September 10, 1933.
37. *Harijan*, March 8, 1935.
38. *Times of India*, March 9, 1938.
39. *Harijan*, August 1, 1936; *Harijan*, December 7, 1935.
40. *Harijan*, November 2, 1934.
41. D G. Tendulkar, *Mahatma*, Vol. III, p. 168.
42. Halm, *Monetary Theory*.
43. In the large scale mechanisied production, it is difficult for producers to correctly calculate the total production and total demand for the product as the producers work independently and in an uncoordinated way. Hence, if the individual producers start feeling that the future is bright (it may be due to prospect of war, opening of trade relations with a new country, wrong calculations, etc.) then the Marginal Efficiency of Capital becomes higher than the rate of interest and a period of boom starts.
44. If the investor feels that it will not be profitable to invest as the demand has fallen short of supply, then the Marginal Efficiency of Capital will fall short of the rate of interest and he will stop investment. The result will be slump.
45. N.K. Bose, *Selections from Gandhi*, Sec. 248.
46. *Young India*, November 13, 1924.
47. *Harijan Bandhu*, September 15, 1935.

48. *Young India*, November 13, 1931.
49. *Harijan*, November 30, 1935.
50. *Speeches and Writings of Mahatma Gandhi*.
51. Pollock, *Economic and Social Consequences of Automation*.
52. Ibid. Also see letter of Richard B. Gregg with comments of Gandhi which appeared in *Young India*, April 15, 1926.
53. *Harijan*, 1934, p. 301; D.G. Tendulkar, *Mahatma*, Vol. II, p. 283.
54. D.G. Tendulkar, *Mahatma*, Vol. IV, pp. 238-39.
55. Ibid, Vol. VII, p. 71-72.
56. M.L. Dantwala, *Gandhism Reconsidered*, p. 24.
57. B.G Ghate, *Changes in the Occupational Distribution of the Population*, Government of India Press.
58. Ibid.
59. *Gide & Rist*, p. 194.
60. Ibid., p. 196 and *Principles*, Vol. II, p. 318.
61. Ibid, p. 192
62. Ibid.
63. Pollock, *Economic and Social Consequences of Automation*.
64. M.L. Dantwala, *Gandhism Reconsidered*, p. 34.
65. M.L. Dantwala, *Gandhism Reconsidered*, p. 31.
66. Prof. D.P Mukerji read a refreshing paper at the UNESCO Seminar on "Machines and Technology" held at Paris in 1953, and presented the Gandhian view-point in a most convincing way.
67. Gandhi was not prepared in 1921 to change even a single word from his writings of 1908 against machines.
68. D.P. Mukerji, *Diversities*, pp. 208-209.
69. D.P. Mukerji, *Diversities*, p. 210.
70. Ibid.
71. D.P. Mukerji, *Diversities*, p. 213-14.
72. D.G. Tendulkar, *Mahatma*, Vol. II, p. 212.
73. D.P. Mukerji, *Diversities*, p. 213.
74. D.G Tendulkar, *Mahatma*, Vol II, p. 212.
75. D.P. Mukerji, *Diversities*, p. 225.
76. *Harijan*, August 31, 1946.

3

The Goal: Anand via Self-purification

Gandhi considered life as one integrated whole. He was not prepared to divided the individual life into water tight compartments of economics, politics, social, etc. So, he tried to fix the goal for human life as a whole.

Gandhi was never a student of economic and political science. He had no formal education of these subjects. Yet he being in the thick of freedom movement and social rejuvenation, knew the meaning and implications of the words such as economic welfare, socialism, growth, human capital, etc. He was never enamoured by them. Further, he had not much respect for different 'isms' such as fudalism, capitalism, socialism, etc., as he believed that each one of them divide society and encourage untruth, hatred, conflict and complexes.

Gandhi had a religious background. This was strengthened by his profound reading of scriptures of different religions, contacts with religious preachers of various religions and indepth discussion and deep medication over various issues as a staunch searcher of truth. All this shaped his concept of the ultimate goal of individual life, the society and the nation. He started with religion but reached to the ultimate conclusion that reading and understanding religious books is not sufficient. Marching on the royal road of spritual advancement, i.e., more and more of self-realisation, self-improvement and self-purification is really what is needed. This will lead to, as Indian saints and scriptures repeatedly say, to the stage of *Anand*, i.e., permanent happiness which is one step before the ultimate goal of salvation.

Gandhi believed that the goal of an individual and the goal of a society cannot be in conflict with each other as westerners believe and say. He never subscribed to the idea of 'Good of Maximum Number.' He believed in the 'Good of All' So, the goal of an individuals and the goal of the collection of individuals, i.e., the society, the nation and the Family of Nations could not be different. They all should strive for one aim and co-operate, suppliment and compliment each other to reach that ultimate truth of life, which accordingly to Gandhi was 'Good of All', i.e. *Anand.*

The western mind, trained in mundane life, will cry aloud that it is not economics. It is religion which is outdated and unscientific. It is therefore, desirable to spell out the logic, i.e., science, behind this Gandhian concept.

When Gandhi had read a lot of scriptures and considered *Gita* as his guide and philosopher and when he talks of self-purification, then it is but natural that he was well versed with the five sheaths, i.e. stages of development of individuals and world.[1] They are –

1. Material Sheath (*Ann Mai Kosh*)
2. Vital or Energy Sheath (*Pran Mai Kosh*)
3. Manas Sheath (*Mano Mai Kosh*)
4. Intellectual Sheath (*Buddhi Mai Kosh*)
5. Permanent Happiness Sheath (*Anand Mai Kosh*)

A brief description of these sheath is given below:

Material Sheath (*Ann Mai Kosh*)

In the evolution of the world, first came the matter in the form of Sun, Moon, Stars, Land, Mountains, Rivers, Ether, etc. Modern science agrees with it and classified them as solids, liquids and gases.

The Hindu seers discovered that matter is essential in many ways. First, it helps in making bodies of flora, fauna, amphibians, mammals, birds, human being; it makes every thing which has life. They discovered five basic elements of nature – earth, water, air, fire and ether. The permutations and combinations of these elements, they thought, produce all types of bodies. For example, water and stone (earth) produce moss. The modern scientists agree with them though they have discovered more then 128 elements todate.

Secondly, the seers called the body, *sthool-sharir* (gross organs). The ancient Hindu *Rishis* opined that matter is essential to keep the body get going. The plants, the animals, the birds and even the human bodies need food, water, air, shelter, etc. which are provided by the matter. So, the importance of the matter cannot be under-estimated.

The Indian *Rishis* believed that in spite of the importance of matter, over emphasis on matter is not good. It is not conducive to permanent happiness. The western scientists, philosophers, sociologists, economists, political scientists, nay all types of thinkers, do not subscribe to this thought. To them matter and happiness are directly related. However, a stage seems to have come when this concept is meeting a challenge in its own citadel. U.S.A. is an affluent society. It is at the peak of material prosperity but the people there are far from being happy. People have to induce sleep by taking pills. Dreaded diseases such as cancer, blood-pressure, heart ailments, AIDS etc., are daily taking increasing toll. Love, faith, confidence and other noble values have already become casualties. Wife doubts her husband, and *vice versa* and parents have no time for children and so is the converse. Majority of crimes are committed by teen-agers. There is hardly any family life. Matter and more matter have made life miserable.

One thing more. The Indian seers seem to ask several pertinent questions. For example, if body is made of matter alone, how is it that every one has different colours and different sizes? How is that some one is born normal and healthy and some one, born with deformities? Why every child has some inborn traits inherited from his parents or even grand parents? These differences show that body is not made of matter alone. There is some things more to it. These wise seers explain this phenomenon with the help of theory of genes and theory of vitality or energy. Westerners seem to agree. Dr. Hargovind Singh Khurana of U.S.A. got Nobel Prize for his work on genes. Several scientists, all over the world, are working on the inner vital organs of human body and discovering startling things which are confirming the views of ancient Indian *Rishis*.

Vital Sheath *(Pran Mai Kosh)*

Ancient Indian seers said that *Ann Mai Kosh* (Material Sheath), i.e., body, which they called *Sthool-Sharir* (gross organs) is made of matter. Inside this *Sthool-Sharir* (gross organs) is another body known as *Sukshma-Sharir* (subtle body). This *Sukshma-Sharir* (subtle body) is also made of matter but has five important organs:

(i) *Gyanandriyas* (Senses of Knowledge) – According to Rishis, they are five – eyes, nose, tongue, ears and skin.
(ii) *Karmendriyas* (Senses of Actions) – Seers said that they are also five – Anus, sex organ, hands, legs and speech.
(iii) *Prans* (Breaths) – They too are five – Breathing, excretion, digestion, blood circulation and nervous system.
(iv) *Manas* – This includes *Kama* (desires) and *Artha* (activities).
(v) *Vivek* (Intellect) – This is different and superior to scientific temper.

These five components of *Sukshma-Sharir* (subtle body) are the most important parts. They exist, as *Rishis* opined, in all living beings, including flora and fauna. The only difference is the stage of their development.

These five components are mechanical, i.e., functional. They function in a most scientific manner. The question arises, why do they function? What makes them work?

It is an admitted fact that none can move, not to say of functioning, without what Indian seers called *Prana* (Energy). The modern scientist may agree to call it energy.

According to physics, energy is of six types:

1. Sound
2. Heat
3. Light
4. Magnetism
5. Friction or mechanics
6. Electricity – hydro or thermal or atomic.

The energy which makes the components of *Sukshma-Sharir* function, appears to be of a different type of energy than these six types. For example, like electricity, it does not repulse or give shocks.

Ancient Indian seers gave a few characteristic of *Prana* energy:

(i) Energy can be associated with any body (or its part, or organ) but it has a separate existence and identity;
(ii) Energy can be transferred from one body (matter) to another; and
(iii) One type of energy can be converted into another type of energy.

The modern scientists will readily agree that these characters of *Prana* energy are found in the six types of energies also which they know of. In spite of these similarities in character, which probably are due to the process by which energy is produced, there are a few dissimilarities.

Modern scientists have found out, though in an imperfect way, that the food which we eat, through digestion process, takes the form of blood. Blood has fats, carbohydrates and proteins. They are burnt with the help of oxygen which is provided through respiration system. This gives energy which we find in cells. In this process carbon dioxide is also produced whose retention in the body is harmful. Hence, it is exhaled out into the atmosphere through respiratory system.

The Indian *Rishis* had laid great emphasis on the type of food which one should eat. Their insistence on *Satvik* food and *Satvik* habits may have some good relation with the quality and quantity of human energy produced, or energy requirements, or both. Similarly, the seers' insistence on deep breathing and *Pranayam*, a technique to control intake, retention and outtake of breath, which means taking oxygen and expelling carbon dioxide, might be influencing the generation of energy. Modern science is agreeing to the importance of *Pranayam*.

Gandhi certainly was wide aware of this Vital Sheath. When he was leaving for England, he took a vow not to eat meat. Then, by his own sweet will, he started experiments on vegetarianism in England which continued throughout his life. He discovered that though milk is full meal yet it is not good for a *Brahamachari*. He reduced his morning breakfast to cure himself of headache. He found out which is the best food for the body and soul. That was the source of his excellent health even at an advanced age.

It is quite revealing and interesting that science is finding out these things today which ancient Indian *Rishis* were saying long back. A few illustrations will be sufficient.

(a) *Mind* is a very complicated part of the human body. Psychologist tell us that it has three parts—conscious, unconscious and subconscious. For the perfect functioning of this most complicated machine of human mind, energy is needed. This energy is generated in the mind itself. Where it is generated, is yet not known. The maximum which science has been able to do is to invent an instrument known as E.E.G. (Electro-Encephalo-Graphy) which can record the current of the mind and help in diagnosis of the disease.

(b) *Heart* is a type of pumping set which pumps blood in arteries. It regulates the flow of blood which is the life line of the whole body. Naturally, the heart must also be working with the help of energy. Recent researches have shown that in the right auricle of the heart, there is a tiny generation set which is known as Pace-Maker. The medical science has invented an instrument known as E.C.G. (Electro-Cardio-Graphy) to measure this energy and through it to diagnose heart disease.

(c) *Eyes* are just like a camera. The image of the object is formed on Retina, the innermost layer of the eye. This image is conveyed to the brain through optic nerves. The energy required for their perception and communication is readily provided partly by the cells of optic nerve, which have energy and partly by the brain. The energy of the eyes are measured by the instrument known as E.R.C. (Electro-Retino-Graphy).

(d) Human body is full of cells. They have electric charge. Extensive studies in cyto-chemistry have established that all the cells have charged ions.

(e) Human body has also innumerable Genes. They are carriers of parental characters and they are inherited by subsequent generations. This phenomenon is termed as heredity. The whole of these activity including reproduction and inheritance of genes is accomplished with the help of energy. This energy is provided by cells.

(i) Harmones play an important role in the human body. The functions of harmones are known – they help in normal functioning of digestive system, circulatory system, excretory system, respiratory system etc., through chemical reactions. Normally, they function with the help of energy.

(g) Enzymes are also important for the human body. They also use energy.

Such instances can be multiplied.

Energy is also found in all living beings: may they be flora or fauna or birds. Here are some examples:

(i) Bats are able to know the location of objects with the help of their particular type of energy. Bats, zoologists tell us, emit magnetic rays to locate objects. Science has taken the idea from bats to develop radar system;

(ii) Electric Ray Fish produces mild electric current which is used to keep away her predators;

(iii) Sea Gulls fly to safe places before the sea storm comes. They are helped by energy currents of some type;

(iv) Termites keep the entrance of their nests in a particular direction with the help of some kind of energy, may be magnetic;

(v) Certain birds migrate from one place to another with the change of weather. They mostly travel by night. It is a settled opinion of the scientists that these birds receive direction with the help of magnetic energy; and

(vi) Owls, Frogs, Snakes—all use special types of energy to locate their preys.

Examples can be multiplied.

Scientists of different fields are working in this new sphere in U.S.A., Italy, France, U.S.S.R. etc. The School of Nancy, the School of Charcot and the School of Mesmarist of U.S.A. have become well-known centres.

Hindu seers felt that the life currents in vitals move through subtle media of ethers.

The functions of this *Sukshma-Sharir* (subtle body) or functional body can be made more efficient if energy from which they are operated can be made more efficient, i.e., its frequency and voltage are regulated to desired specifications. How can it be done? Indian *Rishis* have given a full strategy starting with *Satvik* food to *Satvik* thoughts to *Satvik* actions and some exercises, various forms of which are called *Yoga*, *Dhyana*, *Sadhna* or *Tapa*. Gandhi, therefore, made experiments on what to eat and what not to eat. He realised "supplication, worship, prayer are no superstitions; they are acts more real than the acts of eating, drinking, sitting or walking."

Manas Sheath *(Mano Mai Kosh)*

Besides the *Sthool-Sharir* or *Ann Mai Kosh* (Material Sheath) and *Sukshma-Sharir* or *Pran Mai Kosh* (Vital Sheath) or functional body, there is another body which deals with emotions. This is called *Manas Kosh* or *Manas Sheath.*

This *Manas* Sheath is somewhere located in the mind. This is found in more developed form in a human being than in animals, birds or even plants. Western psychologists call it conscious mind.

Manas Sheath has two main parts or emotions:

(a) *Kama*— It means all desires including sex, wealth, fame, salvation (*Moksh*) etc.

(b) *Artha*— It means all activities—material and non-material, good or bad, social, political, religious, spiritual etc.

Kama or desires lead to *Artha* or activity. This combination is the key to human happiness or unhappiness. Till recently, it was a considered opinion that all physical ailments are due to imbalances or phlegm, wind or gas and bile, or seasonal changes, or infections etc. Hence different types of medical sciences—Allopathy, Homocopathy, Unani or Aurvedic, tried to treat a sick person according to their own systems. However, recent researchers are assigning increasing responsibility to emotional factors. Fear, anger, hatred, envy, jealousy, feeling of insult, insecurity etc., are responsible for several physical problems which cannot be cured by any system of medical science. Headache, migrain, lunacy, nervousness, blood pressure, skin diseases, deformities in wombs, lethargy are some such diseases. On the other hand, good thoughts, respect, confidence, happiness, satisfaction, fearlessness, non-anger, love, auto-suggestion etc., help to improve health and impart younger looks. Hence, greater importance is now being given to psychological treatment.

Scientists have recently invented an instrument known as E.M.B. (Electrical Stimulation of Brain) which is used in brain-washing. The experiments on animals have been quite successful. Due to this instrument it became possible to make cats get afraid of rats.

Indian seers were of the confirmed opinion that man must try to control *Kama* (desires) and sublimate them. Then, he should also try to control his *Artha* (activities) for material advancement and direct most of them to help others. This gives self-satisfaction and inner happiness. This control, the seers opined, was a control of *Dhanna* over *Kama* and *Artha*.

There is not one but several methodologies to achieve this

desired goal. Development of concentration power through *Yoga* or *Bhakti* (devotion) or social service is one way. It is an accepted fact that concentration cheeks disintegration and concentrates powers so that they become more effective. It also improves efficiency. To develop concentration, one must develop determination.

It is here that the role of *Satvik* food, *Satvik* thought, *Satvik* actions, nay *Satvik* life becomes an important.

Gandhi was certainly aware of this sheath. So, after starting with experiments with diet, he slowly moved towards *Brahamacharya*, i.e.., control over five organs and acquire concentration power. Gandhi ultimately took a vow of *Brahamacharya*. This is also well known that he was a social worker par-excellence. With this he mixed Prayer, Fast and *maun* (silence).

Thus, all the three—control over palate, *Brahamacharya* and social work, slowly, added with the other three, transformed Gandhi's entire personality. From a very ordinary man, he developed into an extraordinary super man.

Vivek or Intellectual Sheath *(Buddhi Mai Kosh)*

Ancient Hindu *Rishis*, who were great discoverers, had found out that *Buddhi* has great powers. If it is properly awakened, it sharpens the memory which can remember the events of past lives and foresee future events'; the ears can hear the past and future voices and eyes can see past and future. It can solve the most complicated problems in a minute and guide man to correctly differentiate between right and wrong, from the wider point of view. Till recently even the Indians doubted in the efficiency of the awakening of *Buddhi*.

Psychologist Freud has given three classifications of mind:

(i) The Conscious—It gives awareness of inner and/or outer environment;

(ii) The Subconscious—It pertains to mental activities of which the individual is not aware; and

(iii) The Unconscious—That portion of the psyche which is a store house of memories which are not directly accessible to consciousness, but may be brought into consciousness.

The Western psychologists know much about the conscious mind and any number of experiments have been made to know this part of mind. However, their knowledge till recently was almost negligible about the subconscious mind and still less about the unconscious one. Now they are trying to know about these two minds, specially the unconscious one and the findings are encouraging.

The Indian seers were of the opinion that the conscious mind is mainly concerned with *Ann Mai Kosh* (Material Sheath), *Pran Mai Kosh* (Vital Sheath) and *Mano Mai Kosh* (*Manas* Sheath) i.e., worldly things and individual gains. It helps in the development of an integrated personality through the interplay of Id, Ego and Super-ego. Here, acquired knowledge is confined to matter only. This science develops an analytical power to decide what is right and what is wrong for him or his material world. He takes a narrow view. This we call scientific knowledge and scientific temper.

The Western psychologists are, at present, busy in knowing more about unconscious mind. It is now certain that this part of mind is not concerned with the blood circulation system, respiratory system, digestion system, or any other system concerned with the keeping of the body and mind functional. The medical science has now realised that in the head, there are some centres of magnetism and that they are affected by the North Pole as well as South Pole. The hair when combed quickly, create a magnetic effect on the comb.

The psychologists feel that the unconscious mind has tremendous powers to know the part and to foresee the future, help in solving complicated problems and communicating with other worlds through various senses. This mind becomes more active when the conscious mind is resting, i.e., man is sleeping or when through selected methods, it is made active. A few instances, to prove its powers, can be cited:

(i) Cats are able to know that a building will be destroyed shortly. So, they change their abode well in time;

(ii) Goethe has written in his autobiography that one night, in his sleep, he felt that a severe earthquake had come in Sicily. After sometime, it proved to be correct;

(iii) J. Swift wrote in one of his books that *Mangal* Planet has two moons and the speed of one moon is double than that of the other. This premonition proved to be true in 1877 when Naval Observatory of Washington verified it;

(iv) James Watt was worried on how to make round lead balls for guns. In sleep, he got a clue. He dreamt a storm, rain and round shells hitting his head. When the melted drops of lead were dropped in the water, the process of making round balls was invented;

(v) Iliyas was desperately trying to make a sewing machine. He had developed everything except a needle. One night he dreamt that horsemen, with spears, who had eyes in head, had come to kill him. This premonition gave him an idea of how to make a needle with an eye;

(vi) Neils Bohr, in his dream got an idea of the structure of Atom-nucleus and the rotating electrons; and

(vii) Henry Fehar collected information of about 69 mathematicians. He reached the conclusion that 51 mathematicians got hints in their sleep on the basis of which they could complete their problems.

All these were the wonders of the partly active unconscious mind.

Awakening of the unconscious mind can change the basic character of a man, develop memory and other senses. Here are some illustrations.

(a) French Psychologist Prof. Delgoda, bypassing a current on Temple of a timid animal, Loo Loo, could make him a fearless animal;

(b) Canadian Dr. W.J. Penfield bypassing a current at a particular part of a man could develop his memory to the extent that he could remember even his past life which was stored in a part of his mind; and

(c) Dr. J.V. Rhyne has discovered that without the means of communication, thoughts can travel and influence another man, even when he is at a distance. We sometimes get an idea that a particular visitor will arrive and it proves to be true. We sometimes feel bad and expect some bad news and they come.

Indian scriptures mention a number of persons who had succeeded in awakening this part of their mind, partly or fully, and therefore came to have enormous powers which we call supernatural. Savitri, Anusuia, Damyanti, Gandhari, Sudama, Karna, Kabir, Tulsi, Arvind, Gandhi are some such names. They were not seers who had renounced the world and withdrawn to forests.

How to awaken this part of mind? *Rishis,* past and present, have mentioned a number of methods. Some are:

(i) *Yoga* or *Tapa* or *Sadha* which includes *Satvik* way of life;
(ii) Social service;
(iii) Developing determination and concentration powers through various methods; and
(iv) Adopting human values, social values and spiritual values and go on increasing their quantities.

Obviously, this awakening of mind gives much wider conception of right and wrong than the scientific knowledge and equips a person to have more comprehensive judgement.

Rishis called this awakening of *Chetna* (consciousness) as the fifth dimension. One can imagine how much this fifth dimension of *Chetna* will change the picture of what we see, hear, do, like or dislike.

Gandhi could not be unaware of this Intellectual Sheath when he had not only read religious books but acted upon them. It is evident that Gandhi had developed his intellect and so he could see future and act accordingly. A common man, not blessed with this power was often stunned by his utterances and actions. For example, his work on *Harijan* welfare in 1920 was taken as his angularity but can any body dispute it today. Today there is no dearth of people who will agree with Gandhi that Congress should have been winded up after independence. His admission of the Himalayan Blunder and suddenly withdrawing the movement appeared to be a wrong decision then but who will disagree with him today.

Permanent Happiness Sheath *(Anand Mai Kosh)*

Ancient Indian *Rishis,* who were social scientists, great discoverers and seers had discovered that life comes in a body because of soul; when this soul leaves the body, it stops functioning and the cells stop producing energy. This soul *(Atma)* and super-conscious *(Parmatma)* are one and the same; life, or soul or spirit, is indestructible; the soul leaves a body to enter into another body after a time-interval and this process goes on till it achieves *Moksha* (salvation) i.e., Soul *(Atma)* and super-conscious *(Parmatma)* become one.

Western thinkers, to begin with, did not accept the existence of spirit or soul. However, the recent researches have forced them to have a second thought. Some experiments deserve mention:

(a) Some Para-Psychologists, after mesmerising a person, recorded the occurrence of two or three or even a dozen earlier lives by taking him back to past lives. These readings have withstood the test of authenticity;

(b) Scientific researches are increasingly becoming introverts. For example, study of Atom revealed that Atom is a miniature of solar system; Electrons, Protons and Neutrons form one Atom in which electrons rotate in a set pattern around the nucleus of an Atom which is formed of Protons and Neutrons; the splitting of the Atom releases tremendous energy etc. The questions may be asked; what makes the electrons move? From where does come the tremendous energy when Atom is splitted? The Western scientists have yet to offer an answer. The Hindu seers answer it with the help of their theory of soul and super-conscious, which they also sometimes call as light; and

(c) Botanists have discovered that plants are not lifeless, they have life. Not only this. They can feel various sentiments and react to them. Efforts are being made to utilise them in protecting buildings and catching thieves.

These and many more researches have reduced the vehement antagonism of scientists to the existence of soul.

According to Hindu *Rishis, Anand* (Permanent happiness) starts when the soul *(Atma)* starts realising that it is a part of the super-conscious *(Parmatma)* and begins to integrate with it. With every step towards integration, Anand goes on increasing.

This process of integration starts when there is a proper mixture of the four human sheaths, viz, matter, vitality, *Manas* and *Buddhi,* which are also interdependent. For example, matter is essential but too much importance of matter will be harmful for the development of vitality sheath. Then both matter and vital sheaths are important but *Kama* (desires) and *Artha* (activities) must be channellised towards the goal of permanent happiness. This can come only through the development of *Buddhi* (mind) specially its subconscious and unconscious parts. This alone can give powers for taking the correct decisions (not with the present scientific knowledge). When this is achieved, a stage is set when soul *(Atma)* starts realising the existence of super-conscious *(Parmatma)* and the process of integration starts. This opens the door of permanent happiness or *Anand*.

Thus, the Hindu view of evolution is wholestic and not confined merely to material development or evolution. Permanent happiness cannot be ensured when we confine ourselves only to a lower stage of development i.e. matter.

Certainly, Gandhi was aware, through experiment with Truth, of these five sheaths and so, his insistence on simplicity and not multiplication of want and ultimately not on welfare or socialism but permanent happiness through self-analysis and self-purification. The goal of the individual, the society and the Family of Nations should be this *Anand*, i.e., permant happiness and certainly, in this scheme of things there is no scope of conflict between individual-interest, the social interest and the international interest. All will move in harmony. The conflict that Westerners point out in these three is because the goal is not correct. Material welfare remains only upto the first three sheaths.

A man has two dimensions. In vertical dimension he has a body (material), vitality, a *Manas*, intellect and spirit and at the horizontal plane, he has a family, a society and a Family of Nations. So, to be in the stage of *Anand*, there must be an ideal equilibrium of both horizontal and vertical. Till a perfect equilibrium is achieved, efforts, must be made to have a dynamic equilibrium.

One may exclaim: This is not economics? This is withdrawing to mountains and do all sorts of funny things. This is going back to primitive age. A Gandhi, who is well versed with Gita's Kama Yoga and Anasakti Karma will smile and will plead that it is a way of life in which one stays where one is, performs all the duties but does not get extra enchanted with economic mirages. And there is perfect logic behind all this thought.

Today economists, planners and technocrats are amused at their new slogan of 'Human Capital'. But what they mean is not the qualitative change in the human being, which may lead to their permanent happiness and the social well being, but only increase in their productive skills so that they may become better "Economic Man", Obviously, Gandhi could not subscribe to their concept. He will insist in making a new quality oriented man who may be full with human values such as, Truth, Simplicity, Non-Violence, Self-Control, Dignity of Human Labour, Non-Stealing, etc. Gandhi, through his vast experience, knew that a child starts with his inborn qualities, mainly depending upon his genes and can improve them, if he gets a proper atmosphere and facilities and has the requisite will. For him 'one step forward' on this royal road will be much more than his better earning capacity.

REFERENCE

1. Gupta, S.S., *Integrated Development Plan for India: Goal, Tools and Strategies*, Concept Publishing Company, New Delhi., 1992.

4

The Gandhian Approach

People, including scholars, feel that the approach of Gandhi was at best, intuitional, he being essentially a religious man believing in God and spirit. They argue that most of the decisions were taken by him on the spur of the moment and that they were governed by his inner voice. Sometimes when he could not hear that inner voice, he went on a fast[1] or observed *Maun* (i.e. Silence)[2] which, according to him, helped him in realizing the truth and hearing that faint inner voice. Nothwithstanding the general notion, strengthened quite often by Gandhi's writings and utterances, that he was a believer in intuitionalism[3], a careful and deep study of his life and method of working proves beyond doubt that the approach of Gandhi was neither religious, nor intuitional but very much scientific and rational.

The social scientist would certainly like to know whether Gandhi's approach was micro or macro, whether he studied problems under static conditions or under dyamic conditions and whether he used the tools of inductive analysis or deductive.

Macro and Micro

To this it can be said, that his approach does not fall strictly under any one of the above approaches. It was a peculiar mixture of them all. And if a name is to be given, we can call it eclectic or synthetic. For example, Gandhi used to see things in their entirety, which means that his approach was macro. But this macro was somewhat different from what a social scientist knows. Today social scientists have divided life into different, almost water-tight compartments and the specialist of each compartment thinks only of his compartment, whether he studies it as a whole or in parts. All the economists having macro approach fall in this category. Gandhi, on the other hand, strongly argued that life is one and as such should be studies as a whole.[4] He did not believe in different compartments—political, social, economic and religious, etc., and studied human problems in their entirety and not under the heads of economic problems or social problems or political problems. Thus even when he was busy with the momentous task of achieving political independence for his country, he did not lose sight of social, economic and other problems. His conviction was that all these things do move forward or backward together. Again, the present social scientist is mainly concerned with the problems of his department which are, at best, of national character. He argues that the socio-politico-economic structure of every country is different from that of others and as such every country has its own peculiar traits of seemingly common problems. Gandhi appears to differ with such a belief. He argues that life crosses national boundaries. The basic truths, the basic human problems, the basic human nature are the same all over the world.[5] Whatever differences appear to be there, they are merely superficial and not basic. So, he preaches the surmons of non-violence, simplicity, bread-labour, truth etc., not only for a few selected persons, or for a few countries but for all the people of all the countries. This was his macro approach. Gloriously, this is much wider than what the modern social scientists think. It covers the entire life.

But Gandhi adopted micro approach too. Had it not been so, he would have readily accepted the utilitarian principle of 'greatest good of the greatest number'.[6] Again, while propounding his ideas on the political framework of a country, Gandhi was not prepared to sacrifice the minority for the sake of the majority simply because he was interested as much in individuals as in the bulk.[7] For this very reason, he disagreed with the communist and fascist thinkers who preached that the State is supreme and individual is nothing before it.[8] Gandhi, with all his force, resisted this and went to the extent of saying that in his political set-up, the majority decision will not be thrust upon the minority.[9] Due to this very approach he believed in conversion of heart of the rich and the bad, as also of even enemies and not in their annihilation.[10] A study of Gandhi shows that when he took keen interest in national problems, he took an equally keen interest in the welfare of individuals as well. He became almost a guide, philosopher and friend, a nurse, a cook, a servant of whosoever came in his contact. He believed in raising the moral fibre of individuals and through them to build up a new man and a new society. It was because of this interest in the individual that he mesmerized the largest number of people and won unquestioned loyalty from even those who had nothing in common with him.

Inductive and Deductive

Gandhi used both the inductive and deductive techniques. When he arrived on the political scene of India, he, on the advice of his political Guru, observed silence for a year and utilized this period in going round the country visiting each village and obtaining first hand information of the problems of the individuals, of individual villages and individual cities. On the basis of a general survey of this kind, he formulated his policies. He repeated this feat several times and came to know every nook and corner of this vast country. When in Champaran, he sat down to interview each individual farmer, it was certainly the inductive approach. The same technique was adopted when the Jalianwala-Bagh episode took place. Any number of such instances can be cited to show that Gandhi fruitfully utilized the inductive technique.

But alongside, Gandhi harnessed the deductive method also. His repeated practice of resorting to silence or observing fast, which majority of Indian people, bred and brought up in a religious atmosphere, thought to be a religious practice, was nothing but the technique of concentrating on a problem and using deductive tools. Take for example, his latest fast in Delhi. The division of the country followed by murderous riots, first in Pakistan and thereafter in India, bewildered the Great Mahatma. His faith in oneness of different religions, in religious tolerance, in goodness of man, of amity between Hindus and Muslims was, for the time being, rudely shaken. He wanted to know whether he was wrong or it was just a passing phase of life. For this no data could be collected. No calm thinking was possible. So, the Mahatma resorted to contemplation and used deductive analysis. He returned with the added faith in the correctness of his preachings. His belief in God, i.e. as a moral force or truth, his faith in the supremacy of non-violence, his techniques of non-violent, non-cooperation and *Satyagraha*, his ideas on simplicity and bread-labour or, for the matter of that, his ideas on all the fundamentals of life were philosophical in nature, but they were not the outcome of any survey or inductive analysis but of deductive approach or pure logic. Gandhi mainly used deductive method when dealing with abstract things, the basic fundamentals of life and he freely employed inductive method in tackling the day-to-day problems or testing the results of his theories.

Dynamic and Static

Gandhi was most dynamic in his outlook. His views on machines, for example, underwent a dramatic change from 1924 onward. A sense of limit grew in him.[11] He was deadly opposed to even the smallest 'tools' before 1924 but then he realized his mistake and agreed to use machines. He did not like to propound a theory of his own, or leave behind a sect or 'ism'[12] because he felt that in this changing world nothing except a few fundamentals could be said to be permanent. His autobiography recounts his experiments with truth. The experiments changed according to time and place. The Mahatma who was a firm believer in non-violence agreed not only to administer poison to a dying calf[13] but also to sending an army, equipped with all the modern weapons of destruction, to protect Kashmir against the brutal invasion by Pakistan. Gandhi who first believed that 'there can be non-violence of the weak' changed his opinion after seeing the disturbances of 1947.[14] Scores of such instances can be cited from the life of the Mahatma which will show that he was neither always static in his views nor did he always study problems under dynamic conditions. His views on Untouchability, the *Purdah* System, *Sati* Pratha and the Caste System will bear it out.

However, a close study of Gandhi will show that the man who was most dynamic was static like rock when it came to basic principles of life. We find him most static when we come to his views on God and unity of life, good of all, means and ends, non-violence, simplicity, bread-labour and proper valuation. Gandhi once wrote:

> "At the time of writing, I never think of what I have said before. My aim is not to be consistent with my previous statements on a given question, but to be consistent with truth as it may present itself to me at a given moment. The result has been that I have grown from truth to truth."

Again:

> "Whenever I have been obliged to compare my writings even of 50 years ago with the latest, I have discovered no inconsistency between the two."[15]

Thus, Gandhian approach to problems, in the terms of western social scientists was an admixture of micro-macro, Inductive–Deductive and Statics-Dynamic

xxx xxx xxx

To have a clear understanding of Gandhian approach, one must refer to his mental make up, experiments and conclusions.

Gandhi had read scriptures of a number of religions and yet he selected *Gita* as his guide and philosopher, *Gita*, like other Hindu scriptures, tried to build up a society on the basis of some social values. These values are:

1. *Purity* (Shauch)– It meant cleanliness of body, mind and environment. Today world is worried about pollution and searching methods to purify patables, water, air, atmosphere, etc.

2. *Non-stealing* (Asteya)–It means not only stealing material things or thoughts (copyright has come due to it) but it also means not holding for future. Gandhi gave it a new name, viz., simplicity.

3. *Knowledge confined to matter* (i.e. education or Dhi)

4. *Knowledge of soul* (vidya)–Modern scientist is now struggling to know of it.

5. *Truth* (Satya)–Gandhi called it God or Religion

6. *Self-control* (Brahamacharya)–It meant control of five senses–ear, nose, eyes, tongue and organ. Gandhi realised its importance and started with the control of palate and then, walked on to control sex. Gandhi thought that it helps in transformation of the human personality.

7. *Patience* (Dhriti)–Not to lose calm, composition and balance of mind in adverse circumstances is Patience.

8. *Forgiveness* (*Kshma*)–Not to get provoked and not to retaliate to seek vengeance and to forget the provocation as non-important and have no ill-will against the doer is forgiveness.

9. *Control of Manas* (Dam)–Indian seers talk of Manas, Buddhi and Anand as separate identities. By Manas, they mean a place from

where all the desires originate. On the other hand, Western psychologists divide mind in three parts—the conscious, sub-conscious and unconscious. They know very little about the last two. They think that it is from the conscious mind that the desires and actions originate. Indian seers thought that *Manas* is controlled by Buddhi.

10. *Non-Anger* (*Akrodha*)—To control anger is one thing but not to have anger is another. Non-anger means the later.

To these ten basic moral or social or human values, some more values were added in course of time. Important ones are:

(i) *Renunciation* (*Aparigraha*)—Marx said that love for matter is at the centre of human progress. But then he also felt that it is cause of several ills. He therefore, simultaneously came out with the remedy of abolition of private property. This created an inherent contradiction in Marx's thinking. In the light of this experience, Indian seers concept of renunciation, appears to be better. It meant, out of self-realization to go on giving up love and possession of worldly things.

(ii) *Non-violence* (Ahinsa)

(iii) *Fearlessness and Boldness*

(iv) *Discipline*—Man has body, mind, Manas and soul. Discipline, according to Indian seers, helps an individual, through training to control, develop and bring in unism the body, the mind, and the *Manas*.

(v) *Patriotism*—As per Indian seers, patriotism means giving greater importance to the territorial integrity of the country, its great cultural heritage—value system, customs, traditions, etc.—and the great men of the land, belonging to different walks of life. Preparedness to protect all of them, honour them and try to imbibe their preachings in one's own life is patriotism. Certainly, then patriotism is much wider and nobler than the Western concept.

Gandhi knew all these human values and through his own experiments, selected a few of them, gave a meaning to them in relation of his times and also added a few more. Therefore, it can be said that his approach depended upon the following.

I
GOD AND UNITY OF LIFE

Gandhi is readily accepted as basically a religious man, a believer in

God and a saint. His repeated utterances[16], if read without understanding his philosophy, seem to confirm this view. However, a close study of his writings and utterances on the subject will convince anybody that his God and religion were much different from the conventional ones. To him religions were imperfect and so subject to a process of evolution and reinterpretation.[17] It was because of this imperfection and changing nature of religion that Gandhi opposed conversion and running down of other religions. To quote him:

> "... No one faith is perfect. All faiths are equally dear to their respective votaries. What is wanted, therefore, is living friendly contact among the followers of the great religions of the world and not a clash among them in the fruitless attempt on the part of each community to show the superiority of its faith over the rest..."
> "It follows from what I have said above that India is in no need of conversion of the kind I have in mind. Conversion in self-purification, self-realisation is the crying need of the times. That, however, is not what is ever meant by proselytising. To those who could convert India, might not be said, "Physician heal thyself."[18]
> "The Allah of Islam is the same as the God of Christians and the Ishwara of Hindus... My approach to other religions, therefore, is never as a fault finding critic but as a devotee hoping to find the like beauties in the other religions and wishing to incorporate in my own the good I may find in them and miss in mine."[19]

To Gandhi, religion and God were not meant to achieve the other world. "There is no such thing as the other world. All worlds are one. There is no 'here' and no 'there'."[20]

Then what is religion of Gandhi's concept? To Gandhi, "True religion means good thought and good conduct."[21] Religion "changes one's very nature, which binds one indissolubly to the truth within and which ever purifies."[22] Gandhi's religion is not, therefore, a thing in isolation. It operates on the man, his nature and his institutions. Gandhi, therefore, once wrote: "If I seem to take part in politics, it is only because politics today encircles us like the coils of a snake from which one cannot get out no matter how one tries. I wish to wrestle with the snake. ...I am trying to introduce religion into politics."[23]

Gandhi's religion, like other religions, also rotates round a God. But his God is different. He is not a superhuman, controlling our destinies. For him it is Truth.

"My religion is based on truth and non-violence. Truth is my God. Non-violence is the means of realising him."[24] Again, "In fact it is more correct to say that Truth is God, than to say that God is Truth. But as we cannot do without a ruler or a general, names of God such as King of Kings, or the Almighty are and will remain more usually current. On deeper thinking, however, it will be realised that *Sat* or *Satya* is the only correct and fully significant name for God."[25]

But what is Truth? Explaining the meaning, Gandhi wrote:

> "Generally speaking, observing the law of Truth is merely understood to mean that we must speak the truth. But we in the Ashram understand the word Satya or Truth in a much wider sense. There should be Truth in thought, Truth in speech, and Truth in action."[26]

Gandhi thought that Truth might appear to be relative, changing with time, place and man. "What may appear as truth to one person will often appear as untruth to another person."[27] But this should not detract the seeker. "When there is honest effort, it will be realized that what appears to be different truths are like apparently different countless leaves of the same tree."[28] Sooner or later real truth will come out.[29]

To achieve Truth-God, one must be non-violent. "Truth is my God. Non-violence is the means of realizing Him."[30] Again, "In the march towards Truth, anger, selfishness, hatred etc., naturally give way, for otherwise Truth would be impossible to attain."[31]

Somebody asked Gandhi, "How can we serve God...? Gandhi replied, "Service of His creation is the service of God."[32] Again, "...The immediate service of all human beings becomes a necessary part of the endeavour simply because the only way to find God is to see Him in his creation and be one with it."[33]

Since Gandhi is convinced that God can be realized only through non-violence, i.e. love and service of humanity, he overrules all chances of class-conflict. If everyone is truthful, non-violent and keen to serve humanity, love and homogeneity of interests will be natural outcome. Gandhi wrote:

> "I believe in absolute oneness of God and, therefore, also of humanity. What though we have many bodies? We have but one soul. The rays of the sun are many through refraction. But they have the same source."[34]
>
> "I believe in the essential unity of man and for that matter of all that lives. Therefore, I believe that if one man gains... the whole world gains with him and, if one man falls, the whole world falls to that extent."[35]

When the whole world is one and there is no clash or conflict of just interests, how the life of a man can be divided into different compartments. "I claim that human mind or human society is not divided into watertight compartments called social, political or religious. All act and react upon one another."[36]

II
GOOD OF ALL

It is not only desirable but possible to make each and every individual happy in the true sense of the word. Gandhi was very much influenced by the religious books and preachings of the saints. Hence, his whole outlook is governed by ethical standards. He was not one of the followers of Bentham who believed in the slogan: "the greatest good of the greatest number."[37] For "it means in its nakedness that in order to achieve the supposed good of 51 per cent, the interest of 49 per cent may be, or rather, should be sacrificed. It is heartless doctrine and has done harm to humanity."[38] Gandhi felt convinced that the goal of man's life is happiness which can be realised only by being face to face with God. God can be realised, according to Gandhi, by 'seeing Him in His creation and by being one with it.' In simple terminology it means that happiness can be achieved only by serving others. So, the goal becomes 'the greatest good of all'. Explaining the difference between his goal and that of Bentham, Gandhi wrote:

> "He (the ahimsaist) will strive for the greatest good of all and die in the attempt to realize the ideal... The greatest good of all inevitably includes the good of the greater number, and, therefore, he and the utilitarian will converge at many points in their career but there does come a time when they must part

company, and even work in opposite directions. The utilitarian to be logical will never sacrifice himself. The absolutist will even sacrifice himself."[39]

When this is translated into economics, it will mean the attainment of a social equilibrium, an optimum combination of material and moral progress."[40] In other words, it will mean the establishment of a 'stateless and classless society.'

III
ENDS AND MEANS

In the present materialistic world achievements of ends have become all important. A philosophy has grown that one must achieve aims at any cost. It is argued, if the end is good, do not worry about means, they will take care of themselves. A communist or a facist, or an anarchist, or a dictator, or an army general, therefore, does not mind destroying a few hundred tonnes of foodgrains when people are starving, or shoot down hundreds of countrymen or send a few thousand to concentration camps if this destruction is helpful to him in achieving his goal. This philosophy, in course of time, has vitiated even the ends. Now the ends which are purely for self or party-good are made to appear in the interest of the country and its people. Now neither means nor ends have remained good.

In Gandhian philosophy means are closely connected with ends; they are even convertible terms.[41] He did not believe in the maxim 'the end justifies the means'. He insisted that means should be pure for man has control over means and not on results.[42] Moreover, as the means so the ends.[43] His own experience also showed that whenever he tried to compromise with the means, the progress received a setback. Rajkot affair is an instance.[44] Cases of India and Indonesia can be cited in support. Both won their independence recently. One adopted non-violent means and the other took to arms. The result is that the relations between India and England still are cordial while they are far from satisfactory between Indonesia and Holland.

By this it should not be mistook that Gandhi did not worry about ends. To him both ends and means were equally important and he insisted that both should be equally pure.

To Gandhi, end for 'an individual is self-realization, which will promote good of all. This self-realization can be achieved by self-purification.'[45] To purify oneself, one will have to take vows which are defined by Gandhi as, "To do at any cost something that one ought to do."[46] Gandhi laid down five important vows in the Satyagraha Ashram which are nothing but means. They are: Truth, Non-violence, Non-stealing , Non-possession and *Brahmacharya*.[47] "Taking of a vow does not mean that we are able to observe it completely. From the very beginning, it does mean constant and honest effort in thought, word and deed with a view to its fulfilment."[48] Only through these noble means, lasting peace and progress can come out. It might take slightly more time. This should not deter us because quick results are also short-lived.

IV
NON-VIOLENCE

A close study of the life of Gandhi shows that he had no idea of non-violence and its potentialities till May, 1893. It was only on his way to Pretoria from Durban by train that a 'small' incident forced him to adopt the technique of non-violence as the last and the only alternative, which he then felt was left for him. Gandhi had a first class ticket and a seat booked for him. The train arrived at Martizburg, the capital of Natel, at about 9 p.m. As he had his own bedding, he declined to have one offered by the railway company. Soon after came a passenger. He looked Gandhi up and down. "He saw that I was a coloured man", Gandhi wrote narrating the incident. "This disturbed him." Out he went and came in again with one or two officials. They all kept quiet, when another official came to me and said , 'Come along, you must go to the van compartment.'

> "But I have a first class ticket", said I.
> "That does not matter", rejoined the other. "I tell you, you must go to the van compartment."
> "I tell you, I was permitted to travel in this compartment at Durban, and insist on going on in it."
> "No, you won't," said the official. "You must leave this compartment, or else I shall have to call a police constable to push you out."
> "Yes, you may, I refuse to get out voluntarily."
> "The constable came. He took me by the hand and pushed me

> out. My luggage was also taken out. I refused to go to the other compartment and the train steamed away. I went and sat in the waiting room, keeping my hand bag with me and leaving the other luggage where it was. The railway authorities had taken charge of it."
>
> "It was winter, and winter in the higher region of South Africa is severely cold. Martizburg being at a high altitude the cold was extremely bitter. My overcoat was in my luggage but I did not dare to ask for it lest I should be insulted again, so I sat and shivered. There was no light in the room..."
>
> "I began to think of my duty. Should I fight for my rights or go back to India...It would be cowardice to run back to India without fulfilling my obligation....I should try, if possible to root out the disease...Redress for wrongs. I should seek only to the extent that would be necessary..."[49] ...should I go forward, with God as my helper, and face whatever was in store for me? I decided to stay and suffer. My active non-violence began from that date."[50]

Religious preachers, social leaders and psychologists tell us that man is a bundle of instincts, some noble and some bad. They feel that if efforts are made in the right direction, it is possible to develop the nobler instincts. Religious preachers give there own methods for developing these nobler instincts, which they call *Sadhna* or *Tap* or religious way of life. They offer the temptation of *Moksh* or *Nirvan* or salvation to individuals who, fired by this ideal, follow these methods of self-purification and self-upliftment. The fear of the omnipotent and omnipresent God is also used to keep the desirous on the path of righteousness. Similarly, the leaders of society feel that for proper functioning of the society, it is essential that bulk of the people do not sell themselves to bad instincts. They feel that if a few can be made to lead a noble life—a few because it is not possible for all to ennoble themselves—they will inspire others and thereby save society. These leaders try to use the force of social sanctions for preventing the people from adopting wrong practices. A psychologist on the other hand gives us a scientific analysis of these inborn and acquired instincts. He tries to explain their sources and mode of operation and suggests methods to control and divert them. Pavlov's and Thorndike's researches in applied economics and the new branch of psychology known as psycho-technology bear it our.

The instincts of violence and non-violence are not new. The philosophers of different countries and of different ages wrote voluminous books, giving expressions to their feeling of hatred for violence and love for non-violence. Outstanding among the long galaxy of writers are Valmiki and Vyas of India, Socrates and Plato of Greece, Ehenne dela Boetie, Meijer Wichmann, Roland Holot, Charles Naine, A. Huxley, General Heard, Benjamin Tucker, Ruskin, Calyle and Tolstoy.[51]

Jainism and *Buddhism* the two great religions of India which influenced the Eastern countries, preached non-violence. But these religions never tried to apply the principle of non-violence to solve the problems of this world. Their teachings were confined to personal relations and were reciprocal i.e. men should not do to others what they do not want to be done to themselves. The life and teachings of Jesus were based on love and non-violence. Gandhi respected the Sermons, as he respected the *Gita* because both preached the philosophy of non-violence. "What the Sermon describes in a graphic manner, The *Bhagvadgita* reduces to a scientific formula... Today supposing I was deprived of *Gita* and forgot all its contents but had a copy of the Sermon, I should derive the same joy from it as I do from the *Gita*."[52]

The life of Jesus is full of incidents which go to prove his unshaken faith in non-violence. To quote a few instances, at the time of his arrest, Peter drew his sword and chopped off the ear of the priest's servant. Master, seeing this, said to Peter, "Put up again the sword in its place, for all that take the sword shall 'perish with the sword."[53] Again at the Cross, the votary of *Ahimsa* burst out, "Father, forgive them for they know not what they do."[54]

The Chinese religion, one of the oldest in the world, also had a long tradition of non-violence. "The three Chinese religions, Confucianism, Taoism and Buddhism are pacific.[55]

Judaism and its scriptures, old Testament, Mishna and Talmud, kept up preaching non-violence.[56]

Anselm Bellegarigue, the French revolutionary of 19th century came up with the 'theory of calm' This theory is based on non-violence and non-cooperation. Anselm thought that all governments were based on violence and as such should not be helped by the believers in non-violence.

Similarly, Henry David Thoreau, the well known American anarchist refused to pay taxes as a revolt against the slavery in

America. His stand was also based on non-violence and non-cooperation.

The Quaker State in Pennsylvania, which was established in 1682 and lasted for 70 years, was administered without any military.

Before Gandhi used the technique of non-violence to win political freedom for India it was considered a noble instinct, the development of which was desirable. However, it was felt that it was meant only to purify onself, having no other aim or purpose and it could not be practised or employed by the majority of the people. Albert Schweitzer has aptly remarked, "The ancient Indian Ahimsa is an expression of world and life negation. It sets before it no aims that are to be realised in the world, but is simply the most profound effort to attain to the state of keeping completely pure from the world".[57] The greatest contribution of Gandhi is that he made non-violence a commodity for mass use and brought it down from the high towers to earth to be employed in service of humanity. He gave it an aim, a purpose. Gandhi made it a beacon-light for the common man, a light which should give guidance to him in all the walks of life, be it political, economic, religious or social. He made it a complete code for all persons and for all nations. "We have to make truth and non-violence, not matters for mere individual practice but for practice by groups and communities and nations. That, at any rate is my dream. I shall live and die in trying to realise it. My faith helps me to discover new truths everyday. *Ahimsa* is the attribute of the soul, and therefore is to be practised by everybody in all the affairs of life. If it cannot be practised in all departments, it has no practical value."[58] Again, "Some friends have told me that truth and non-violence have no place in politics and worldly affairs. I do not agree. I have no use for them as a means of individual salvation. Their introduction and application in everyday life has been my experiment all long."[59]

Gandhi widened the meaning and purpose of non-violence. So it is necessary to understand its meaning clearly.

The three words — Violence, Anti-violence and Non-violence — are very different from each other but still they are taken to be closely allied. Violence is the use of force (physical or unjust) to achieve selfish interest which may enhance human misery. Richard B. Gregg[60] includes pride, anger, killing, wounding, fighting, exploitation, tempting to evil etc., in the category of violence. According to Gandhi, "Exploitation is the essence of violence."[61]

Anti-violence, on the other hand, is diametrically opposed to violence. It indicates, "Love, forgiveness, friendliness, peace, kindliness, civility, frankness, service, protection, philanthropy, generosity and so on."[62] Benevolence, i.e. generosity and unselfishness are the key notes of anti-violence. It is thus a thing which can be practised only by the saints. An ordinary man cannot always afford to be generous, unselfish and working for the good of others.

The term non-violence or *Ahimsa* gives the impression of being a negative doctrine. But it has two aspects, one is negative and the other positive. In its negative sense it means refraining from *Himsa*, i.e. violence.

> "*Ahimsa* does not simply mean non-killing. *Himsa* means causing pain to, or killing any life out of anger, or from a selfish purpose, or with the intention of injuring it. Refraining from so doing is *Ahimsa*."[63]

This aspect of non-violence aims at maximum human welfare as it attempts to reduce killing, pain, anger, selfishness etc. from this world.

But from this negative aspect of *Ahimsa*, it should not be misunderstood that killing always means violence. Only that killing or causing pain to another, which is motivated out of anger or selfishness or with the intention of injuring one, is violence. Kaka Kalelkar has given as interesting illustration to establish the truth of this statement from the life of the greatest votary of *Ahimsa* of this age.

> "One day a calf fell ill. We did all we could to relieve its sufferings. We called in experts on animal diseases from villages. We called in the vet. All to no purpose. The calf went steadily from bad to worse."
>
> "The suffering of the poor dumb creature became so intolerable, even to the onlookers, that *Bapu* (Gandhi) called us together and suggested that we should give it the merciful relief of death. It is the height of cruelty, he pleaded, to go on prolonging its agony like this."
>
> "A keen discussion arose. Shri Vallabh Bhai Patel come over from Ahmedabad and said, "This calf can not last longer than

> two or three days at the most but if you kill it, you will bring a regular hornets' nest about your ears. The whole Hindus community will be shocked to the depths. We are just leaving for Bombay to collect funds—not a pie shall we get to bless ourselves with. Our work will suffer terribly, *Bapu*."
> "Bapu heard him out in grave silence, appreciating his difficulties. Then he said, "What you say is perfectly correct. But it is impossible for us to sit still and do nothing while that calf writhes away its last moments in agony. I believe that it would be sheer wickedness to deny to a fellow creature the last and most solemn service which we can render to it."
> "Then a Parsi Doctor was called, and he administered peace to the suffering calf."[64]

Thus, according to Gandhi, killing is not always violence and in its positive form, *Ahimsa* means the largest love, greatest charity."[65] This aspect of non-violence is to convert even the enemy to once own side so that aggression and fear may go from this world and man may be able to lead a happier and more peaceful life.

Gandhi was a firm believer in truth, fearlessness and love. He loved even his enemies and never tried to take advantage of their difficulties. In his life he continuously demonstrated his faith in this positive aspect of non-violence.

Indians in Africa were subject to many unfair laws. "In 1906, the Government of Transvaal introduced a bill in the legislature which required every Indian to be registered by finger print, like criminals, and to produce his certificate of registration upon demand by any police officer at any time. Failure to register meant deportation, and refusal to produce the certificate would be punished by fine..."

> "...Under the leadership of an Indian lawyer, M.K. Gandhi, they held meetings of protest and asked for hearings on the bill. But the Government ruthlessly passed it. Thereupon, the leading Indians at a huge mass meeting took an oath that they would all refuse to register and would go to jail rather than obey the law..."
> "They stuck to their resolve and Gandhi and many others went to jail..."
> "Not long after that, in 1913, an European judge in the Transvaal Supreme Court made a court decision which

> invalidated all Hindu and Muslim marriages and thus rendered all the Indian children illegitimate and incapable of inheriting property. This roused all the Indian women. A group of them, at Gandhi's suggestion, crossed from Transwal to Natal mines which were worked by Indian labourers. The women were imprisoned. But the men, numbering about five thousand, all came out on strike as a protest against this court decision about marriages and against a very heavy and oppressive head tax which practically kept them in slavery. Under Gandhi's leadership they started a march on foot across the border into Transvaal, by way of non-violent protest. It was against the law to cross the boundary line in either direction without permission.
>
> "During the march, Gandhi was arrested three times, released on bail twice, and finally put in jail. The border was crossed and the army continued, leaderless, but still non-violent. Finally they were all arrested and taken back by train to Natal...
>
> "They were impounded at the mines and beaten and ill treated. Still they remained firm and non-violent."
>
> "Just then a strike broke out among the European railwaymen in South Africa. Gandhi saw that the Government was in a very difficult situation, but instead of taking advantage of the incident, he chivalrously suspended the Indian struggle until the railway strike was over, an act which won much admiration for the Indians."[66]

The unfair laws were withdrawn and so Gandhi could convert the enemy through the positive aspect of non-violence

This is not the only example of the positive aspect of non-violence. Gandhi's help to Britishers during the First World War in spite of the continuous struggle for freedom; India's willingness in recent years to settle differences with Pakistan in spite of her aggressive attitude; are but a few examples sufficient to demonstrate the practicability of the positive aspect of non-violence.

Non-violence, according to Gandhi, can be of three types. The best and of the highest order, is 'Enlightened non-violence'. This can be practised by a brave person who can raise the plank of his morality to a very high order by accepting non-violence as a creed. "Those who accept non-violence as a creed would never surrender their sense of humanity and brotherhood even in the midst of conflict of interests and would ever try to convert and not coerce their adversary."[67]

The second type of non-violence can be called the 'passive non-violence of the weak'. Here the person, who practices it, adopts it as a policy to achieve some desired end and is liable to give it up after the fulfilment of the purpose for which it was adopted. This type of *Ahimsa* is "not as effective as the thorough going non-violence of the brave."[68]

Gandhi, after the communal disturbances of 1947 revised his opinion about the 'passive non-violence of the weak.' He wrote, "There was no such thing as non-violence of the weak. Non-violence and weakness was a contradiction in terms."[69]

The third and the worst type of non-violence is known as 'passive non-violence of the coward'. The person who practices it, does not adopt it either as a creed or as a policy. He takes shelter behind non-violence out of his helplessness. Gandhi gave a beautiful illustration to demonstrate the 'Passive non-violence of the coward'.

> "The people of a village near Bettia told me that they had run away whilst the police were looting their houses and molesting their women folk. When they said that they had run away because I had told them to be non-violent, I hung my head in shame."[70]

Gandhi condemned this type of non-violence. He even condemned the coward.

> "Cowardice is impotence worse than violence. The coward desires revenge but being afraid to die, he looks to others, may be the Government of the day, to do the work of defence for him. A coward is less than a man. He does not deserve to be a member of society of men and women"[71]

So he concludes:

> "Cowardice and *Ahimsa* do not go together any more than water and fire."[72]

How non-violence worked in the political sphere in India, is now a well-known historical fact. This, however, has raised several important questions: First, can this policy of non-violence be of any use after the country has achieved independence? In other words, can it be of any use in facing an armed aggression from a foreign Government? Secondly, can an army, like a violent one, be trained of non-violent soldiers? And lastly, is the policy of non-violence of any use in the sphere of economics? The answer to the first two questions has been given by Mr. Richard B. Gregg in his famous and most authoritative book *The Power of Non-violence* the summary of which is presented in Appendix I. The answer to the third question has been presented in the following chapters but here it will suffice to explain the meaning of non-violence in the economic sphere.

.Gandhi being interested in human welfare was judging everything with the scale of happiness. He acclaimed everything as good, nice, right and non-violent if it led to human happiness and discarded everything as bad, inhuman and violent if it added to human misery. His whole economic thinking was based on this one particular notion.

Mass production with the help of complicated machines, whether Government controlled and owned or otherwise, leads humanity to misery. In the first stage it divides society into two sections of the 'haves' and 'have-nots' which have opposite interests. In the second stage it leads to exploitation of other countries and ultimately to wars and vast destruction of man and material. Gandhi, therefore, called such production as violent. He said,

> "...An increase in the number of mills and cities will certainly not contribute to the prosperity of Indian millions. On the contrary it will bring further poverty to the unemployed and all the diseases that follow in the wake of starvation. If town dwellers can look upon such a spectable with equanimity there is nothing more to be said. In such an event it will be the reign of violence in India, not a reign of truth and *Ahimsa*..."[73]

Gandhi's non-violence in its negative aspect, will persuade producers to refrain from exploiting the labourers and spreading misery. It will convert the capitalists into trustees..

> "By the non-violent methods we seek not to destroy the capitalist, we week to destroy capitalism. We invite the capitalist to regard himself as a trustee for those on whom he

> depends for the making, the retention and the increase of his capital"[74]

And in the positive aspect, non-violence will create a spirit in producers to help the labourers and exploited ones in improving their lot, and thus narrow down the gulf between the two. Once Gandhi wrote,

> "...The relation between mill agents and mill hands ought to be one of the father and children or as between blood brothers. I have often heard the mill-owners of Ahmedabad refer to themselves as 'masters' and their employees as their 'servants'. Such loose talk should be out of fashion in a place like Ahmedabad which prides itself on its love of religion and love of *Ahimsa*. For that attitude is a negation of *Ahimsa* inasmuch as our ideal demands that all our power, all our wealth and all our brain should be devoted solely to the welfare of those who through their own ignorance and our false notions of things, are styled labourers or servants..."[75]

Thus, Gandhi tried to construct a structure of production which may be non-violent, i.e. beneficial to the general masses.

The desire to raise the standard of living by increasing the number of wants also decreases human happiness, and, therefore, is violent. High standard of living is violent because the persons consuming a large number of commodities do not increase their happiness in the same proportion in which they multiply their wants while they certainly do decrease the happiness of others by leaving very little for them."[76] Again, attempts to raise the standard of living by one may mean reduction of necessary articles for another. The present world bears testimony to it. It is due to this reason that Gandhi called over-eating 'a theft' as it deprived some one of his food. Of course, if supply of goods would have been in abundance it would have been different. But as we know, this is a 'world of scarcity' where the 'problem of choice arises'. Any attempt to led a luxurious life by one adds to the miseries of others and so one is violent. Therefore, Gandhi said:

> "If we are to be non-violent, we must then not wish for anything on this earth which the meanest or the lowest of human beings

cannot have."[77]
"Civilization in the real (economic) sense of the term, consist not in the multiplication, but in the deliberate and voluntary restriction of wants. This alone promotes real happiness and contentment and increases the capacity for service."[78]
"The religion of *Ahimsa* consists in allowing others the maximum of convenience at maximum of inconvenience to us, even at the risk of life."[79]

The introduction of money gave an impetus to exchange as money became a medium of exchange and a standard of value. But money brought several vices with it. It increased exploitation and reduced human happiness.

> "...What is a man, if he is not a thief, who openly charges as much as he can for the goods he sells? If the reply be that the buyer is a willing dupe, it begs the question. In reality the buyer is helpless rather than willing. The stealing referred to is one of the systems of a deep rooted disease of society. It is symptomatic of the eternal strife between the moneyed few and the many paupers."[80]

Hence money and too much exchange never appealed to Mahatma Gandhi. He called excessive use of money as violent.

The present methods of dividing the produce among different factors of production is also violent according to Gandhi. The technique adopted tries to give a unit of factor the share which is in accordance with the contribution made by it. Naturally it leads to glaring inequalities of income and leaves little share for other less efficient units of production. One leads a luxurious life and the other starves. Thus the method of distribution is also violent and should be replaced by a non-violent one, in which such glaring inequalities of income may not exist.

> "Inequalities, unintelligence and uneven opportunities will last till the end of time. A man living on the bank of a river has anyway more opportunity of growing crops than one living in a desert. But if inequalities stare us in the face, the essential equality too is not to be missed. Every man has an equal right for the necessaries of life even as birds and beasts have..."[81]

How can this equal distribution be brought about through non-violent means?

> "The first step towards it is for him who has made this ideal a part of his being to bring about the necessary changes in his personal life. He would reduce his wants to a minimum, bearing in mind the poverty of India...When he has done all that is possible in his won life; then only will he be in a position to preach this ideal among his associates and neighbours."[82]

Such then briefly is Gandhi's application of non-violence to economics.

V
SIMPLICITY

Gandhi, like religious preachers, philosophers and noble men of different times[83] and countries, was a believer in the philosophy of 'simple living and high thinking' and wanted to build his socio-politico-economic structure on it.

The idea of simplicity, i.e. "the deliberate and voluntary restrictions of wants"[84] differs with forced poverty and in its ideal form means complete renunciation or non-possession. The idea of simplicity or deliberate and voluntary restriction of wants or non-possession probably came to Gandhi from stealing. In common parley stealing means to take anything belonging to another without his permission.[85] Even taking away something in the belief that it is nobody's property[86] might be included in theft. However, Gandhi wanted to stretch the meaning of theft further. He said:

> "It is theft to take something from another even with his permission, if we have no real need of it."[87]

Further,

> "If we devote some thought to the subject, we shall find that we can get rid of quite a number of our wants. One who follows the observance of non-stealing will bring about a progressive reduction of his own wants."[88]

Non-stealing means not only reduction of present wants but also not bothering for the future wants. Gandhi wrote:

> "One, who observes the principle of non-stealing, will refuse to bother himself about things to be acquired in the future."[89]

Again,

> "Possession implies provision for the future. A seeker after Truth, a follower of Law of Love cannot hold anything against tomorrow."[90]

A person wedded to non-stealing, will reduce his present wants but what should he do of his already acquired possessions? Gandhi evolved his theory of trusteeship and wanted a man to hold this property in trust for the benefit of the society.[91]

Thus, simplicity, or non-stealing, or non-possess of Gandhi's concept means reducing present wants to minimum, not accumulating things for the future use and to hold the already acquired surplus things as a trustee for the society.

Obviously, the idea of absolute non-possession or simplicity is unattainable in its fulness. "Only the fewest possible, if any at all," Gandhi observed, "can reach this ideal. We ordinary seekers may not be repelled by the seeming impossibility. But we must keep the ideal constantly in view, and in the light thereof, critically examine our possessions and try to reduce them."[92] Gandhi did not worry about the ultimate goal or future. For him one step was enough.[93] Gandhi was also aware of the difficulties involved in it.

> "I cannot tell you with truth that, when this belief came to me, I discarded everything immediately. I must confess to you that progress at first was slow. And now, as I recall those days of struggle, I remember that it was also painful in the beginning. A time came when it became a matter of positive joy to give up those things...Exploring the cause of that joy, I found that, if I kept anything as my own, I had to defend it against the whole world ...And, then I said to myself: Possession seems to me to be a crime...[94]

Certain illustrations can be given from the life of Gandhi himself to show his faith in simplicity.

"The Government had fixed upon the monthly sum of Rs.150 for Bapu's expenses, because he was a State prisoner. Major Martin, the Jail Superintendent, brought a whole lot of furniture, crockery and all sorts of utensils the very first day. 'For whom have you brouhgt all this?' asked Bapu, 'Take it away please.' Major Martin was puzzled. He said, propitiatingly, 'I have written and told the Government that at least 300 rupees a month should be spent on an honoured guest, like you. I have every hope that Government will agree.' Bapu said, 'That is all very well. But after all, all the money would come from the Indian Treasury, would it not? I do not want to increase the burden on my country. I hope that my boarding expenses will not come to more than 35 rupees a month. Had my health permitted, I would have eaten 'C' class food. But to my shame, fruit is for me a sheer necessity; so is goat's milk.' So all the paraphernalia of comfort was sent away."[95]

When Gandhi came to India as a full-fledged Barrister, he always walked to the court from his house.

"When Bapu sat down to write, he would take up the letters he had received, carefully cut out the parts of the letter paper that had not been written on, and write his answers on them."[96]

"In England, in the winter of 1931, he went about without much additional covering and without even boots or shoes when others shivered with cold in spite of their overcoats and other woollen dresses."[97]

* * *

It may well be asked why Gandhi wanted to make everyone a Sadhu? Or why he wanted to turn the clock back?[98]

The aim of life, even the westerners wedded to the present materialistic philosophy of life will agree, is to promote one's own happiness to the maximum and if possible also to promote the happiness of others. Gandhi felt that there cannot be any clash of just interest of an individual and the society and so he felt it is possible to promote one's own happiness along with the happiness of others. If this basic point is conceded, the logic behind simple living will become clear like crystal.

Gandhi seems to start with an examination of the results of the Western philosophy which is a materialistic one. He inquires, 'Is man's happiness increasing in the same proportion in which his belongings are increasing?[99] The answer is apparent. "As it is, the rich are discontented not less than the poor. The poor man would fain become a millionaire, and the millionaire, a multi-millionaire."[100] Again, "The human mind is like a restless bird, the more it gets the more it wants and still remains unsatisfied."[101] C.E.M. Joad seems to agree with such a view. He observes, "It is significant that the suicide rate among the unemployed rich is the highest."[102]

The man who is always trying to multiply his wants, even beyond a minimum limit, does not only make himself unhappy but also brings unhappiness and misery on other as, the great economist Robbins tellsu s, 'means are limited.' Gandhi wrote, "Our ignorance or negligence of the Divine Law, which gives to man from day to day his daily bread and no more, has given rise to inequalities with all the miseries attendant upon them. The rich have a superfluous store of things which they do not need, and which are, therefore, neglected and wasted; while millions are starved to death for want of sustenance."[103] Herman Finer, a well known authority on political science agrees: "Men are today ruled by the ideal of the High Standard of Living...This greed is at the root of most of the major political problems, domestic and international, of the present day...[104]

Gandhi felt that voluntary poverty enables one to understand the difficulties and problem of lesser fortunate ones. A rich man, like the Queen of Louis XVI of France who when told that the people in Paris had no bread to eat, might ask: "Why do they not eat cake then?" Victor Hugo was right when he remarked, "He who does not weep, does not see." Romain Rolland also observed, "He who suffers has a chance of awakening to the suffering of others."[105]

"The deliberate and voluntary restriction of wants which promotes real happiness and contentment," Gandhi observed, "also increases the capacity of service."[106] Again, "Love and exclusive possession can never go together."[107] The philosophy of *Yajna*[108] is based on it. *Gita* has also said, "He who eats without offering Yajna, eats stolen food."[109]

Arnold Toynbee, the famous historian, speaks of corporate benefits of simple way of life, "No doubt we have a far greater capacity to reconstruct as well as to destroy than the Chinese and the Roman had. On the other hand, a simpler social structure has a far greater spontaneous recuperative power than a more complicated one has...[110]

Multiplication of wants brings uneven distribution of wealth and the artificial complexes of inferiority and superiority which are based on possession of wealth and not virtues.

The excessive love of the possessive impulses excludes creative impulse and makes life a drudgery. But voluntary poverty increases the power of resistance of the body and soul, while multiplicity of wants decreases it. Multiplication of wants is against the law of Nature. Gandhi wrote, "He never creates more than what is strictly needed for the moment."[111]

The difference between a beast and a man lies in that one wants more and the other tries to reduce his wants[112] for others.

This much about the meaning of simplicity in the realm of economics.

In the political sphere it will mean reducing power, i.e. establishing village republic or *Ram Rajya*.

In the present types of Government, whole authority is vested in one central body composed of a few persons, whether elected by the people or self-styled dictators. This renders indispensable an expensive political and administrative machinery, and heavy militarization which consume a greater part of the State revenues and complicate financial entanglements. This robs life, freedom of action, occupation, food, clothes, house etc. It is due to this that Gandhi was against excessive centralization of power. "I look upon an increase in the power of the State with the greatest fear, because although while apparently doing good by minimising exploitation, it does the greatest harm to mankind by destroying individuality, which lies in the root of all progress. We know of so many cases where men have adopted trusteeship, but none where the State has really lived for the poor."[113] Gandhi, therefore, wanted to decentralize power by converting every village into a self-sufficient republic having its own legislature, executive and judiciary, all combined into one. Under such a decentralization, opportunity will be granted to all for the maximum growth of individuality and perfect freedom of action and choice will be ensured.

VI
BREAD-LABOUR

Gandhi left Johannesberg for Natal via Durban. Mr. Polak came to see him off at the station and left with him Ruskin's 'Unto This Last'.

The book gripped Gandhi. He could not get any sleep that night. He decided to change his life according to the ideals of that book. He even later translated it entitling it, *Sarvodaya*. The book revealed three principles to Gandhi:

> "1. That the good of the individual is contained in the good of all.
> 2. That a lawyer's work has the same value as the barber's.
> 3. That a life of labour, i.e. the life of the tiller of the soil and the handicraftsman is the life worth living."[114]

Gandhi knew the first one. The second he had dimly realised. The third had never occurred to him.[115] "Unto This Last" made it clear as daylight for me that the second and the third were contained in the first. I arose with the dawn, ready to reduce these principles to practice."[116] Though the idea, that 'to live man must work' came to Gandhi after reading Ruskin's "Unto This Last", it took root only after he had read Tolstoy's writings on Bread-labour.[117] The religious books of different faiths watered the roots and helped in the sprouting of leaves. For instance the *Bible* says: 'In the sweat of thy brow shalt thou eat thy bread.'[118] The same principle has been set forth in the Third Chapter of the *Gita*, where we are told that he who eats without offering sacrifice eats stolen food. Sacrifice here can only mean bread-labour.[119] Gandhi's own experiences, first in Africa at Phoenix Settlement and Tolstoy Farm and later in India at Sabarmati Ashram[120] and thereafter in his wanderings and experiments in non-violence[121] and self-help[122], richly manured it and helped it into becoming a tree loaded with sweet fruits. Probably Gandhi's concept that 'whoever eats more than is enough to sustaining the body is a thief' strengthened, as a corollary to it, the faith in Bread-labour. He once wrote, "I believe that a man has no right to receive anything more than his keep, and that every one who labours is entitled to a living wage."[123] The idea of Bread-labour was neither new, nor was it a peculiarity of Indian soil. It was also far from being a theoretical concept of an arm-chair politician. It had germinated equally well in all soils through the different ages.

Bread-labour is composed of two words—Bread and Labour. As such it implies that every one should earn his bread with his physical labour. Gandhi wrote: "Man must earn his bread by labouring with his own hand.[124]

Gandhi, being a realist, knew that it is an ideal which is difficult to be achieved in the present world.[125] But he felt that it was a good ideal and one must strive to achieve it.[126] He felt that by propagating the ideal he will convert many and will certainly educate those millions who though observing it are still thinking in the other direction and so remain unhappy and their labour becomes less fruitful.[127] In fact, he wanted to stop the mad craze for white collar jobs and check the feeling of hatred towards physical labour. He wanted to restore physical labour to its old glory and real dignity which it had been robbed of by capital. Gandhi wrote, "Under my system it is a labour which is the current coin, not metal."[128] Gandhi, therefore, wanted that everyone, whether rich or poor, must do some productive physical labour. However, Gandhi would not insist that it should be sufficient to enable one to earn one's bread. He wrote, "It is not, therefore, necessary to earn one's living by Bread-labour, taking the word in its broader sense. But every one must perform some useful body labour."[129]

Physical exercises taken to induce hunger will not be considered as Bread-labour by Gandhi. Labour must be productive. He wrote, "If everyone, whether rich or poor, has thus to take exercise in some shape or form, why should it not assume the form of productive, i.e. Bread-labour."[130]

Physical labour done out of ignorance or compulsion can also not be termed as Bread-labour. The reason is clear. "Compulsory obedience to a master is a state of slavery, willing obedience to one's father is the glory of the sonship. Similarly, compulsory obedience to the law of Bread-labour breeds poverty, disease and discontent. It is a state of slavery. Willing obedience to it must bring contentment and health."[131]

Gandhi felt that there is no tussle between intellectual labour and Bread-labour. "Mere mental, that is intellectual labour is for the soul and is its own satisfaction"[132] Again, "The needs of the body must be supplied by the body. 'Render unto Caesar that which is Caesar's'.[133] Intellectual labour might be "infinitely superior to bodily labour, but it never is or can be a substitute for it, even as intellectual food though far superior to the grains we eat never can be a substitute for them."[134]

Thus, voluntary useful physical labour is Bread-labour. If it becomes 'intelligent' also, it becomes the highest form of social service.[135] Explaining it Gandhi wrote:

> "The adjective 'intelligent' has been prefixed to 'labour' in order to show that labour to be social service must have that definite purpose behind it otherwise every labourer can be said to render social service. He does in a way, but what is meant here is something much more than that. A person who labours for the general good of all serves society and is worthy of the hire. Therefore, such Bread-labour is not different from social service."[136]

But why should every one do some physical labour? J.C. Kumarappa, the noted Gandhian economist, has given a very fitting answer to this query. He tells us, "like Physiocrats and Adam Smith, that man's institutions, to be permanent, must be in keeping with the laws of Nature. 'Work' in Nature consists in the effort put forth by the various factors—insentient and sentient—which cooperate to complete this cycle."[137] Earthworms, birds, bees, all work in this sense and in return get just sufficient to feed themselves. That is their wages.[138] The history of early civilization when man began to make tools out of stones, confirms it.[139] He further tells us that work consists of routine and rest, progress and pleasure."[140] We should not isolate anyone of these from the others. It is unfortunate that man used his freewill to break up work, against law of Nature, "into its component parts, passing on the routine to those who are helpless to resist and appropriating to the strong the pleasures to be derived from work."[141] The result was ruin. The civilizations of Greece and Rome were based on such misappropriation and so they perished. The modern materialistic world is also repeating it and is on the threshold of ruin and destruction. The continuous struggle between labour and capital on the one hand, and between labourers and capitalists themselves on the other, and each trying to annihilate the other proves it. Not only this. One has forced idleness, grinding poverty, drudgery and disease and the other has to take exercise to induce hunger and still he suffers with tensions, heart diseases and nervous breakdown. Gandhi summed up this in his own inimitable style.

> "Nature compels animals to work and live naturally. We have so debased our working classes that they cannot work and live naturally..."
> "Work and culture cannot be separated then?

"No. They tried to do it in ancient Rome and failed miserably."[142]

Gandhi felt that the conflict between labour and capital can be eliminated only when, in economic terminology, capital is not divorced of labour, or every one voluntarily takes to some useful physical labour. He enquired, 'Why should I, who have no need to work for food, spin?' Soon came the answer, "Because I am eating what does not belong to me. I am living on the spoilation of my countrymen. Trace the course of every pice that finds its way into your pocket and you will realize the truth of what I write..."[143] His entire opposition to machines rests on this theory.

Gandhi was pained to see that the rich, who have exploited the labour and continue to do so and avoid physical labour, themselves, want to ameliorate poverty by donations. He called it 'hypocrisy and a sham' of the rich.[144] Gandhi went to the 'Marble Palace' in Calcutta and saw that the owners were feeding beggars, even the able-bodied ones. He called it 'misplaced charity' and he would stop all such *sadavrat* if he has the power to do so.[145] Even doles to refugees were not proper.[146] The same idea was repeated by him under the title, 'A Shame', in *Harijan* of March 1, 1935 and *Young India* where he wrote, "I must refuse to insult the naked by giving them clothes they do not need, instead of giving them work which they sorely need. I will not commit the sin of becoming their patron, but on learning that I had associated in impoverising them, I would give them neither crumbs nor cost of clothing, but the best of my food and clothes and associate with them in work."[147]

When every one takes to useful bodily labour, the will to exploit will automatically go and the man will revert back to the useful handicraft which Gandhi wanted to revive. He felt that agriculture, spinning, weaving, carpentry, smithy, etc, which are connected with some primary needs will flourish if all take to physical labour of the productive nature.[148]

Love for Bread-labour will not only provide work to the unemployed manual labourers[149] but will also solve to a very great extent, the present problem of the educated unemployed whose number, unfortunately, is sharply rising in every country. Gandhi wrote, "We the educated classes have lost the art of labour for our bread. With the wages of weavers, carders and spinners rising daily, there is certainly no bread problem...We must not think of earning a livelihood by desk work merely."[150]

When even the rich take to some useful physical labour, they will come to know of the problems and difficulties of millions of labourers. When they become labourers themselves, the invidious distinctions of rank would be abolished.[151]

Gandhi believed that the law of Bread-labour did help in reducing wants. "If we did so, our wants would be minimized, our food would be simple. We would then eat to live not live to eat."[152] It might sound strange but Gandhi from his own experience knew it and so challenged the non-believer. "Let anyone who doubts the accuracy of this proposition, try to sweat for his bread...discover that many things he took were superfluities."[153]

When everyone will be engaged in useful physical labour, not only the wants will be reduced but also the production will increase. These two things, naturally will reduce scarcity and solve the problems of over-population, disease and misery. Gandhi wrote, "If all laboured for their bread and no more, than there would be enough food and enough leisure for all, then there would be no cry of over-population, no disease, and no such misery as we see around."[154]

Gandhi knew that "those who get all that leisure – both the working and intellectual classes – do not make the best use of it. In fact, we too often find the idle mind being turned into the Devil's workshop."[155] The western economists, psychologists and medical men are busy in treating the ills of this idle leisure. Gandhi, by preaching the utility of Bread-labour was trying to solve this problem of leisure. Gandhi pleaded thus, "It will cease to be monotonous when they realise that they not only earn a few coppers but preserve their own health and that of their countrymen.[156]

Gandhi believed that Bread-labour would improve the health[157] of the pursuers and would sharpen their intellect and thereby improve the quality of intellectual work. In his own words, "Intellectual work is important and has an undoubted place in the scheme of life. But what I insist on is the necessity of physical labour. No man, I claim, ought to be free from that obligation. It will serve to improve even the quality of his intellectual output."[158]

Bread-labour is a great character builder. It makes one non-violent, i.e. a nobler man. "Thirty-four years of continuous experience and experimenting in truth and non-violence have convinced me that non-violence cannot be sustained unless it is linked to conscious body labour."[159]

It helps one to 'worship truth' and makes the observance of *Brahmacharya* a natural act."[160]

Gandhi felt that if one-tenth of humanity, which at present is not doing physical labour, starts doing it, the world will become much more happier, healthier and peaceful.[161] Gandhi would, therefore, prefer it even to contemplation,[162] and he will make it a qualification of a voter.[163]

VII
ON VALUATION

We, in life, are called upon to pronounce judgements constantly.[164] So in order to be able to pronounce correct judgements, it is necessary to have a correct standard of valuation.

There are different kinds of standards for valuing various kinds of goods.[165] These standards are accurate and well defined and the articles to which they are to be applied are also well known. For example you cannot weigh wheat by the number of grains or the cloth by counting threads or bamboos by their length.

In spite of these standards, the value of a commodity may differ from person to person, or place to place, or time to time. A rupee in the pocket of a rich person may not be so valuable to him as it may be in the pocket of a hungry man. Again, the utility, i.e. value of a banana to a person, who has already consumed six may not be equal to the utility of the first banana which he consumed. It will, therefore, be a mistake to apply the same standard of valuation to different person, to different places and at different times.[166]

The existing different standards of valuation can be grouped into two main headings—self-centred standard and altruistic standard. When "we judge things in relation to ourselves we say it is self-centred and when measured against an external, or abstract ideal and in relation to others, it is said to be altruistic."[167] But to lead to any degree of permanence it is necessary that the standard of value must be based on something apart from the person valuing, i.e. it should be altruistic standard.

Besides the necessity of a standard of valuation, its importance is very great in our lives as "the standard of values applied and the method used impress their characteristic trait on their users. The spirit of the most predominant value that prevails amongst a people will colour a whole civilization for centuries. Hence the great importance of choosing our standard consciously and deliberately."[168] For example, the great civilizations of Egypt, Babylon, Greece and Rome were built predominantly on self-centred and transient valuation, and so were swept away with the tides of time. But, on the other hand, the equally old civilizations of India and China were founded on altruistic and objective values and so are able to stand and face the mighty storm of time and invaders.[169]

In the present set up, gold the self-centred standard has become the only standard of valuation. It is due to this reason that various phrases like: 'High standard of living', 'Raising the national income', 'Increasing productive power and efficiency', 'Will it pay', have become so familiar to our ears.

The absurdity of adopting money as the standard of valuation will become obvious when we see that land is being daily transferred from food crops such as wheat, maize, pulses, etc., to cash crops, such as tobacco, cotton and jute inspite of the hungry millions. We are struck with surprise when we see that man, in order to quench his thirst for gold, makes his neighbours' children weep because their stretched tiny hands could not get milk. The love of gold reduces a man to a hunter who goes around the world hunting nations in order to preserve his markets. A very illustrative example is offered by the popular story of the greedy King Midas. He wanted to have so much wealth that he worshipped the Sun-God in order to have a boon of his choice. The God was propitiated and the boon of his choice was granted. Whatever thing the king will touch will turn into gold. The king was very much pleased. But was he really happy for long? He soon realised to his utter dismay that the boon became a curse. He wanted to eat, but food was turned into gold, he wanted to kiss his daughter, but she was reduced to a statue of gold. Therefore, he very soon wanted to get rid of the boon. Gandhi has similarly pointed out that the large scale production helped by the modern intricate machines and centralised political set-up is a boon to humanity, like the boon of Sun-God to King Midas, for which it was paining and striving from the very beginning but on achieving the same humanity is realizing that it is turning everything it touches into money leaving the rest to a miserable lot. Ruskin also criticised this idea very bitterly:

"So far as I know, there is not in history record of anything so disgraceful to the human intellect as the modern idea of the *commerical text* 'Buy in the cheapest market' and 'Sell in the dearest', represents, or under any circumstances could represent, an available principle of national economy. Buy in the cheapest market? – Yes; but what made your market cheap? Charcoal may be cheap among your roof timbers after a fire, and bricks may be cheap in your streets after an earthquake; but fire and earthquake may not, therefore, be national profits. Sell in the dearest? – Yes, truly; but what made your market dear? You sold your bread well today: Was it to a dying man who gave his last coin for it and will never need bread more."[170]

Gandhi, all along his life, was giving relative values to different things. A few illustrations can be given here:

In the present age, politics is considered to be everything and other equally important, or even much more valuable things are kept subordinate to it. Gandhi wanted to reduce this undue importance given to politics. "My work of social reform" he said, "was in no way less or subordinate to political work. The fact is, that when I saw that to a certain extent my social work would be impossible without the help of political work, I took to the latter and only the extent that it helped the former."[171] Thus he made politics a means to achieve the social aims and thereby, struck the true valuation between them.

It was not only in politics and social work that he attached relative values, but he gave practically everything its value in relation to other things. It is a general notion that "End justifies the means" Gandhi condemned this view and in a graphical way said, "The means may be likened to a seed, the end to a tree; and there is just the same inviolable connection between the means and the end as there is between the seed and the tree."[172]

Again, "We have always control over the means and never on the end."[173] So it is better to take care of what is in the hand – the means, rather than the end. World Wars, First and Second, were fought under the pretext of achieving equality, democracy and justice, indeed admirable ends. Even wicked and bad means were adopted to attain this noble aim. But alas! the aim is yet far off while the wrong means have given tremendous fillip to selfishness, ill-will, jealousy, fraud and everything bad. Does it not prove the gross failure of the maxim, "End Justifies the means?"

Besides giving values to different things Gandhi also gave us the standard of valuation which is not 'self-centred' but 'altruistic' and objective. His standard of valuation is indeed 'morality' i.e. real good of man. He applies the standard of morality to everything, be it economics, religion or politics. "That economic is untrue which ignores or disregards moral values. The extension of the law of non-violence in the domain of economics means nothing less than the introduction of moral values as a factor to be considered in regulating international commerce."[174] Again, "True religion and true morality are inseparably bound up with each other. Religion is to morality what water is to the seed that is sown in the soil."[175] Similarly, "There are some who think that morality has nothing to do with politics . . . But in 1920, we stuck an entirely new departure and we declared that since truth and non-violence were the sole means to be employed by the Congress to reach its goal, self-purification was necessary even in political life."

By making 'morality' the standard of valuation Gandhi has struck at the very root of greed, selfishness, jealousy and exploitation. To Gandhi 'man is the supreme consideration' and 'life is more than money'. "It is cheaper to kill our aged parents who can do no work and who are a drag on our slender resources. It is also cheaper to kill our children whom we have to maintain without getting anything in return. But we kill neither our parents nor our children, but consider it a privilege to maintain them, no matter what their maintenance costs us."[176] J.C. Kumarappa has also expressed similar sentiments. "A robber murders a child, takes away its necklace and offers it for sale. Who will care to buy that necklace knowing the history behind it? That ornament represent not merely so much tolas of gold but the blood of the innocent child. No one who abhores the murder of a child would wish to possess that article, howsoever cheap it may be offered."[177] The same will apply to the other article exposed for sale. If they are stained with the guilt of exploitation, none should like to purchase them. Swadeshi movement in India was based on above valuations. Insistence on *Khaddar* came out of it:

> "*Khadi* represents human values, mill cloth represents mere metallic value."[178] Again, "*Khaddar* economics is wholly different from the ordinary. The latter takes no note of the human factor. The former concerns itself with the human."[179]

Gandhi does not want people blindly to accept his standard of valuation or the relative values given by him to the different things. He wants people to make their own standards. But he also wants that the people who want to set up their won laboratory should possess some qualities. "Those who have made experiments have come to the conclusion that strict preliminary discipline is necessary to qualify a person to make experiments in the spiritual realm."[180]

REFERENCES

1. Gandhi was the first person to use the technique of fasts to settle political and social issues and to purify self. He undertook a number of fasts, important ones being those of September 20, 1932, Aug. 7, 1934, May 8, 1933, March 3, 1939, Feb. 10, 1943, Jan 13, 1948. He also undertook 3 days fast to boost the morale of striking labourers of Ahmedabad and 7 days fast as a penance for his carelessness. See *Harijan* December 13, 1940; Mira, *Gleanings*, p. 9; *Harijan*, Dec. 9, 1939, Bapu's letter to Mira, p. 26; *Autobiography*.
2. Gandhi observed silence regularly. When he was stuck up with special problems, he took to special *Mauns*. Besides this, he observed silence for one year on the advice of his *Guru* and again for one year in 1926. This silence meant that he stopped making public statements and only studied problems.
3. *Young India*, III, p. 350; *Vishal Bharat* (Hindi) Oct. 1938, p. 401; Speeches, Appendix II, p. 40
4. *Harijan*, December, 24, 1938; *Autobiography*, p. 591; J.H. Holmes, *Mahatma Gandhi*, p. 83.
5. It was due to such a realization that he did not differentiate between religions and did not hold that there will be or should be any clash of interests between man and nation. He was not a believer in the theory of class conflict. *Yeravada Mandir*, Chap. X, XI; *Young India*, October 20, 1927; *Young India*, March 26, 1931.
6. *Diary*, I, p. 201; *Young India*, II, p. 956.
7. Young India, I, p. 860, 864-65; *Young India*, II, p. 227; *Harijan*, July 1, 1939; Gandhi's statement on the break-down of Gandhi-Jinnah talks, September 28, 1944.
8. *Harijan*, February, 1, 1942; *Young India*, May 1, 1920.
9. *Young India*, I, p. 864-65.
10. *Young India*, March 26, 1931; *Harijan*, August 31, 1947.
11. D.P. Mukerji, *Diversities*, p. 212-213.
12. *Harijan*, March 2, 1940.
13. Kaka Kalelkar, *Stray Glimpses of Bapu*, p. 77.
14. *Harijan*, July 27, 1947.
15. *Harijan*, September 30, 1939.
16. *Young India*, III, p. 350; *Speeches*, Appendix II, p. 40; *Harijan*, May 14, 1938; *Harijan*, July 20, 1947; *Harijan*, November 14, 1936; *Young India*, II, p. 65; *Harijan*, December 10, 1938.
17. *Yervada Mandir*, Chapter X.
18. *Young India*, April 23, 1931.

19. *Harijan*, August 12, 1938; *Hind Swaraj*, p. 23-24.
20. *Harijan*, July, 26, 1942.
21. *Young India*, January 9, 1930.
22. *Young India*, May 12, 1920.
23. *Speeches*, p. 807; Romain Rolland, *Mahatma Gandhi*, p. 98.
24. *Young India*, January 8, 1928; *Young India*, December 6, 1928.
25. *Young India*, July 30, 1931; *My Experiments with Truth*, p. 4.
26. Ibid.
27. Ibid.
28. Ibid.
29. Ibid.
30. *Young India*, January 8, 1924.
31. M.K. Gandhi, *My Experiments with Truth*, p. 428.
32. *Harijan*, August 22, 1936.
33. *Harijan*, August 29, 1936.
34. *Young India*, September 25, 1924.
35. *Young India*, December 4, 1924.
36. *Young India*, March 2, 1922.
37. It is clear from Gandhi's autobiography (p. 40) that he knew about Bentham's Theory of Utility.
38. *Diary*, I, p. 201. Keneth Rivett in his *Economic Thought of Mahatma Gandhi* holds that Gandhi knew nothing about Utilitarianism (p. 3) but this view is apparently coloured.
39. *Young India*, II, p. 956.
40. Dr. T.K.N. Unnithan's *Gandhi and Free India*, (p. 46); Richard B. Gregg's essay in *Mahatma Gandhi : Essays and Reflections on His Life and Work*, edited by S. Radhakrishnan (p. 80-86).
41. *Young India*, II, p. 435.
42. Pattabhi Sitaramayya, *History of the Congress*, p. 979.
43. *Young India*, II, p. 364; *Hind Swaraj*, p. 60.
44. Gopi Nath Dhawan, *The Political Philosophy of Mahatma Gandhi*, p. 60.
45. M.K. Gandhi, *Autobiography*, II, p. 592.
46. *Yervada Mandir*, p. 75.
47. Gopi Nath Dhawan, *The Political Philosophy of Mahatma Gandhi*, p. 62.
48. *Yervada Mandir*, p. 27.
49. M.K. Gandhi, *An Autobiography*, p. 80-81.
50. D.G. Tenduldar, *Mahatma*, Vol. I, p. 44.
51. Gopi Nath Dhawan, *The Political Philosophy of Mahatma Gandhi*, p. 38.
52. *Young India*, December 31, 1931, and December 22, 1927.
53. *Matthew*, XXVI, p. 52.
54. *Luke*, XXIII, p. 34.
55. Gopi Nath Dhawan, *The Political Philosophy of Mahatma Gandhi*, p. 22.
56. Ibid, p. 24.
57. Albert Schweitzer, *Indian Thought and Its Development*, p. 224.
58. *Harijan*, June 2, 1940.
59. *Amrit Bazar Patrika*, June 30, 1944.
60. Richard B. Gregg, *The Power of Non-violence*, p. 282.
61. *Harijan*, November 4, 1939.
62. K.G. Mashruwala, *Practical Non-violence*, p. 9.
63. *Young India*, November 4, 1926, p. 385.

64. Kaka Kalelkar, *Stray Glimpses of Bapu*, p. 77.
65. *Speeches and Writings of Mahatma Gandhi*, G.A. Natesan & Co., p. 356.
66. Richard B. Gregg, *The Power of Non-violence*, p. 5-7.
67. *Harijan*, August 31, 1947, p. 302.
68. Gopi Nath Dhawan, *The Political Philosophy of Mahatma Gandhi*, p79.
69. *Harijan*, July 27, 1947, p. 253.
70. Richard B. Gregg, *Power of Non-violence*, p. 254.
71. *Harijan*, September 15, 1946.
72. *Harijan*, November 4, 1939, p. 331.
73. *S.T.C.*, p. 5.
74. *Young India*, March 26, 1931.
75. *Young India*, May 10, 1928.
76. Prof. Robbins admits that means are scarce which have alternative uses.
77. *Ceylon*, p. 132.
78. *Yervada Mandir*, p. 36.
79. *Harijan*, December 2, 1922, p. 422.
80. *Harijan*, July 21, 1946.
81. *Young India*, March 26, 1931.
82. *Harijan*, August 25, 1940, p. 260.
83. "Man cannot serve both God and Mammon" Jesus, *Matthew* 6:24. Buddhism and Hindhu Religion agree with it. "Possessions are our limitations," Tagore, *Sadhna*, p. 16. "Our philosophy is where treasure lies," said Will Durant. In the present age men are 'demented with the mania of obtaining' to quote the caustic remark of Walt Whitman. K.M. Munshi and N.C. Aiyer, *Gandhi's View of Life*, p. 143; Romain Rolland, *Soul Enchanted*; Harman Finer, *The Theory and Practice of Modern Government*; Arnold Toynbee, *International Affairs*, October, 1947; Dean Inge, *More Lay Thoughts of a Dean and Plato Symposium*.
84. Quoted by Nehru in *An Autobiography*, p. 510.
85. *Yervada Mandir*, Chap. V.
86. Ibid.
87. Ibid.
88. Ibid.
89. Ibid.
90. Ibid, Chap. VI.
91. Gopi Nath Dhawan, *The Political Philosophy of Mahatma Gandhi*, p. 94.
92. *Yervada Mandir*, Chap. VI.
93. *Harijan*, April 20, 1934.
94. Address delivered at the Guild House, London, September 23, 1931 – *Speeches and Writings of Mahatma Gandhi*, p. 106.
95. Kaka Kalelkar, *Stray Glimpses of Bapu*, p. 86-87.
96. Ibid, p. 88.
97. K.M. Munshi and N.C. Aiyer, *Gandhi's View of Life*, p. 149.
98. We have already discussed the evil consequences of multiplication of wants. However, a brief repetition may not be out of place.
99. *Speeches and Writings of Mahatma Gandhi*, G.A. Natesan & Co., p. 350.
100. *Yervada Mandir*, Chapter VI.
101. Ibid.
102. C.E.M. Joad, *Counter Attack from the East*, p. 252.
103. *Yervada Mandir*, Chapter VI.

104. Herman Finer, *The Theory and Practice of Modern Government*, Vol. I, p. 47.
105. Quoted in K.M. Munshi and N.C. Aiyer, *Gandhi's View of Life*, p. 143-144.
106. Quoted by Nehru in *An Autobiography*, p. 510.
107. *Modern Review*, October, 1935.
108. "Yajna means an act directed to the welfare of other, done without desiring any return for it." *Yervada Mandir*, Chap. XV.
109. *Yervada Mandir*, Chap XIV.
110. Arnold Toynbee, *International Affairs*, 1947, p. 468.
111. *Yervada Mandir*, Chap. VI.
112. Ibid, Chap. XV.
113. N.K. Bose, *Studies in Gandhism*, p. 204.
114. M.K. Gandhi, *The Story of My Experiments with Truth*, Chap. XVIII.
115. Ibid.
116. Ibid.
117. *Yervada Mandir*, Chap. IX.
118. Ibid.
119. M.K. Gandhi, *Socialism of My Conception*, p.63-64, Vol 1,.
120. *Harijan*, November 14, 1948 and November 28, 1948.
121. *Harijan*, January 27, 1940.
122. *Young India*, May 13, 1926.
123. *Ashram Observances in Action*, p. 60.
124. *Yervada Mandir*, p. 50.
125. *Harijan*, August, 3, 1935.
126. *Harijan*, June, 29, 1935.
127. *Ashram Observances in Action*, Translated from Gujarati by V.G.D.
128. R.K. Prabhu and U.R. Rao, *The Mind of Mahatma Gandhi*, p. 133.
129. *Young India*, November 5, 1925.
130. *Yervada Mandir*, Chap. IX.
131. *Harijan*, June 29, 1935.
132. Ibid.
133. Ibid.
134. *Harijan*, October 15, 1925.
135. *Harijan*, June 1, 1935.
136. Ibid.
137. J.C. Kumarappa, *Economy of Permanence*, p. 3.
138. Ibid., p. 4.
139. Ibid., p. 88.
140. Ibid.
141. Ibid., p. 89.
142. *Harijan*, August 1, 1936.
143. *Young India*, October 13, 1921.
144. *Young India*, September 20, 1928.
145. *Young India*, August 13, 1925.
146. *Harijan*, March 2, 1947.
147. *Harijan*, October 13, 1921.
148. Gopi Nath Dhawan, *Political Philosophy of Mahatma Gandhi*, p. 100.
149. *Harijan*, December 19, 1936; *Yervada Mandir*, Chap. IX.
150. *Young India*, August 25, 1921.
151. *Yervada Mandir*, Chap. IX.
152. *Harijan*, June 29, 1935.

153. Ibid.
154. *Harijan*, June 29, 1935.
155. *Harijan*, August 1, 1936.
156. *Harijan*, March 8, 1935.
157. By rendering a willing obedience of it, they enjoy good health as well as perfect peace and develop their capacities for service, *Ashram Observances in Action*, p. 60.
158. *Harijan*, February 2, 1947.
159. Harijan, January 27, 1940.
160. *Yervada Mandir*, Chap. IX.
161. *Yervada Mandir*, p. 50.
162. *Harijan*, November 2, 1935.
163. *Harijan*, March 2, 1947.
164. For instance, we have to say whether water is fresh and pure, or is unhygienic; the food is well cooked or is half cooked; the shirt is well tailored or not; a flower is fragrant or not; is it good to be healthy and strong; is wealth everything; what is the value of truth and non-violence in our life, etc.
165. We have the standard of Pound to weigh wheat and iron : the yard stick of inches to measure cloth and wool; the numbers to count eggs and bamboos.
166. The following illustrations will clarify the point :

    In Mysore, sandal wood is considered as a very cheap thing and so is used for constructing huts even by the poor. But this cannot be used by the rich in other parts of the country because of its high cost. Thus, with place, the value differs.

    Meat, fish and eggs are considered valuable by those who have a taste for them. But these things have no value for the vegetarians. The idea of value thus differs from person to person.

    Value may also change with time. A piece of land which was considered of little value some 30 years back in New Delhi is considered a valuable possession today. Again, groundnut crop was not considered so valuable before the invention of Hydration process. Similarly, petroleum and its by-products were of little value before the invention of engines, cars, etc.

    "A professor of Economics will say that price mechanism controls supply and demand, the cheaper the articles the greater the demand and so on. Is this always true? In the outside world 'the economic man' does not exist. A woman who wishes to buy a *Saree*, does not call for the cheapest article. She has her own ideas of colour combination, texture, etc., and she would purchase that which fulfils most of her notions. Similarly, a prince who prides on being exclusive, may buy up a whole stock of ties of the same pattern that a dealer may have so that no one else may be seen wearing a tie like that. Again, a petroleum company may buy up a patent of a vegetable oil burning lamp paying a fabulous price for it, and leave the patent unexploited in a pigeon hole in its office, to prevent anyone else bringing out a lamp that may adversely affect the sales of its kerosene oil by creating a demand for a substitute. Such and many other deviations from the academic standards of economics there are that vitiate our unconditional acceptance of them."

    —J.C. Kumarappa, *Economy of Permanence*, p. 39-40.
167. *Harijan*, p.27
168. *Harijan*, p.35
169. Ibid., p. 34.

170. Quoted by S.N. Agarwal, *The Gandhian Plan*, p. 28.
171. *Young India*, August 6, 1931, p. 203.
172. *H.S.*, p. 60.
173. *History of the Congress*, p. 979.
174. *Young India*, December 26, 1924, p. 421.
175. *E.R.* p. 49.
176. *Harijan*, December 10, 1938.
177. J.C. Kumarappa, *Economy of Permanence*, p. 32.
178. *Harijan*, February 9, 1934.
179. *Harijan*, July, 16, 1931.
180. *Young India*, January 23, 1930.

5

Some Problems of Production

A careful study of the trends and developments in almost all the countries of the world since the invention of the first machine, some 400 years back, reveals in spite of great diversities, certain common factors. The power of the machine enamoured man and he, without bothering to stop and think for a moment, fell all out for industrialization thinking that it alone was the symbol of progress and could bring permanent happiness. When, on the one side the industrialized countries are vying with each other to industrialize themselves further in an increasingly shorter period, on the other, the underdeveloped or developing economies also want to join in the race and make their presence felt. This love for industrialization has brought in its wake, the ever-increasing large scale mechanised production, centralization, growth of cities and decline in the importance of villages, a growing demand for all important managerial and technician class, change in ownership from individual ownership to State ownership, through partnership, joint stock companies and cooperative ownership, dispute whether production should be motivated by profit motive or welfare motive (not knowing what this welfare really means), and the ever-increasing responsibility of the State in controlling and regulating things. Since these changes are readily adopted in search of human happiness, we are faced with certain problems created by these changes. For example, we are called upon to fight the demands of unemployment, of uneven distribution of wealth, of exploitation (of the poor by the rich, of labour by the capitalist and of one nation by another) of imperialism and colonialism, of world wars, of booms and slumps with all the evils associated with them, of food shortage and famines, of over-production and under-production, of military alliances, of hatred and jealousies, etc. Industrialization has accelerated the tempo of life and added to its tensions, but the goal of human happiness, of peace and prosperity, of plenty, of increasing leisure for artistic and noble pursuits still continues to evade man. Despite the talk of different types of economies—capitalist, socialist and mixed—and of the countries being on the different stages of development, the dream remains a distant reality. The world has not become a happier and nobler place to live in.

Gandhi, out and out a practical man, wedded to 'untainted' human happiness, saw all these changes and their consequences. Naturally he could not remain a silent spectator to these changes much less be a party to them. He, through his utterances, writings and actions, started giving a new picture of the production system of India of his dreams—a system which may work as a model for other countries of the world. It will, therefore, be advisable to study the views of Gandhi on some important problems connected with the production system of his dreams.

I
AIM—ESTABLISHMENT OF SERVICE ECONOMY

Unlike other economists trained in the western way of thinking, the greatest Gandhian economist, J.C. Kumarappa, in keeping with the spirit of his master, has enumerated five type of economies[1] based on division of society according to their approaches:

1. *Parasitic Economy*—An economy, wherein there is consumption without production and destruction of the source of supplies, is known as parasitic economy. The tiger produces nothing and destroys the source of supply. The tiger is parasitic.

2. *Predatory Economy*—In predatory economy there is consumption without production but the source of supply is not destroyed. The monkey does not produce but does not destroy the trees which give fruit.

Both these economies are self-centred having no sense of duty.

3. *Enterprising Economy*—In enterprising economy rights are balanced with duties, one produces for consuming and one has a right to private property. The abode of the little birds in the house is an example. It builds its nest and enjoys the shelter that it has produced.

4. *Gregarious Economy*—When production is not only for own personal consumption but for general consumption and people live like one family, it is gregarious economy.

The bee collects honey and deposits it for others. It is the gregarious state of economy.

5. *Service Economy*—In service economy , the duty is supreme and none bothers about the rights. The bird picks up grain and instead of eating itself, feeds its younger one's without expecting any reward either in the future, or in the present.

The world has yet to see the last two types of economies though the socialists claim that they have established a gregarious economy.

The aim of Gandhi was to establish a service economy, which he called *Sarvodaya Economy*. He felt that only this economy would be able to bring in permanent happiness for all. Obviously, this economy will be a happy blending of 'productive efficiency' and 'ability to subserve the main social requirements'.[2] The readings of the planning wing of the All India Khadi and Village Industries Board confirm it. "I do not believe that the spiritual law works on a field of its own. On the contrary, it expresses itself only through the ordinary activities of life. It thus affects the economic, the social and political fields".[3] Again, "Civilization is that mode of conduct which points out to man the path of duty. Performance of duty and observance of morality are convertible terms. To observe morality is to attain mastery over mind and other passions".[4]

II
INDUSTRIALIZATION VS. SELF-SUFFICIENCY
i.e. Centralization vs. Decentralization

There appears little scope for doubt that if the aim of economy is fixed as to put duty before right, to serve others without bothering for the reward, to have a happy blending of material progress with moral progress, the mad race for unlimited industrialization would automatically cease. The evils, the world has seen because of this craze for industralization, made Gandhi an opponent of industrialization. It will be worthwhile to quote him here:

> "As I look at Russia where the apothesis of industrialization has been reached, the life there does not appeal to me, to use the language of the *Bible*, 'What shall it avail a man if he gain

> the whole world and lose his soul'."[5]
> "But all do not think like me. Pandit Nehru wants industrialization, because he thinks that if it is socialized, it would be free from evils of capitalism. My own view is that the evils are inherent in industrialization and no amount of socialization can eradicate them."[6]
> "The future of industrialization is dark... And if the future of industrialization is dark for the west, will it not be darker for India."[7]
> "I have seen the wreckage which lies at the end of this road."[8]

Gandhi, therefore, wanted to replace the mad race for unlimited industrialization with regional self-sufficiency. "We shall have to see that the villages become first of all self-contained..."[9]

Explaining the meaning of self-sufficiency, Gandhi wrote:

> "But mind you my idea of self-sufficiency is not a narrow one. There is no scope for selfishness and arrogance in my self-sufficiency. I am not preaching isolation... We have to mix with people even as sugar mixes itself with milk."[10]

Gandhi was not against industries. He wanted to revive and encourage them in India. However, he only wanted to put a limit on them. In his own words:

> "Every village (has) to produce and use all its necessaries and in addition, produce a certain percentage as its contribution to the requirements of the cities."[11]

Hence, industrialization will cease to be the goal. Regional self-sufficiency will take its place.

If the goal of rapid, unbridled industrialization is changed, with it would also disappear the emphasis on centralization. Gandhi opined:

> "Centralization as a system is inconsistent with non-violent structure of society."[12] "I suggest that, if India is to evolve along non-violent lines, it will have to decentralize many things. Centralization cannot be sustained and defended without adequate force."[13]

Mr. Henry Ford appears to agree with Gandhi: "Whenever it is possible, a policy of decentralization ought to be adopted...The thing is not only reasonable and practicable, but it is becoming absolutely necessary."[14]

Gandhi wanted to revive 'Agrarain' civilization. In his own words:

> "There are two schools of thought current in the world. One wants to divide the world into citics and the other into villages. The village civilization and the city civilization are totally different things. One depends on machinery and industrialization and the other on handicrafts. We have given preference to the latter."[15]

Harrison Brown agree with Gandhi.[16] The reasons are not far to seek: "We are inheritors of a rural civilization. The vastness of our country, the vastness of the population, the situation and the climate of the country have in my opinion destined it for a rural civilization."[17] Again, "Many of us believe, and I am one of them, that through our civilization we have a message to deliver to the world."[18]

III
PLACE OF MACHINES

Mahatma Gandhi was against the use of more and more complicated machines because of their inherent defects. But it does not mean that his opposition was either indiscriminate or total. To quote him:

> "It is not true that I desire the destruction of all machinery, or that I am working in that direction."[19]

Again,

> "How can I be 'against machinery' when I know that even this body is a most delicate piece of machinery? The spinning wheel itself is a machine; a little tooth-pick is a machine."[20]

Gandhi simply wanted to impose a limit on the use of machinery. He said, "My object is not to destroy the machine but to impose limitations to it."[21] Again, "I am aiming not at eradication of all machinery but limitation."[22] And the limit according to Gandhi is that the use of machinery should not result in unemployment or exploitation of the poor. Explaining it he says,

> "I have no objection if all things required by my country could be produced with the labour of 30,000 instead of that of three crores. But those three crores must not be rendered idle or unemployed."[23]

Gandhi will , therefore, protect and even encourage any machine which does not deprive masses of men of the opportunity of labour, but which helps the individual and adds to his efficiency and which a man can handle without being its slave.

The saint of India was not against mass production, but he was against mass production of the present type. He wrote:

> "I envisage mass production certainly, but not based on force. After all, the message of the spinning wheel is that. It is mass production, but mass production in people's own homes. If you multiply individual production to millions of time, would it not give you mass production on a tremendous scale."[24]

It appears Gandhi was in complete conformity with the views of Nym Wales, who said, "The extent of mechanisation and the size of the industrial plant depend upon the relative security and cost of labour and capital. Under present conditions it is more profitable in China to use more labour power and less equipment."

IV
PATTERN OF PRODUCTION

From the times of Plato, ownership of wealth has been a subject matter of profound thinking. With the development of society, the concept of wealth has been undergoing a continuous change. And now it is taken for granted that if private ownership is not kept under some sort of control, and is permitted to function freely it is bound to create unemployment, exploitation of the weak, social injustice and so many other evils which will make life into worth living.

The government of a capitalist country wants to control the

private ownership with the help of monetary and fiscal policies, corrective legislation and establishment of a public sector. In other words, the economist feels that a mixed economy will be able maintain all the virtues of private ownership and minimise its vices. In such an economy where private and public sectors are working side by side, efficiency will be highest; imputation of prices will be possible; factors will move to those places where they are most efficient; freedom of production, consumption and occupation will exist; production will be maximum at the minimum cost; and so on. At the same time, the weak will be protected by the State; differences in income will be scaled down; employment will increase, welfare schemes will ensure minimum standard; public interest will be safeguarded through the nationalization of key industries etc. Thus, democratic governments are attempting to introduce mixed economy in place of a purely capitalist one.

The communists object to this type of mixed economy. They feel that this control over private ownership will not be sufficient to correct the grave inequalities of wealth, check the exploitation of the poor by the rich, improve the employment position and ensure a minimum standard for all. They think that, the misnomer of a mixed economy is merely an 'eye wash', a make-shift, and, an appeal to the more fortunate ones to show a little more charity. In a capitalist set-up, the rich are most powerful. They are at the helm of affairs. may it be the State, religion, or society and, therefore, they will never do anything which may be against their interests.

The communists, after condemning the capitalistic system and all its forms, come forward with a new technique—the technique of socialization of all means of production and abolition of all private ownership. In this new set-up, they tell us, production will not be guided by the profit motive but will be directed by the State's Central Planning Authority to those channels where it will be of maximum social benefit. In such a communistic state, there will be no place for exploitation, unemployment, grave inequalities of income etc., and a minimum standard of living will be ensured to all. The country will become a paradise, and life, worth living.

To this, the followers of another camp take serious objection. They tell us that the idea of nationalization is mooted out mainly because of the excessive exploitation of labour by 'haves' and the desire of thinkers to save the labour from the tyranny of the mill-owners. Marx, with all his catch phraseology and magic way of putting things in such a wonderful way that even unscientific thoughts may appear scientific, gave it a new meaning and importance. He made it as the essential part of and an important means to socialism. The initial success of the experiment in Russia, not so much in the form of levelling down of the inequalities of wealth or minimising the exploitation of labour and improving its standard of living, but in the form of the military might, scientific advancement and pace of industrial development, which were mainly due to other factors and not nationalization alone, has persuaded even the governments and economists of the free world to agrees to the partial, if not total, nationalization of industries and growing State control. However, at present a rethinking is going on and it will be worthwhile to analyse it here briefly.

Nationalization is, in fact, nothing but "Governmentalization". It is a technique to make a powerful State all the more powerful by making it a capitalist also. Certainly this increase in the power of the State cannot be, and time has proved that it is not, in the interest of employees for whose welfare the medicine was prescribed, as the enemy has emerged out more powerful than becoming weak. In 1953, the British Trade Union Congress appointed a committee to study the condition of labour in nationalized industries vis-a-vis private industries. The report of the committee clearly shows that the condition of the labour in nationalized industries was in no way better, and at places it was worse than that in the privately owned and managed industries. When this was the achievement in a democratic country having a powerful political party of labour, what will be the position of labour in a communist economy where the State is all powerful, can be anybody's guess. When the disparities in incomes in the U.S.A. are in the ratio of 1:15, they still continue to be 1:80 in the blessed country where the experiment was started first. And to add to this, the concentration camps, the merciless butchery of 'agents of capitalist' and the denial of right to unite or strike have their own tales to tell. The labour got nothing in bargain but lost freedom also.

It was given out that nationalization would lead to socialization where not only basic needs of all would be met but something more would also be given. How unfortunate it appears that when in the U.S.A., Australia, Canada, to name only a few countries, where agriculture still continues to be in the hands of individuals, the problem is how to dispose of the surplus grains, in the countries where land has been nationalized and the Government has paid the maximum attention to it, famine conditions continued to prevail. Russia, in spite of the best efforts of Khrushchev and others, since 1955 had to import huge quantities of food from the U.S.A. and Australia to save the hungry millions from death. China, in spite of the "Great Leap Forward", had to admit its failure and resort to import of rice and food. Similarly, East Germany, Czechoslavakia and Poland—all communist countries—imported foodgrains from their known enemies of the free world. A study in Russia has revealed that the private owned farms, which are now about 36 per cent of the total land, produced more than double of the land which is under collective ownership. All this forces one to conclude that in the public sector, in spite of the increased facilities, the production, specially in the sphere of agriculture (relatively speaking), remains less than that in the private sector.

Nationalization was considered as an essential part and an important means to socialism. However, now people feel that real socialism cannot come till a new man is not created. And if we can create this new man, certainly he will not need the aid of nationalization for socialization. So, why have it? The recent collapse of USSR has clearly demonstrated this truth.

Whether nationalized industries are really in the hands of people or they are managed by the party or group in power for their own ends can be decided by applying three tests, viz., Is there a public control? Is there a public administration and is there public accountability? Unfortunately, a study both of the free and communist countries, has revealed that these three tests do not justify nationalization. Probably it was because of this that the idea of Public Corporations was mooted out in England and daily it is becoming more and more popular with other countries also.

It is now admitted that in nationalized economies, the factors of production do not necessarily move where they are most efficient or wanting, that in the absence of drive given by profit motive, efficiency goes down and costs go up, that correct imputation of prices is not possible, that individuality and individual initiative are not tolerated and life is rigidly regimented. Indeed, people are called upon to pay a heavy price for a mirage. Probably it is because of this that enthusiasm of nationalization is slowly dying out. B.C. Roberts reflected the attitude of Trade Unions of England towards nationalization in these words:

> "...The change in the attitude of the unions is a fundamental one. They are not prepared, at this stage, to recommend that nationalization should be carried much farther..."

Anthony Crossland, a labour M.P., wrote in December, 1959 issue of 'Socialist Commentary' that nationalization has not ceased to be an important means to socialism but "is now less central to socialist strategy." The opinions of G.D.H. Cole, Bevan, and scores of other eminent economists can also be cited in support. The manifestos, programmes, and utterances of the socialists and labour unions of Holland, Switzerland, Sweden and Austria clearly show that they too are not enthusiastic about the scheme of nationalization. De-nationalization of coal and steel industries in U.K. shows in what direction the wind is blowing.

A glance at the seemingly divergent systems—capitalism, communism and mixed economy—reveals an interesting fact, i.e., there are more things common in them rather different. For example, in all the three, faith is pinned up on the use of more and more complicated machines. Naturally, when large scale production with the help of complicated machines is carried out, it results in vast differences of incomes between different groups and increases exploitation of one class by another. It is immaterial whether this class is called 'Capitalist' or 'Managerial'. The only differences in these patterns is one of degree of exploitation. Again, the three are based on material progress, and hence emphasise multiplication of wants. They completely ignore moral, spiritual or human side. Hence, they cannot be said to be either perfect system of production or those opposed to each other in substance.

The question arises to which camp does Gandhi belong? Does he prefer a purely capitalist economy with no state control, or a mixed economy with some state control or a communist state with complete state control or an entirely new pattern of production.

Gandhi, being the democrat of all democrats, has come forward with a new plan according to which individual freedom would be ensured to the maximum, but at the same time, misuse of it would not be permitted. He would retain individual ownership so long as it does not come in conflict with social welfare. It is a new type of mixed economy which, if a name is to be given to it, can be called a Pragmatic Economy or Labour Oriented Economy. Gandhi said, "Under my system it is labour which is the current coin, not metal."[25]

In the ideal economy of Gandhi's concept, agrarian civilization will be revived, emphasis will be laid on decentralization of power, economic as well as political, and regional self-sufficiency in matters of basic needs will be aimed at. Naturally, under this type of economy, emphasis will shift from industries to agriculture. Gandhi was of the firm opinion that the basis of economic life is land. Therefore, in Gandhian pattern of production, agriculture comes first and industries next.

In Gandhi's pragmatic economy, three sectors will function side by side. They are

(1) Private sector where production will be carried on by small and independent producers with the help of 'useful machines'.
(2) Trusteeship sector where production will be under trust control and will be carried out with the help of 'useful machines'.
(3) Public sector where production will be under state control. Here the latest and most up-to-date complicated machines shall be harnessed in production.

Private Sector

In order to ensure the minimum exploitation and maximum peace it is necessary that production should be on the small scale and with the help of those 'useful machines' which may help man to increase his efficiency and earning capacity as may reduce all the monotony and drudgery of the work. But at the same time, it should not result in exploitation of any one else.

Besides the use of small, selected machines and small scale production, it is necessary that production should be reverted back to the places where consumers reside. In other words, the production apparatus should be scattered in different localities and should not be permitted to concentrate in certain regions. This will give birth to self-sufficient localities which was the aim of Mahatma Gandhi. He once wrote, "...Industrialization on a mass scale will necessarily lead to passive or active exploitation of the villages as the problem of competition and marketing comes in. Therefore, we have to concentrate on the village self-contained, manufacturing mainly for use."[26]

The production in private sector, which will be concentrated in self-sufficient localities will be carried out by two types of persons

(a) The farmers whose primary work will be to cultivate the land and secondary work will be to produce goods such as cloth, paper, oil, paddy husking, pottery, toy, cutlery, bamboo and cane work, rope making, tiles and brick making etc. in their spare time.

(b) The persons whose main and only work will be to run the cottage industries and meet the needs of the villagers.

(c) The peasantry's first concern will be to grow its own food crops. The farmers in growing these crops will use the recently invented machines sparingly, as they may oust many men and bullocks from the land. Mirabehn, writing in the *Hindustan Times* has rightly struck a compromise between the use of machines and of methods of cultivation when she says, "I would, therefore, advocate the use of tractors for bringing waste land under cultivation where it is situated in large blocks and is otherwise suitable. But after the land is reclaimed, I would not for a moment suggest that it should remain permanently under mechanical cultivation. The bullock is in every way economical. The bullock is fed from the products of the land, and gives in return valuable cow-dung which is used for fuel and for manure. The bullock can also be used for all kinds of work—carting, water lifting and the like, whereas the tractor has to have expensive oil purchased for it from the *bazaar* and it gives nothing back from its belly."

In India agriculture does not provide employment throughout the year. For several months in a year the farmer is completely idle and even the remaining months, except during the sowing and harvesting time, he is partially unemployed. During this period of forced idleness, he is wasting most of his time in gossips and litigation. The need of subsidiary industries, therefore, is greatly felt, specially in the backward countries of Asia. Gandhi himself said, "Hand spinning does not...compete with...any existing type of industry...The sole claim advanced on its behalf is that it alone offers an immediate, practicable and permanent solution of that problem of problems that confronts India, viz. the enforced idleness for nearly six months in the year of an over-whelming majority of India's population owing to lack of a suitable supplementary occupation to agriculture..."[27] And it is for this reason that production, in private sector, will be shifted from cities to the villagers where it will provide subsidiary work for the farmers in their idle period.

These subsidiary cottage industries can be many—cotton ginning, oil pressing, mat making, fruit preservation, paper making, toy making, pottery, cane work, rope making etc. The only criteria of choosing these industries should be that it may not be necessary to work them all the year round and they may not require much capital or training to run them. Gandhi feels that *Charkha*—the spinning wheel—fulfils all these conditions and is ideally suited as a subsidiary industry. Therefore he selected it as a symbol.

The other part of private sector will constitute of the cottage industries which will be working all the year round and producing anything which the climate, supply of raw material, opportunity to dispose of the produce, technical skill etc., permit. Here some firms will be owned by individuals, some by two or three persons and some by a number of persons. It all will depend upon the capital one can invest. But in every case the size of the firm will not be large enough as to enable its owners to oust the other producers from the field. The owners will be permitted to employ few labourers, the number not exceeding a certain limit (which will be fixed by the Government of the country from time to time).

The production carried out in cities will also be on the same pattern but because of the existence of mental workers in the cities another type of subsidiary industries will grow up. These subsidiary cottage industries will be working all the year round and for only a few limited hours every day as their sole purpose will be to provide an opportunity to the mental workers to do some physical work so that they may recognize the importance of Bread-labour.

The *Panchayats* in villages or cities will keep an eye over these small firms and will take strong action against the offenders of the rules laid women by them regarding the size of the firm, number of people employed, types of machines employed etc. But the action taken by *Panchayats* will be non-violent in nature. The sanctions which effectively can be applied will be boycott of the goods, social boycott of owners of the firm etc. No one, who is familiar with the *Swadeshi* movement of India, will ever deny the power of these non-violent methods.

The Gandhian social structure will try to raise the moral plan of the general public through the education system of *varna-vyavastha*, and will make them believers in non-violence, simplicity and Bread-labour. The impressions thus carved on the people will not permit them after some time, when the impressions have become deep and permanent, to exploit their neighbour or stand erect against the non-violent sanctions applied against them, after they had broken the general code of behaviour.

This type of private sector will retain all the virtues of a capitalistc system—freedom of occupation, consumption and production; possibility of correct imputation of prices as factors will be purchased and sold in open market, movement of factors where they are most efficient, maximization of production, profit incentive to reduce cost and improve efficiency etc. Besides this, it will have certain other advantages to its credit. As production will be carried out on a small scale and under *Panchayat's* observation, chances of exploitation will be minimum. This decentralized production will remove class conflict, increase the earning capacity of the poor people and reduce the power to amass wealth. This will also save time and the middle man's profit as it will establish a direct relation between producers and consumers.

Trusteeship Sector

But in spite of small scale, decentralized production and self-sufficient units, it may be possible in some cases that one person may be able to exploit others and amass wealth. A few of such cases may be :

(a) A few commodities, by their very nature, cannot be produced on a small scale. The production of these commodities will naturally place the owner in a unique position. As he will not get sufficient amount of the competition, he will be able to exploit the ownership for his personal ends.

(b) The production of a few commodities requires special technical knowledge and training. The person who has this training and knowledge may be able to exploit people as it will not be possible for other producers to start production in a short period and compete with him.

(c) The owners of small firms may combine and start enjoying the benefits of monopoly by keeping down the production and artificially raising the prices.

(d) Some producers, in spite of people's preference for small scale production, may carry on with production on large scale and exploit the public.

(e) Some persons, due to their peculiar circumstances, may be in a position to exploit others and may be using these circumstances for their benefit at the cost of others. For example, a landlord and a factory owner, with no hand in production, belong to this group of people.

(f) Any other such reason which may place special power in the hands of a few to exploit others.

Before trying to answer the remedy suggested by Mahatma Gandhi to meet such cases effectively, it will not be out of place here to understand his ideas on exploitation.

Gandhi feels that every one should earn his bread by his own labour. There should be no place for unearned incomes. But if some persons are able to earn without working, may it be due to ownership of property or other similar reasons, it is exploitation of the poor. Again, if a person is able to earn more than twelve times the income of the poorest man in the society, it will be termed as exploitation. The difference in income is permissible because of the differences in efficiency of the persons. Even in Soviet Russia, the difference in maximum and minimum incomes was more than this. Burn in his 'Managerial Revolution' writes, "the upper 11 to 12 per cent of the Soviet population receives approximately 50 per cent of the national income."

Mahatma Gandhi wanted to check exploitation with the least violence. Therefore, at the very outset he could not possibly prescribe the bitter pill of nationalization to meet effectively the above mentioned cases. He felt that when some reformer lost faith in his method of conversion, the technique of what is known as scientific socialism was born. But he was a reformer made of another stuff and so was trying to solve the same problem that faces the scientific socialists in a different way. Gandhi repeatedly said that his approach is always and only through non-violence. The medicine prescribed by him was in terms of the principle of trusteeship. Trusteeship gives one more chance to the capitalist to stop exploitation. It is only after the failure of trusteeship that the firm is nationalized in the interest of the society.

The theory of trusteeship can briefly be summarised as follows

The capitalist, who is found exploiting the people, is made the trustee of the property and so would be expected to use the property, after deducting his maximum permissible income, for the public sake. Gandhi wrote, "When an individual had more than his proportionate portion he became a trustee of that portion for God's people."[28] Again, "What I expect of you, therefore, is that you should hold all your riches as a trust to be used solely in the interest of those who sweat for you, and to whose industry and labour you owe all your position and prosperity."[29]

But who will be the owner of this trust property? Will the ownership vest in the State, or in an association of a voluntary character like village communes and municipalities which may, of course, derive their final authority from the State made laws? To this Gandhi replied, "That question involved some confusion of thought. Legal ownership in the transformed condition was vested in the trustee, not in the State. It was in order to a void confiscation that the doctrine of trusteeship came into play, retaining for society the ability of the original owner in his own right."[30] Thus ownership will vest in the same person and he will be permitted to manage it in the way, he thinks best. The only difference will be that he will not be permitted to misuse the property, as the incentive to commit social crimes will be taken away by not permitting him to retain money beyond the maximum limit. The accounts department of the village Panchayats will be easily able to find out the real income of the trustee from the trust. If it is more than the trustee is entitled to keep, it will be distributed among the owners of others factors of production in proportion to their remuneration.

What will become of the trust property after the death of the trustee, or when he wants to get rid of it by passing it over to others? To this Gandhi replied that the choice of naming the successor "should be given to the original owner who became the first trustee, but the choice must be finalised by the State. Such arrangement puts a check on the State as well as the individual."[31] It is, therefore, not necessary that trust property will pass from father to son, in every case, or can be sold our to any one.

If the capitalist, in spite of becoming a trustee betrays his trust then what will happen? We know about the legally appointed trustees, such as a guardian over a minor's property. He exploits the property for his own use and is reluctant to return it. Same is true of U.N.O. A few countries have been put under the trust and care of the powerful ones who wish to continue their hold on them under one pretext or the other. So, it can be asked : "How then Gandhi will perform a miracle?"

Late Prof. S.K. Rudra, the noted economist. did not agree with the Gandhian Theory of Trusteeship. "The criterion of all economic endeavour is the service of the community, whether achieved through private profit or some other technique. The Gandhian economic philosophy too, would seem to point this way with its doctrine of trusteeship. There is much to commend this view. But it is doubtful if there arc not grave drawbacks attached to the system...to expect people to act according to this principle though ethically supreme, actually will not render substantial and continuous results." To this Mahatma seems to have answered, "My theory of trusteeship is no makeshift, certainly no camouflage. I am confident that it will survive all other theories. It has the sanction of philosophy and religion behind it. That possessors of wealth have not acted upto the theory does not prove its falsity; it proves the weakness of the wealthy. No other way is compatible with non-violence."[32] Further, "I adhere to my doctrine of trusteeship in spite of all the ridicule that has been poured upon it."[33]

Probably, while discussing the theory of trusteeship, critics have forgotten the Gandhian structure of the State and society, which may go a long way in solving many problems. In small self-sufficient units, like villages or cities, it will not be very late to find out the unsocial design of a trustee. And it is a matter of general agreement that exploitation is possible only so far as the consumers are ignorant of this fact. But if in spite of it, the trustee does not stop exploitation, every sort of non-violent pressure will be put on him by the society and the State. Social boycott and non-cooperation will immediately be applied against the offender by the society. Consumers will stop to purchase from him. Owners of factors will refuse to cooperate in production. The result will be, in the absence of large markets to dispose of goods and purchase factors, the trustee will be forced to follow the right track. Some one asked Gandhi, "how will you bring about the trusteeship? Is it by persuasion?" To this he replied, "Not merely by verbal persuasion. I will concentrate on my means. My means are non-cooperation. No person can amass wealth without the cooperation, willing or forced, of the people concerned."[34] And if, in spite of these sanctions a trustee is adamant, the State will dethrone him and the property will go under the trust of another person or it will be nationalized.

The Gandhian theory of Trusteeship is a positive improvement over the Marxist method of socialization of the whole economic structure. Besides being less violent in character, it retains the freedom of occupation, consumption and production, and thus ensures the right of development of individual personality, which is completely lacking in a communist State. It is also more just and scientific in fixing the upper limit of income as it takes into consideration the Index Number and economic prosperity of the country and region.

But in spite of these differences, there is some common meeting around between the Gandhian and Communist ways of thinking. Both aim at scaling down the differences of income, both feel that production should not be left solely to the direction and management of the individual, may he be a trustee or a manager, both realise the importance of keeping social interest above individual interest etc.

The Gandhian concept of Trusteeship, unlike the capitalist system, does not permit an owner to misuse his wealth. He is the owner of only that portion of the income which is necessary for his existence, it being fixed by the State. There cannot exist glaring inequalities of incomes and exploitation in the Gandhian system. On the one hand it keeps a check on exploitation and on the other it strikes at the very root of misery and chaos by trying to convert the present man into a self-sufficient and decent man believing in non-violence and dignity of labour. But Gandhi and a capitalist, both want to retain individual freedom and initiative.

Public Sector

Gandhi was against reckless wholesale nationalization, because it represents violence.[35] However, he being a realist, will agree to nationalize a few industries or firms provided prerequisites of nationalization are fulfilled. One of the prerequisites, and the most important one, is a good Central Government manned by tried patriots who can be trusted to hold the interest of the millions as their first care. "Nationalization presupposes that real power rests with the people, i.e. with the masses. When the Government of the land is in the hands of such tried patriots who will be trusted to hold the interests of the millions as their first care, then alone can we claim to have a National Government and 'Nationalization' will then ensure that the interests of the masses will be taken care of."[36] Obviously, this Central Government will be a federation of *Panchayats* and will be effectively controlled by them.

The second pre-requisite is that only those industries or firms will be nationalized which are producing consumption goods for masses and not those which are serving a selected few. Nationalization of Airways, on this ground, will not be justifiable. The logic is clear, "The funds available to the Government should be earmarked for the provision of facilities for the masses and hence we cannot divert them for the betterment of airways Let private enterprise go on as they have done. Some 'haves' will exploit other 'haves'..."[37]

Only those firms of the private sector or trusteeship sector shall be nationalized which, in spite of warnings, have failed to improve. Somebody asked Mahatma Gandhi, "If you are assured that a person would never be a trustee in the sense in which you would like to have him, do you not think that the State would be justified in taking away those things from him, with the minimum of violence." To this Gandhi replied, "Yes, the State will, as a matter of fact; take away these things, and I think it will be justified if it used the minimum of violence...I would be very happy indeed if the people concerned behaved as trustees, but if they fail, I believe we shall have to deprive them of their possession through the State with the minimum exercise of violence."[38]

These are in nutshell the ideas of Gandhi regarding nationalization of the trust property. He wanted to avoid it to the maximum, but if it became unavoidable he would never hesitate in nationalizing it though he felt that it involved some violence. But since it would have to be done in the interest of the general masses, it is pardonable.

One thing is worth noticing here: even when the Mahatma recommends nationalization, it does not apply to the industry as a whole. Individual cases are to be tested on their separate merits and only such trustees as are found guilty of the breach of trust, will be deprived of their trust property. For example, if Mr. X is a trustee of a cotton spinning and weaving factory (of course of a small size) and is not discharging his trust well, then the factory will be nationalized. But other trustees or individuals, who are running their factories, in keeping with the Gandhian ideology, will not be touched. The industry as a whole will not be nationalized. Only the firm will be affected.

With nationalization is closely knit the question of compensation. Does Gandhi believe in giving compensation or not? It can be well argued that if a trustee, who claims the ownership of the property, is unwilling to fulfil the obligations of a trustee, and is removed, naturally, he loses the right of compensation. But to take this stand always will not be correct. Gandhi felt that individual cases should be studied separately and the question whether compensation is to be given or not should be decided according to their respective merits. The amount of compensation should also depend upon individual cases. Gandhi wrote in *Young India*, "... I said at the Round Table Conference that every vested interest must be subjected to scrutiny, and confiscation ordered if neccessary...with or without compensation as the case demands."[39]

Regarding the public utility concerns and basic industries, Gandhi wrote:

> "The heavy machinery for work of public utility, which cannot be undertaken by human labour, has its inevitable place, but all that would be owned by the State and used entirely for the benefit of the people."[40]

Explaining the point, he wrote:

> "...If we could have electricity in every village home, I should not mind villagers plying their implements and tools with the help of electricity. But then the village communities or state would own power houses just as they have their grazing pastures."[41]

Gandhi would agree to nationalize a new key industries also. But only those key industries will be nationalized the goods of which cannot be produced on a small scale. In the words of Gandhi:

> "The key industries which the national needs may be centralized. But then I would not choose anything as a key industry that can be taken up the villages with a little organizing."[42]

Thus Gandhian public sector will have three types of industries and firms:

1. Firms whose owners, in spite of repeated reminders, continue to betray the trust.

2. Public utility concerns such as transport and communication, health and sanitation, education, banking and insurance, statistics

and research.

3. Key industries which cannot be run on small scale such as defence industries, power generating industries, mining metallurgy and forestry, machine tools, heavy engineering, heavy chemicals, fertilizers and pharmaceuticals.

REFERENCES

1. J.C. Kumarappa, *Gandhian Economic Thought*, p. 9-11.
2. M.P. Desai, *Planning for Basic National Recovery*, p. 8.
3. M.K. Gandhi, *Non-violence in Peace and War*, p. 30-31
4. M.K. Gandhi, *Hindu Dharma*, p. 57.
5. D.G. Tendulkar, *Mahatma*, Vol. IV, p. 8.
6. Ibid., Vol. V, . 147.
7. C. Rajagopalacharya and J.C. Kumarappa, *The Nations Voice*, p. 190.
8. Ibid.
9. G.D. Tendulkar, *Mahatma*, Vol. IV. p. 8, Vol. V, p. 11.
10. N.K. Bose, *Selections from Gandhi*, vide S.N. Jha, *Gandhian Economic Thought*, p. 168.
11. M.K. Gandhi, *Economic and Industrial Life and Relations*, Vol. I, p. liv.
12. N.K. Bose, *Selections from Gandhi*, Sec. 248.
13. Ibid., p. 246.
14. Richard B. Gregg, *A Philosophy of Indian Economic Development*, p. 37.
15. N.K. Bose, *Selections from Gandhi*, Sec. 366.
16. S.N. Jha, *Gandhian Economic Thought*, p. 131.
17. N.K. Bose, *Selections from Gandhi*, Sec. 187.
18. Ibid., p. 7.
19. *Young India*, January 19, 1921.
20. *Young India*, November 13, 1924, p. 377; Vincent Sheen, *Lead Kindly Light*, Chap. IV, p. 65.
21. *Young India*, November 3, 1924.
22. M.K. Gandhi, *Cent Percent Swadeshi*, p. 104.
23. *Harijan Bandhu*, February 27, 1938; *Harijan*, Feburary, 12 1938.
24. *Harijan*, November 2, 1934
25. G.D. Tendulkar, *Mahatma*, Vol. III, p. 169.
26. N.K. Bose, *Selections from Gandhi*, p. 244-45.
27. *Young India*, October 21, 1926.
28. *Harijan*, February 23, 1947.
29. *Young India*, May 10, 1928.
30. *Harijan*, February 16, 1947.
31. *Harijan*, February 16, 1947.
32. *Yervada Mandir*, p. 45-9.
33. K.R. Khosla, *Mahatma Gandhi: Life Through Pictures*, p. 58.
34. C. Rajagopalacharya and J.C. Kumarappa, *The Nation's Voice*, p. 190.
35. M.K. Gandhi, *Economic and Industrial Life and Relations*, Vol. I, p. 124.
36. J.C. Kumarappa, *The Gandhian Economy and the Way to Realize It*, p. 76.
37. Ibid., p. 77.

38. N.K. Bose, *Studies in Gandhism*; M.L. Dantwala, *Gandhism Reconsidered*, p. 57.
39. M.K. Gandhi, *Economic and Industrial Life and Relations*, Vol. I, p. 124.
40. *Cent Percent Swadeshi*, quoted by M.L. Dantwala, *Gandhism Reconsidered*, p. 40.
41. *Harijan*, June 22, 1935.
42. G.D. Tendulkar, *Mahatma*, Vol. II, p. 277.

6

Some Allied Problems

In the foregoing pages, an attempt has been made to study the views of Gandhi on two problems connected with the industrial development, viz., attitude towards technological changes and patterns of production. Some more problems are also associated with the industrial development. It will be in the fitness of things to study these problems from the Gandhian point of view.

It is now being realized that for a speedy development of the country, it is essential that the quantity of the population and its rate of growth should be linked with the requirements. It is for this reason that now greater emphasis is being placed on population planning by every country of the world. It will, therefore, be worthwhile to study the views of Gandhi on the problem of population.

The present day industrialization has clearly demonstrated that the relation between labour and capital is far from being satisfactory. Each is trying to liquidate the other. No economic system—Capitalism, Communism, Socialism, Fascism, Nazism and now U.N.O.—has so far been able to resolve the ever-growing differences between the employer and the employee and restore a climate of peace, love and mutual understanding. It will be worthwhile to know, from the Gandhin view-point, where the malady lies and what would be done to create in the industry a family atmosphere and a spirit of 'live' and 'let live.' While studying the problem of labour-capital relations it will be but natural to know the views of Gandhi on some practical problems, like Trade Unions and State Legislation.

I
GANDHI AND THE POPULATION PROBLEMS

Malthus was the first economist to tell the world in a scientific way, some 106 years back, that population is increasing at a very fast rate and, if unchecked, will soon outnumber the supply of food and consequently the natural calamities (Positive Checks in his words) will follow. Natural calamities are bad and so they should be prevented. Malthus suggested, as an alternative, Preventive Checks, first in the form of 'Moral Restraint', but thereafter seemed to be inclined to consider the "Evils and Vices"[1] also.

After Malthus, a large number of demographical researches have been undertaken and either Malthus has been rediscovered or criticised or alternative theories suggested.[2] All this has made Governments and peoples more cautious and population planning minded.[3] But in spite of all these scientific studies, one is constrained to say that mainly the quantitative aspect of the problem with reference to individual nations has been studied and practically no attention has been paid or is being paid even now to the qualitative aspect.

It appears Gandhi was one with Malthus about natural calamities. He, in another reference, observed, "I share the belief with the whole world, civilized and uncivilized, that calamities such as the Bihar one (Earthquake) come to mankind as chastisement for their sins. . ."

Gandhi realised that the emphasis of the Westerners on the quantitative aspect of population and efforts to control its growth by artificial methods are not every proper and that they may lead to disasterous results. For example, use of contraceptives is undermining the heath of Westerners because it encourages excessive indulgence and is also encouraging pre-marital sexual relations. Again, in Japan the technique of abortion is practised on a large scale. All this has adverse effects and creates new tensions. Gandhi has written exhaustively on the subject and has also cited authorities. A few extracted will be of interest:

> "Procreation is a natural phenomenon indeed, but within specific limits. A transgression of these limits imperils womankind, emasculates the race, induces disease, puts a premium on vice and makes world ungodly."[4]

"If contraceptives are resorted to, fightful results will follow. Men and women will be living for sex alone. They will become soft-brained, unhinged, in fact, mental and moral wrecks."[5]

Gandhi quotes the conclusions of William R. Thurston which are based on his personal observation and the data which he obtained from physicians, statistics of social hygiene and medical statistcs:

(a) "It causes the woman to become highly nervous, prematurely aged, diseased, irritable, restless, discontented and incapable of properly caring for children."
(b) "Among the poorer classes, it leads to the propagation of many children who are not wanted."
(c) "Among the higher classes, unrestrained sexual intercourse leads to the practice of contraception and abortions." "If contraceptive methods, under the name of 'birth-control' or any other name are taught to the majority of the women of the masses, the race will become generally diseased, demoralized, depraved, and will eventually perish."
(d) "The excessive sexual intercourse drains the male of the vitality necessary for earning a good living." "At present there are approximately 2,000,000 more widows in the United States than there are widowers. Comparatively few of these are war widows."[6]

Gandhi further explains his opposition in these words:

"Artificial methods are like putting a premium upon vice. They make man and woman reckless. And respectability that is being given to the methods must hasten the dissolution of the restraint that public opinion puts upon one. Adoption of artificial methods must result in imbecility and nervous prostration. The remedy will be found to be worse than the disease..."[7]

Again,
"The protagonists of contraceptives have almost set up self-indulgence as their ideal...unlimited self-indulgence, as everybody would admit, can only result in certain destruction of the individual or the race concerned."[8]

> "As it is, man has sufficiently degraded her (the woman) for his lust, and a artificial methods, no matter how well meaning the advocates may be, will still further degrade her."[9]

There is another objection"

> "Assuming that birth-control by artificial aids is justifiable under certain conditions, it seems to be utterly impracticable of application among the millions..."[10]

At least the experience of under-developed countries of Asia and Africa confirms this view.

Gandhi on Quantitative Controls

But this does not mean that Gandhi was against all types of quantitative controls of population. The difference between him and the Westerners is that he wanted to control the growth of population irrespective of the size, the natural resources and the stage of development of the country and through less injurious methods. This is evident from his views on marriage and *Brahmacharya* or celibacy.

Gandhi at his own cost has come to know of the pitfalls of early marriage – he was married at the age of thirteen.[11] So he was against child marriage or early marriage.[12] Gandhi, therefore, asked people not to marry their children till they were grown up and capable of sharing the responsibilities of their family. His sermon in favour of late marriages was not only for the thickly populated countries like India and China. It was a universal formula. Surely, late marriages are bound to affect the rate of growth of population adversely.

The second formula which Gandhi gave to control the quantity of population was self-control, i.e. *Brahmacharya* or celibacy. This idea struck to him because of Mr. Hill[13] and was fanned by the preaching of the saints and the study of religious books. But for Gandhi, the meaning of *Brahmacharya* was different from the prevailing one. It meant not only control of sex before marriage but also during the married life.[14] Not only this. It meant, besides control of desire for sex, a complete control of self. To quote him:

> "...Let us remember the root meaning of *Brahmacharya*, *Brahmacharya* means *Charya* or course of conduct adopted to

> the search of *Brahma* or Truth. From this etymological meaning arises the special meaning, viz. control of all the senses. We must forget the incomplete definition which restricts itself to the sexual aspect only...[15]

> "*Brahmacharya* is not mere mechanical celibacy, it means complete control over all the senses and freedom from lust in thought, word and deed. As such it is the royal road to self-realization or attainment of *Brahma*... "[16]

Gandhi admitted that to observe *Brahmacharya* is not an easy job. He himself had to try hard to achieve it. So he lays down a code of conduct, based on his own experience, for observing *Brahmacharya*:

The first thing is to control palate. To quote:

> "Control of the palate is the first essential in the observance of the vow. I found that complete control of the palate made the observance very easy, and so I now pursued dietic experiments not merely from the vegetarian's but also from the *Brahmacharya's* point of view. As the result of these experiments I saw that *Brahmachari's* food should be limited, simple, spiceless, and if possible, uncooked."[17]

Other pre-requisites of *Brahmacharya*, according to Gandhi, are control of senses, clean companions and prayer. In Gandhi's own words:

> "A *Brahmachari* must need to control his palate. He must eat to live and not for enjoyment. He must see only clean things and close his eyes before anything unclean. A *Brahmachari* will likewise hear to nothing obscene or unclean, smell no strong, stimulating things. The smell of clean earth is far sweeter than the fragrance of artificial scents and essences...The third step is to have clean companions – clean friends and clean books ... The last and not the least is prayer...[18]

Exploding the myth that *Brahmacharya*, i.e. self-control is very difficult to practise and is meant only for *Sadhus* and *Sanyasins*, Gandhi quoted Western and ancient Indian authorities.[19]

To conclude, Gandhi did believe in planning quantitative aspect of population but, unlike other economists, he abhorred prevelant preventive checks and advocated the tools of late marriage and self-control, i.e. *Brahmacharya*.

Qualitative Aspect of the Problem

Although no economist of the world has tried to propound a theory of population discussing the qualitative aspect of the problem, yet none will dispute its importance for a country's socio-politico-economic progress. Gandhi was the first economist to draw our attention to this neglected aspect of the problem. His views on *Brahmacharya*, i.e. self-control, education and socio-politico-economic set-up give a clue to it.

Gandhi was opposed to the different artificial methods of birth-control, because he felt convinced – and he has cited many authorities in his support – that they are injurious for the society. He, therefore, suggested, as an alternative, two methods – late marriages and *Brahmacharya*, i.e. self-control. Self-control, before the marriage and during the married life will not only keep in check the growth of population but will also improve the quality of the population.

Gandhi felt convinced that till the people of a country are not healthy, they will not be able to serve properly either themselves or their society, their country and humanity at large. And no amount of good food, pure air and fresh water can improve their health without self-restraint. So by popularising *Brahmacharya*, Gandhi was trying to improve the health of the people. To quote him:

> "Many are the keys to health, and they are all quite essential; but one thing needful, above all others, is *Brahmacharya*... There can be no doubt that men and women can never be virile or strong unless they observe true *Brahmacharya*."[20]

Gandhi's own experience confirmed it.

> "*Brahmacharya* teaches self-control not only of desire for sex but also of other senses. This all around self-control raises the moral fibre of the nation and removes vanity, anger, fear and jealousy from the people."[21]

Hindu religious books tell us that *Brahmacharya* raises the intelligence of the person who practises it and helps in the integration of his personality. *Sadhus* and *Sanyasins* confirm it. Gandhi also believed in it. Explaining the cause of it, he wrote:

> "All power comes from the preservation and sublimation of the vitality that is responsible for creation of life. If the vitality is husbanded instead of being dissipated, it is transmuted into creative energy of the highest order...Hence perfectly controlled thought is itself power of the highest potency and can become self-acting."[22]

Gandhi quotes William Lebtus Here's article 'Generation and Regeneration' to elaborate the point. Some of the extracts from this article can be quoted here with profit:

> "All bodies perform two functions, viz. 'internal reproduction for the building up of the body, and external reproduction for the continuance of the species'. The processes he names regeneration and generation respectively."
>
> "The regenerative process—internal reproduction—is fundamental for the individual and, therefore, necessary and primary, the generative process is due to a superfluity of cells and is, therefore, secondary...The law of life, then, at this level is to feed the germ cells firstly for regeneration and secondly for generation. In case of deficiency, regeneration must take the first place and generation be suspended."[23]
>
> "Among civilized human beings sexuai intercourse is practised vastly more than is necessary for the production of the next generation and is carried on at the expense of internal reproduction, bringing disease, death and more in its train."[24]
>
> "The process of regeneration is not and cannot be mechanistic in character, but like the primitive fission is vitalistic. That is to say, it exhibits intelligence and will. To suppose that life separates, differentiates and segregates by a process that is purely mechanists is inconceivable. True, these fundamental processes are so far removed from our present consciousness as to seem to be uncontrolled by the human or animal will. But a moment's reflection will show, that just as the will of the full developed human being directs his external

movements and actions in accordance with the guidance of the intellect, this, indeed being its function, so the earlier processes of the gradual organization of the body must, within the limits provided by environment, be allowed to be directed by a kind of will guided by a kind of intelligence. This is now known to psychologists as 'the unconscious.' It is a part of our self-disconnected from our normal daily thinking, but intensely awake and alert in regard to its own functions so much so that it never for a moment subsides into sleep as the consciousness does."[25]

Some Other Fundamental Changes

Gandhi being a practical man, knew it well that to improve the quality of man and to make him obey the rules of *Brahmacharya*, mere preaching of *Brahmacharya* will not do. The preaching must be supported with some more fundamental changes. So, through education and new socio-politico-economic set-up, Gandhi wanted to make a new man who will be truthful, non-violent, of simple habits, hardworking disciplined and strong, in short a first-rate moralist.

Through a new scheme of education, Gandhi wanted to integrate the body, mind and soul of the students, develop their faculties and raise their moral standards. He, therefore, advocated a knowledge of the 3 R's but said that it should be round some craft such as weaving and spinning, agriculture, animal husbandry, carpentry, etc. The Wardha Scheme' of Education is a pioneer work in the direction

Socio-politico-economic set-up is also to be reorganized so that the fine models made by education are not later disfigured. So Gandhi wanted a new type of political system, a system which he described as *Ram Rajya** i.e. "Sovereignty of the people based on pure moral authority"[26] or *Panchayati Raj*. In this political set-up, village republic will be federated and there will be maximum decentralization of power. The rule of majority will have a narrow application and everyone will be enjoying full liberty but no licence.

The social set-up will also have to be overhauled—Gandhi like Robert Owen, wanted to change the atmosphere of the people and so he made bold experiments in organising Phoenix settlement and

* For details, see Chap. IX

Tolstoy farm in South Africa, *Sevashram* (known as *Satyagrah Ashrama*) and Wardha Ashram in India. His non-violent sanctions—*Satyagrah*, i.e., non-violent non-cooperation, picketing and fast—were potential weapons in the armoury to convert a die-hard. His insistence on non-violence and truth, even in politics, his preaching of simplicity, bread-labour, *Brahmacharya*, equality of man, and his experiments with diet and self-control give a clue of the direction in which he wanted to take his people.

Gandhi wanted to replace the Gospel of Mammon with the Goddess of satisfaction. His memorable speech delivered in the Physics Lecture Theater of the Muir College, Allahabad, on December 22, 1916, still rings in the ears of the students of Economics interested in real progress. Gandhi posed the question: "Does economic progress clash with real progress?"[27] Soon came the answer: " 'You cannot serve God and Mammon' is an economic truth of the highest value. We have to make our choice. Western nations are groaning under the heels of the monster—God of Materialism. Their moral growth has become stunted.[28] So he wanted to build up a new economic world where wants will be minimum, villages will be self-sufficient in all the basic requirements, production will be carried out in houses, internal and international trade will be minimum and exploitation will be non-existent.

International Migration of Population

So much about the long-term solution of the problem. But what can be done in a short period to reduce the pressure of a very large population in countries like India and China. Even the protagonists of artificial methods of birth-control are unable to suggest a solution. So it will be worthwhile to turn towards Gandhi.

When Gandhi reached Africa he found that the condition of Indians there was very bad. They were badly treated by their European masters. He also came to know that they were invited by the whites for developing their own trade and business. This pained him. So he started thinking about problems of the Indian residing in Africa. While thinking about them he hit at the idea of international migration of population and the problems connected with it .

Gandhi, in course of his visits to Europe and Africa as also during the struggles in Africa and India, observed that due to rapid advancement in the means of transport and communication, the world is shrinking and people are becoming more and more cosmopolitan in outlook,[29] but at the same time due to fast growing destructive power of armament, nations are becoming super-sensitive and unduly narrow in outlook.[30] He also observed that while on the one hand free movement of capital [31] is increasing, on the other movement of people – the living beings – is restricted.[32] These tendencies, together with the disproportionate distribution of population of the world in different countries, looking to the distribution of area,[33] are creating tensions, both internal and international.[34] The indiscriminate increase of trade relations are likely to increase these tensions.[35] All this made Gandhi think in terms of equitable distribution of population all over the world, removal of restrictions on international movement of population, duties of emigrants etc. Incidentally these ideas solve the problems not only of the countries having large population but also of the thinly populated countries like U.S.A., U.S.S.R., Canada etc. If migration of population is carried out on the basis of mutual gains, the international relations will also improve and it will also bring the Mulatto dream nearer realization. Hence, Gandhi preached free international movement of population. His stand was based partly on psychological grounds and partly on economic and political grounds.

Gandhi tells us, through his utterances and actions in South Africa, that international migration of population is profitable only when (1) this migration is in the interest of the people of both the countries, (2) the countrymen receive the immigrants as their own brothers and not as labourers and inferiors, and (3) immigrants adopt the country they are migrating to as their own.[36]

The above discussion clearly shows that Mahatma Gandhi believed in planning the population of not only of individual countries but of the world as a whole. He wanted to control the rate of growth of population but was certainly against the modern artificial methods. He suggested *Brahmacharya* i.e. self-control as an alternative because on the one hand, it avoids the evils of the modern methods of birth-control and, on the other, improves the quality of the population – health, self-control, intelligence etc. – and thereby integrates the individual personality. Gandhi, as a first rate humanist and believer in equality of men, also suggests the method of international migration of population to solve, in short period, the problems of both the countries – over-populated and under-populated. Certainly these ideas are more important and dynamic than those ever propounded by any economist of the world.

II
LABOUR CAPITAL RELATIONS

A review of events of the last three or four hundred years will convince any body that the panacea of large scale mechanized industrialization for all ills has not been able to cure any disease but has created new ones, the most important and recent in the industrial spheres being the growing bitterness between labour and capital. The continuing war, sometimes cold and sometimes hot, leaves no place for doubt. A Gandhi will naturally like to know what has gone wrong that the feeling between labour and capital, which had been rather cordial in the earlier days, are now becoming more and more bitter so much so that one started thinking of annihilating the other. One talks of growing automation, rationalizaton and scientific management and the other of dictatorship of proletariate and nationalization.

Mr. R.H. Tawney thinks that concentration of wealth or power or both, which the rapid industrial development of the present type has brought in its wake, is mainly responsible for the growing deterioration in labour-capital relations. He writes: "In an industrial society, the tendency of economic power is not to be dispersed among numerous small centres of energy, but to be massed in blocks. Lord Melchett smiles, and there is sunshine in ten thousand homes. Mr. Margan frowns and the population of two continents is plunged in gloom"[37]

This concentration has reduced one time small but free and contented entrepreneurs into wage-earners depending on the mercy of their masters and so always grumbling. H.S. Kirkaldy has rightly remarked: "The problems of industrial relations arise with and from the divorce of the worker from the ownership of the instruments and materials of productions."[38] This divorce of ownership has injected the feelings of master and servant, of superiority and inferiority,[39] and has thus spoiled the relations. With these complexes when the labourer sees that in spite of working very hard, he is unable to satisfy even his bare necessities of life and on the other hand the owner of machines, the master, without doing much is able to live in luxury, he naturally feels sore. The bitterness increases. The love for power and money has made the modern industrial plant so much unwieldy that the employer has lost all contacts with his labour. Labour has come to be known by number and not by names. Naturally, the employer does not know the difficulties, personal, social and official, of his employees, nor is he aware of their qualities and defects, aspirations and desperations. In the absence of this knowledge, selection, placement and maintenance of the working men as also the ways and means of sharing certain phases of marginal control with employees become faulty. Dodd has rightly remarked, "Industrial unrest is merely the manifestation of mal-adjustments which obtain in the intricate relation of men to jobs, of management to men and both to the broader aspects of our economic and political system."[40]

When the employer is ignorant of his workers and he starts with a pre-possessed mind that they are lazy, inefficient, dishonest, bad, disinterested in industry and pure mercenaries, the labour in the absence of any first hand information about his master, whom he hardly sees once a year and knows only through the stories of brutality or luxury, also starts with a fixed nation that his master is necessarily an evil, an exploiter and parasite. Acting with a per-possessed mind, with indifference and antagonism, the chances of misunderstanding each other are widened and the slightest wrong step sparks off the powder.

Recent psycho-technological researches have focussed attention on some psychological problems."[41] Human nature, we are told, is a composite of inborn and acquired characteristics which have become so closely interwoven as to be almost inseparable. In spite of diversity in human nature, habits and certain basic traits, like nature for possession, self-assertion, escape or to meet obstructions with anger; and the emotions of fear, worry, anger, love and hate are common to all men. Nature, emotions and habits are basically noble. It is also possible to control and develop human personality through transformation, repression and direction. Dodd has said, "Human nature conceived as the sum of inherent and acquired characteristics exhibited in behaviour, does change and develop both in the life of the individual and that of the race."[42] It is unfortunate that till recently study of the human side of labour has been criminally neglected and this had led to the present tensions, distrust and ill-will in the industrial sphere. Soman has wisely concluded: "The workers' whole nature must be intelligently understood, properly stimulated and rightly directed, if industry is to function peacefully"[43] because "labour is not a commodity." Probably, it is because of these psycho-technological researches that the labourer's nature of possession is being satisfied by giving him a share in profit and management; his herd nature by allowing him to organize unions, clubs and other associations; and his parental nature by assuring him a good house, medical aid, schools and games for him and his children. Yet much is left untouched.

Insistence on rights by both labour and capital, without bothering about their duties, has also contributed to the malady. According to the western ideology, which is extrovert, each party organize itself with the eye on the cake. One wants more profits and the other grudges it and puts a counter claim in the form of higher wage, more bonus and lesser hours of work. None seems to bother about duties. Soon this insistence on rights, devoid of duties, take the form of a class-conflict in which hatred, jealousy, ill-will, violence and other vices freely flourish.

The idea of class-conflict pre-supposes the divergence of interests and heterogeneity in life. It is on this wrong understanding that slogans like 'the greatest good of the greatest number' and others have been coined as it is logically concluded that good of all, due to divergence of interests, is not possible. Hence, tensions and conflicts in industrial relations are taken as normal phenomena.

The communist tells us that 'conflict' is the very essence of progress. He harnesses the tools of materialistic interpretation of history to prove his point. He suggests his labour friends that if they want to improve their condition and establish the dictatorship of the proletariate, they must not insist that means must be pure. The ends justify the means. This philosophy has not been only accepted in the communist and fellow-travellers world but has won a good number of friends in the other world also as this preaching comes handy for serving selfish ends. But unfortunately this has, to use the Marxian terminolgoy, seeds of self-destruction. "Destructive means employed engender corresponding counter means and so forth *ad-infinitum*. As the Buddha put it: "If hatred responds to hatred, when and where ...will hatred end?"[44] So we notice labour-capital strife taking the most ugly turns. Huxley also agrees when he writes, "Our personal experience and the study of history make it abundantly clear that the means whereby we try to achieve something are at least as important as the end, we wish to attain. Indeed they are seen more important."[45]

Leadership, whether of labour or of capital, can either fan the flames or extinguish them. G.D.H. Cole has rightly observed, "The workers crave for a personal leader even as they need a personal God."[46] If they get an ambitious, selfish, mean and unwise leader, violence and strike will become matters of daily occurrence. On the other hand, a sober, and disciplined leader wedded to all round development of labour will try to minimise the area of war. History bears testimony to it.

To conclude, industrial peace has been disturbed, according to experts from the West, because of concentration of power and wealth, neglect of 'human producers of profit', loss of personal contact between the employer and the employee and consequently wrong selection, placement, training and facilities of workers, pre-possessed mind, no efforts to understand human nature and develop it, insistence on rights and negligence of duties, indifference towards pure means, faulty leadership and presumption of divergence of interests.

Modern experts, seeing the deteriorating labour-capital relations and disturbed industrial peace and the price which nations are paying, tried to remedy the evil. However, a perusal of the different types of socio-politico-economies – Capitalism, Communism, Socialism, Nazism and Fascism – will show that the problem has continued to persist and even grow. For example, in capitalist economies, in spite of growing interference by the State and passing of ever-increasing labour laws – the schemes of bonus, profit-sharing and participation in management and other welfare schemes – the relations between labour and capital continue to be bad and both are pitted against each other as sworn enemies. Communism tried to solve the dispute by eliminating one party to the dispute. However, in doing so, it seated a more powerful enemy on the throne in the form of State Capitalism,"[47] which has robbed labour of all freedom and has started using labour union for strengthening itself. The inequalities of income continue of exist.[48] The idea that State will 'wither away' still remains a distant reality because in the words of Stalin, "the State cannot wither away in a single socialist country before the world revolution because of the necessities imposed by capitalist encirclement."[49] Nazism and Fascism have also failed and they, like a communist government have only ruthlessly suppressed labour. Socialism whether democratic or otherwise, being neither this nor that, has also not done anything spectacular so far. Sorokin was right when he observed, "With the decline of Capitalism and the rise of various totalitarian systems of economy, various brands of the latter are offered as radical cures for war. However, different these brands may be in their secondary traits, they are similar in essence."[50]

What then is the Gandhian technique and tradition to establish and maintain peaceful industrial relations? A study of Gandhi's scattered writings utterances and actions gives a clue to his way of thinking. Let us examine them here briefly.

Gandhi's association with labour dates back to 1906 when he took up the cause of indentured Indian labourers in South Africa. At home, it was because of his efforts that Indian Emigration Act, which had legalized the indenture system of Indian labourers, was repealed; the exploitation and misery of indigo peasants of Champaran were put to an end; and *Satyagraha* of Kheda (Gujarat) peasants and strike of Ahmedabad mill workers were led to a successful conclusion. It was he who, for the first time in India, organised a labour union at Ahmedabad on non-violent lines and gave a new impetus and direction to the labour movement of the country. It was he amongst the political leaders who was ever keen to associate himself with even the most down-trodden labourer viz., sweepers and other depressed classes and, therefore, started calling them and himself a Harijan. All this made him the uncrowned king of the Indian labourers, may they be agricultural labourers, factory workers or others. His association with the biggest industrialists of the country are also well known. He became an adviser to most of them and his advice became the last word to many of them, specially to Jamna Lal Bajaj and the Birlas. It can, therefore, be safely said that Gandhi's views on labour-capital relations are neither imaginary nor idealistic. They cannot be dismissed light heartedly as they are based on his personal intimate knoweldge of both, labour and capital, and a lot of study on the subject. It is almost certain that he was well acquainted with the western outlook, thinking and efforts.

Gandhi wanted to knock out the very basis of the labour-capital conflict by calling a halt to the mad craze for machines and automation[51] and by organizing production on non-violent lines; the bulk of which may to be carried on in private sector with the help of small scale units, some of which in trusteeship sector having those units which were misbehaving and the rest of which in the public sector, consisting of large scale enterprises of basic, key, and public utility concerns.[52] Obviously, when the size of plant is small, the power to exploit will accordingly be less and the opportunities to know each other will be greater. This decentralization of power and consequently of wealth will go a long way in restoring permanent peace and amity in industrial relations. The experiments in decentralization of Sweden, Japan and of Switzerland and the opinion of Henry Ford[53] bear testimony to the correctness of Gandhi's views and show which way the wind, even in the West, has started blowing.

Gandhi, as has been already said, was against unlimited material progress. He was of the confirmed opinion that material progress and happiness part company after a certain minimum is reached. His memorable lecture on December 22, 1916 in the Muir College still rings in the ears. He reminded his audience that material progress beyond a limit does not promote real progress but retards it. He repeated the theme a hundred times.[54]

When the emphasis from unlimited material progress and so excessive selfishness shifts to reasonable material progress and human happiness, nine-tenth of the trouble will automatically vanish. Mr. J.A. Hobson rightly felt that the evils of capitalism are, really speaking, the evils of 'impropriety'.[55] With a view to remove 'improprieties' Gandhi wanted to fix the maximum and minimum limits of income. He wanted that labourers must be assured a 'living wage'.[56] Explaining the meaning of this 'living wage', he told the All India Village Industries Association, "We should ensure all workmen with whom we deal, a wage which would give them a reasonably balanced diet. That a meal may cost an anna and half in Bihar and four annas in Gujarat and six annas in Bombay was a different question...A balanced diet must be devised."[57] Probably his method of calculating this living wage resembled the method followed by the Trade Boards and Wage Boards in United Kingdom.[58]

An interesting problem was posed to Gandhi. He was asked, 'when the labourer works in a factory should the minimum wage be a living wage for him alone or should it be a living wage for his family?' Gandhi was keen observer of human psychology. He knew that tensions of a labourer, who has a herd-instinct, can never be satisfied till he is able to feed his family members properly. Gandhi, therefore, opined that the living wage must be sufficient for the family and not for the labourer alone.[59]

It is important to note here that Gandhi did not want "anything more for workers and peasants than enough to eat and house, and clothe themselves and live in ordinary comforts as self-respecting human beings".[60] The logic is clear. Any wage beyond this living wage will not promote human happiness and will result in a never ending struggle between labour and capital because then there will be no end to demands.

When the labourers are paid only a living wage, then the mill owners cannot be allowed to live in unlimited luxury. Gandhi wrote: "Just as it is proposed to fix a decent minimum living wage, even so a limit should be fixed for the maximum income that could be allowed to any person in society. The difference between such minimum and maximum incomes should be reasonable and equitable and variable from time to time so much so that the tendency would be towards obliteration the difference."[61] To begin with, the differences can be only to a maximum of 1:20.[62] Then, as the nation progresses towards the ideal, the differences will be scaled down not by increasing the income of the labourers but by reducing the income of the better off. Is it not ideal socialism?

Gandhi was a firm believer in unity in life. Class collaboration and not class struggle was his objective. With reference to industrial relations Gandhi wrote:

> "I have always said that my ideal is that capital and labour should supplement and help each other. They should be a great family living in unity and harmony."[63]
>
> "The relation between mill agents and mill-hands ought to be one of father and children or as between blood brothers."[64]
>
> "Our socialism or communism should be based on non-violence, on harmony, on cooperation of labour and capital, landlord and tenant."[65]

Gandhi felt that conflict arises when one wants to appropriate more than one needs. The greed is at the root of it. With changed outlook and restrictions on greed, the area of conflict will automatically narrow down. Moreover, the feelings that the other is not important, and the exaggerated notion about ones own importance also breed conflict. Gandhi, therefore, wanted to make both labour and capital realise that each is ineffective without the other. To labourers he said:

> "Labour possesses the key to production but lacks talents to

> run the mills. You could not run it even if you had a million rupee."[66]

And to the employers he warned:

> "Capital would be helpless without labour. All mills would be at a standstill, if labourers were not there to work them. There is no doubt that you are helpless without labour."[67]

So he advised both to work in harmony. "My advice to the employer would be that they should willingly regard workers as the real owners of the concern which they fancy they have created."[68] Again, " in my opinion, the mill-hands are as much the proprietors of the mills as the shareholders and when the mill-owners realise that the mill-hands are as much mill-owners as they are, there will be no quarrel between them."[69] Gandhi, therefore, pleads for the participation of labour in the management. "It is vital to the well being of industry that workmen should be regarded as having every right to possess an accurate knowledge of the transactions of the mill."[70] It was with this background that Gandhi suggested the employers to offer the labourers full control of the concern in case of a strike. He felt that it will disarm opposition and win sympathy for the employer and ultimately turn out to be in his own interest. This psychological treatment will satisfy, to a very great extent, the acquisitive nature of the labourers and relieve tensions. Scanlan Plan of U.S.A. and the experiments of Yugoslavia, West Germany, France, Sweden and U.K. in the workers' participation in management have been started with this purpose in view."[71]

Gandhi was greatly influenced by Ruskin and Tolstoy. He, therefore, became a believer in the law of bread-labour. He felt that when a millionaire has to 'induce hunger by taking exercise', when one gets tired if "he rolls in his bed all day along", when "9/10 humanity lives by tilling soil", and when the negligence of this golden rule has created complexes of superiority and inferiority and "invidious distinctions of rank", it will be ideal if the remaining 1/10 starts earning its living by bodily labour.[72] Love for bread-labour will obliterate the distinctions of rank as the employer will come to know and realise the difficulties of his labourers and improve their "physical and mental health."

Whatever little scope for dispute is still left in industrial sphere, will be finished by stressing the importance of purity of means and insistence on duties rather than rights. Gandhi insisted that the means, both of labour and capital, should be pure because we reap as we sow,[73] and we have control over means and not on ends. His pure means are truth, non-violence, self-purification and *Satyagraha*. When both labour and capital are truthful, they will be prepared to hear the other's case and enter into an agreement which is just and honourable for both. There is experimental basis for the belief that industrial workers will seldom revolt against an employer whose employment policies and practices are founded upon priciples of fair play."[74] Non-violence and self-purification, i.e. self-reform[75] are great soul forces and help in conversion of heart of the exploiter and the bad. And if due to sheer ill-luck, justice is denied to a party, its non-violent non-cooperation i.e. strike will win it justice speedily, withour creating heat, ill-will and the feeling of winning or losing. The life of Gandhi, whether in the field of politics, social reforms or industry, bears testimony to it. We won our independence through non-violence and we find that our terms with Englishmen have become more cordial than what they had been before.

To Gandhi, duties were more important than rights.

> "The capitalists and the Zamindars talk of their rights, the labourer on the other hand of his, the prince of his divine right to rule, the *ryot* of his right to resist it. If all simply insist on rights, and not on duties, there will be utter confusion and chaos." Hence..."if instead of insisting on rights, every one does his duty, immediately the rule of order will be established among mankind."[76]

The duty of labour, according to Gandhi, is to work honestly and the duty of capital to treat the labour as equal partners and to act as trustees. If both insist on their respective duties, naturally the chances of a struggle, based on duties will be non-existent.

The Mahatma of India, thus tried to permanently resove the fight between labour and capital in his own way which has its roots in morality. A westerner may smile at it and call it an Utopian dream. One can only remind such a westerner of the words of Toynbee that "there is no inevitability of failure, if the challenge is properly met," and repeat the apt comment of A. Huxley, "Sooner or later it will be realised that this dreamer had his feet firmly planted on the ground, and that the idealist was the most practical of men."[77] Gandhi, who was too aware of such types of comments also said, "I am not a visionary. I claim to be a practical idealist."[78]

III
LABOUR UNIONS

The history of labour unions is not very old. It dates back to the 18th century when in England the first labour union was organised. The Industrial Revolution uprooted people from their homes and gave a permanent labour force to the country depending solely on industrial concerns. Soon it was realised that the classical concept of homogeneity of interests is no more correct and in order to protect the labour from excessive exploitation collective bargaining is a must. Thus, labour unions were formed as a measure of self-defence to protect their economic interests. The aim continues to be the same even today. There seems to be no evidence, at least on record, to show that labour unions were formed to satisfy the herd-instinct of the labourers or their pugnacity. So even today labour unions do not concentrate their activities on the mental, physical or moral upliftment of the labour and their dependents. Its main emphasis continues to be on the economic betterment to secure higher wages, more bonus and D.A., share in the profit, lesser hours of work etc. Recently, they have also started to call a halt to the schemes having potentialities of labour-saving and so furthering exploitation of labour. Their opposition to rationalization, scientific management and automation is primarily based on it.

The weapons used by the modern labour unions to protect their economic interests are collective bargaining, go slow, and strike. They have come to realize that the stake of the capitalist, when the wheels start stopping, is more and so he can be forced to come to terms. Normally, the labourers are no believers either in the purity of means or of justice. They get violent because they are fed on the ideas that might is right, conflicts are a natural phenomena of the industrial life, self is supreme, the end justifies the means, happiness is directly related with material progress etc.

The reaction to all such thinking is that the capitalists have also started organizing themselves in strong unions known as Millowners Associations. The strength is thus met with added strength. Not only this. They have started introducing more and more labour-saving devices in order to get rid, to the maximum, of labour troubles. By creating artificial gulfs between the labour ranks, mainly based on monetary standard, they are also attempting to break their unity and create in them group and sub-groups having seemingly divergent economic interests. The hatred, jealousy, ill-will, class-conflicts which were first found to be between labour and capital only are finding their way in labour ranks and files also. The technique to encourage more than one union, having different political associations and aspirations, is widening rather than bridging the gulf. The threat of lock-out is demonstrating to the labourers that the interest in keeping the wheels moving is not of the capitalists alone but also of the labour. It might be true that the loss to a capitalist for the days a factory remains closed might be greater but then his bearing capacity is also equally great. On the other hand, the labour cannot stand the strain of starvation for long. They crack and give way which proves more injurious.

Thus, a war of nerves goes on between labour and capital and the trade unions have only tried to intensify the war and slightly change the tactics of war but have not done much either to improve the lot of the labour or to bridge the gulf between labour and capital.

The Mahatma of India, because of his associations with labour and capital, first hand information of the working of the unions and mills and a deep study of the subject, soon realized that the present type of labour unions will not do. So, he launched a new experiment at Ahmedabad where he organised a labour union on a purely non-violent line having many aims, methods and philosophy. It will be worthwhile to closely examine this great experiment of Gandhi.

One of the aims of Gandhi's labour union was the economic betterment of its members. But this aim was neither permanent[79] nor of paramount importance. Gandhi believed that multiplicity of wants did not bring happiness, it rather retarded it after a minimum level had been reached.[80] So, he came forward with his theory of living wage.[81] He wanted that labourer should get only just sufficient in which he and his family members are able to satisfy the bare necessities of life.[82] In order to make labour independent of shackles of slavery, he wanted that they must pick up some subsidiary occupation which will mean better utilization of their idle time, additional income, lesser dependence on employers and satisfaction of the creative, acquisitive and curiosity instincts. His *charkha* programme is mainly based on these ideas. He, all along his life, also experimented with other cottage type industries which can be run at will with very little technical know-how and capital.[83]

The second aim, and an important one of the labour union of Gandhi's concept, was to create an atmosphere of amity and goodwill in industrial life. He wanted to replace the idea of class-conflict with homogeneity of interest. Gandhi stated a truth when he wrote:

> "The whole reason why labour so often fails is that instead of sterilizing capital, as I have suggested, labour wants to seize that capital and become capitalist itself in the worst sense of the term. And the capitalist, therefore, who is properly entrenched and organized, finding among the labourers also candidates for the same office, makes use of a portion of these to suppress labour. If we really were not under this hypnotic spell, everyone of us, men and women, would recognize this rock-bottom truth without the slightest difficulty."[84]

Gandhi, therefore, wanted labour to leave the capitalist's mentality and realize that sticking to material progress alone will not take it anywhere. He argued that life is one. There is complete unity in its different departments. So is mother nature. Gandhi said that labour without capital is useless and capital without labour is ineffective.[85] Both are like two wheels of a cart or two legs of a man. Why then should there be any scope for class conflict in the economic and more so in industrial life? The trouble arises when we want to appropriate more than our just share. Gandhi wanted labour unions to change this too much materialistic mentality of labourers. He wanted that "the relation between mill-agents and mill-hands ought to be one of father and childern or as between blood-brothers."[86] This ideal can be achieved only when one does not prize 'material progress' even at the cost of 'real progress' or one is prepared to do one's duty while claiming just rights and insists on purity of means. Gandhi was continuously repeating: "If the labour alone can understand its rights and responsibilities and confine itself to the purest means, both capital and labour must gain. But two things are essential. Both the demands and means adopted to enforce them must be just and clear."

Gandhi was wide aware of the defects and drawbacks of labour. He knew that not only economically but also physically, mentally and morally it is backward. He, therefore, thought that the primary duty of a labour union is to work for the all round development of its members. The activities of the labour union of Ahmedabad, whose leader Gandhi was, throws a flood-light on the point. Gandhi himself described the activities of the Ahmedabad labour union in these words:

> "Ahmedabad labour union is a model for all India to copy...It has its hospital, its schools for the children of the mill-hands, its classes for adults, its own priniting press and Khadi depot, and its own residential quarters. It influences the municipal policy of the city."[87]

Gandhi insisted that labour unions should "aim to raise the moral and intellectual height of labour and thus by sheer merit...make labour master of the means of production instead of being the slave that it is."[88] He felt that poverty or idleness is the mother of vices. So he wanted unions to train up workers to a supplementary occupation.[89]

Gandhi wanted labour unions to work in such a way that every member of the unions may become a dyanamic living force and the complexes within him may vanish. He must not consider himself inferior either to his co-workers or even to his employers.[90] He must consider himself to be a co-partner in the concern.[91] And this is possible only when he is well educated, physically fit, morally high and emotionally integrated. The labourers, therefore, must be made believers in truth, non-violence, simplicity, dignity of labour and self-purification. Gandhi, through his own experiences and experiments, laid down a path on which a man, willing to cultivate these virtues, can succeed in attaining the goal. Of course, one should not worry about the degree of proficiency one achieves as, for Gandhi, one step is enough. It is not important how much one gets. The important thing is that one is on the right track and has a will to keep to it. The agrument that these virtues cannot be practised on a mass scale did not appeal to him. He tried to make them instruments of mass use. To quote him, "Some friends have told me that truth and non-violence have no place in politics and wordly affairs. I do not agree. I have no use for them as a means of individual salvation. Their introduction and application in everyday life has been my experiment all along."[92] Again, "It is a profound error to suppose that whilst the law is good enough for individual it is not for masses of mankind."[93]

Gandhi, after laying down these aims and objects of an ideal trade union, also formulated certain rules of their guidance. The important topics are: One trade, one union; away from politics, on leaders, on duty, non-violent, non-cooperation, rules of strike, preparedness to negotiate even when in the thick of fight and arbitration. It will be better to briefly study them here.

Gandhi had seen the evil consequences of the mutual rivalries of labour unions. They, in order to win cheap popularity, leave their main work, which is always a difficult one, and indulge in personal bickerings, character assassination, unholy alliances and unwanted opposition. This is neither good for the workers, nor for the industry and the country. Gandhi, therefore, pleaded that there should be only one union for an industry and the membership should be obligatory.[94]

It is an unfortunate commentary on the labour unions that most of them not only in India but in foreign countries also, are politics oriented. Labour Party of U.K is a glaring example of it. Gandhi felt that the main object of a labour union is to safeguard the interest of its members and to help in their all round development. For this outside asistance[95], more so of political powers, is hardly needed. Search for such outside help brings many troubles. So he advised his labour friends, "...I am strongly against the exploitation of labour organization for political purposes." Again. "In my opinion, it will be a most serious mistake to make use of labour strikes for such a purpose. I do not deny that such strikes can serve political ends. But they do not fall within the plan for non-violent non-cooperation. It is a most dangerous thing to make political use of labour..."[96] "Strike for economic betterment should never have a political end as an ulterior motive. Such a mixture never advances the political end and generally brings trouble upon the strikers..."[97]

Since Gandhi wanted to keep labour unions away from politics and outside help, he certainly could not agree to the leadership of outsiders. The leaders must come from among the workers themselves so that they may be able to know their real difficulties according to their relative importance, their limitations and resources, their weaknesses and strong points, aspirations and desperations and may suffer and gain with them. When Gandhi was leading the Ahmedabad mill workers he realized to his agony that the striking workers had to be an outsider and so he had to undertake a fast to convince them that he was one with them.

A labour leader, according to Gandhi, must not only belong to labour ranks but also be an ideal man. He must be wedded to truth and non-violence,[98] so that he may be able to raise the moral plane of his follower; he should have unlimited capacity to suffer for the cause[99]; must have control over all senses[100] so that he may have controlled thought, action and speech; he must be selfless and devoted to the cause to the extent that he may even be prepared to oppose his followers, if he thinks that they are wrong;[101] he must not differentiate between his followers on the basis of colour, caste, creed, language, sex, etc.[102] and must not nurture ill-will against his employer.[103] Such an ideal labour-leader will be able to inspire confidence amongst his followeres and arise them to any height and secure anything for them. To comment that it is impossible to get such an ideal leader is not very proper. Such perfect leaders may not be available in the beginning, though there is no dearth of really good people in the world, but if the goal is clear and the efforts are there, then in due course of time, such leaders will be born. History bears testimony to it.

Gandhi felt that it is the duty of labour unions to see that their members discharge their duties honestly. Gandhi said,"...We should assure to the mill flawless work, careful handling of machinery and minimum waste of material and stores,"[104] becasue, like Robert Owen, he left that an increase in efficiency of the workers will surely bring greater share to them also.

Gandhi believed that in his socio-politico-economic set-up, there can hardly be any scope for differences between labour and capital as both will insist on their "just claims and no more". Since his ideal will not be achieved in a day, it is very likely that the differences between labour and capital may arise. In such a situation, labour unions should not rush to use the last weapon in the armoury of war, viz. non-violent, non-cooperation and fast. It should be used only when all other avenues such as negotiation, conciliation and arbitration have been exhausted. "Such strikes can only take place when every other legitimate means has been adopted and failed."[105] The working of Ahmedabad mill union bears testimony to it as in 32 years only one strike took place there. Gandhi was of the firm view that even during a shooting war, the doors for negotiations and arbitration should always be kept open. In his own words,

> "The *Satyagrahi* whilst he is ever ready for fight, must be equally eager for peace. He must welcome any honourable opportunity for peace."[106] "As a *Satyagrahi* I must always allow my cards to be examined and re-examined at all times and make reparations if an error is discovered."[107]

Throughout his life, Gandhi was waging a struggle for independence but was ever ready to sit round a table and discuss.

Gandhi while acceding to the right to labour unions to strike work[108] pleaded that it must be taken only when six conditions are fulfilled, viz.

1. The cause of the strike must be just.
2. There should be practical unanimity among the strikers.
3. Strikers should never depend upon public subscription or other charity.
4. A strike is no remedy when there is enough other labour to replace the strikers.
5. Strikers must fix an unalterable minimum demand and declare it before embarking upon their strike.
6. There is no room in a non-violent strike for violence in the shape of intimidation, incendiarism, etc.[109]

Gandhi felt that in certain cases the weapons of fast, which is much more powerful than strike because it reforms the other by self-starvation[110] can be used only by those who have undergone previous training.[111]

These, in brief, are the aims and objects, methods and general rules for guidance of the trade unions of Gandhian concept. The history of Ahmedabad mills unions demonstrates that such unions can exist and serve the cause of all labour, capital, industry and country better than their counterparts born and brought up in Western Ideology.

IV
LABOUR LEGISLATION

Love for large scale mechanised production has not only divided society into 'haves' and 'have-nots' and pitted them one against the other in a never ending bout, but also has forced the empire—the

State—to come to the rescue of labour which in spite of its union continues to get thrashings at the hand of capitalists. It was Robert Owen who, moved by nobler sentiments, for the first time tried to help the bleeding labour by introducing certain reforms in his factory and thus made his factory a Mecca for the visitors from all over Europe. It was the result of his experiments and continuous efforts that the first labour legislation was passed in 1819 in England. Thereafter, the State which for 200 years was a silent spectator to exploitation, suddenly woke up to its responsibilities, or to put it the other way realized that there was one more sphere to exercise its authortity. Hence, a flood of labour legislation followed, some to better the economic condition[112] and others to look after the bodily ailments.[113] It will be in the fitness of things to know Gandhi's views on such labour legislation.

A Gandhi will say that the talk of labour legislation pre-supposes certain things. It pre-supposes that production will be carried on with the help of machines and the size of the plant will be large. Obviously, in this production pattern the owners of means of production will have immense power to exploit others and in their selfishness, they will not hesitate to use this power. Thus, logically it is acceded that there will always be two classes—haves and have-nots, whose interests will be divergent, mill-owners always exploiting and mill-hands unable to defend themselves always being exploited. Thus, classes, divergence of interest and exploitation are permanent things and the State, realising this fact, only tries to reduce exploitation by means of legislation.

The philosophy of labour legislation also pre-supposes that not only are the labourers weak and unable to help themselves today but will continue to remain so far all times to come. So they will need State help permanently.

Lastly, this has also been pre-supposed that the State with all its poweres and influence will remain for ever and be always required to distribute justice. Amusingly enough, it has been presumed that in spite of the concentration of power, the State, whether democratic, commuistic, socialistic or totalitarian will remain impartial and just, always supporting the weak and downtrodden.

It is rather surprising the Gandhi, who has written on almost everything under the Sun, has hardly written or said anything on this topic. It cannot be assumed that he was ignorant of this development. His silence, therefore, can be interpreted to mean that he did not deem it necessary to express his views on this topic, which probably he considered useless. However, in spite of his silence, some idea of his reactions can be had from his views on the State and its functions, production pattern, place of machines and large scale enterprises, his classless society and a new man and material progress or real progress etc.

Gandhi was not in favour of centralisation of either power or wealth. He, therefore, came out with his theory of decentralisation. He, like, an anarchist, believed in Statelessness. He wanted to build *Ram Rajya* i.e., an ideal State by federating independent village republics, known in India as *Panchayats*. In Gandhi's own words: "...Every village will be a republic or *Panchayats* having full powers. This does not exclude dependence on and willing help from neighbours or from the world..."[114] *Ram Rajya* will be a federation of small village republics because "the State represents violence in a concentrated and organized form. The individual has a soul, but as the State is a soulless machine, it can never be weaned from violence to which it owes its very existence."[115] Gandhi, therefore, was in favour of decentralization of power and was keen to build a State based on non-violence and truth. To quote him, "By political independence I do not mean an imitation of the British House of Commons, or the Soviet rule of Russia, or... We must have our suited to ours... I have described it as *Ram Raj*, i.e. sovereignty of the people based on pure moral authority."[116] Again, "*Swaraj* is synonymous with *Ram Raj*—the establishment of Kingdom of Righteousness on earth."[117] This cannot be established till every individual has not self-control. "And without rule over self there can be no *Swaraj* or *Ram Raj*. Rule of all without rule of one-self would prove to be as deceptive and disappointing as a painted toy-mango, charming to look at outwardly but hollow and empty within.[118] Consequently "in the ideal State, therefore, there is no political power because there is no State,"[119] and class war will be foreign.[120] Government will not interfere, or interfere only when it is imperative.

Just as Gandhi wanted to decentralise political power so he wanted to decentralize economic power and wealth. He, therefore, contemplated a production pattern in which three sectors will function side by side. Bulk of the production shall be carried on under private sector with the help of small units using only those machines which are "useful servants". Trusteeship sector will have those concerns of private sector which have failed to behave properly and which have been given an opportunity to correct themselves before administering the bitter pill of nationalization. The third will be public sector having large scale enterprises of public utility, key and basic industries. Obviously, in this production pattern the power to exploit others will be the minimum.[121]

As has been discussed earlier, in such a production pattern, not only will the power to exploit the 'have-nots' be the minimum but also the 'have-nots' will organize themselves in strong labour unions, will be satisfied with a living wage and will insist on pure means, – truth, non-violence, bread-labour and self-purification.[122] Such a labour force will become, in due course, a powerful force whom it will be impossible to exploit.

Gandhi wanted to create a new man. This new man will not aspire for 'material progress' but will search for 'real progress'. He will be truthful, non-violent and a believer in simplicity and bread-labour. This new man will be created with the help of a new type of education and a new socio-politico-economic set-up. The science of Etiology tells us that such a man can be created. This man will not be a believer in exploitation because he will not be governed by excessive selfishness.[123] Thus, neither capital nor labour will like to exploit each other.

In the light of the above well known ideas of Gandhi, on socio-politico-economic problems, it is quite logical to conclude that Gandhi was not in favour of any labour legislation for the industries in private sector. Here the power and desire to exploit others will be minimum and the so-called weak party will not be so weak as to allow its exploitation. The same can be said about the industries under public sector where the State itself will be the owner and manager and will be governed not by profit motive but, as Gandhi called it, "Love Motive'. These industries will be managed by the representatives of labour, consumers and the State. With the labour participation in management as equal partners, and the absence of any will to exploit them, the need for any labour legislation shall be hardly felt. However, it may be conceivable that the Government may be required, because of legal requirements, to enact such legislation as may enable it to force the decisions of the Managing Boards. Trusteeship sector is a sector which is not permanent by its very nature. Some of the firms, which persist in misbehaving, shall be nationalised and others, which improve, will revert back to the private sector. Thus, labour legislation of a permanent nature will not be required for the firms of this sector also.

REFERENCES

1. By 'evils' or 'vices' Malthus meant the use of contraceptives, resort to abortion, etc. There is a controversy going on. Gide and Rist believe that 'there is no reason to believe, however, that, were Malthus now alive, he would not be a Neo-Malthusian.' On the other hand, quite a few economists believe that seeing the changing world, growing poverty which is source of all evils, consent of Catholic Church to Dr. Stope's Rhythmic method and the milder tone of the edition of 'Essays' it can be imagined that Malthus would have changed.
2. Francis Place (Principles of Population) agreed with Malthus while Godwin (Essays) refused to accept the behaviour of population as put forward by Malthus. Bestiat in France and Carey in U.S.A. challenged the principle of diminishing returns in land and gave an optimistic tinge to the population theory. Sir Edward Wet (Essays) held that as population grew, labour became more productive due to specialization. Sidgewick (Principles) laid the foundation of Optimum theory which was later systematized by Cannon and popularised by Carr Saunders. Thomas Doubledy (The True Law of Population) made an assault on classicalists by bringing in the idea of standard of living and reached the conclusion that among the rich, population decreases while amongst the poor it increases. Sir Archibald Alison developed the point further. Senior, thinking on the same lines, looked upon the future of population with less concern than that was shown by Malthus. Raymond Pearl (The Biology of Population) argued that the population growth typically takes the form of a flattened sloping 'S' shape curve. The western sociologists are worrying about eugenic aspect of population. They argue that in better placed persons, the rate of reproduction is less than unity while among the poors it is more than one. The overall effect of it is that the quality of population is steadily going down.
3. Population Planning normally means the control on the growth of population. However, in some cases it also means the reverse. Hilter's Germany and Mussolini's Italy are examples.
4. *Young India*, April 29, 1926.
5. *Amrita Bazar Patrika*, January 12, 1935.
6. *Young India*, September 27, 1928.
7. *Young India*, March 12, 1925.
8. *Harijan*, November 12, 1936.
9. *Young India*, April 2, 1925.
10. *Harijan*, September 14, 1935.
11. M.K. Gandhi, *Autobiography*, p. 6.
12. "It is my painful duty to have to record here my marriage at the age of thirteen. As I see the youngsters of the same age about me who are under my care, and think of my own marriage, I am inclined to pity myself and to congratulate them on having escaped my lot. I can see no moral argument in support of such a preposterously early marriage." Again, "Little did I dream then that one day I shall severely criticise my father for having married me as a

child." (*Autobiography*, p. 8).

13. "I have already referred to Dr. Allinson's birth control propaganda. If it had some temporary effect on me, Mr. Hill's opposition to those methods and his advocacy of internal efforts as opposed to outward means, in a word, of self-control had a far greater effect, which in due time came to be abiding. Seeing, therefore, that I did not desire more children I began to strive after self-control. There was endless difficulty in the task. We began to sleep in separate beds. I decided to retire to bed only after the day's work had left me completely exhausted." (*Autobiography*, p. 150).
14. "Marriage is natural thing in life, and to consider it derogatory in any sense is wholly wrong. The idea is to look upon marriage as a sacrament and, therefore, to lead a life of self-restraint in the married state." (*Harijan*, March 22, 1942.

    "Marriage, for the satisfaction of sexual appetite is no marriage. It is VYABHICHARA—concupiscence, (Todays) ceremony, therefore, means that the sexual act is permitted only when there is a clear desire by both for a child. The whole conception is sacred. The act has, therefore, to be performed prayerfulty...Such union may only be once in life-time, if no other child is desired. Those who are not normally and physically healthy have no business to unite, and if they do, it is VYABHICHARA—concupiscence. You must unlearn the lesson, if you have learnt it before, that marriage is for the satisfaction of animal appetite." (*Young India*, April 24, 1927).

    "Those who want to perform national service, or those who want to have a glimpse of the real religious life, must lead a celebate life, no matter if married or unmarried. Marriage but brings a woman close together with a man, and they become friends in a special sense, never to be parted either in this life...I do not think that, in our conception of marriage, our lusts should necessarily enter." (*Young India*, December 2, 1921).
15. *Young India*, September 3, 1931.
16. *Young India*, April 29, 1926.
17. M.K. Gandhi, *Autobiography*, p. 152.
18. *Young India*, April 29. 1926.
19. "I venture to claim that by judicious treatment it is possible to observe self-control without much difficulty. Indeed it is a claim put forth not merely by me but German and other nature cure practitioners. The latter teach that water treatment or earth compresses and a non-heating and chiefly fruitarian diet soothe the nervous system and bring animal passions under easy subjection, whilst they, at the same time, invigorate the system. The same result is claimed by *Raja-Yogis* for scientifically regulated *pranayama*, without reference to the higher practices. Neither the western nor the ancient Indian treatment is intended for *sanyasin* but essential for the house holder." (*Young India*, April 2, 1925).
20. M.K. Gandhi, *Self-Restraint vs Self-Indulgence*, p. 51-53, 1958.
21. Ibid.
22. *Harijan*, July 23, 1938.
23. *Self-Restraint vs Self-Indulgence*, p. 37-40, 1958.
24. Ibid.
25. Ibid.
26. *Harijan*, January 2, 1957, p. 374.
27. D.G. Tendulkar, *Mahatma*, Vol. I, p. 237.

28. Ibid, p. 240.
29. For example, the League of Nations was founded to settle the disputes of nations through an international agency. United Nations Organization with its all organs (IMF, World Bank, UNESCO, etc.) is also devoted to solve individual and international problems through the forum of family of nations. Happenings on Kashmir, Korea, Egypt, Hungary, U2 flights over Russia and Congo, etc., and their quick reaction all over the world bear testimony to it.
30. The theories of self-preservation, balance of power, tussels between India and Pakistan, U.S.A. and Cuba, China and India, and China and U.S.A., and rules of Exports-Imports, Passports and Visa, etc., are only a few examples of the growing nationalism.
31. For example, capital is freely flowing in India from a number of friendly countries like U.S.A., Canada, England, West Germany, Japan and U.S.S.R. and India is not the only country which is receiving these foreign aids and loans. Moreover, several industries are being established in India, as in other countries also, by the foreign capitalists. And now huge amounts are also being lent out by the World Bank.
32. For example, to great resentment of Japan, U.S.A. made the Immigration Law in 1924. The apartheid of South Africa and immigration rules of every country should be eye openers. It is most surprising to note that countries like U.S.A., Canada and Australia, whose present stage of progress is due to the immigrants, turned nationalists, should now shut their doors to outsiders.
33. W.S. Waytinoky in his book, *World Population and Production*, p. 48-49 has given the following data:

Country	Population in Millions	Area (in 000 Miles)
China	463.5	3773
U.S.A.	151.7	3034
Canada & New Found Land	13.8	3858
U.S.S.R.	193.0	8632
New Guinea	1.1	93
United Kingdom	50.6	95

G.H.T. Kimble, in his book *World's Open Spaces* has calculated the immigration potential of different countries. On the basis of these calculations, the following Chart has been prepared which will show that Gandhi was right when he preached *international migration of population:*

	Region	Population (In Mill.)	Land Area 000 Sq. Mils.	Density	Population Capacity in Millions	% Cultivated Area to Total Area	Immigration Capacity in Millions
1.	Siberia	14.3	4352	5	75	3	60.7
2.	Manchuria .	43.0	462	93	75	15.1	32.0

3.	Indonesia	30.0	683	43	150	N.A.	120.0
4.	Philippines	20.2	114	17.7	100	12.5	79.8
5.	Australia	8.4	2975	2.8	20-60	1.32	11.6-51.6
6.	New Zealand	1.9	103	17.6	20	2.9	18.1
7.	Africa	200.0	10384	19.0	1650-2300	N.A.	1450-2100
8.	U.S.A.	154.0	2974	51.5	300-500	18.57	146-346
9.	Canada	14.0	3457	4	100-250	2.7	80-236
10.	Argentina	17.6	1079	16	150	10.75	132.4
11.	Brazil	53.3	3291	16.5	430-1200	8	376.7-1146.7

34. When an over-populated country is unable to export its surplus population to other countries its people remain poor and the efforts to improve the condition result either in revolution at home or aggression abroad. China is a living example of it. When industrially advanced countries are unable to dispose of their entire produce at home, they try to establish trade relations with backward countries and ultimately colonise them. This leads to misery, world wars, complexes.
35. Prof. Y. Tusrumi, participating in the UNESCO. Seminar on 'Gandhian Outlook and Techniques' on January 16, 1953 aptly commented:
"It is the proportion of the population of the world to the area which they inhabit, and the lack of free movement which create difficult tensions. Take for instance, the case of Japan at the moment. In 1924 we had a very deplorable experience when the American Government passed the Anti-Asiatic Immigration Law. For seventeen long years, we had the so called "Gentlemen's Agreement" between America and Japan by which Japan promised to restrict the entry of Japanese labour into America. Later when the Anti-Asiatic Immigration Law was being passed, Japan almost implored the American Government not to pass the Bill and leave the matter in the hands of Japanese Government. We promised that if this were done, we would see that not one emigrant goes to America...
"It was not a matter of Economics or Law, but just a matter of Psychology. Japan, since 1868, had one ambition—to be equal with the nations of the West...The internal change was the result of the shock of our self-respect given by this American Law—I had then already predicted and, unfortunately it came true ten years later, that Japan may become militaristic."
36. Several incidents can be cited in support of these conclusions. Gandhi in South Africa; tried hard to get equal rights for Indian labourers—right to vote, right to live wherever they wanted, right to do whatever they liked. The series of *Satyagraha* movements organised by him and the petitions submitted to the Government of Africa, African Legislature and the Government of England are few of the efforts in the direction. When Gandhi was fighting for the equal rights for Indians, he was also preaching them to be loyal to the country of adoption. His first speech in Pretoria asking his audience to be truthful in business, to forget distinctions, to learn English and to be hygienic in habits';

as also his loyalty to the country, his participation first in Boer War of 1899 and then in Zulu Rebellion of 1906, his withdrawal of *Satyagraha* when the country was threatened with a general Railway strike are a few examples, out of many, to corroborate the point.

37. R.H. Towney, *Equality*, p. 233 vide R.H. Soman, *Peaceful Industrial Relations*, p. 101.
38. H.S. Kirkaldy, *The Spirit of Industrial Relations*, p. 5 vide Soman, Peaceful Industrial Relations, p. 5.
39. Physical labour is looked down upon and the rich avoid it. Gandhi said "There is a world-wide conflict between capital and labour and the poor envy the rich. If all work for their bread, distinction of rank would be obliterated." vide R.N. Bose, *Studies in Gandhism*, p. 1.
40. Watkins and Dodd, *The Management of Labour Relations*, p. 6.
41. R.J. Soman. *Peaceful Industrial Relations*, p. 151-173 has made a very able summary of this psychological aspect.
42. Watkins and Dodd, *The Management of Labour Relations*, p. 90.
43. R.J. Soman, *Peaceful Industrial Relations*, p. 162.
44. Keyserling, G.H. vide *Mahatma Gandhi*, edited by Dr. S. Radhakrishnan, p. 184-85.
45. A. Huxley, *Ends and Means*, p. 52.
46. G.D.H. Cole and Margaret, *A Guide to Modern Politics*, p. 348-49.
47. A. Huxley, *Ends and Means*, p. 50 and A. Gide's aritcle on *God that Failed*.
48. Gregg, R.B., *Which Way Lies Hope*, p. 39 and James Burnhan in *The Managerial Revolution*, p. 102; R.J. Soman, *Peaceful Industrial Relations*, p. 114-15 has given charts to show the disparities in incomes.
49. Quoted in *The Strategy and Tactics of World Communism*, by Committee of Foreign Affairs, p. 12.
50. P.A. Sorokin, *The Reconstruction of Humanity*, p. 31.
51. See Chap. II.
52. See Chap. V.
53. M.R. Masani, *Cooperative in a Planned Economy*, p. 11, has quoted it at length.
54. D.G. Tendulkar, *Mahatma*, Vol. IV; *Yervada Mandir*, p. 34; *Hind Swaraj*; *Harijan*, August 29, 1936.
55. R.J. Soman, *Peaceful Industrial Relations*, p. 132.
56. "I am not concerned with the name. Call it the minimum wage, if that expression sounds sweeter. Living wage to my mind is the most accurate description for irreducible wage." (*Harijan*, February 13, 1937)
57. *Harijan*, August 31, 1935.
58. Sir Hector Hethington has described it giving two tests, viz., "a wage which avoids the reproach of 'sweating', in other words a wage on which at least maintenance is possible and rates offered to workers in comparable occupations are equivalent."
59. Bose, R.N., *Gandhian Technique and Tradition*, p. 48.
60 *Young India*, April 2, 1931.
61. Quoted in Pyare Lal, *Gandhian Technique in the Modern World*, p. 31.
62. All India Congress Committee, *Report of the Economic Programme Committee*, 1918, p. 43; R.N. Bose, *Gandhian Technique and Traditions*, p. 51, however, places the maximum disparity to 1 : 12. Also see the Bonus Agreement between Ahmedabad Textile Labour Association and Mill

Owner's Association of June 27, 1955 which lays down certain important principles on the point.

63. *Young India*, August 20, 1925.
64. *Young India*, May 10, 1928.
65. *Amrit Bazar Patrika*, August 2, 1934 vide N.K. Bose, p. 90.
66. *Harijan*, November 7, 1936.
67. Ibid.
68. *Harijan*, March 31, 1946.
69. *Young India*, August, 1927.
70. *Harijan*, February 13, 1937.
71. Bose, R.N., *Gandhian Technique and Tradition*, Appendix V, p. 204-17.
72. *Yervada Mandir*, p. 50.
73. *Young India*, December, 26. 1924.
74. Watkins and Dodd, *The Management of Labour Relations*, p. 108.
75. Anger and fear are two emotions which stimulate pugnacity. The strikes and lock-out are the media of expression for this impulse. In industry pugnacity can be neutralised if this instinct is made to fight social evils like gambling, insanitation, illiteracy, drinking, etc. Gandhi, therefore, was attacking the problem psychologically when he was pleading for self-purification." Soman, *Peaceful Industrial Relations*, p. 171-72.
76. Bose, R.N. *Gandhian Technique and Tradition*, p. 58.
77. vide *Vishwa Bharti*, Gandhi Memorial Peace Number.
78. *Young India*, August 11, 1920.
79. Gandhi, through his socio-politico-economic set-up, wanted to make a new man who will refuse to exploit others and be exploited by others. Moreover, in his production-pattern, the scope of exploitation will be minimum. So, labour unions, to protect economic interests will be required only for the duration of transitory period which will depend on the ability of the advocates of the Gandhian order and strong headedness of those who are to be persuaded.
80. See earlier Chap.
81. See earlier Section.
82. Ibid.
83. All India Village Industries Association, etc., have done useful work in this direction.
84. *Young India*, January 14, 1932.
85. See earlier Section
86. *Young India*, May 10, 1928.
87. R.N. Bose, *Gandhian Technique and Tradition*, p. 15, Also see the *Chart of Activities of Ahmedabad Textile Labour Union*, given in Appendix II.
88. *Hindustan Standard*, October 28, 1944.
89. M.K. Gandhi, *Constructive Programme*, p. 2, 28.
90. *Yervada Mandir*, p. 50; see previous Section.
91. *Harijan*, November 7, 1936, *Young India*, May 10, 1923, and see Section II, Chap. VI.
92. *Amrit Bazar Patrika*, June 30, 1944.
93. *Harijan*, September 5, 1936.
94. R.N. Bose, *Gandhian Technique and Tradition*, p. 24.
95. "I have been a labourer like you ever since I entered public life...I have also come to the conclusion that you have to help yourselves, no one from outside can help you."

96. *Young India*, February 16, 1921.
97. *Harijan*, August 11, 1948; also see *Is India Different*, p. 25
98. Gopi Nath Dhawan, *The Political Philosophy of Mahatma Gandhi*, p. 187.
99. Mahadev Desai, *A Righteous Struggle*, p. 27.
100. *Harijan*, July 23, 1938.
101. Mahadev Desai, *A Righteous Struggle*, p. 13, 15; *Young India*, March 26, 1931.
102. Ibid., p. 13, 58.
103. Ibid.
104. vide R.N. Bose, *Gandhian Technique and Tradition*, p. 90; *Speeches and Writings of Mahatma Gandhi*, 4th Edition, G.A. Natesan & Co., p. 104-05
105. *Young India*, March 19, 1931; Soman, *Peaceful Industrial Relations*, p. 181.
106. Ibid.
107. *Harijan*, March 11, 1939.
108. *Young India*, April 24, 1920.
109. *Young India*, February 16, September 22, 1921.
110 *Gandhiji's Political Method* In *Mahatma Gandhi*, edited by S. Radhakrishnan, p. 298-99.
111. *Harijan*, March 18, 1939.
112. Such as Minimum Wages Act, Bonus Act, Profit Sharing Act, Dearness Allowance Act, Old Age Pension Act, Unemployment Benefit Act.
113. Employees State Insurance Act giving the benefit of accident, medical aid, maternity aid; provisions of the Factory Act forcing the employees to have safety devices, fixing the hours of work, minimum age, canteen, etc.
114. *Harijan*, Jule 28, 1946, p. 236.
115. N.K. Bose, *Studies in Gandhism*, p. 202-04.
116. *Harijan*, January 2, p. 374.
117. *Young India*, May 4, 1921.
118. *Harijan*, November 21, 1936.
119. *Young India*, July 2, 1931.
120. *Amrit Bazar Patrika*, August 2, 1934.
121. For details, see previous Chap
122. See for details previous Chap., Section III.
123. See previous Chap.

7

Money, Markets and Trade

The invention of Money is considered as a fundamental one around which economic science clusters. We are told, "Money is a symbol or token of credit, that is to say, of human trust in relation to human needs and desires... As a symbol, money is exceedingly useful and powerful in human affairs. All symbols are psychologically carriers of energy.[1] Credit or expectancy is itself a most potent energizer.[2] The subtle power of money credit has been one of the major causes and agencies for the immense development of the past five hundred years in science, machinery, industry, transportation and commerce."[3] Thus, money removed the difficulties of barter system and made exchange easier and thereby widened the demand for goods. By acting as a store of value it helped in accumulation and mobility of capital and by making it possible to make advance payments and by solving the problem of distribution, it encouraged large scale production and division of labour and thereby made it possible to increase the supply of goods. Consequently, the size of markets changed from local to international. For sometime, it was felt that there was nothing which money could not do. It is a passport to heaven. It is because of money that man is able to distribute his income on different goods and services in the way he likes and thus maximise his gains. Again, it is money which has brought to the door of man a large number of goods and services and has given him additional power to purchase them and thereby raise his standard of living, i.e., happiness.

However, it is also realized that if money has given so many advantages, it has not failed to create problems as well. "Although money is a symbol of trust, it is capable of expressing only a small part of either the quality or extent of human trust... the money acts mechanically like an axe to trim off and cripple the trust, and like a sieve to strain away the finer feelings associated with trust which give it quality and help sustain its existence."[4] It brought in its trail many vices. It has been called upon to fulfil many functions some of which "deal with simple concrete things and other with intangible and very complex ideas and judgments. This ambiguity of functions, and, therefore, of meaning, confuses people's minds, and, therefore, helps to make the money system easy to abuse and difficult to control."[5] Capitalism, division of society, class-conflict, international trade, imperialism and world wars are the inevitable results of the invention of money. It is because of money, which gave profit motive, that production of luxury articles is carried on where due to the scarcity of bare necessities of life, millions are called upon to starve. Booms and Slumps, with all their evil consequences, are the creation of money which has disturbed the natural and simple equilibrium of demand and supply by giving birth to round about production, middleman, cut-throat competition, monopolies, combinations, trusts, artificial hoarding, artificial demand, over production, under-production etc. Unemployment and the miseries attached with it are also a gift of money. Money, in short, has badly betrayed the trust.

If these, in nutshell, are the views on money and markets of even western economists who equate material progress with happiness, it certainly is worthwhile to know how they tried to remedy the evil and how Gandhi wanted to tackle the problem.

Western philosophers are of the opinion that evils of money and markets can be well controlled by imposing more and more restrictions on both. The State was, therefore, given power to control the quantity of currency and credit. But the goal before a Monetary Authority remained undecided. Some want it to be price stability, some argue in favour of exchange stability, some insist on full employment, and a new school wants neutral money. Not only the goal is uncertain but also the effectiveness of means is debatable. The result is that the power of State is increasing day by day, but the goal of peace, prosperity, happiness and equality still continues to evade man.

The history bears out that the state betrayed the trust in one more way. It misused its power to print notes and create money. Keyness, to fight unemployment and depression came out with the technique of deficit financing. The states now use these tool to fight wars, to plan economic development and to meet their ever increasing expenses. This normally leads the country into the trap of inflation and debt. The solution has proved equally bad.

Government were also empowered to control markets. International Trade ceased to remain a free trade. Old Mercantilism appeared in a new garb and a war of restrictions is going on in spite of the U.N.O., International Monetary Fur.·l. World Bank and International Agreements. The story of interna' trade is not much different. Artificial barriers on the movement ›f goods within a country are also raised under pretext of zonal sys ·m, rationing and price control, rationalization and scientific management, licensing system, planning etc. The troubled man, who willy-nilly surrendered his rights to the State under the able guidance of the all knowing economist is amazed, alarmed and much more unhappy than what he used to be. The remedy has been worse than the disease itself. The poor man has also surrendered his liberty to the State who now refuses to return it back.

Recently, more so after the debacle of mighty U.S.S.R., the sole super power U.S.A, with the help of GATT, U.N.O and its allied agencies is trying to dominate the economies of other countries. This love for money may now lead to economic imperialism.

Let us now turn to the Eastern prescription which Gandhi wanted to administer.

Gandhi wanted to reduce the size of markets of essential consumption goods by decreasing their supply and demand. He, therefore, pleaded that the size of plants should be small,[6] and only those machines should be used which will serve as a servant.[7] His production pattern and insistence on decentralization very clearly give this idea.[8] In such a set-up, the scope for mass production is mainly through masses,[9] and not machines. Gandhi also held that multiplicity of wants beyond a minimum limit would not promote happiness.[10] He, therefore, preached the law of simplicity.[11] The outcome of small production units and minimum wants will give regional self-sufficiency though not individual self-sufficiency. To quote Gandhi:

> "...We have to concentrate on the villages being self-contained, manufacturing mainly for use..."[12]
>
> "...My idea of village *Swaraj* is that it is a complete republic, independent of its neighbours for its vital wants, and yet

interdependent for many others in which dependence is necessary."[13]

"...What is necessary is to make the village self-sufficient and self-reliant. But mind you, my idea of self-sufficiency is not a narrow one, there is no scope for selfishness and arrogance in my self-sufficiency."[14]

"...Villages collectively, not the villager individually, will become self-contained so far as their clothing requirements are concerned..."[15]

And according to Shri S.N. Agarwal, "the regional unit of economic self-sufficiency will differ with different commodities."[16] But Gandhi's idea of self-sufficiency in basic requirements does not mean isolation.

"...I am not preaching isolation, we have (to) be humble as the dust for the fulfilment of our cause. We have to mix with people even as sugar mixes itself with milk."[17]

"That a man ought to be able to satisfy most of his essential needs himself is obvious, but it is no less obvious to me that when self-sufficiency is carried to the length of isolating oneself from society it almost amounts to sin."[18]

But where does 'self-dependence' end and 'inter-dependence' start? Gandhi wanted to apply the criterion of self-respect to determine their respective spheres. "Self-dependence is a necessary ideal so long as and to the extent that it is an aid to one's self-respect and spiritual discipline. It becomes an obsession and a hindrance when it is pushed beyond that limit. On the other hand inter-dependence when it is not inconsistent with one's self-respect is necessary."[19]

Thus, in Gandhian set-up the size of a market of essential consumption goods will be very small, generally coinciding with a village or a group of villages within a short radius. However, the markets for other commodities might be of a bigger size, they may be even international. To quote Gandhi: "Then every village of India will almost be a self-supporting and self-contained unit exchanging only such necessary commodities with other villages where they are not locally producible."[20] In Gandhian life, the preference to purchase or sell things will be strictly on a priority basis. Immediate neighbours will get priority over the distant ones. Defining *Swadeshi*, Gandhi wrote: "It follows that *Swadeshi* was that spirit which dictated man to serve his next door neighbour to the exclusion of any other. The condition... was that the neighbour thus served had in his turn to serve his own neighbour..."[21] Again, "In that of economics I should use only things that are produced by my immediate neighbours..."[22] And if things are not available within the country, Gandhi will not hesitate to purchase them from abroad. "I buy from every part of the world what is needed for my growth."[23] "To reject foreign manufactures mainly because they are foreign and to go on wasting national time and money to provide manufacturers in one's country for which it is not suited would be criminal folly and a negation of *Swadeshi* spirit."[24]

Similarly, he will allow the disposal of the country's surplus goods in foreign countries.

Gandhi was not a follower of Adam Smith in international trade. He was a believer of protective trade. "Free trade may be good for England which dumps down her manufactures among helpless people and wishes her wants to be supplied from outside at the cheapest rate. But free trade has ruined India's peasantry... Moreover, no new trade can compete with foreign trade without protection."[25]

Gandhi wanted protective trade not out of ill-will or hatred: "I would not countenance the boycott of a single foreign article out of ill-will or a feeling of hatred."[26] It was because of the well known infant industry argument that he wanted protective trade. "To talk of no discrimination between Indian interest and English or European is to perpetuate Indian heritage. What is equality of rights between a giant and a dwarf? Before one can think of equality between unequals, the dwarf must be raised to the height of the giant."[27] Thus protective trade is not a permanent policy with Gandhi.

Gandhi did not try to give 'an exhaustive catalogue' of articles which can be imported in his scheme of things.[28] He only laid down a general principle, "I buy from every part of the world that is needed for my growth. I refuse to buy from any body anything however nice or beautiful, if it interferes with my growth or injures those whom Nature has made my first care."[29] Again, "My economic creed is a complete taboo in respect of all foreign commodities whose importation is likely to prove harmful to our indigenous interests."[30]

Thus, Gandhi will not import or purchase a thing from his neighbour, whether of his own country or of outside, simply because the product is cheap or best. "The rule of the best and the cheapest is not always true. Just as we do not give up our country for one with a better climate but endeavour to improve our own, so also may we not discard *Swadeshi* for better or cheaper things"[31]

Obviously, these ideas of Gandhi on international trade are more dynamic than those of either Adam Smith or Fedric List or Mercantilists or Neo-Mercantilists, because Gandhi wanted protective trade only so long as the country was not able to stand the vice of dumping.[32] He did neither want exchange control. He wanted the international trade to be simple, limited and for mutual gain. However, this trade will not be left to the sole discretion of individuals. According to the known Gandhian Economist, S.N. Agarwal, "Just as individual or a village community should be the agent for internal trade so a nation should be the agent for international trade."[33]

This should not give the idea that Gandhi was against middlemen and wanted to liquidate them. Replying to Shri Jetha Lal Govind, Gandhi wrote,"...He has set before him an ambitious ideal that did not obtain in our country probably at any time even in the past. The cultivator had always to depend for certain necessaries of life on the middleman and it seems to me that this is just as it should be."[34] Gandhi did "not want to take away from the middleman his occupation, but only to give a new orientation to it and to change his mental outlook."[35] Gandhi hoped to do it with his new socio-politico-economic set-up.

When the size of markets for the necessary consumption goods will be small, when different regions of the country will mainly be confined to luxury or comfort articles or the capital goods produced by the State for the welfare of the people, when international trade will not be based on "cheapness" but on "growth" principles, when the mass production will be through masses and not labour-saving devices and large size plants, when wants will be minimum and the goal will be 'to live and let others live happily', then the importance of money will automatically go down. It will cease to be the master, the controller of the destinies of the millions. It will not be the sole measurement of value. "Money has its use as much as labour. After all money is a token of exchange...The moment labour recognizes its own dignity, money will find its rightful place, i.e. it will be held in trust for labour. For labour is more than money."[36] Even taxes will not be necessarily paid in cash. "I have always held that whatever may be said in favour of cash payment of taxes, its introduction injured the nation to the extent that the system of stocking grain in the village was disturbed."[37] Wages will also be paid partly in cash and partly in kind.[38] The importance of capital will be negligible as very little capital will be required and it will be realized that labour is capital and there is no conflict between the two.[39]

With the changed importance of money and the limitation of the size of markets in the way that production and consumption are carried out in the same area, price fluctuations will no longer remain a problem. "There is no question of high or low prices when a nations's economies are put on a sound basis..."[40] This is because the law of supply and demand is replaced with the law by manufacturing enough for the supply.[41]

These ideas on money, size of markets, role of international trade and *Swadeshi* by the Father of the Nation should force our leaders and Government to pause and think again on permitting multi-national companies to invade India, to sign G.A.T.T. and other trade agreements, to go on, like a mad man, after hi-technology and latest giant machines. Will, all this, be in the interest of Indian masses? Will it help in promoting regional self-safficiency? Will it remove or even reduce unemployment? Will it help in our growth? Will it promote our national pride? Will it be patriotism?

REFERENCES

1. W.A. White, *Mechanism of Character Formation*, p. 113. 114, 333.
2. S.A. Reeve, *Modern Economic Tendencies*, Chap. V.
3. H.D. Macleod, *Theory of Credit*, Vol. I, p. 75. 88, 90; quoted by Richard B. Gregg, *A Philosophy of Indian Economic Development*, p. 57.
4. Richard B. Gregg, *A Philosophy of Indian Economic Development*, p. 57.
5. Ibid, p. 58.
6. See Chap. V.
7. Ibid.
8. Ibid.
9. *Harijan*, November 2, 1934, "It is mass production, but mass production in people's own homes. If you multiply individual production to millions of times, would it not give you mass production on a tremendous scale."
10. See Chap II.
11. See Chap. IV.

12. *Harijan*, August 29, 1936.
13. *Harijan*, July 26, 1942.
14. *Hind Swaraj*, December 6, 1944.
15. *Young India*, April 25, 1925.
16. S.N. Agarwal, *A Gandhian Plan*, p. 93.
17. *Young India*, April 25, 1925.
18. *Young India*, March 21, 1929.
19. Ibid.
20. M.K. Gandhi, *Economic and Industrial Life and Relations*, Vol. II, p. 69.
21. Ibid., p. 57.
22. Ibid., p. 64.
23. Ibid. p. 78.
24. *Young India*, June 18, 1931, vide, S.N. Agarwal, *The Gandhian Plan*, p. 97.
25. *Young India*, May 15, 1924.
26. *Young India*, November 15, 1928.
27. *Young India*, March 26, 1931.
28. M.K. Gandhi. *Economic and Industrial Life and Relations*, Vol. II, p. 70.
29. Ibid., p. 78.
30. Ibid., p. 84; also *Young India*, March 23, 1929.
31. Ibid., p. 84.
32. Gandhi advised his American friends not to resort to dumping because it is neither in their own interest nor of others. If they are able to produce surplus, they should gift if out to the needy ones. vide Tendulkar, *Mahatma*, Vol. III, pp. 168-69.
33. S.N. Agarwal, *The Gandhian Plan*, p. 97.
34. *Young India*, March 21, 1929.
35. Ibid.
36. *Harijan*, October 16, 1945, Gandhi was impressed by the scheme of Yarn currency tried at Gopuri (Wardha). *Harijan*, March 23, 1942, vide S.N. Agarwal, *A Gandhian Plan*, p. 102.
37. *Harijan*, December 28, 1947.
38. Vide S.N. Jha, *Gandhian Economic Thought*, p. 216.
39. M.K. Gandhi, *Economic and Industrial Life and Relations*, Vol. II, p. 140; also see N.K. Bose, *Selections from Gandhi*, Sec 259.
40. *Harijan*, December 28, 1947.
41. M.K. Gandhi, *Economic and Industrial Life and Relations*, Vol. II. p. 99.

8

On Distribution

With the advent of Industrial Revolution, the problems connected with distribution started assuming an ever-increasing importance. In the academic world not only new theories of the method of determining the share of different factors of production were invented and debated but also the problems connected with unequal distribution of wealth and its consequences started receiving attention. Mahatma Gandhi was not concerned with the first aspect of the problem which probably was too academic and uninteresting for him but he was certainly interested in the second problem. He felt that one of the important causes of the present day unrest and unhappiness can be traced in the faulty method of distribution of wealth. Today the distribution of wealth among the various factors of production takes place in such a way that a few get the major share of the produce and thus live in luxury, while the majority gets so little that it is never able to satisfy even its minimum requirement of life. Hence, Gandhi wanted to change the method of distribution.

Marxist and fellow travellers were, like Gandhi, not satisfied with the capitalistic method of distribution and so they suggested that State must become supreme in matters of distribution also. The State should decide what commodities and in what quantity must individuals be allowed to consume. They thought that by making State supreme, a more equitable distribution of wealth shall be possible and none will be allowed to die in hunger or live in misery. Bulk of the masses will maintain almost the same standard of living. However, it has now been seen in actual life that in spite of making the State supreme equal distribution of wealth has not been possible, and the masses are in no way better off than their counterparts in the free world. In some cases they have become worse. Moreover, while achieving very little in bargain they have lost their freedoms. And now the all powerful state apparatus has fallen apart. There is no U.S.S.R. Gandhi could, therefore, never agree to the State supremacy and the method of distribution evolved in the communist world.

Gandhi wanted, not "equitable distribution but equal distribution of wealth,"[1] so that the "social optimum"[2] and "complete economic equality of all individuals"[3] can be achieved. Gandhi wrote:

> "I have no doubt that if India is to live an exemplary life of independence which would be the envy of the world, all the *Bhangis*, lawyers, teachers, merchants and other would get the same wage for an honest day's work."[4]

Gandhi, as has been made amply clear elsewhere, was not for a blind material progress. He wanted to mix material progress with moral progress in such an ideal ratio that it promote happiness of all and not only of either a few or the majority. He called it a "real progress" or "social equilibrium."[5] This is amply clear in his ideas on distributions also. Gandhi wanted equal distribution of wealth and for this he propounded a theory, which can be called the theory of equality.

Before studying the theory of 'Equality' it will be better to repeat that in the Gandhian set-up, the problems of distribution, unlike what they are in the present world, will be least important. In the Gandhian way of life, neither the people will have a desire to exploit others nor will they be in a position to do so. Bulk of the production will be carried on a small scale or in the form of cottage type industries using such machines as will only relieve back-breaking labour and will not give sufficient powers of exploitation.

The Theory of Equality

Explaining the Theory of Equality of Gandhi, *Harijan* wrote:

> "Economic equality of his conception did not mean that every one would literally have the same amount. It simply meant that everybody should have enough for him or her needs. For instance, he required two shawls in winter whereas his grand nephew Kannu Gandhi, who stayed with him and like his own

> son, did not require any warm clothing whatsoever. Gandhi required goat's milk, oranges and other fruits. Kannu could do with ordinary food. Kannu was a young man, whereas he was an old man of 76; the monthly expense of his food was far more than that of Kannu, but that did not mean that there was economic inequality between them. The elephant requires a thousand times more food than the ant, but that is not an indication of inequality. So the real meaning of economic equality was to each according to his need."

Here a question crops up, viz. "How the entrepreneur will know the minimum requirements of the owners of the various factors of production at different places and at different times?' To this it can be said that the Government through the help of its statisticians and experts will be publishing, from time to time, the value of the minimum requirements of the owners of the various factors. Of course, while calculating this minimum several factors such as number of family members and their age and state of health, prevalent price level of various goods, existing normal standards of living etc. will have to be kept in mind by the statisticians of the Government. Naturally, such publications by the Government will serve as an index of minimum wages to the entrepreneur as well as the unions of the owner of various factors.

But how can equal distribution of the Gandhian type be brought about through non-violence?

Gandhi felt that the existing economic systems are such that not only the rich exit but they thrive and their number increases while the poor get poorer. Gandhi, therefore, wanted that the rich should themselves renounce their extra wealth, because material progress of the rich, beyond a limit, is highly immoral and it retards real progress. However, if they fail to behave properly they should be forced to do so. On the other hand, the poor should be encouraged and helped to have material progress upto a point as it increases their moral fibre and promotes happiness. Thus a social optimum must be achieved. To achieve this social optimum Gandhi suggested the following measures, the idea of which can be had through his scattered writings and speeches.

Theory of Self-Renunciation or Trusteeship

Gandhi came in contact with Jamna Lal Bajaj who, partly due to his grand-father's insults and partly due to associations with Gandhi held his property as a trust for the poor. This gave the idea of possible change of heart of the rich. The Hindu philosophy of renunciation, which was successfully and willingly practised by our ancestors for centuries, confirms this view. So, Gandhi held that for a capitalist society, where accumulation of wealth has already taken place, and chances are that some new persons may become successful in acquiring huge fortunes, the rich should, by their own accord, become trustees of their properties and so help in non-violent redistribution of wealth.[6]

Role of Labour Unions

Gandhi felt that so long as a really non-violent society is not established and production is carried on a large scale, labour unions will be a necessity. He thought that labour organised in a strong union on his lines will be able to keep a check on the greed of the rich and through non-violent non-cooperation and *Satyagraha* will, on the one hand, be able to convert them into trustees and, on the other help in improving the lot of labourers. However, he felt that in an ideal state there will be no conflict between labour and capital as their interests are not opposed to each other but are complementary to each other.[7]

Role of the State

Gandhi was in a way an anarchist who believed in no State. But till that ideal state of statelessness is achieved, he wanted that the State, which will be mainly controlled by peasants,[8] should help through legislations, regulations, taxation and expenditures on social services in reducing the inequalities of wealth. His ideas on profit sharing and minimum wages are a pointer in the direction.

Method of Production

In the Gandhian set-up the power to exploit others and accumulate wealth beyond all reasonable limits will ultimately have to go. The production in private sector will be mainly carried on either in the form of cottage industries or small scale enterprises. Obviously, this will take away from the owners of the plants the power to amass wealth. Whatever extra wealth they will be able to collect will have to be shared with the labour because of the labour unions and the State pressure.

A New Society

Gandhi dreamt of making a new society and a man who will not be interested in exploiting others and will not allow others to exploit him. His goal of life will be to promote his own happiness and help others in becoming happier. The mad craze for material progress beyond all reasonable limits will no longer attract this new man. This man, Gandhi thought, can be produced with the help of education and new surroundings. He, therefore, came out with a scheme of socio-politico-economic set-up and a new educational system.[9]

These, then in brief , are the ideas of Gandhi on distribution. Apparently, Gandhi was right in suggesting that the payment to the factors of production be made according to their minimum requirements and not according to marginal productivity. But some one may say that this principal of equality may be used to justify the glaring differences of income of the prince and the pauper. To this Gandhi said:

> "...that will be idle sophistry and travesty of my argument...the contrast between the rich and the poor today is a painful sight. The poor villagers are exploited by the foreign Government (and by their own Government) and also by their own countrymen – the city dwellers. They produce the food and go hungry. They produce milk and their children have to go without it. It is disgraceful. Every one must have a balanced diet, a decent house to live in, facilities for the eduction of one's children and adequate medical relief."[10]

He did not want to taboo everything above and beyond the bare necessities.

REFERENCES

1. T.K.N. Unnithan, *Gandhi and Free India*, p. 86.
2. Ibid., p. 85.
3. Ibid.
4. *Harijan*, March 16, 1947, vide *Towards Non-violent Socialism*, op. cit. 24.
5. Article 4, R.B. Gregg in the Book of Essays on M. Gandhi edited by S. Radhakrishnan, p. 80-86.
6. The theory of trusteeship has been discussed in some detalis in Chap. V.
7. For details on Labour Unions, see Chap. VI.
8. See Chap. IX.
9. See Chap. IX.
10. Ibid.

9

Gandhi's Socio-political Set-up

Till recently there had beed a trend towards excessive specialisation. Life had been broken and divided into different compartments—social, political, economic, legal, ethical, literary, artistic etc., and experts of each branch studied only the problems of their own respective spheres and remained unconcerned with those of others. This was the era of micro-analysis. However, soon it was realized that in spite of this departmentalisation and excessive specialization, there was a running thread common to all and that changes in economic life of a country affected its social and political life, and on the other hand, changes in social and political life influenced the economic conditions of its prople. In Russia, the entire social and political structure underwent a radical change when attempts were made to scale down the glaring inequalities of income and to stop economic exploitation of man by man. Similarly, with changes in political thinking in England, the economic life also underwent changes. The same is happening in India. With the increase in industries, commerce and trade, the village life has started cracking and the contented villagers of yesterday have started demanding more and more political and social rights today. Keeping in view this infallible inter-connection that the well-known economist, Maurice Dobb, observed, "...I should be the first and most vehement in denying that economic factors...can be separated from their social background and from political implications."[1] Today, no country, therefore, plans only its economic life. Social and political changes are also planned in such a way as may help strengthen the economic changes.[2] Gandhi was aware of this inter-connection of different aspects of life. He, while fighting for the freedom of the country, continuoulsy made efforts to reform society and change the economic pattern. He repeatedly gave vent to these feelings. "The whole gamut of man's activities today constitutes an indivisible whole. You cannot divide social, economic and purely religious work into water-tight compartments."[3] It will be in the fitness of things to briefly study here the political and social ideas of Gandhi because they have an important bearing on his economic ideas. Moreover, without them his economic ideas look idealistic, lacking in reality.

It may be repeated here that Gandhi laid down certain fundamental principles for guiding life. The principles are: Truth, primarity and purity of means, non-violence, simplicity, i.e. decentralisation; bread-labour and proper valuation. Gandhi was most static and uncompromising as far as these fundamental principles were concerned. He wanted to raise his socio-politico-economic structure on them. Therefore, while discussing his political or social set-up, we cannot lose sight of these principles.

I
POLITICAL IDEAS

The Political Philosophy, as it has grown in the West, tries to answer three questions: First, how the State has originated? Secondly, what is the basis of political obligations – is it 'will' or 'force'? In other words, what is the place of a State? Is it an end in itself or is it a means and the end is the man? And lastly, what are the functions of a State? It is unfortunate, though very common, that no unanimity of opinions exists on any of the above questions. We, at present, are not much concerned with the first question because it is more or less one of historical importance. It is generally accepted that man is a social being and as such he wants to live in society. When he lives in society, a State [4] slowly comes up.

The second question is the most controversial one, and has not been settled as yet. There are mainly "two distinct streams of thought."[5] The early Greeks felt that "The State was the supreme fact of life, and the efforts and actions of the individuals had to flow into it just as a river flows into the sea."[6] These thinkers made monarchs all powerful and the slogans like 'King can do no wrong' and others were coined. The German School led by Hegel revived this theory. He wrote that "The existence of the State is the movement of God in the world."[7] These and many other philosophers thus made the State all-powerful and subordinated the 'man' and the 'will' of the people to it.

Rousseau regarded the State as a social contract to fulfil the 'General Will'. The State was thus relegated to the back seat and the man, the individual, was pushed forward. Rousseau is, therefore, known as the founder of the democracies of the world. However, he was not very clear and he introduced certain ethical and spiritual concepts. This made him not very much acceptable. It was the English idealist, T.H. Green, who scientifically and philosophically proceeded to prove that the State was not the end but only means to an end. He naturally gave the 'will', rather than 'force', an importance.

When these two groups were busy in matching their strengths, the Industrial Revolution brought about certain important changes in the social fabric of the nations. Societies got divided into two classes of 'haves' and 'have-nots' with seemingly divergent interests. This brought to the scene the socialist thinkers of different brands, notably Karl Marx. These philosophers agreed that man is important but they argued that to serve his interest, it is essential that in the beginning the State must be made all-powerful. They held that after putting the man on the right track, the State will 'wither away'. Thus, the State and the Force were made means to achieve the ultimate goal of classless society. The believers in 'will' and 'man' do not agree with this prescription. They argue that the State having once tasted the fruits of absolute power will never agree to renounce those rights. Prof. A. Huxley has remarked: "...such a highly centralized dictatorial state may be smashed by war or overturned by revolution from below; there is not the smallest reason to suppose that it will 'wither away.'[8] John Gunther agrees with it, "Russia may become a dictatorship not of but over the proletariate."[9]

Count Coudenhove Kalergi has brilliantly summed up these controversies by calling these two schools as 'The Spartan Ideal of Totalitarian State' and 'The Athenian ideal of Totalitarian Man'. In Sparta, man lives for the sake of the State; in Athens, State lived for the sake of man.[10]

It is now more and more realized that insistence on either 'Force' or 'Will' will not do. "The aim should be a poise between Liberty and Authority. The State should facilitate, promote and strengthen mutual accommodation of individual and group welfare. The individual should perform his duty towards the State and the State should safeguard the rights of the individual and enable him to develop his personality to the fullest possible extent.[11] Prof. Towney agrees with it.

The third controversy flows from the second one. If the State is the means and not an end, and the 'Will" is to prevail, then the functions of the State should be miminum. J.S. Mill, who was an individualist, held that the State has to perform only police functions, viz. to protect the State from foreign invasions, to maintain law and order within the country and to administer justice. On the other hand, if the State is 'end' and the 'force' and not the 'will' is important, then the functions of the State should be limitless. It must be in complete command.

Before the twentieth century, wars were not total; they were only regional. Hence the principle of Balance of Power was invented and practised. The war of 1914-18 changed the complex of a war. It became a world war. The principle of Balance of Power could no longer deliver the goods. The League of Nations had to be created to settle international disputes through negotiation, conciliation and arbitration. The second war brought with it more destructive weapons. The totalitarian Governments which wanted war either to establish the supremacy of their race or to convert a civil war into a world or regional war to liberate the labouring classes, soon realised that war will no longer serve them. They too had to accept the U.N.O. and its obligations. The functions of a State in international relations have thus undergone changes.

In the post-Second World War period, the world slowly got divided into two power blocks–Free World and Communist World. A sort of cold war stated. Some countries, intheir own interest, in their own interest, tried to organise a third block. But economic compulsions resulted in the unexpected sudden collapse of mighty Russia. So, all the previous alignments became meaningless. Now U.S.A. is trying to assume the position of super-dictator in the world affairs. The U.N.O. and other international agencies, it appears, have become servants of all powerful U.S.A. In the light of these ideas of modern political philosophy and recent developments, let us study the political framework of Gandhi and see whether his ideas were primitive and he wanted to revert the clock back or they were ultra-modern having philosophical basis and realistic touch.

Let us start with two negative statements saying what Gandhi was not and then come to his positive ideas.

It is wrong to try to fix up Gandhi in one of the existing holes. He was neither a conservative nor a liberal, a socialist, a radical, a communist or an anarchist. He was something of them all but not all of some one of them. For example, he was a conservative because he valued the great human heritage handed down to us by our ancestors both in religion and in social life. He was not ready to summarily dismiss the sayings and writings of the saints by calling them 'superstitions". He was not willing to give up those old social values and traditions, which kept up our civilization intact, in spite of repeated invasions from outside and disruptions from within, simply because they were old.

Gandhi spared no pains in persuading his opponents and followers to his own line of thinking by discussions. He sat, untiring on the prayer ground, preaching people to be reasonable, patient and searching for truth. And if the art of persuasion by reason is the essence of the liberal creed,[12] Gandhi was the first among the liberals.

Gandhi never adhered to the established theories of socialism though he always called himself a socialist.[13] But if socialism tells us that the accumulation of wealth at the cost of the hungry millions is unjust and that service of the poor and the community should precede the selfish ends. Gandhi can easily be called a 'convinced socializer.'

Gandhi was a radical in the sense that he wanted to remove all evils, be they in the form of caste-system or untouchability, or foreign domination. However, he wanted removal of all evils from the root. Half-hearted attempts, or minor reforms could never satisfy him.

Gandhi was also a communist? If communism means accepting certin ortheox Marxian doctrines, such as materialistic interpretation of History, dictatorhsip of the proletariate, class-conflict, establishment of a classless socitey by violent means, overthrowing of Governments in neighbouring countries through revolution, State ownership, centralization of power and abolition of money, then Gandhi was not a communist. But if scaling down the differences in income, minimising exploitation, granting equal opportunities to all, establishment of a happy classless society is the aim of communism, then Gandhi can be called a first-rate communist. The difference between him and a communist in the prevalent sense was only of approach and not of ends.

Gandhi, like an anarchist, hated the growing power of the State because "The State represents violence in a concentrated and organized form. The individual has a soul, but as the State is a soulless machine, it can never be weaned from violence to which it owes its very existence.[14] But he differed from the anarchists as regards their disobedience of the laws of the land, considered immoral. He felt that disobedience of the rules, though they may be evil, should be reserved for those occasions when one is prepared to die rather than obey.

It is just possible that some critic may say that if Gandhi was something of everything, he was only a 'muddle-headed fool, from whom we can have nothing to learn'. To refute this, Horace Alexander's conclusion can be cited: "I believe that in every human being who is not seriously limited in his personality, there is in fact some element of most, if not of all, of these seemingly contradictory attitudes to life. In my own experience, at least, I have noted again and again that men who are extremely radical in their politics may be ultra-conservative in art or in some aspect of their personal lives... Now, the great merit of Gandhi is that he is such a complete man that he can recognize the need for some element of everyone of these priciple in the life of the community. Without being wholly, he can and does strike a balance among them all."[15]

The second negative statement is that Gandhi neither fully believed in Parliamentary Democracy of England, or in the Presidential system of the U.S.A. nor in the Soviet Rule of Russia. He wrote: "By political independence I do not mean an imitation of the British House of Commons, or the Soviet Rule of Russia, or the Fascist Rule of Italy, or the Nazi Rule of Germany. They have systems suited to their genius. We must have ours, suited to ours."[16] Why was Gandhi against the prevalent systems? Probably he knew their defects and the views of experts also. Democracy is at the cross-roads, to use Prof. Tawney's phrase, because it has become 'acquisitive society.' Lord Bryce, after studying six major democracies of the world, found them to suffer from six major evils: (1) influence of money in perverting legislation and administration, (2) the tendency to make politics into a profession, (3) the abuse of the doctrine of equality and failure to appreciate the value of administrative skill, (4) extravagance in administration, (5) the tendency of legislators and political official to play for votes in the passing of laws and in tolerating breaches of order, and (6) the undue power of party organization. Even Bernard Shaw, pointing out the defects of the electioneering system described election meetings as "scandalous and disgusting spectacles at which sane and sober men yell senselessly until any dispassionate stranger looking at them would believe that he was in a lunatic asylum for exceptionally dreadful cures of mental derangement." "The older I grow", continued Shaw, "the more I feel such exhibitions to be as part of the serious business of the Government of a nation, entirely intolerable and disgraceful to human nature and civic decency."[17] When this is the opinion of experts, if Gandhi called democracy a 'Mobocracy',[18] probably he was not much wrong. His observation that "Western democracy as it functions today is diluted Nazism or Fascism...At best it is merely a cloak to hide the Nazi or Fascist tendencies of Imperialism,"[19] appears to be correct.

Since Gandhi was not in favour of the present type of democracies where the State is not taken to be an 'end' but a 'means' and the 'will' rather than the 'force' is given preference, how could he agree to totalitarian type of Government, where 'man' and his will' have hardly any place and the State becomes an 'end' in itself. Gandhi remarked: "But from what I know of Bolshevism it not only does not preclude the use of force but freely sanctions it for the expropriation of private property and maintaining the collective state ownership of the same. And if that is so, I have no hesitation in saying that the Bolshevik regime in its present form cannot last for long."[20]

> "Their (communists) philosophy, as they have declared it to me, I cannot subscribe to."[21]

Again, "Socialism and communism of the west are based on certain conception which are fundamentally different from ours. One such conception is their belief in essential selfishness of human nature. I do not subscribe to it for I know the essential difference between man and the brute."[22]

Now it can be enquired: What type of Government Gandhi wanted to give to his people? Gandhi, as is well known, was an individualist, who wanted to give maximum liberty to each and every individual for his growth but certainly he was against granting a licence for exploiting others. To quote Gandhi:

> "I value individual freedom but you must not forget that man is essentially a socail being... unrestricted individualism is the law

of the beast of the jungle... willing submission to social restraint for the sake of the well-being of the whole society enriches both the individual and the society."[23]

Again,

> "The highest form of freedom carries with it the greatest measure of discipline and humility. Freedom that comes from discipline and humility cannot be denied. Unbridled licence is a sign of vulgarity, injurious alike to self and one's neighbours."[24]

To Gandhi man was the end and the State was needed only to help and serve him. Once man achieves his moral height, the State shall no longer be needed and a truly stateless society shall be established.

> "In truth a Government that is ideal governs the least. It is no self-government that leaves nothing for the people to do. This is pupilage – our present State. But if we are to attain *Swaraj*, a large number of us must outgrow enforced nonage and feel our adolescence. We must govern ourselves."[25]

Gandhi also believed in purity of means,[26] and wanted to concentrate on means because he held that as we sow so we reap and that there is an infallible interconnection between the two.[27] Hence, Gandhi, like the English Idealist, T.H. Green, preferred "will" and not the "force".

> "A Government in an instrument of service only in so far as it is based upon the will and consent of the people. It is an instrument of oppression when it enforces submission at the point of the bayonet."[28]

He like the communist wanted that the State should wither away but he did not prefer to make it most powerful to achieve the ultimate goal.[29] Centralization of power was a sin and a violence to him. Gandhi, therefore, wanted a democratic Government based on Non-violence and decentralization of power where man is supreme and the State is only a servant. He called it *Ram Rajya*. To quote him:

> "It can be religiously translated as Kingdom of God on earth. Politically translated, it is perfect democracy in which inequality based on possession and non-possession, colour, race, creed or sex vanishes. In it, land and State belong to the people. Justice is prompt, perfect and cheap, and therefore, there is freedom of worship and of speech and of the press-all this because of the reign of the self—imposed law of moral restraint. Such a State must be based on truth and non-violence and must consist of prosperous, happy and self-contained villages and village communities."[30]

Gandhi gave us the picture of his village republic in the following words:

> "The Government of the village will be conducted by *Panchayat* of five persons, annually elected by the adult villagers, male and female, possessing minimum prescribed qualifications. This will have all the authority and jurisdiction required. Since there will be no system of punishment in the accepted sense, this *Panchayat* will be the legislature, judiciary and executive combined to operate for its year of office. Any village can become such a republic today without much interference even from the present Government whose sole effective connection with the village is the exaction of the village revenue."[31]

It will be wrong to suppose that these village republics will be isolated entities. Even in the past, they were not so. "The rural republics gradually passed into larger political organizations on a federal basis rising layer upon layer from the lower rural stratifications on broad basis of popular self-government. Dr. Radhakumud Mookerji mentions how these different administrative units, one above the other, were known as *Sabha, Mahasahba* and *Nattar*."[32]

So, Gandhi non-violent State, or *Ram Rajya* will be a federation of self-governing autonomous village republics. This federation will be brought about, according to G.N. Dhawan, not by coercion or compulsion but by the voluntary offer of every village republic to join such a federation. The work of the central authority will only be to coordinate the work of the different village republics and to supervise and manage things of common interest as Education, Basic Industries, Health, Currency, Banking, etc. The central authority will have no power to enforce its decisions on village republics except the moral pressure or power of persuasion.

Gandhi's idea of the village republic is neither new nor primitive. Prince Kropothin in his *Mutual Aid* has given a good account of such village republic which functioned in different countries of Europe before the Industrial Revolution. R.C. Dutta in *The Economic history of India* has observed that India developed and preserved these village republics for the longest period. In *Manu-Smriti*, and *Shanti-Parva* of the *Mahabharat*, the reference to *Gramsanghas* is not uncommon and Kautilya in his *Arthashastra* also describes them. Reference to *Janapada*, which was a kind of federation of numerous village republics, is found in *Valmiki Ramayan* too. Chinese travellers, Heiun Tsang and Fa Hien, also gave their account. *Rigveda*, *Jatakas*, *Vishnu* and *Manu-Smritis*, *Dharma-Sutras* and even archaeological excavation bear testimony to the fact that in ancient India, a village republic was the basic unit of administration and was autonomous to a very great extent.[32]

The idea of decentralization of power is most modern. Prof, Joad, for instance, wants that "the State must be cut up and its functions distributed. It would seem, then, that the machinery of Government must be reduced in scale; it must be made manageable by being made local."[34] Prof. Cole observed, in his 'Fabian Socialism', "If we want to diffuse widely among ordinary men and women, a capacity for collective activity and an understanding of public affairs, we must set out to build our society upon little democracies..." Aldous Huxley,[35] Roy Glenday,[36] Prof. Adams,[37] Prof. Laski,[38] Lewis Mumford, Lord Bryce[39] and scores of others are all in favour of decentralization of political power."

"As to the franchise, he (Gandhi) swore by the franchise of all adult, male and female, above the age of twenty-one or even eighteen. He would bar old men like himself. They were of no use as voters. India and the rest of the world did not belong to those who were on the point of dying. 'To them belongs death, life to the young. Thus he would have a bar against persons beyond a certain age, say fifty, as he would against youngsters below eighteen."[40]

But the age alone would not make one a voter. He must be also prepared to do manual work. According to Gandhi, the qualification for voters, "would be neither property nor position but manual work – literacy or property test has proved to be illusive. Manual work gives an opportunity to all who wish to take part in the Government and the well-being of the State."[41] In the small constituencies, elections will not be difficult or expensive. Those villagers who command universal respect will be chosen as a matter of course. However, Gandhi favoured indirect elections for Provincial and Central Governments.[42]

In Gandhi's 'non-violent state' or *Ram Rajya* majority decision will not always be binding on the minority. To quote him: "The rule of majority has a narrow application, i.e. one should yield to the majority in matters of detail. But it is slavery to be amenable to the majority, no matters what its decisions are. Democracy is not a state in which people act like sheep. Under democracy, individual liberty of opinion and actions is jealously guarded. I, therefore, believe that the minority has a perfect right to act differently from the majority."[43] Again, "The rule of majority does not mean it should suppress the opinion of even an individual, if it is sound. An individual opinion has greater weight than the opinion of many, if that opinion is sound. That is my view of real democracy."[44] In the case of difference of opinion, the only course open for majority as well as minority will be to convert the opponents through negotiations and persuasion.

In the political set-up of Gandhi, the functions of the State will be minimum and efforts will be made to reduce them further as the moral fibre of the people goes up.[45]

The existing judicial system, which is famous for its proverbial delays and uncertainties, will no longer be required in its present form in a Gandhian State. With the rise in moral standards and decentralization of industries and commerce, litigation will automatically be reduced and the genuine difference of opinion of two parties will easily be settled by the village *Panchayats* which may be more conversant with the actual facts being nearer to the place of dispute.[46] Thus Courts, Judges and lawyers will have limited existence as very few cases will be referred to the law courts. Gandhi on the basis of his experience as a lawyer preached the inevitable conclusion that in the present set-up the lawyers work towards increasing litigation and not for getting justice and ending disputes. Hence he wanted to minimise them.

Take the question of punishment of criminals. In 1947, Gandhi said:

> "...all criminals should be treated as patients and the jails should be the hospitals admitting this class of patients for treatment and cure. No one commits crime for the fun of it. It is a sign of a diseased mind. The causes of a particular disease should be investigated and removed. But the outlook of the jail staff should be that of a physician and nurse in a hospital. The prisoners should feel that the official are their friends. They were there to help them to regain their mental health and not to harass them in any way."[47]

Thus Gandhi thought that by constructing a non-violent society, based on morality, crimes can be reduced. But he knew that it will not be possible to convert all criminals into decent people or check future growth of them.[48] So he advocated the method of social boycott for keeping the criminals in check. The second method suggested was that of sending them to a hospital or reformatory for curing them of their disease.[49] And this work of keeping a check on criminals and running the reformatories can best be done by the village republics.

In a truly non-violent state, there will not be many occasions for violent conflicts between groups. Police, therefore, will only be required to meet dacoits, robbers and few violent outbreaks. The police force will be very small as compared to the present one and will be recruited from among the villagers themselves. It will consist of "believers in non-violence."[50] They will be mere reformers than the preventors of crime.[51] Thus maintenance of police will be a function of the village republics and not of the central authority.

Similarly, the other functions of the central authority such as framing of laws, exercising control over the executive, local administration etc., will be passed over to the village republics as education becomes more extensive and morality of individuals rises. The Centre, on the other hand, will be incharge of only those functions which are of general importance such as Defence, External Affairs, Transport, Irrigation, Higher Education, Foreign Trade, Currency and Banking etc. The Centre will perform these functions with the consent of the village republics whose representatives will be members of the Central Parliament. This consent will be acquired by moral pressure or through persuasion.

The non-violent decentralised state of Gandhi's concept will not be a state in isolation. It will endeavour, "to live on the friendliest terms with its neighbours, whether they be great powers or small nations.[52] It shall share its moral and material resources with other nations.[53] It will try to live on equal footings with other nations.[54] Thus, Gandhi's state will try to liquidate exploitation of weaker nations by stronger nations.[55] Gandhi will not mind International Agencies to settle international disputes but this settlement will have to be on the basis of peaceful means[56] Gandhi was in favour of raising an international force of non-violent soldiers for controlling violent out breaks.

Gandhi's decentralized state will be free from all the defects of the present type of Government. The decentralization of authority and converting of every village into a republic will improve the efficiency of the administration, reduce its expenses and keep a better check on the elected representatives as they will be under continuous observation of the people who can unseat them at any time. This type of Government, with a high moral sense of the people, will ensure a perfect Government.

This, in short, gives Gandhi's idea of *Ram Rajya*.

Dr. Gopali Nath Dhawan calls *Ram Rajya* of Mahatma Gandhi a 'Non-violent State'. " By a non-violent state we mean the State that is predominantly non-violent. The completely non-violent state would no longer be a state. It would then be the stateless society and society can be stateless when it is completely or almost completely non-violent. This is an ideal that may not be fully realized. What we may get in actual practive may be predominantly non-violent state advancing towards, though perhaps never reaching, the stateless stage."[57]

"In this structure composed of innumerable villages, life will not be a pyramid with the apex sustained by the bottom. But it will be a concentric circle whose centre will be the individual always ready to persih for the village, the later ready to perish for the circle of villages till at last the whole becomes one life composed of individuals. The outer most circumference will not yield power to crush the inner circle but will give strength to all within and derive its own strength from it."[58]

II
THE SOCIETY OF GANDHI'S CONCEPT

Gandhi made his appearance on the Indian scene as a political leader and not as a social reformer. It was during his toils and troubles that he realised that life is one[59] and for making people ready for a political struggle it is essential to remove the social evils which, in course of time, have crept into the Indian social fibre and have degraded it from its ideal form. Gandhi had widely read Hindu scriptures[60] and was very much influenced by them. He had a good knowledge of other religions[61] also. He could see, on the basis of this comparative study and practical experience of life, that the old Hindu social order was one of the best as it was based on the happy combination of material and psychological factors.[62] He, therefore, wanted to restore Hindu society to its old vigour by removing its rigidity and defects. His untiring crusade against untouchability[63], superiority and inferiority of *Varna*,[64] *Pardah-system, Sati-Pratha*,[65] child marriage[66], dowry system[67], gambling, institution of *Dev Dasi* and animal sacrifics,[68] prostitution[69] and beggary [70] and pleading for widow marriage[71], girls education[72], prohibition,[73] religious tolerance[74], etc. show that he was untiringly working for the restoration of the Hindu society to its old elasticity and glory.

Gandhi never bothered to trace the origin of the society or to find out the revolution of relationship of man and society.[75] He accepted society as a reality and proceeded to define its goal, which according to him, was *Sarvodaya*. In his own words:

> "A votary of *Ahimsa* cannot subscribe to the utilitarian formula (of the greatest good of the greatest number). He will strive for the greatest good of all and die in the attempt to realize the idea. He will, therefore, be willing to die so that others may live... The greatest good of all inevitably includes the good of the greatest number, and therefore, he and the utilitarian will converge in many points in their career, but there does come a time when they must part company, and even work in opposit directions. The utilitarian to be logical will never sacrifice himself, the absolutist will even sacrifice himself,"[76]

Gandhi wanted to establish *Ram Rajya* i.e. Stateless society[77] in the political sphere; classless society[78] in the social sphere and neodemocratic socialism[79] in the economic sphere. He was convinced that decentralization of power and wealth and consequently no complexes and no exploitation alone can give a permanent, happy social order.

In order to build such an ideal society, it is essential that a new man must be made, and not any particular aspect of the society be reorganised.[80] Karl Mannheim also agrees with it when he writes: "It is only by remaking the man himself that the reconstruction of society is possible.[81]

Gandhi wanted to create a new man whose "mission is to strive after perfection, which is self-realization."[82] Again: "What I want to achieve – what I have been striving and pining to achieve these thirty years, is self-realization..."[83] And this self-realization can come only when man attains to truthfulness, non-violence, to simple living, and bread-labour. Ashramites were, therefore, required to take seven vows: Truth, Non-Violence, *Brahmacharya*, Control of Palate, Fearlessness, Non-stealing and Non-possession.[84]

Gandhi believed that the understandings, attitudes, skills, habits and ideals necessary for the above qualities can be developed in a child through proper education. So, he came forward with his new scheme of education popularly known as the Wardha Scheme,[85] the most important factor of which was free and compulsory primary education centring round a craft.

Being a realist, Gandhi knew that even after a new man is made, the chances are that he may degenerate. He also realised that till such a man is evolved, something must be done to keep adults in control. So, he agreed to take the help of the state in making good social laws, though he ultimately puts faith in his social sanctions – civil disobedience, non-violent non-cooperation, picketing and fasts.[86]

But he did not lose sight of the most important problem, i.e. what is the relation between man and the society. Gandhi did not believe in either absolute freedom for the individuals or complete subjugation of the individuals. He felt that the society must help in the development of individuality and character of its members and the members must serve society by observing social restraints. In his own words:

> "I value individual freedom but you must not forget that man is essentially a social being. He has risen to the present status by

> learning to adjust his individualism. Individualism is the law of the beast of the jungle. We have learnt to strike the mean between individual freedom and social restraint for the sake of the well-being of the whole society of which one is a member."[87]

Gandhi wanted to revive reciprocity in relationship through *Varna* and *Ashrama*. A brief description of both will not be out of place here.

Varna

Defining *Varna*, Gandhi worte: "*Varna* means predetermination of the choice of man's profession. The law of *Varna* is that a man shall follow the profession of his ancestors for earning his livelihood. Every child naturally follows the 'colour' of his father, or chooses his father's profession. *Varna*, therefore, is in a way the law of heredity. *Varna* is not a thing that is super-imposed on Hindus, but men who were trustees for their welfare discovered the law for them. It is not a human invention but an immutable law of nature – the statement of a tendency that is ever present and at work like Newton's law of gravitation. Just as the law of gravitation existed even before it was discovered so did the law of *Varna*. It was given to Hindus to discover that law."[88] Thus, in modern terminology, *Varna* gave Hindu society division of labour for earning one's own livelihood with the only difference that it was based on hereditary profession while at present no such strings are attached to it.

Gandhi thought that four broad divisions of the society in *Brahamins, Kshatriyas, Vaishyas* and *Shudras* are sufficient but he was not against further sub-division. In his own words:

> "The different professions can easily be brought under the four main divisions – that of teaching, of defending, of wealth producing, and of manual service."[89]

Again,

> "*Varnas* were originally four. It was an intelligent and intelligible division. But the number is no part of the law of *Varna*."[90]

It is wrong to think that *Varna* and caste are one and the same thing. Gandhi wrote, "*Varna*... has nothing in common with caste as we know it today."[91] *Varna* is also different from the modern classes because it is not based on power or wealth. It is simply a broad division of labour.

When *Varna* and caste are not the same and four *Varnas* can be further splitted into sub-*Varnas,* the question of superiority and inferiority of one or the other hardly arises. Gandhi wrote:

> "...It would be quite right for any brainy carpenter to become a lawyer..."[92]

Again,

> "... I regard *Varnashrama* as a healthy division of work based on birth... there is no question with me of superiority or inferiority. It is purely a question of duty."[93]

Gandhi, therefore, felt that intercaste marriages are not prohibited by *Varna*.[94] Gandhi will even encourage persons of one *Varna* to take the duties of other *Varna* provided it is not motivated by greed or love for fame, and by a will to serve humanity. To quote Gandhi:

> "He may do anything he likes so long as he does it for love of service. But he who changes profession from time to time for the sake of gaining wealth degrades himself and falls from *Varna*."[95]

Varna Dharma has many advantages. It channelises the energies of a young man, from the very beginning to a set goal and helps him in acquiring efficiency in it. It avoids cut-throat competition, waste of time and energy, and affords sufficient time to be put to better uses. In Gandhi's own words:

> "... He (man) must not devote the chief part of his life to making experiments in finding out what occupation will best suit him for earning his livelihood. On the countrary, he will recognize that it is best for him to follow his father's

occupation, and devote his spare time and talent to qualifying himself for the task to which mankind is called."[96]

"You will realize that if all of us follow this law of *Varna*, we would limit our material ambition, and our energy would be set free for exploring those vast fields whereby and where through we can know God. You will at once then see that nine-tenth of the activities that are today going on throughout the world and which are engrossing our attention would fall into disuse."[97]

"In my opinion the law of *Varna* alone makes life livable by all and restores to ambition the only object worthy of it, namely, self-realization."[98]

Gandhi felt that Hindu civilization has survived the Egyptian the Assyrian and the Babylonian because of this institution.[99] *Varna* is not a human invention, but an immutable law of nature. Just as by discovering and applying certain laws of nature, the people of the west have easily increased their material possessions so Hindus by their discovery of this irresistable social tendency (*Varna Dharma*) have been able to achieve in the spiritual field what no other nation in the world has achieved.[100]

Ashrama

To train a man in the service of society and make him an ideal man, the Hindu saints divided the span of life into four equal parts, each part known as one *Astrama*. The child was to be educated and trained to be a good citizen. This training went for 25 years and every youth was made a *Brahachari* in thought, word and deed.[101] He was thus made a disciplined soldier ready to enter the second span of life known as *Grihasthashrama* where he enjoys material things, sexual life and leads a family life. "And because the whole conception of Hinduism is to make man better than what he is, and draw him nearer to his Maker, the *Rishis* set a limit even to *Grihasthashrama*."[102] The man is thus required to enter the third stage, the *Vanaprasthashrama*, where he starts winding up his personal and family afffairs and devotes more and more time to social service. And when he has become quite old, with no family liabilities, and unable to take part in active social service, he enters the last phase of his life, viz. *Sanyasashrama* where he passes most of his time in meditation.

Gandhi felt, "*Ashrama* is a necessary corollary"[103] to *Varna*, and "the institution of four *Ashramas* enables one the better to fulfil the purpose of life for which the law of *Varna* is a necessity."[104] Thus both *Varna* and *Ashrama* were to supplement each other. It is, however, unfortunate that when the *Varna* became distorted, *Ashrama* altogether disappeared"[105] Gandhi wanted to revive both in their old dynamic and pure form.

Thus *Varnasharma* is a code of conduct for every individual, who by observing it will not only enrich himself but also serve his fellow-beings. The present conflict between the interests of the individual and the society will automatically be resolved by these two social institutions—*Varna* and *Ashrama*.

REFERENCES

1. Maurice Dobb, *Some Aspects of Economic Life*, p. 1.
2. See A. Kardiner, *The Individual and His Society*, p. 251, 291; J.B. Gittler, *Social Adjustments to Technological Innovations*, p. 116; P.C. Bebarta, *Technical Changes of Social Adjustments*, Seminar Paper, Vol. II, 1955-59; S.C. Dube, *India's Changing Villages—Human Factors in Community Development*, p. 144-45 and also D.N. Majumdar *Rural Profile*, p. 1. All these authorities clearly bring home the fact that culture is conceived as a configuration of functionally interlocked consellations of material and non-material traits. Any alteration in a particular cultural trait upsets the whole configuration.
3. D.G. Tendulkar, *Mahatma*, p. 387.
4. A State is defined as having a territory, a definite population, a Government and the people owning allegiance to the Government. These are taken as the conditions of Statehood for becoming a Member of the Family of Nations.
5. S.N. Agarwal, *Gandhian Constitution for Free India*, p. 18.
6. Giechrist, *Principles of Political Sciences*, p. 460, quoted by S.N. Agarwal, p. 16.
7. A Huxley, *Ends and Means*, p. 63.
8. Ibid
9. John Gunther, *Inside Europe*, p. 574.
10. S.N. Agarwal, *Gandhian Constitution*, p. 19.
11. Ibid.
12. Article of Horace Alexander, *Social and Political Ideas of Mahatma Gandhi*, p. 7.
13. For example, socialists feel that the authority of the State should continuously increase in order to stop the exploitation of the weak. But Gandhi doubts whether the remedy will be better than the disease as the seeds of exploitation are deep rooted in a system based on centralisation. So he favours decentralisation and minimisation of the authority of the State.
14. M.K. Gandhi, *Sarvodaya*, p. 74.
15. Horace Alexander, *Social and Political Ideas of Mahatma Gandhi*, p. 6.
16. *Harijan*, January 2, 1937.
17. S.N. Agarwal, *Gandhian Constitution*, p. 30-31.

18. Ibid., p. 31.
19. S.N. Agarwal, *Gandhian Constitution*, p. 31.
20. *Young India*, May 1, 1920.
21. *Harijan*, January 26, 1941.
22. *Amrit Bazar Patrika*, August 2, 1934.
23. *Young India*, June 3, 1926.
24. *Harijan*, May 27, 1925.
25. *Young India*, August 27, 1925.
26. *Satyagraha in South Africa*, p. 480; *Harijan*, September 22, 1940.
27. *Young India*, December 26, 1924; *Harijan*, February 28, 1937.
28. *Young India*, October 22, 1919.
29. M.K. Gandhi, *Sarvodaya*, p. 74.
30. G.N. Dhawan, *The Political Philosophy of Mahatma Gandhi*; *Hindu*, June 22, 1945.
31. *Harijan*, July 26, 1942.
32. S.N. Agarwal, *Gandhian Constitution*, p. 68.
33. Ibid.
34. Joad, *Modern Political Theory*, p. 120-21.
35. A. Huxley, *Ends and Means*, p. 63.
36. Roy Glenday, *The Future of Economic Society*, p. 251.
37. Adams, *The Modern State*, p. 235.
38. Laski, *An Introduction to Politics*, p. 53.
39. Lord Bryce, *Modern Democracies*, Part II, p. 489.
40. *Harijan*, March 2, 1947.
41. *Young India*, Vol. II, p. 435-36.
42. Gandhi suggested indirect elections in the Round Table Conference held in early thirtees and again advocated it in 1942.
43. *Young India*, Vol. I, p. 864-65.
44. Gandhi's Statement on the Breakdown of Gandhi-Jinnah Talks, September 28, 1944.
45. G.N. Dhawan has discussed this point at length.
46. *Young India*, Vol. II, p. 436.
47. *Harijan*, November 2, 1947, p. 396.
48. *Harijan*, July 31, 1937.
49. *Harijan*, April 27, 1940.
50. *Harijan*, September 1, 1940.
51. K.G. Mashruwala, *Practical Non-violence*, p. 21.
52. *Harijan*, April 20, 1940.
53. *Young India*, March 26, 1931, V. I,II, p. 438, V. I,II, p. 1292; Mahadev Desai, *Gandhian Indian Villagers*, p. 170.
54. *Harijan*, February 11, 1939.
55. *Young India*, Vol. III, p. 548.
56. Speech in Geneva in 1931 on League on Nations, quoted by B. Sharga, *Gandhi*, p. 389-90.
57. G.N. Dhawan, *Political Philosophy of Mahatma Gandhi*, p. 314.
58. *Harijan*, July 12, 1948, p. 236.
59. D.G. Tendulkar, *Mahatma*, p. 387.
60. Ray, B.G., *Gandhian Ethics*, p. 3-4; Krishnamurti, Y.G., *Gandhian Era in World Politics*, p. 66.
61. *Young India*, October 6, 1921.

62. Mahadeva Prasad, *Social Philosophy of Mahatma Gandhi.*
63. *Yervada Mandir*, p. 33-34.
64. *Harijan*, March 6, 1937, September 28, 1934; *Young India*, January 4, 1931.
65. *Young India*, May 12, 1931.
66. M.K. Gandhi, *Autobiography*, p. 6, 8.
67. *Young India*, January 15, 1927.
68. *Young India*, November 21, 1929; *Harijan* April 5, 1942.
69. *Young India*, November 17, 1921, December 18, 1921, April 16, 1922.
70. M.K. Gandhi, *My Experiments with Truth*, p. 530; *Young India*, August 13, 1925.
71. *Young India*, May 2, 1929; *Harijan*, June 22, 1935.
72. *Young India*, February 23, 1922, January 12, 1925, April 12, 1926, April 22, 1926, January 6, 1927; *Harijan*, August 18, 1940.
73. *Harijan*, June 15, 1935; *Young India*, April 27, 1921.
74. *Yervada Mandir*, Chap. X, XI.
75. There are mainly two theories : (i) The Contract Theory, and (ii) The Organismic Theory. Maciver, R.M. in his *Society*, p. 41-70 has given a beautiful summary of the present theories and views of great sociologists.
76. *Young India*, December 2, 1926.
77. M.K. Gandhi, *Sarvodaya*, p. 74; *Young India*, August 27, 1925; *Hindu*, June 22, 1945.
78. Mahadeva Prasad, *Social Philosophy of Mahatma Gandhi*, p. 244.
79. *Harijan*, April 20, 1940, February 20, 1937; *Young India*, November 15, 1928.
80. Mahadeva Prasad, *Social Philosophy of Mahatma Gandhi*, p. 3.
81. K. Mannheim, *Man and Society*, p. 15.
82. *Harijan*, June 22, 1935.
83. M.K. Gandhi, *My Experiments with Truth*, p. 4.
84. Mahadeva Prasad, *Social Philosophy of Mahatma Gandhi*, p. 38; *Yervada Mandir*.
85. See Chap. 10.
86. See Appendix.
87. *Harijan*, May 27, 1939.
88. *Young India*, November 24, 1927, November 17, 1927, October 20, 1927.
89. *Young India*, November 24, 1927.
90. *Young India*, November 17, 1927.
91. *Young India*, November 17, 1927, October 20, 1927.
92. *Young India*, November, 24, 1927.
93. *Young India*., April 23, 1925.
94. *Young India*, November 17, 1937.
95. *Young India*, November 24, 1927.
96. *Young India*., November 17, 1927.
97. *Young India*, October 20, 1927.
98. *Young India*, November, 17, 1927.
99. *Young India*, October, 20, 1927.
100. *Young India*, November 24, 1927.
101. *Young India*, October 20, 1927.
102. Ibid.
103. Ibid.
104. *Young India*, November 17, 1927.
105. *Young India*, October 20, 1927.

10

Gandhi's Concept of Education

The political and social set-ups of Gandhi's concept are useful aid and help to his economic set-up, but the real key to it is his educational philosophy. Through education Gandhi wanted to build up a new man having a high moral sense, and through his socio-politico-economic set-up he wanted to prevent him from degenerating into a materialistic being. In a way the success or failure of Gandhi largely hinges on his ability to create such a new man, which in its own turn, depends on his educational philosophy. It is, therefore, essential to study his ideas on education.

A very erroneous notion, unfortunately quite common, is that Gandhi had neither read the works of ancient or modern educationists or philosophers of education, nor had he made any experiments in the field, he having remained extremely preoccupied with his political and social activities. By charging Gandhi of lacking in first-hand information in the field of education, these critics want to paint him as a visionary with no touch of reality. It may, however, be pointed out that the truth is rather otherwise. Like the greatest educational philosopher of the 20th century, Prof. J. Dewy, Gandhi had experimented with his ideas at Phoenix Settlement and Tolstoy Farm in Africa and Sabarmati Ashram in Inida. He also founded the Gujarat Vidyapith in 1920. His association with students, teachers and educationists cannot be simply questioned. He was also a copious reader and there are proofs to show that he had read a lot both of eastern and western philosophy on education.[1] His ideas on Basic Education on which topic he has mainly written, and on University Education, therefore, deserve serious attention. They are practical, life-oriented and not mere academic researches of an arm-chair theorist.

What is the aim of Education? The western experts on education give us two divergent aims. One set of them feels that the society is all important and the individual must live and work for the society. Thus, they want to make society, i.e., the State, all-powerful and a controller, regulator and director of the lives of the people—the Individual and Individualism had no place in this thinking. These experts think that Education is an important medium to achieve this goal. By a properly chalked out educational programme individuals can be made to believe that the State is supreme and they can be prepared to sacrifice their ownselves for it. Ancient Sparta furnishes a perfect example of it. In Athens this aim of Education continued to be kept in view. Prof. Munroe points out, "The pleasures of private life whether amusement in sports and games, attendance upon the theatre or social gatherings for eating and drinking were controlled, for social ends, by the Athenians...The State and the entire social life became a School..."[2] France of Napoleon, Germany of Hitler and Italy of Mussolini are further instances. And now Russia and the entire communist block is wedded to this philosophy. In England the social aim of education takes a less extreme form. As Prof. James Ross puts it, "Social service is the aim in education. Schools ought to stress the duties and responsibilities of the individual citizens; they ought to train their pupils in a spirit of cheerful, willing and effective service.[3] But Sir Percy Nunn attributes the social aim of education at present to Hegel. "From the idealism of Hegel more than from any other source, the Prussian mind derived its fanatical belief in the absolute value of the State, its deadly doctrine that the State can admit no moral anthority greater than its own, and that the University should be used as an instrument to engrain these notions into the soul of the whole people."[4]

According to others, the aim of education is peda-centric, or psychological or individual. Sir Percy Nunn argues that the individual and not the state is important. He wants his education system to be such "under which individiality is most completely developed."[5] Eucken[6] agrees with it.

Three observations can be made regarding these aims of education. First, it is rather unfortunate that the western educationists feel that these two aims are not complementary and supplementary to each other but are rather competitive, and we have to choose either the one of the other. Secondly, both the aims want to develop the intellect of the educated and, therefore, they concentrate on importing knowledge of the 3 R's. Thirdly, both the aims want to use education for the attainment of material progress alone.

A study of the ancient *Gurukul* system of India will show that the aim of education was to develop the personality of the educated to the maximum while giving him literary training also and to make him a useful citizen who may abide by the just rules of the society and in turn give it something good. In the western terminology, we can say, there was a synthesis of both the individual and social aims. However, it is to be noted here that this education was not for the masses but only for a selected few. It was given not in the society but outside society in lonely places. It was not matter-oriented and it did not believe either in text books or in unlimited liberty of students. It revolved round a teacher who was a dynamic living force and whose place was only next to God, above that of a father.

In the light of the above knowledge, we will proceed to know the aim of education of Gandhi's concept.

Gandhi was essentially a believer in God. But the concept of his God was much different from what is commonly understood in these days. To him God was not a superhuman controlling our destinies. For him God was Truth[7] and Non-violence.[8] Just as a scientist is in search of Truth, so Gandhi was in search of Truth. For him Truth may differ with time, space and person. It could be served not be retiring to the Himalayas but by serving His Creation:[9]

> "...the only way to find God is to see Him in His Creation and be one with it. This can only be done by serving all. I am a part and parcel of the whole, and I cannot find Him apart from the rest of humanity."[10]

"Man becomes great exactly in the degree in which he works for the welfare of his fellow-men."[11]

Self-realization i.e. *Moksh* can be had only through the service of humanity.[12] The ultimate aim of one's life should be self-realization, i.e., utmost development of heart, hand and head (3 H)[13] when this goal can be achieved only through the medium of serving humanity, and living nearer home and in the midst of society, Gandhi could not find out any real conflict between the just interests of individual and the society and between one society and other societies. To Gandhi, all become one, helping and supporting each other.[14]

This, in short, was the philosophy of life of Gandhi. This

philosophy of life is reflected in his educational philosophy. Gandhi, to begin with, wanted that education should be such as may lead to self-realization. In his own words:

> "The motto of the Gujarat Vidyapith (whose founder was Gandhi himself) is *Sa Vidya Ya Vimuktaye* It means that is knowledge which is (leads to) salvation."[15]

The ancient word for a *vidyarthi* (student) is *Brahmachari*, because all his study and activity had as their objective the search of *Brahman*..."[16] Gandhi was a realist. His experiments in Education at Tolstoy Farm and Sabarmati Ashram convinced him that his ultimate aim of education was beyond the reach and even conception of an average man wedded so much to self and to material progress. He was not prepared to commit the mistake of his ancestors who made education for a few chosen ones. He, on the other hand, wanted to make education compulsory and so also free for all the children between the age of 7 and 14 years. He also did not think it practicable to shift schools to outside cities and villages, away from life. So, a sense of limit grew in him. He, while keeping this ultimate aim of education, gave us some more aims of education which might be called immediate aims or sub-aims.[17] These aims, at first sight, might look opposed to each other but when seen in proper perspective will ideally fit in a complete whole. John Dewy will immediately agree with this view because he compares the aim of education to a landscape which seems to differ when seen from top of the hill and different points of the hill.

The immediate aims of Education of Gandhi's concept are a peculiar mixture of individual and social aims. He wanted the fullest development of the individual and his personality and also wanted that the good of society, nay of the world, may be promoted. He, therefore, gives us the following immediate or sub-aims of education:

(1) Education should help in the all round harmonious development of the students. This all round development is possible only when literary education is supplemented with the development of body and soul. To quote Gandhi:

> "Man is neither mere intellect, nor the gross animal body, nor the heart or soul alone. A proper and harmonious combination of all the three is required for the making of the whole man and

> constitutes the true economics of education."[18]
>
> "I hold that true education of the intellect can only come through a proper exercise and training of the bodily organs e.g. hands, feet, eyes, ears, nose etc. In other words an intelligent use of the bodily organs in a child provides the best and the quickest way of developing his intellect. But unless the development of the mind and body goes hand in hand, with a corresponding awakening of the soul, the former alone would prove to be a poor lopsided affair...A proper and all round development of the mind, therefore, can take place only when it proceeds *pari passu* with the education of the physical and spiritual faculties of the child. They constitute an indivisible whole."[19]
>
> "Literary education is of no value, if it is not able to build up a sound character."[20]

Gandhi attached far more importance to the cultural side of education than to the literary. Addressing the girl students he said:

> "Culture is the foundation. It should show itself in the smallest details of your conduct and personal behaviour...Inner culture must be reflected in your speech, the way in which you treat visitors and guests, and behave towards one another and your teachers and elders."[21]

Dr. Radhakrishnan argeed with Gandhi. "Mere knowledge which gratifies curiosity is different from culture which refines personality."[22] "A man's culture is not to be judge by the amount of tabulated information which he has at his command but by the quality of mind which he brings to bear on the facts of life."[23] Cardinal Newman has called it "philosophical habit."[24]

"Purity of personal life is the one indispensable condition for building up a sound education."[25] And this purity can only come when the students are believers in God, i.e. Truth and Non-violence, have a pure heart, lead a simple life and believe in dignity of labour. In other words, they become real *Brahmacharis*.

To sum up, Gandhi was the prince among individualists. He wanted a homogeneous all round development—physical, mental, cultural and moral of the educated. "True education is that which draws out and simulates the spiritual, intellectual and physical faculties of the children."[26]

(2) He wanted to base education, on indigenous culture,[27] because otherwise it would make the educated "unfit for the service of the community"[28] and make them, "foreigners in their own land".[29] Education, therefore, must reflect national conditions[30] and be so revolutionized as to answer the wants of the poorest villager.[31] Criticising the present system of education, Gandhi observed: "The greatest drawback of the present system of education is that it does not bear the stamp of reality, that the children do not react to the varying wants of the country. True education must correspond to the surrounding circumstances or it is not a healthy growth.[32]

Gandhi thought that the social aim of education does not come in conflict with the individual aim. Man is to serve society[33] and society is to help man.[34] The good of one lies in the good of the other. There is no question of superiority of inferiority. Gandhi's greatness lies in this synthesis of aims. He says: "I value individual freedom, but you must not forget that man is essentially a social being. He has risen to his present status by learning to adjust his individualism to the requirements of social progress. Unrestricted individualism is the law of the beast of the jungle. We have learnt to strike the means between individual freedom and social restraint. Willing submission to social restraint for the sake of the well-being of the whole society, enriches both the individual and the society of which one is a member."[35]

So much about the aims of education. Now we turn to the Gandhian technique to give practical shape to these aims. Here it will suffice to mention only a few important methods which Gandhi wanted to harness for the fulfilment of the aim of education of his concept.

(1) Gandhi was aware of the Science of Etiology. He felt that during the impressionable age of 7 to 14 years, proper education can sow the seeds which he wanted to sow in a child. These seeds, in course of time, will take the form of fragment trees. Gandhi was aware that it shall not be possible to cover the entire child population and mould it to his line of thinking without making education compulsory and free. He, therefore, wanted the State to make education free and compulsory. His Wardha Scheme of Education bears testimony to it.

(2) Gandhi knew the importance of bread. He was also aware of the problems—unawareness of students about their future career,

cut-throat competition, unemployment and low wages etc.—of this materialistic world. Gandhi also knew that it was essential to have a living wage to keep the body and soul together. Gandhi was also aware of the high cost of education. Therefore, he wanted to make education self-supporting. "Such education, taken as a whole, can best be self-supporting; in fact, self-support is the acid test of reality."[36] By self-supporting he meant two things. First, it must be able to meet the current expenses of education. Gandhi said, *Nai Talim* without the self-supporting basis would, therefore, be like a lifeless body."[37] Again, "My *Nai Talim* is not dependent on money. The running expenses of this education should come from the educational process itself. Whatever the criticism, may be, I know that the only education is that which is self-supporting."[38] "But this does not mean that this basic education will be self-supporting from the very start. But taking the entire period of seven years, covered by the basic education plan, income and expenditure must balance each other."[39] Nor does it mean that it will also cover capital expenditure. "Land, building and equipment are not intended to be covered by the proceeds of the pupil's labour."[40] Education should be self-supporting in matters of salaries of teachers and other current expenses. The logic behind this self-sufficiency is not far to seek. Gandhi wanted to make primary education compulsory as well as free so that he may be able to mould the new generation to his ideas. For this, huge amounts were required which no nation, more so a poor one, could afford.

How painful it is that in the land of Gandhi, where leaders after leaders, swear by him, none bothered to know his views on education and introduce them. And now, under the impact of liberalization and globalization, efforts are made to make education self-supporting. Here again, it is self-supporting in a different sense.

The second meaning of self-supporting is that the student who may go out after 7 years schooling may not be required to get his name registered with Employment Exchanges and waste valuable time and energy in seeking a job and in the process lose self-confidence and self-respect. Gandhi wrote:

> "The child at the age of 14, that is after finishing a seven year course, should be discharged as an earning unit...You impart education and simultaneously cut at the root of unemployment."[41]

Education should not only serve as an insurance against unemployment but also make workers more efficient in their respective occupations,[42] and avoid unnecessary cut-throat competition.

Gandhi wanted to achieve the aim of self-supporting education by imparting education round a craft.[43] He felt that the present method of imparting education through books is lifeless. If it is imparted round a craft, education will not become self-supporting but also more lively. The student should be taught the why and wherefore of every process.[44] Thus, he will acquire knowledge of geography, history, economics, commerce, science and so many other subjects in a more pictorial way.

Gandhi felt that the produce of students must be marketed by the State.

(3) Gandhi was sorry to see that in modern times the teacher has been relegated to the back seat and the text-books have acquired undue importance. The teacher has become only a friend of the students and a mercenary and he has ceased to be their guide, philosopher and controller. Gandhi, therefore, wanted education to revolve round a teacher and not books. "I have always felf that the true text-book for the pupil is his teacher,"[45] because "children take in much more and with less labour through their ears than through their eyes."[46] Again, "I do not believe that this (education of the heart) can be imparted through books. It can only be done through the living touch of the teacher."[47] Gandhi felt that 75 per cent of the text-books will have to be consigned to the scrap-heap[48], because they have become commercial propositions and more important than teachers who have originality.[49]

In existing Indian conditions one will have to wait and ponder from where to get teachers of Gandhiji's concept. Today teachers have not only become mercinary but have degenerated into a soul-less machine who have nothing to do with the character building of their students and setting an example by their own conduct.

(4) Gandhi, unlike the western educationists, was not in favour of unlimited liberty of students. He believed in restricting their librerty because no training is possible without discipline and restrictions.[50] Gandhi wanted to make students *Brahmacharis* and *Tapaswis*.[51]

(5) Gandhi was convinced that the only useful medium of instruction can be the mother-tongue because a foreign language

"deprives them of the spiritual and social heritage of the nation, and renders them to that extent unfit for the service of the country."[52] The students can learn much quickly and with ease when taught through their mother-tongue.

(6) It appears Gandhi was not much concerned about higher education. He was prepared to accept that it may be left for the chosen few who are really brilliant. However, he wanted that the higher education should not be a costly one[53] and it should not be at the expense of the poor taxpayers.[54] He wanted to leave it mainly in the hands of private enterprize[55] but remodelled and brought into line with the basic education.[56]

This in brief, is the educational philosophy of Gandhji through which he hoped to create a new man.

A reading of Gandhian Philosophy gives the impression that Gandhi laid equal importance, if not more, to informal education. He wanted to build a new man, full of moral values and a developed and integrated personality. This could be done, as was done in ancient India, with the help of informal education which was given first at home by family atmosphere and traditions and then in locality, in society and also by observing festivals designed for it. Gandhi would have added electronic media, cinema, cultural shows etc. to it. But then all of this could not be allowed to have a commercial orientation. Character building and money do not go together.

REFERENCES

1. M.S. Patel, *The Educational Philosophy of Mahatma Gandhi*, Chap. V and VI.
2. Paul Munroe, *A Brief Course in the History of Education*, p. 44.
3. Prof. James Ross, *Groundwork of Educational Theory*, p. 43-44.
4. Sir Percy Nunn, *Education : Its Data and First Principles*, p. 3.
5. Ibid., p. 4.
6. Euken, *Life's Basis and Life's Ideal*, p. 371.
7. *My Experiments with Truth*, p. 4, 308, *Young India*, April 3, 1924, March 5, 1925.
8. *Young India*, April 3, 1924; *Harijan*, July 29, 1940, *Yervada Mandir*, p. 13.
9. *Harijan*, August 22, 1936.
10. Ibid, August 29, 1936.
11. M.K. Gandhi, *Ethical Religion*, p. 56.
12. *Harijan*, August 29, 1936.
13. *Young India*, September 1, 1921.
14. "I believe in the absolute oneness of God and, therefore, also of humanity. What though we have many bodies we have but one soul. The rays of the sun

are many through refraction. But they have the same source." (*Young India*, September 25, 1924, December 4, 1924; N.K. Bose, *Selections from Gandhi*, p. 27).

15. *Young India*, March 20, 1930.
16. *Young India*, September 8, 1927; M.K. Gandhi, *To the Students*, p. 188.
17. M.S. Patel, *The Educational Philosophy of Mahatma Gandhi*, p. 45.
18. *Harijan*, December 19, 1938.
19. *Harijan*, April 17, 1937.
20. *Speeches and Writings of Mahatma Gandhi*, p. 213, 214; *Young India*, June 1, 1921, June 21, 1928.
21. Mahatma Gandhi, *To the Students*, p. 291.
22. Dr. S. Radhakrishnan. *Freedom and Culture*, p. 22.
23. Ibid, p. 23.
24. M.S. Patel, *The Educational Philosophy of M.K. Gandhi*, p. 31.
25. *Young India*, September 8, 1927.
26. *Harijan*, September 11, 1937.
27. *Young India*, September, 1921.
28. Mahatma Gandhi, *My Experiment with Truth*, p. 414.
29. *Young India*, February 4, 1920.
30. *Young India*, March 12, 1925.
31. *Harijan*, August 21, 1937.
32. *Young India*, March 12, 1925; *Young India*, December 23, 1926.
33. *Young India*, November 14, 1929; December 4, 1929.
34. *Young India*, March 26, 1931.
35. *Harijan*, May 27, 1939.
36. *Harijan*, October 2, 1937.
37. *Harijan*, August 26, 1946.
38. *Harijan*, March 2, 1947.
39. *Harijan*, August 25, 1946.
40. *Harijan*, October 30, 1937.
41. *Harijan*, September 18, 1937; *Harijan*, September 11, 1937.
42. *Harijan*, September 18, 1937; *Harijan*, September 11, 1937.
43. Ibid.
44. *Harijan*., July 31, 1937.
45. Mahatma Gandhi. *My Experiments with Truth*, p. 412.
46. Ibid.
47. *Young India*, September 1, 1921.
48. *Harijan*, September 9, 1939.
49. Ibid.
50. *Young India*, July 21, 1927.
51. *Young India*, February 28, 1929.
52. Mahatma Gandhi, *My Experiment with Truth*, p. 414.
53. *Young India*, February 10, 1927.
54. *Harijan*, March 9, 1940.
55. G. N. Dhawan, *The Political Philosophy of Mahatma Gandhi*, p. 362.
56. Ibid.

11

Conclusion

There is no dearth of people who label Gandhian teachings as impracticable. The most charitable amongst them, however, accede, though with great difficulty, that the Gandhian teachings may be practised only by industrially backward countries having a large population. But certainly, in their opinion, the Gandhian way of life has no meaning for the countries of the West. They argue that East is East and West is West, and both will never meet. We have to examine the validity of this type of statements.

There are others who distort Gandhian way to life, either intentionally or under a genuine mistake. One of such distortion is arithmetical in character. "Communism and Gandhism are regarded by them as two equations made up of several constituent quantities, which can be subtracted from one and added to the other with a change of signs without injuring the equation." "Communism," they define, "is Gandhism plus violence and Gandhism is communism minus violence." We must carefully analyse such statements also.

The following pages, therefore, have been devoted to these two important questions—'Was Gandhi an Utopian thinker?' and 'is the Gandhian system superior to other systems?'

I
GANDHI—NO UTOPIAN

Several people, a few of them even well-read and well-meaning dub Gandhi as an Utopian thinker preaching theories and a line of action which are difficult to practise in day-to-day life even by the most determined disciples, not to say by an average man. Was Gandhi really teaching us something which is impracticable? Let us analyse the question in some details on the basis of hard facts.

People in general hold that everything is not fine in the kingdom of capitalism and Marxism or communism of today. They may go a step further and suggest that in the one, the fears of exploitation of not so happily placed countrymen; in the other the loss of individual liberty; and in both, the chances of imperialism and world wars do not leave these systems as desirable ones. So the systems must be changed. Probably, it is an outcome of this deep-rooted urge for a change that the new capitalism is no more what the old one used to be and that Marxism is busy in changing colours—from Marxism to Khrushchevism through Leninism and Stalinism. But in spite of these changes in both schools, much that is desired remains unfulfilled. So what is to be done? The frail saint of India, deeply interested in human welfare, gave us an entirely new prescription based on a deep study, scientific analysis and vast experience. It is better to try this new prescription rather than to die by taking the medicines which have proved to be injourious.

A man sitting at the shore of a turbulent sea cannot boast of knowing either the real roughness of the sea or its might. A ship tossed and destroyed by the mighty waves can only know the real roughness and might of the sea. A man who is known to indulge in anti-religious activities and who, for a moment, has not cared to look round and realise the might and kindness of God, is generally not accepted as an authority on the existence of God. To know God, to realise God and His greatness, one has to pass through a mill. It is the practical experience which can only show whether God exists or does not exist. Similarly, without adopting the way of life outlined by the Mahatma of India, one cannot and should not have the right to discard it as impracticable. Was Marxian system, before it was successfully practised in U.S.S.R. with certain modifications, not considered as an Utopian system. But who will call it so now in spite of U.S.S.R. present state of affairs.

Yes! it may be acceded here at the beginning that none imagines that the Gandhian way is practicable in its entirety in all the countries and at all times. Gandhi himself knew it. His autobiography is entitled "My Experiments with Truth" for this very reason. He made changes on the basis of his experiences. He was dynamic and not static in his thinking. He refused to propound a thesis giving his views on life and discouraged the use of the word 'Gandhism'. To quote him:

> "There is no such thing as 'Gandhism', and I do not want to leave any sect after me. I have simply tried in my own way to apply the eternal truth to our daily life and problems."[1]

His opposition to machine was total upto 1924, but experience showed him that total abolition of machinery was not possible at the time. So, a sense of limit grew in him and his opposition to machinery changed from total to partial. To quote from the interview given to Shri Ram Chandran in October, 1924:

> "R: Are you against all machinery?
> G: How can I be...What I object to is the *craze for machinery, not machinery as such*...
> R: But I was not thinking just now of the practical side. Ideally would you not rule out all machinery? When you except the sewing machines, you will have to make exceptions of the bicycle, the motor car etc.
> G: No, I don't because they do not satisfy any of the primary wants of man...Ideally, however, I would rule out all machinery, even as I would reject this very body, which is not helpful to salvation and seek the absolute liberation of the soul. From that point of view, I would reject all machinery, but machines will remain because like the body, they are inevitable."

The flexibility or dynamism of Gandhi should not be mistaken for his compromise with fundamentals. He was firm as a rock on his fundamentals. Only in the application of these fundamental principles he used discretion and allowed flexibility according to the nature of the problem and time.

Obviously, the dynamism of Gandhi forces us to accede that his way of life cannot be purely theoretical. It must have, and in quite large quantity, the elements of reality.

Gandhi looked at life as an integral whole. He never divided life into water-tight compartments—economic, political, social etc. He announced, "The whole gamut of man's activities today constituted an indivisible whole. You cannot divide social, economic, political and purely religious work into water-tight compartments."[2] It was this realisation due to which Gandhi gave us a few fundamental principles of life—truth, non-violence, simplicity, bread-labour etc.—which are applicable equally to the so-called all branches of life. Will a theorist speak like this? The acceptance of the integrity of life is now conceded by all those whom we consider as practical thinkers. Then, why put a different stamp on Gandhi alone?

Probably, some feel that the adherence to these fundamental principle made Gandhi a theoretical man, as non-violence, truth, simplicity etc., cannot be practised by an average man. The question is: Was Gandhi originating in them quite new principle of life or are they old notions which he revived? A glance at the history of various religions and societies will convince any body that there are nothing new which Gandhi was preaching. He himself admitted, "I represent no new truth."[3] Again, "I never claimed to be the one original *Satyagrahi*."[4] Let us take non-violent non-cooperation for example. Jainism, Buddhism, religious sects and teachers, especially the devotional saints who preached the *Bhakti-Marga*, three Chinese religions—Confucianism, Taoism and Buddhism, Rome of 5th Century B.C., Judaism, Christianity and Jesus—all preached non-violence and *Satyagraha*. But we never dubbed these religions or religious preachers as Utopian. We never called Thoreau, Tolstoy, Fox, Barclay, William Penn, Ruskin, to name only a few, ideal thinkers lacking reality. Then, why should we label Gandhi as an Utopian? Should we simply condemn him because he tried to throw a new light on many an old truth, or because he tried to apply the well established and accepted old doctrines on an almost universal scale?

A pertinent question may be asked here. Gandhi worked to build up an ideal man and an ideal society on the foundation of some basic principles such as truth, non-violence, simplicity, bread-labour etc. Are these basic principles Utopion? Are they illogical? Ancient Indian seers proponded most of these principles. They were repeatedly debated and their truth and logic tested. There were six philosophies in ancient India. All of them verified their logic, truth and practicability. The man and the way of life that was developed in ancient India and whose traces persisted even after repeated all round invasions for centuries, confirms that there is nothing Utopian in these basic principles and an ideal society can certainly be built based on them. Gandhi, in his humble way tried to repeat the performance. How can then he be called Utopian?

A counter-question may be posed. Is it really bad to be an Utopian? Has there been no economist with elements of Utopian in his writings? A peep into the galaxy of economists does not support it.[5] All leading economists – Marshall, Keynes, Galbraith and Marx, to name a few, – imagined that soon a stage will be reached when economic problems will cease to bother us. There will be plenty for everybody. When this stage has been reached, emphasis will be shifted from material rewards to non-material ones – more leisure, work for love of it, education etc.

Take, for instance, Marshall. That great supporter of classical doctrines tried to think about the condition of a society and its workers, when a free economy reaches the stage of maturity. In 1873, he spoke of "Future of working class" and imagined that method of production will become so efficient as to increase output materially and thereby reduce hours of work and make work lovable. Not only this, large amounts will be spent on education which will be of sufficient depth and duration. Marshall returns to this thought in 1907 and speaks about employers and other better off classes. He pleads with these upper classes to stop showy and wasteful expenditure and prize material rewards lower than non-material rewards. He asks his brother economists to propagate the principles of economic chivalry.

Thus Marshall imagines that after a certain stage of economic development emphasis will shift from more production to elimination of unpleasant and hard work, reduction of hours, universal education "and the inculcation of economic chivalry that will value material rewards less than non-material ones and spread a code of conduct that will be ethical, and not just economic, in its approach to economic activity." Truly an arresting picture, which continues to evade us.

Keynes, who gave a vigorous new lease of life to classical economics, also dreams in "Essays in Persuasion" that a day is not far off when due to science and technological advancement and investigation in new equipment "The problem of want and poverty and the economic struggle between classes and nations" would come to an end and "the economic problems will take the back seat where it belongs and that the arena of the heart and head will be occupited or re-occupied by our real problems – the problems of life and of human relations, of creation and behaviour and religion."

Keynes tells us that when this stage has been reached, the problem will not be how to meet the absolute needs but "how to occupy leisure which science and compound interest will have won for him (man) to live wisely and agreeably and well." This day has not come.

Prof. Galbraith does not want to lag behind Marshall and Keynes. The only difference between him and the two giants is that while they imagined about an affluent society, he actually lives in it. To quote him, "More die in the United States of too much food than of too little... For many women and some men, clothing has ceased to be related to protection from exposure and has become like plumage, almost exclusively erratic..." 'In this worship for production, non-material needs that glaringly cry out for redress remain neglected.' "Alcohol, comic books and mouth wash all bask under the superior reputation of the market; schools, judges and municipal swimming pool lie under the evil reputation of bad things.' So, Prof. Galbraith wants that after society has solved the problem of production, the goal should become the elimination of toil and change the nature of work to make it agreeable and helpful in the fulfilment of personality and make education the means to achieve it. This problem of production is evading a solution.

Karl Marx was no less visionary than his counterparts of the bourgeois world. He dreamt of establishing a classless society where want and misery will be non-existent and new problems concerning intellectual and spitritual development will arise. To quote him:

> "In a higher phase of communist society, after the enslaving subordination of individuals under the division of labour, and therefore, also the anti-thesis between mental and physical labour has vanished; after labour, from a mere means of life, has of itself become the prime necessity of life; after the productive resources have also increased with the all round development of the individual and all the springs of cooperative wealth flow more abundantly; only then can the narrow horizon of the bourgeois law be fully left behind and society can inscribe on its banner; "from each according to his ability, to each according to his needs."[6]

U.S.S.R tried to put Marx ideas in practive and what has happened today. Mighty Russia is no more. It has fallen to pieces. We have never dubbed these known economists as mere Utopians. Then, why give a different treatment to Gandhi? All these economists of repute have acceded that after the stage of economic maturity has been achieved, material problems will become less important and non-material things will receive greater attention. If the Mahatma of India wants to start with the so-called non-material things first because he feels that material needs are insatible, would we be justified in calling him impracticable? Is it wise on our part?

One thing more. The Known Utopains of yesterday have become realists of today. Robert Owen was condemned in the most strong words, when he launched his experiment of reforms in his factroy. But today we honour him as the pioneer of Factory Legislation. Again, when his experiment of new colonies failed, people laughed at him. But now everybody accepts the importance of science of Etiology. The western world laughed at Marx and his disciples when Lenin tried to implement his Master's preachings in U.S.S.R. soon after the revolution. The new economic policy was hailed on the realisation that Marxism was not practicable. But who will challenge Marx's theory today. Similarly, Gandhi may be called a saint, a day dreamer today, but no wonder if soon a day may come when his ideas would become a reality.

Gandhi was a very ordinary man to begin with. There was nothing to show in early days of his life that he would acquire even one hundredth of the greatness which he actually did. Gandhi's greatness, besides many other reasons, was due to the fact that he was out and out a realist. When he emerged on the Indian Political Scene, he, unlike other politicains, decided to keep silence till he had known India. He took extensive and intensive tours and felt the pulse of the masses. It was only after he had come to know India and her people, that he chalked out a political programme and asked people to follow him. It was his realistic approach to life that enabled him to realise that no political advancement is possible without social rejuvenation. So, he tried to remove the stigmas of untouchabilty, *Pardah System, Sati Pratha,* Child marriage and other social evils from the Hindu society. There is not a single suggestion which the Mahatma of India gave to his people without himself actually practising it. How can such a man be labelled, a day-dreamer, an Utopian?

Gandhi used to say that one should try to pin up one's ideals pretty high so that real efforts will have to be made to achieave them. If ideals are low, real achievement will be quite low. Gandhi, therefore, gave us ideals which, to a stranger, appear to be imaginary. But seeing them in the context of Gandhi's thinking, they appear to be reasonable.

Gandhian Economics is not just a series of disjointed precepts or maxims, not a mere inventory of urgent reforms and remedial measures, but a whole system of thought like capitalism or Marxism. It has an ideology, a method and a programme. The whole system is based on simplicity, equality, self-sufficient village units, nationalization of basic and key industries and theory of trusteeship. The above five points solve all such problems relating to labour, capital, production, distribution, profit and structure of society as are baffling the present day world and causing so much blood shed, misery, starvation, deaths, wars and have deluded us so far in fmding a fair and just solution.

Gandhi's Economic Philosophy is based on the 'goodness of human nature'. But it can be said that in this materialistic world human nature cannot be changed. And if this is correct, it appears that the whole economic structure, envisaged by Gandhi, will tumble down. Take, for example, his principle of simplicity. If man's nature cannot be changed, how would it be possible to revert to samll scale production? How would it be feasible to construct small self-sufficient village republics? Again, if the thirst for more wealth and the hunger to pile up huge stores, when the neighbour is hungry, thristy and frustrated, cannot be stopped, how would it be possible to construct a non-violent society, check exploitation and accumulation of wealth? To speak of human values, when cut-throat competition is the rule rather than the exception, seems to be vague and futile. Who can or would care for his neighbour when one is busy in piling up wealth for oneself? When mass production, multiplication of wants, ever-increasing thirst for wealth and power are the pillars of economic structure, the growth of a class depending on unearned incomes is quite natural. Dignity of labour can hardly be recognised in such a society. The whole society would go the way it is going, it would act as it is acing. No change can be introduced, no valuable results can be achieved.

The main point in the above argument seems to be—'can we change human nature? Critics say 'NO', but Gandhi says, 'YES'. History seems to favour Gandhi. When Lenin and Stalin could change human nature, when machine could revolutionise human thinking, why then Gandhi should fail? Why he with all his humanity, with all his moral force coupled with dynamic political and social reforms, through the process of proper education and training, may not be able to mould people in his own way of life? why the followers of one, who could make millions of his countrymen stand, march and die, on his one word, should fail to change human nature? When the magic man of the age, could single-handed snatch freedom for India and shake the world with his simple but majestic utterances, why should his followers fail, assisted as they are by the press, radios, platform and good-natured persons, scattered all over the world?

The Gandhian idea of economic organization is not an Utopian one; it rather offers a practical and lasting solution of the internal economic conflicts as well as international wars. Those who decry such ideas as chimerical and visionary should vividly recollect the horrors of total wars. If we are really eager that these horrors should not occur in future, we must reconstruct our economic structure from top to bottom on the lines indicated by Gandhi, taking truth, simplicity, non-violence, decentralization and bread-labour as the corner stones of such an economic structure. Else we choose hell, if we reject Gandhian Utopia. In order to build our economic structure on the lines suggested by Mahatma Gandhi, we will have to train up people according to a new code of morality. We will have to build our world on the same lines on which the Hindu society was built up by its spiritual preachers.

II
"JIU JITSU"

It is often said that the present world is divided between two rival blocks—capitalism, which is led by the wealthy U.S.A., and communism, which is controlled mainly by Russia though now militant China is trying to snatch the reins. However, the followers of Gandhi feel that the tussle between capitalism and communism is not serious, as both have so many fundamental things in common. Both pin down their faith on matter and so both are materialistic in outlook. One has individual capitalism and the other has state capitalism. Both thrive on hatred. In the one, the rich capitalist class exploits the weak and poor class; while in the other, the working class wants to eliminate the employer class. Both believe in large scale mechanised production and consequently both want foreign markets to dispose of their surplus products and acquire cheap raw material. This naturally leads them to acquire colonies, under one label or the other. Both believe that happiness depends upon multiplicity of wants. Both believe with a slight difference of degree, in violence. Hence the present mad race for armaments. It is because of these fundamental similarities that the Gandhites opine that both the systems are influencing each other, with the result that the capitalism of today is much different from the capitalism of the nineteenth century and that communism has lost its original shape like a hat being worn by several persons. Today people have started thinking and even saying that the day is not far off when the difference between these two systems will become indistinct. The fate of Russia confirms it.

For the last fifty years, serious students of International Relations have started taking note of the rising third force led by Mr. Nehru of India. A few people, mostly outside India, have taken note of a new ideology, revived by the frail saint of India, which has the potentialities of developing into a powerful force. I am referring to the Gandhian way of life. The philosophers, specially having a fair knowledge of the Eastern Philosophy, after studying the outlines of Gandhian way of life, are bound to repeat the words of Vinoba Bhave: "...though the Gandhian ideology stands nowhere in an organised form, yet inasmuch as it is impregnated with the virily of right thinking. I believe that ultimately it will be Gandhism with which communism will have its trial of strength."[7] There are fundamental differences between Gandhi and Marx and, therefore, to raise the solgans like the one "Gandhism is communism minus violence" is not only wrong but certainly misleading. This is true that both the great men of the century were passionately interested in the welfare of masses, the 'have-nots', but their love for the 'have-nots' was like two mothers, one indiscreet, who overlooks the far-reaching effects of her excessive love, and the other discreet and careful. This is because of the realisation of these fundamental differences between Marxism and Gandhism that Red China thought it proper to invade India in spite of the declared aim of India to establish a Socialist Society under the leadership of the disciple of Gandhi.

It will be in the fitness of things to analyse here the difference between Marxism and Gandhism and to try to pronounce judgment. Hence, in the following pages, an attempt would be made to compare the two ways of life under three main headings—social, political and economic set-ups.

The Social Set-up

It is said that Marx read Hegel's 'Dialectical Idealism' very carefully and turned it upside down. Consequently he believed in matter and environment instead of ideas, and ignored the existence of a thing like 'Spirit'. He laughed at the so-called 'Moral Principles' and propounded a thesis that "the End Justifies the Means". He also told us that a careful study of History and Science tells us that life, with its social environments, has appeared and developed according to a set pattern and is bound to proceed in a set direction. He, therefore, pleaded with people to cooperate with one another to bring the last stage of development speedily without worrying about the means. Thus, love of matter, conflict, violence, elimination of classes, regimentation of life to achieve the goal and absence of the importance of the individual, religion and moral principles have become essential elements of a communist society.

To a person trained in the Gandhian ideology, this social set-up appears to be of no good. He aruges that by making matter supreme, Marx injected the feelings of hatred and class-conflict in the society. Here the poor hate the rich not because they hate wealth but because they have not been able to amass wealth themselves. But hatred is not a virtue, specially when it is based on one's own incapability. Hatred is a passion, a mental deformity, and not a perfect development of reason and sentiments. Moreover, it generates heat in the mind and creates tensions having psychological and physical repercussions.

Gandhi, like the Buddha and other saints, was convinced that spirit or soul is superior and different from matter. He, therefore, tried to build up a social set-up based on the love of the spirit. When every one is to love the spirit, he is bound to value life and other human beings. In that case, the question of hatred simply does not arise. To quote Gandhi:

> "It is my firm belief that it is love that sustains the earth. There only is life where there is love. Life without love is death."
>
> "Hatred ever kills,—love never dies. Such is the vast difference between the two. What is obtained by love is retained for all time. What is obtained by hatred proves a burden in reality, for it increases hatred."
>
> "True love is boundless like the ocean and rising and swelling

within one. It spreads itself out and crossing all boundaries and frontiers envelops the whole world."

Marx after creating hatred and class-conflict talks because there is no other way out—of elimination of the rich class and establishment of a classless society. But is it possible to abolish classes? Experience shows that the present classes may be abolished but then their place is soon taken by new classes. In Russia the 'Capitalists' class has been abolished but its place has been taken by more powerful classes—the politicians, the managerial class and the class of military commanders. Not only this. Even the workers class is having sub-classes—agricultural workers class, factory workers class and intellectual workers class. Of them all, the privileges and powers of the factory workers are the most and those of the agricultural workers the least. The incomes of these classes and sub-classes also vary sufficiently. When nature has not made all equal, how can man make them equal?

When love is the basis of the Gandhian society, the question of trying to eliminate the classes (which one is unable to do) simply does not arise. Hence, Gandhi talks not of class-conflict and elimination of classes but of class harmony and cooperation amongst classes. His theories of *Vama—Vyavastha* and Trusteeship fully bear it out. Gandhi explain that *Vama—Vyavastha* is not only for the Hindu religion but for the whole world. "It is natural to man in his regenerate statc.[8] He, therefore, gives a new interpretation to the old concept of *Vama—Vyavastha* in the following words:

"The law of *Vama* means that everyone shall follow as a matter of *dharma*—duty—the hereditary calling of his forefathers in so far as it is not inconsistent with fundamental ethics. He will earn his livelihood by following that calling. He may not hoard riches, but devote the balance for the good of the people."[9]

Again,

"(*Vama*) established certain spheres of action for certain people with certain tendencies. This avoided all unworthy competition. While recognising limitations the law of *Vama* admitted of no distinctions of high and low."[10]

Obviously *Varna – Vyavastha* wants to eliminate cut-throat competition and take the fullest advantage of the hereditary capacities of the people. But this does not mean that there will be rigidities of distinctions in *Varna – Vyavastha*. It will be a system in which cooperation between different *Varnas* will be more and life will be harmonious. Every member of the society, irrespective of his *Varna*, will be motivated with the principle of trusteeship, which even in the modern international Law, has been accepted as a sound principle. Hence, in the Gandhian-Society, exploitation will be non-existent.

Marx with the help of history and science has announced that both our goal and path are predetermined and hence fixed. So, there is riged schooling and no freedom of action in a communist society. If some 'misguided' person due to his selfish interests, wants to behave in an independent way, it becomes the duty of the more 'sensible' comrades to purify him by arranging for him a pleasure trip to Siberia or by brain-washing communes. And if a comrade country is misled by the false propaganda of the imperialists, the mighty forces must liberate their brethren. But unfortunately for Marx and his ardent supporters, recent researches have proved beyond doubt that neither science nor history has yet fixed a definite goal. Life is neither so static not so colourless as they had conceived of. But a Mao would not care for science and history to be created by the bootlickers of the imperialists.

When Marx believed that the world is moving towards a predetermined goal of classless and stateless society, it was natural for him to advise people to cooperate so that the goal might be achieved at the earliest. He was, therefore, indifferent towards means; he loved violence and revolution and laughed at religion and moral principles.

Gandhi, on the other hand, was not certain about the future of the world. He talked only of 'One Step Forward' and was always ready to revise his ideas and actions in the light of new experiences. In such a state of affairs, how could Gandhi ask people to take to violence and revolution? How could he be indifferent towards means? He firmly believed that no society, worth its name, could thrive if every member of it resorted to violence, fraud, untruth, opportunism etc. These means, instead of helping the society to advance on the path of progress, are bound to lead it to regard human beings as means rather than ends and to deaden their finer feelings, all this resulting in oppression and cruelty. The story of the communist countries amply testifies to it.

One thing more; Violence cannot be regarded as a weapon of the masses and cannot be adopted permanently, So, if the people are forced to take it up, it is bound to degenerate people into wild beasts and to recoil on them after they have eliminated the enemy. So, Gandhi talked of non-violence and stressed the importance of means. To quote him:

> "The means may be likened to a seed, the end to a tree; and there is just the same inviolable connection between the means and the end, as there is between the seed and the tree."[11]

"If one takes care of the means, the end will take care of itself."[12]

Since Gandhi wants to build up a society based on non-violence and purety of means, undoubtedly he also wants to grant complete freedom of thoughts, speech, action and worship to every member of the society. There is no scope for rigid schooling and slogans like the one 'society is supreme' in a Gandhian society.

Obviously, Gandhian social set-up is a thousand times superior to the Marxian society. Recent happenings have proved it.

The Political Set-up

This difference between Marx and Gandhi is as well obvious in respect of political set-up they envisaged. For example, Marx believed in dictatorship (may it be of the proletariate). He argued that to establish a stateless and classless society, the first requisite is to make the state supreme and all-powerful. Hence, democracy and the individual have no place in a Marxist state. There is complete centralisation of power and criticism of authority is not even conceivable.

A Gandhite will argue that to reach a state of statelessness through centralization of power is a contradiction in itself. Once the State becomes all-powerful, it will certainly not try to liquidate itself. Not only this, it will become a worse tyrant than the dictators known for their brutality. The history of the countries wedded to Marxian ideology seems to confirm it. Gandhi, therefore, talked of democracy and decentralization of power. He propounded the theory of village republics. He went even a step ahead and pleaded that even the majority decisions should not be always binding on the minority. Surely, in such a political set-up, the question of violence and exploitation simply cannot arise and criticism of publicmen will be welcomed.

Marx believed that a communist state cannot live and thrive till it helps in accelerating the pace of violent revolutions in the neighbouring countries and ultimately succeeds in establishing the dictatorship of the proletariate in those countries also. This process should go on till the entire world becomes a camp follower. It refuses to permit a neighbour to manage its own affairs according to its own liking and even looks down upon the nations that want to achieve the same goal through other routes. Thus, according to Marx, a Marxist State should spend huge sums on arming large forces with the most deadly weapons, even if it is at the cost of the poor man's consumption. Not only this, it should pursue a policy of isolationism so that its plans, projects and actual conditions of the people may remain a top-secret.

Gandhi, on the other hand, believed in 'live and let live' policy. He never wanted to interfere with the way of life of the people of other countries, even if it was for their good. He believed in complete freedom of self and others. He was also against violence and arms race. To quote him:

> "No empire intoxicated with the red wine of power and plunder of weaker races has yet lived long in this world..."[13]
> "I would not only try to convert but would not even secretly pray that anyone should embrace my faith..."[14]
> "In my opinion, it is impossible for one to be an internationalist without being a nationalist...Indian nationalism has, I hope, struck a different path. It wants to organise itself or to find full expression for the benefit and service of humanity at large..."[15]
> "Some nation will have to dare to disarm herself and take large risks..."[16]
> "The non-violent state will endeavour to live on the friendliest terms with its neighbours, whether they be great powers or small nations, and shall covet no foreign territory."[17]

All this clearly shows that the political set-up of Gandhi's concept is much more liberal, much more flexible than, and very much superior to, the Marxian system.

The Economic Set-up

Both Marx and Gandhi were interested in the welfare of the masses and were keen to make them more happy. However, their concepts of 'happiness' and the standards to measure them were poles asunder. Marx build this entire socio-politico-economic structure on love of matter. Consequently he felf that "happiness depends upon the quantity of material things which one is able to get." Like the other western economists Marx thought of more wants, greater satisfaction, more happiness.

Gandhi, on the other hand, felt convinced that soul and not matter is important. So, he started with love of soul, i.e. life. Consequently, he felt that the western method of measuring happiness is not good. It is true that to keep body intact, it is essential to satisy the minimum material requirements, but to have a passion for them will certainly not lead to happiness. Prof. J.K. Mehta has very convincingly differentiated between 'pleasure' and happiness' and has argued that minimisation of wants will only lead to happiness while multiplicity of wants will only give us pleasure which is of a very temporary nature. Gandhi elaborated this theme in his lecture at Allahabad and reached the inevitable conclusion that material advancement without limit does not increase moral progress in the same proportion. He cited cases to prove it. Our experience also confirms it.

When multiplicity of wants becomes the corner-stone of happiness in a Marxist or capitalist society, the technique of production also becomes almost fixed. Large scale mechanised production becomes the automatic choice. In this respect, the only difference between capitalism and Marxism centres round the ownership of the powerful means of production. Capitalism believes in democracy and so leaves ownership in the hands of the individuals while Marx is anxious to minimise the exploitation of the 'have-nots' within the country and so talks of public ownership, though in so doing he asks the 'have-nots' to surrender their independence in the bargain.

Mahatma Gandhi did not believe in the multiplicity of wants beyond a reasonable limit and so he did not like large scale mechanised production. He argues that once you give yourself to large scale mechanised production you have to accept its evil consequences also. Large scale mechanised production is bound to divide society and the world into the exploiter and the exploited. By nationalising the means of production you can only minimise the exploitation within the four walls of the country but you cannot prevent the exploitation of the weaker and industrially backward nations by the powerful and industrially advanced nations. The history of the last 200 years confirms this. Wheels of the giant machines can continue to rotate only when extra production can be pushed outside the country and raw material acquired from there. The subjugation of nations under one pretext or the other becomes an inevitable truth. And with subjugation start other evils, including wars. Gandhi points out that imperialism and world wars do not add to the happiness of the human race. So, he wants mass production but not through large scale mechanised units. He pleads for a large number of small scale units having practically no capacity to exploit others. Obviously, in such an order, the problems of the 'have-nots', slave nations and mighty world wars will not arise.

Not only this. Large scale mechanised production, irrespective of its ownership, is bound to create many more mighty problems. As has been argued earlier, it brings many social evils in its trail: the average man's power to judge, decide and act for himself decreases; the worker loses the sense of achievement and joy in his work; diseases multiply; and hatred, jealousy, group rivalry coupled with the sobbing of the unemployed, half-clad and half-fed people does not cease and the entire population is robbed of all its freedom and is converted into tame animals. Gandhi was not prepared to run after this mirage. So, he rightly pleaded the case of cottage and small scale industries.

A Marxist argues that in his scheme of production, allocation of resources is ideal and the efficiency is of a very high order. To many this may appear to be a tall claim, specially after the revolt of Hungary, the shake up of the Russian economy at the hand of Khrushchev and the reliable information coming out from Peking about the Great Leap Forward. But even if it is conceded, it does not prove its supremacy over the Gandhian system. When every one is his own master and is sufficiently enlightened, efficiency is bound to be a very high order and the allocation of resources will be no problem.

In the Gandhian set-up, middlemen will have practically no

place and the question of exploitation of consumers will hardly arise. When wants are minimum and the size of producing units is small, the area of markets is bound to be limited and exchange will not be a great problem. Both capitalism and communism cannot boast of these advantages. In the one there is freedom of consumption but there is lot of exploitation; while in the other, even the freedom of consumption has been denied.

Marx boasts of a better method of distribution. He gives us the enchanting slogan of "each according to his needs". But he does not openly tell us who will decide these needs. Will the worker himself determine it or somebody else will do the favour of calculating it for him. If the so-called Marxist societies are any guide, it can safely be said that the distribution of the national produce amongst the owners of the factors of production is arbitrary. Moreover, the myth of a better and even distribution of income in Marxist society has also been sufficiently exploded by the inner stories of the communist countries.

In the Gandhian set-up, distribition will not be a great headache. When bulk of the workers is its own master, when wants are minimum and when the size of the producing units is small, great disparities of incomes cannot simply exist and everyone will get sufficient to satisfy his needs.

The troubles connected with labour-capital relations will also be non-existent in the Gandhian set-up because here neither the capital will have the power nor the will to exploit others and the labour will also be neither ignorant nor weak to permit their exploitation. As such, need of labour legislation will not be felt in a Gandhian set-up and the role of trade unions will be entirely different from what it is today. Both labour and capital will live like blood relations and not enemies. Will it not be a better life?

To sum up, we can safely say that the Gandhian way of life is superior to the other existing systems—Capitalism, as well as Communism. Not only is the Gandhian way of life superior but it is also practicable. The only thing needed is to give it a fair trial. Let us hope the day is not far off, when some wearied nation will catch up the idea and build a new model which will emanate light and rays of hope for the bleeding humanity of today.

III
THE INDIAN SCENE

This study will remain incomplete without a peep into the post-independence state of affairs in the land of Gandhi.

The political heir of Gandhi, Pt. Jawahar Lal Nehru, took up the reins of India in 1947. His close and trusted associates, who were with him in the thick and thin of the political freedom movement and social rejuvenation, also joined him as Ministers. The All India Congress party with which Gandhi was associated has now ruled the country for almost half a century. So, it will be worthwhile to know what the followers of Gandhi, who are never tired of cashing his name have done to take the country on the Gandhian path.

Gandhi was not enamoured by the goal of 'Welfare' He wanted that every citizen should remain in perpetual happiness which does not come with economic prosperity alone. So, his goal was ANAND. Unfortunately the goal that was set before independent India by Gandhi's followers was *Welfare.* This was the beginning of the casualty. During the last fifty years, we could not achieve welfare, what to say of even thinking of Anand.

Gandhi called himself a socialist. But his socialism was not that of West. It had the roots in the Indian Culture which pleaded for simplicity, non-stealing and self-renunciation. Gandhi gave it new name of non-violence and simplicity. He wanted to built up a society on this Indian brand of socialism. The Indian leaders, in their wisdom, and ironically in the name of Gandhi, prescribed in the Indian Constitution, "We, the people of India, having solemnly resolved to constitute India into a "Sovereign Socialist Secular Democratic Republic". This was the second blunder. And now in the name of new economic policy, this socialism is being given a silent burial keeping it intact in the constitution.

Gandhi wanted to build a new India and its moral-oriented people on the fundamentals of Truth, Non-violence, Simplicity, Bread-labour, *Brahmacharya*, etc. He would have never agreed to make gold the GOD of man. But unfortunately, under the evil influence of Western way of thinking and action, exactly contrary to Gandhi's preaching has been done. Gandhi, had said, as the means so the ends. Now we are reaping the harvest. No wonder that common man is finding himself unsafe. Violence, kidnapping, land grabbing, drug-trafficking, murders, rapes, etc., which are natural outcome of money culture, has pervaded the land of Gandhi.

Gandhi wanted mass production with the help of masses, tiny machines and limited capital. It would have left villages intact and broken the backbone of poverty and unemployment. The leaders in their wisdom did exactly the opposite. They imparted machines, technical know-how and foreign investment. Recently, in our wild craze for speedy industrialisation, in the name of liberalization and globalization, we have opened the doors of India to foreign investors, foreign super machines, foreign hi-technology and foreign engineers and technocrats. Swadeshi has been given a silent burial. The economic imperialism has been given an impetus by inviting dozens of East India Companies. This has already started breaking villages. Unemployment is not likely to be reduced and the numbers of people living below the poverty line may increase. It appears, India has sold it soul.

Gandhi would agree to nationalisation of firms (not an industry) only as a last resort. He may agree to public owned industries in case of defence and key industries. Under the influence of USSR, we were enamoured by Public sector. So, Government established units after units. They all turned out to be white elephants. Mirage of socialism, like USSR, has also been broken in India. Now we are trying to find out excuses to sell these units of Public sector.

Contrary to Gandhi's preaching, we tried to become a carbon copy of West, not only in dress, language, eating habits, mannerism etc. but also in copying their labour legislation. We also encouraged Western type of Trade Unions. Today a stage has come when work culture has gone and worst type of exploitation by the employees of their employer and thereby nation has started. Future of India seems to be bleak.

Our population was big enough and it is also increasing at a fast rate. We are sinking billions on population control and yet the population is increasing. Again, we like Westerners, are talking of 'Human Capital' and spending crores to improve it. The results are eluding us. All this is multiplying our socio-politico-economic problems. This appears to be the result of not agreeing to Gandhian techniques of population planning.

It is clear that we have given up the Gandhian idea which was in tune with our culture of village self-sufficiency and village Republics. We have borrowed, with vengeance, the idea of machines, mass production with the help of machine and wider and still wider markets from west thinking it to be passport to heaven. With the recent love of liberalization and globalization we have made the best efforts to open up our markets to the world community. Knowledgeable patriots believe that this glamour will last for a few years and then day of judgement will start approaching.

These anti-Gandhi actions, in the name of Gandhi, are increasing poverty of masses and making few rich, richer. Even the mirage of welfare and socialism seems to be evading us. Gandhi was right when he said that we have control over means and not the ends and as we sow, so we harvest. The western method of production and distribution have added to our misery.

This, in nut shell, are the doings and achievements on the economic front of the followers of the Gandhi, in the land of Gandhi. The picture is more gloomy in the political and social life. Every thing appears to be anti-Gandhi. We could not achieve responsible western democracy of England and have, in bargain, criminalised politics. Same is true of social life. Old values have been destroyed and the new good values of even west could not be imbibed. The society has now all the vices of the east, west and some thing more.

We have lost sufficiently in the past forty seven years of independence but yet there seems to be some hope left. Let us not only take the name of Gandhi but start acting on his advice. This alone will be in line with our glorious past, culture and way of life and will prove a beacon light to the weeping humanity of the World.

REFERENCES

1. Tendulkar, *Mahatma*, Vol. IV, p. 66-67.
2. Ibid., Vol. II, p. 212.
3. *Young India*, Vol. I, p. 567.
4. *Young India* Vol. II, p. 367.
5. Dr. V.K.R.V. Rao, the then Director, Institute of Economic Growth, Delhi, read a very refreshing paper on "Some Reflections on the Economic Utopia" on November 8, 1960 in Paris under the auspices of the Institute de Science Economic Appliquee. The following pages are based on this paper.
6. Marx and Engels, *Communist Manifesto*, p. 20.
7. K.G. Mashruwala, *Gandhi and Marx*, p. 15.
8. *Conversation*, p. 61.
9. *Harijan*, September 28, 1934, p. 260-61.
10. N.K. Bose, *Studies in Gandhism*, p. 205.
11. *Hind Swaraj*, p. 60.
12. *Harijan*, February 11, 1939, p. 8.

13. *Young India*, February 23, 1922.
14. *Young India*, June 27, 1927.
15. *Young India*, June 18, 1925.
16. *Young India*, Vol. II, p. 863.
17. *Harijan*, April 20, 1940, p. 96.

APPENDIX–I

SYMBOL OF SMALL SCALE INDUSTRIES – *CHARKHA*

Gandhi's name is associated with *Khadi*. He wanted to revive this age old home industry of India by impressing upon the masses the need of wearing *Khadi*. He said that *Khadi* is a symbol of democracy as it will scale down the glaring inequalities of wealth and will better the condition of poor labourers. Indians followed his lead of wearing *Khadi* – not because they believed in the soundness of the economy of the *Khaddar* but because of the national sentiments which were tied with it by *Bapu*. *Khadi* came into vogue. Hand-woven and hand-spun cloth became a symbol of national movement. *Charkha* and handloom restarted working in the houses of the poor craftsmen. But soon after independence this love for *Khadi* began dying out fast. People are reverting back to mill cloth. *Khadi* is losing its importance. The purpose of this chapter, therefore, is to show that *Khadi* – symbol of decentralized production – is a sound economic proposition and that it should be encouraged even now to ensure peace and prosperity.

That *Khadi* cannot stand in competition with the mill-made cloth, is a popular belief. It is charged of being costlier. Let us test the validity of this criticism. The following figures published in *Hand Spinning and Hand Weaving* will throw some light on the point.[1]

	Mill Power	*Hand Power*
Hours of work in one year	2,920	2,720
Output per spindle	100-120 lbs.	90 lbs.
Count of yard	15	15
Cost of spindle	Rs. 100	Rs. 3, 4
Percentage of spindle efficiency relative to costs	100	2,400
And similarly hours of work in one year	2,920	2,920
Outturn per loom	12,000 yds.	21,00 yds.
Cost of loom	Rs. 900	Rs. 20
Percentage of loom efficiency relative to costs	100	450

These figures are slightly different from the figures submitted by Ahmedabad Mill Manager. According to him "hand spindle efficiency relative to costs is 1158 per cent and the comparative handloom efficiency relative to costs is 220 per cent."[2] But still it shows that a handloom or *Charkha* is much more efficient than a power-driven loom or spindle.

Probably some one may say, "What have we to do with these data when in actual life we find that the mill cloth, besides being better in quality, is cheaper than the hand-spun and hand-woven cloth? Here one overlooks two important facts. First, the tools used by the craftsmen are very much inferior, being outdated. If slight improvement can be done in these tools, as has been done in Japan and now in India, the output will increase and the cost will decrease. Secondly, the poser of the question has a narrow outlook, it being confined to only his own self. He, however, overlooks the immense social cost which the society has to pay to see the wheels of the giant mills rotating. For example while comparing the cost of mill-cloth with that of the hand-spun and hand-woven cloth, the costs of the following items should be added to the cost of mill-cloth or they should be subtracted from the cost of *Khaddar*—

The cost of erecting power-generating stations, developing transport and communication systems, basic industries, constructing factories and purchasing machinery.

In order to construct a modern cloth mill, factories are to be constructed. Besides this, power is to be produced without which these machines cannot work. All these constructions requie big capital. This capital is to be borrowed, either from the rich people or from other countries. But borrowing is not a desirable thing. It leads to difficulties. Mr. Ford in his book, *Today and Tomorrow* writes: "when business goes into debt, it owes a divided allegiance. The scavengers of finance, when they wish to put a business out of the running, or secure it for themselves, always begin with the debt method. Once on the road, the business has two masters to serve, the public and the speculative financer, it will scrimp the one to serve the other, and the public will be hurt, for debt leaves no choice of allegiance."[3] Thus the evil consequences of borrowing should also be credited to the cost of mill cloth.

Strangely enough, according to the investigations of the Indian Textile Journal, if the cost of erecting a spinning mill is spent on the hand driven spindles, the production will be about 11 times more than the mill production.[4] Thus the cost of this loss for extra production should also be accounted for in the bare cost of the mill cloth.

The cost of national commercial rivalries followed by imperialism, wars and slums should also be added to the cost of mill cloth. Mass production results in wars and destruction of innumerable men and material. Man is degraded to the position of a beast. Is this not the cost of a mill? Then why should not it be added to the cost of the cloth produced by a mill.

It is an indisputable fact that the use of machine increases unemployment in the country. The present history of the world bears witness to it. Even in U.S.A. which is said to be the most advanced and highly industrialised country of the world, unemployment is ever on the increase. The pressure of unemployment was so bitterly felt in U.K. that men with intelligence came forward with various schemes of helping unemployed persons. The government adopted these schemes to a certain extent according to its financial capacity. Similarly in U.S.S.R. which claims a stage of full employment, vigorous attempts are being made to capture new markets which may enable it to keep its people employed. This ever increasing problem of unemployment is solely due to the use of present type of machines which can work much faster than man. It is these labour saving machines which are responsible for the ever-growing unemployment. The mill-cloth also throws thousands out of employment. These unemployed labourers still need food, clothes and shelter. These necessities of life are now provided to them by the State in some degree. The State, in order to maintain these able-bodied workers, of whom any nation can be proud raises taxes.[5] Therefore, the amount of the taxes, which is spent on the unemployed workers should also be added to the cost of the mill-cloth.

Further, those persons who are forced to remain unemployed if they had not been thrown out of employment, would have been spending more on consumption goods. This extra expenditure on goods would have resulted in the expansion of the industries. Thus more production, and greater prosperity would have been the result. The value of the production which we are sacrificing due to big mills producing cloth, should also be added to the cost of mill-made cloth.

In conclusion we can say that the real cost of mill-cloth is much more than the cost of hand-spun and hand-woven cloth, provided we add the above-mentioned costs, to the bare cost of the raw materials and wages.

Some more arguments are put forward against *Khadi* and for the matter of that, against all types of goods that are produced on small scale. One of them is that the wages of the workers producing cloth with the help of simple implements is much less than the wages of the workers working in a mill. This argument is also as shallow as the previous one. Gandhi repeatedly said that the people should take to spinning and weaving as a hobby, a part-time job. The workers should devote their leisure hours in the production of *Khadi*. Thus the question of comparing wages does not arise at all. But let us suppose, for argument's sake, that all the requirements of the cloth are supplied by the craftsmen working on their *Charkha* and handloom, for the full day. Then does the criticism hold good? No, even then it is wrong to say that the wages of a labourer will be less than the wages he would have got in a cloth mill. Recent investigation in South India have shown that the workers have earned about 66 p.c. of their family income by working on the old type of *Charkha* and handloom. And these incomes are bound to increase if the workers are better trained and the quality of *Charkha* and handloom is improved.

Besides the wages, the worker will be getting several other advantages which he would have not got in a factory. For instance, he gets a job at his own house, at his own place. Moreover, he is not made to stand all the noise and slum of a factory. These real advantages of worker should be added to this money wages while comparing them with the wages he would have got while working in a factory. Can somebody still put the argument with equal force?

Yet another argument put forward against *Khaddar* is that it will ruin the mills of foreign countries like Japan and England. The closing down of the foreign mills will create unemployment in those countries. This, in its turn, will affect the relations of the two countries, which will worsen. But this seems to be only a face saving argument. In the first place, production of *Khadi* cannot speedily be increased. It takes time to increase the supply of hand-spun and hand-woven cloth and, therefore, ample opportunity will be given to foreign countries to transfer their capital from cloth industry to other industries. Thus they will be able to counter-balance the decrease of employment in cloth industry with the increase in employment in other industries. Secondly, righting of an old wrong is not a bad thing even when it may result in temporary suffering. And nobody will ever say that one country should not try to raise the standard of its people, simply because it will cause a little of inconvenience to a few people living in another country. Therefore, this argument also does not sound good.

Khadi, incidentally, also means a greater equidistribution of wealth and an increase in purchasing power. Purchasing power can be increased by lowering the prices and increasing the wages of the labourers, i.e. by having a greater equidistribution of wealth, *Khadi*, which is produced by a craftsman, brings more money to him but at the same time it reduces profits of big capitalists. Thus capitalists' income decreases, which the condition of craftmen improves. This results in greater equidistribution of wealth. Mr. C. Rajagopalachari has rightly remarked, "You cannot distribute wealth equally after producting it. You would not succeed in getting men to agree to it. But you can so produce wealth as to secure equable distribution before producing it."[6]

In conclusion, we may only say that the *Khadi* programme put forward by Gandhi is a wise step to save humanity from a disaster. It is not good only on humanitarian considerations, but it stands the test of economics also. Its cost of production is in no case greater than the cost of mill-made cloth as it has low fixed charge, low power costs, low expenses for repair, maintenance and depreciation, low inventory charges, rapid turn-over of material and product, little or no storage and transportation costs. At the same time *Khadi* ensures employment to a greater number of people and it encourages equidistribution of wealth and greater purchasing power in the hands of people. What more can be expected? And it is these advantages of decentralized production over large scale production which strangely enough have made people like Mr. Ford, to decentralise their factories. Mr. Ford is of the view that "big business, keeping service to the public always in mind, must scatter through the country not only to obtain the lowest cost but also to spend the money of production among the people who purchase the product."[7]

REFERENCES

1. Richard B. Gregg, *Economics of Khaddar*, p. 25. Gandhi has written a lot on the subject. His two articles published in *Young India*, October 21 and 28, 1936 deserve special attention.
2. Richard B. Gregg, *Economics of Khaddar*, p. 25.

3. Ford, *Today and Tomorrow*, p. 32-33, quoted by Richard B. Gregg, *Economics of Khaddar*, p. 26.
4. Reproduced in *Young India*, September 3, 1925 in Article called 'Mills vs the Spinning Wheel'.
5. Richard B. Gregg, on the basis of reliable data calculates that tax due to unemployment in agriculture comes to Rs. 5/7/0 per capita if we take the daily wage to be 3 annas per day. "Thus the annual cost of agricultural unemployment is seen to be greater than any of these other great national expenses or incomes," Richard B. Gregg, *The Economics of Khaddar*, p. 31-32.
6. *Young India*, May 24, 1928.
7. Quoted by Richard B. Gregg, *Economics of Khaddar*, p. 53.

APPENDIX – II

CHART OF ACTIVITIES OF AHMEDABAD TEXTILE LABOUR UNION

Chapter I *Union Development*

(1) Propaganda and organization:
- (a) Departmental unions
- (b) Ward unions

(2) Vigilance:
- (a) Departmental
- (b) Ward

Chapter II *Conditions of Work and Disputes*

(1) Conditions

(2) Complaints:
- (a) Departmental unions – Groups A,B,C
- (b) Ward unions

(3) Action under the Bombay Industrial Disputes Act

(4) Arbitration

(5) Labour legislaion

Chapter III *Trade Benefits*

(1) Victimization benefit

(2) Legal aid:
- (a) Industrial
- (b) General

(3) Strike aid

(4) Help in compensation of accidents

(5) Employment aids:
- (a) Secondary occupations
- (b) Other aids

Chapter IV *Social Centres*

(1) Recreation

(2) Health

(3) Instruction:

(a) Libraries and reading rooms
(b) Visual education

(4) Miscellaneous

Chapter V *Social Betterment*

(1) Education:
(a) Day schools, (b) Night schools,
.(c) Adult literacy classes, (d) Nursery school,
(e) Girls' hostel, (f) General

(2) Medical aid
(3) Cheap credit and savings
(4) Work for backward communities
(5) Cheap stores
(6) Welfare work among women
(7) Miscellaneous

Chapter VI *Civic*

(1) Civic conditions
(2) Municipal complaints
(3) Labour representation in the municipality

Chapter VII *Information Bureaus*

(1) Library
(2) Cuttings
(3) Bibliography and references
(4) Investigations
(5) Compilation

Chapter VIII *Publicity*

(1) Periodical:
(a) Majur Sandesh
(2) Miscellaneous

Chapter IX *Relations with Other Sections of Lobour*

(1) Local
(2) Textile federation
(3) Other centres

Chapter X *Office Administration*

(1) Constitution of bye-laws
(2) Returns and procedure under Govt. Acts and Rules
(3) Organization of work:
(a) Plan and time studies
(b) Distribution of work
(c) Rules and instructions
(4) Staff

(5) Records
(6) Reports
(7) Other arrangements
(8) Office information
(9) Central correspondence
(10) Cash
(11) Stationery stores and stock
(12) Accounts

Chapter XI (*Press*) (2) *Studio*

Chapter XII Ahmedabad Taxtile Industry's Research Association. A short note from a booklet published by the Ahemedabad Textile Industry's Research Association on the occasion of the opening ceremony of the Centre by Prime Minister Nehru.

A textile research laboratory, created and sustained by the co-operative effort of the industry and the Govt. of India was envisaged by the Ahmedabad Millowners' Association as early as 1944. This idea could come into fruition only in 1947, following the Income-tax Act Amendment, whereby manufacturing concerns could include in their revenue expenditure contributions made towards the capital and recurring expenses of recognized research institutions. Soon after in December, 1947, the Ahmedabad Textile Industry's Research Association was registered. Its 71 founder members, who were all members of the Ahmedabad Milliowners' Association, made an initial contribution of rupees fifty lacs. The Govt. of India then contributed rupees nineteen lacs, and promised to bear during the first five years, half the recurring expenses of the Association, up to a maximum of rupees one lakh and a half in any one year. The member mills contribute annually one anna per installed spindle and rupees two and a half per installed loom.

The development of ATIRA and the completion of a number of research projects created a new problem. Increasing demands for implementation in industry could not be satisfied without seriously handicapping the programme of research and development in the laboratory. A Liaison Division has, therefore, been recently created to take over the responsibility of implementation and to maintain a two-way channel of communication between the research laboratory and the industry.

The creation of separate Technology Division was deferred till the arrival, recently of textile machinery for the pilot mill. However, the Physics and Physical Chemistry Division and Statistics Division have been actively engaged in the study of several technological problems.

As early as the second year of ATIRA, the great value of operational research in effecting economy in mill working was strikingly demonstrated by the Quality Control programme. Other research programmes in the fields of Human Relations, Chemistry, Physics and Technology soon demonstrated the wide applicability of the scientific method. The Council of Administration decided in 1952 that it was desirable that these results be placed at the disposal of industry, not only in the region around Ahmedabad but throughout the country. With this in view steps were taken to amend the constitution and in 1953, membership was thrown open to mills all over India.

ATIRA's research programmes is based on,

(a) Problems referred by industry.
(b) Scientific developments, the details of the application of which require to be worked out to suit local conditions.
(c) Ideas originating from research workers at ATIRA.

The research programme of ATIRA may broadly be classified as operational, applied and fundamental. Operational research, aimed at standardization and rationalization of existing processes and work methods in the industry, and applied research designed to introduce developments of practical use to industry, have to be tested under mill conditions. For these, the field of experimentation extends from laboratory to the mill. Fundamental research, on the other hand, deals with the understanding of men, materials and processes in industry. It has a very direct bearing on applied and operational research, though its results may not be obvious soon nor its practical use immediate. Fundamental research enables practical problems to be viewed by a purely empirical approach, and is thus a very fruitful source of new ideas.

The following are examples of research work carried out by the Association:

(a) Machine interference
(b) An analysis of attitudes of workers
(c) Training within industry for supervisors

(d) Motivation to work
(e) Group form incentives
(f) Workloads and working conditions
(g) Job description manual
(h) Job evaluation
(i) Work-physiology studies
(j) Illumination

APPENDIX—III

NON-VIOLENT SANCTIONS

The purpose of non-violent sanctions is to persuade the wrong-doer to follow the path of truth and righteousness. The one who applies them against the wrong-doer, therefore, insists on *Satyagraha*. Gandhi defined it in the following words:

> "Its root meaning is holding on to truth: hence truth force. I have also called it love force or soul force...I discovered in the earliest stages that pursuit of truth did not admit of violence being inflicted on one's opponent but that he must be weaned from error by patience and sympathy. For what appears to be truth to the one may appear to be error to the other. And patience means self-suffering. So, the doctrine came to mean vindication of truth not by infliction of suffering on the opponent but one's own self."[1]

A person, trying to mould another person on the path of truth, connot afford to be guided by hatred and selfish motives. "The conditions necessary for the success of *Satyagraha*," said Gandhi, are "(1) the *Satyagrahi* should not have any hatred in his heart against the opponent, (2) the issue must be true and substantial, (3) the *Satyagrahi* must be prepared to suffer till the end."[2]

It will be wrong to compare Gandhian *Satyagraha* with the pacifist movement of Europe and America. Mr. C.E.M. Joad, a pronounced pacifist, has upheld the war in a B.B.C. Speech in 1940. The pacifist opposes war by all means but when once it is declared he supports it and he shifts the blame of the war on others. But Gandhi's *Satyagraha* can never take to violent means and will never charge others for it.

To uphold truth and make others to follow the path of truth and righteousness, Gandhi suggested certain effective remedies; they are:

1. Civil Disobedience
2. Boycott – Social, Economic and Political
3. Pickcting
4. Fasts

Civil Disobedience

"I have found that it is our first duty to render voluntary obedience to law, but whilst doing that duty I have also seen that when law fosters untruth it becomes a duty to disobey it. How may this be done? We can do so by never swerving from truth and suffering the consequences of our disobcdiencc. That is civil disobedience."[3]

Gandhi successfully practised the sanction of civil disobedience against the Governments of South Africa as well as of India. It is needless to name them here. But from this, it should not be concluded that civil disobedience can be used only for political issues. It is equally applicable in social, and economical spheres.

Application of sanctions of civil disobedience requires great discipline, faith, unity and courage to suffer in the persons applying them. The breaking of law is no joke. One has to stand trials, *lathi* charges, shooting and all sorts of humiliation. But more the suffering the greater is the demoralizing effect on the other party. And sooner or later a stage is reached when the other party cannot stand this moral force. It cracks and gives way.

Boycott or Non-cooperation

It is not always necessary that only laws – political, social and economic – may be wrong and unjust. It is equally possible that certain actions of individuals and groups may be unjust. To meet this challenge, Gandhi originated the technique of boycott. Suppose a producer is exploiting the consumers as well as the factors of production of a country by artificially raising the prices and lowering the remuneration of the factors. This action of the producer, though unjust, is not due to any laws of the land. Similar is the case with untouchability in India. Gandhi demonstrated to the world that by non-cooperation and boycott the sufferers can get justice for themselves. If consumers may refuse to purchase goods from this producer, what other alternative he will have except to lower the price. If untouchables may refuse to render service to the society, say clean the cities, till they are treated at par with other sections of the society, they will be able to get equal rights.

Boycott and non-cooperation whether in social, political or economic field, can achieve success, but demands great sacrifice. Consumers, who may refuse to purchase the goods, may have to go without them for a long time. Untouchables, who have refused to clean the cities, may have to go empty stomach for a number of days. But this self-suffering is bound to raise their moral and unite them while it will have a great deterrent effect on the other party.

Picketing

Sometimes it becomes necessary to persuade others to cooperate in the civil disobedience movement, or the movement of non-cooperation. It is here that picketing works. Gandhi's volunteers' picketing at the shops of wine and foreign goods is famous. This picketing persuaded, of course by non-violent ways, the purchasers of wine and foreign goods not to go in for them. Probably, no one can collect sufficient courage to pass over the floor of the lying bodies to reach the wine shop. What other alternative is left except to be moved and swept away with the sentiments of the deep-devoted volunteers?

Here again, the suffering, self-invited suffering, is the keynote of success.

Fasts

Fasting, though new to the western mind, is very old in our country. Even today, on certain fixed days, ladies and gents of the family fast. The common belief is that by fasting nobler instincts of a man wake up and he is purified.

Gandhi by introducing fasting as one of the effective weapons of non-violent sanction achieved two ends. First, it helps in making the non-violent resister feel that he is morally better than his opponent. This has an intensifying effect on his actions. Secondly, the sight of a hungry man, who has refused the meals, not because he cannot get them, but in order to correct the wrong-doers, wins the sympathy of the onlookers. Onlookers start considering him a hero, a noble soul. And when we consider some one as our hero, we try to imitate him. Therefore, onlookers start imitating him and slowly but surely start helping him. This brings more courage and force to the non-violent resister and finally brings about the desired success.

Gandhi felt that fasts helps in one more way. It purifies the soul and see the truth. So, Gandhi look innumerable fasts to purify himself and thereafter decide his future course of action.

REFERENCES

1. *Young India*, January 14, 1920, vide M.K. Gandhi, *Satyagraha*, p. 6.
2. *Harijan*, March 31, 1946.
3. *Young India*, September 13, 1919.

APPENDIX-IV

BLUE-PRINT OF GANDHIAN SOCIAL SET-UP

The Indian society, in spite of its respective religious denominations, has by and large, similar social evils. The difference, if any, is of degree only. The reason for this commonness is that almost all belong to the stock of Hindus and even now are governed by almost the same culture, traditions,customs etc. It can, therefore, be concluded that the Indian Society can be rejuvenated on the basis of some principles.

Social Strategy

During the past forty years, Indian leaders tried to achieve political unity through the doctrine of secularism. It appears that they have failed miserably. It is apparent that in this land of multi-religions, political unity can be achieved only through social unity and not *vice versa*. It is time that efforts be made to develop principles on the basis of which a new united Indian social order may be constructed.

Man is a social animal. He has the herd instinct, he wants to live in a group. So, to satisfy this instinct and also to refine man, gradually society with its network of social institutions—family, marriage, religion, educational institutions etc.—came into existence. With scientific advancement followed by industrialisation, the real aim of life got blurred and materialism was allowed to take over the reins under the impression that materialism and happiness are interchangeable terms. In this mad race for materialism, man became hard pressed for time. Further, new thinking also raised doubts on the utility of the society and its institutions. So, knowingly or unknowingly, functions of the social institutions were transferred to the new hired institutions. For example, the function of the family to rear a child was transferred to baby sitters, child-minders, creche and residential schools, and of recreation, which was also a family function, to TV, V.C.R., toys, etc. and marriage became mainly a luxury to satisfy sex hunger and soon the new ways were found and the old concepts of celibacy and faith, love for partner were given a silent burial. Religion was called a disease and an opium and was slowly made untouchable. Its place was given to secularism, atheism and Marxism.

If we want to change the goal from maximum satisfaction of wants to *Anand*, i.e., where none lives in either misery or excessive luxury and all have the opportunities of optimum development of their respective personalities in an integrated and balanced way so that they may have an enduring happiness, we will have to revive the old social institutions, keeping their basic characteristics intact while changing their forms as per needs of time. This is essential for continuity sake. In doing so, we will have to remember:

(a) That life is one. Society and its social institutions are an essential part of life. They are as important as the other parts—political, economic etc.—are.
(b) That all the segments of life, which go to make the whole life, should be so designed as to work in perfect unison with each other. All should supplement and complement each other and also compete with each other to achieve the goal of *Anand*.
(c) That all the segments of life—social, political, economic etc.—can play a frictionless role only when they are built on common foundations.
(d) That society and its institutions are not an end in themselves. They are means to an end, and the end is the goal of *Anand*. So, the modern concept that society or the state is supreme and the individual is unimportant will have to be changed. Both will have to co-exist on equal and respectable terms.

To re-construct society on healthy lines, the pages of Indian history have to be turned over to draw some lessons.

Society in Harmony with Nature

The Indian seers observed the following characteristics of nature:

1. Nature moves onward in a gradual and systematic manner.

It evolves. It is dynamic.

2. Nature is moving in a set direction probably to reach a particular destination.
3. Nature's onward movements are cyclic.
4. Nature in India, is never extreme. It takes a moderate course.
5. Nature affects man in a number of ways.

The history of nature, as told by the modern scientists, is that first came lifeless matter. More than 128 basic elements have been discovered so far. Ancient seers talked of five elements of nature – earth, fire, air, water and ether, and said that they made life. The modern scientist agrees and says that permutations and combinations of these lifeless elements produce life. Probably, first came moss. With the gradual evolution, then came flora. Small plants came first followed by bigger plants. Modern botanists admit that plants have not only life, they have even power to feel, think and react. In the process of evolution, then came fauna. First came small insects, followed by the bigger ones, birds and then animals. And thereafter, appeared man. It appears, in this process of evolution, a better man or a super-man is to come. So, nature is slowly moving towards a set goal. Man and his institutions – social, political and economic – should help nature.

Modern scientists have also discovered that nature, specially cosmic, has cyclic movements. Earth rotates in a cyclic motion on a cyclic path. This gives the cycle of day and night and the cycle of various seasons which have a profound effect on man. The moon also rotates in a cyclic motion giving a fifteen day cycle. Modern zoologists have discovered a close co-relationship between cyclic movement of the moon and reproduction of animal world. And the doctors have discovered a co-relation between the mad man's madness and the moon's fifteen day cycle, the movements of stars and planets are also cyclic. Thus, it appears, all move onward in a systematic manner, on a cyclic path and in a cyclic motion. It means that while moving onward, they have ups and downs. After achieving optimum height, downward trend starts and when a maximum downfall has been achieved, the upward trend starts. And this goes on.

Nature, specially in India, takes a moderate course. There is neither extreme heat nor extreme cold. There is neither too much rainfall nor scanty rainfall. There are neither too long days nor too long nights.

It is apparent that mother nature has a profound effect on man. For example, man was born because of nature (matter) and his physical existence also depends on nature. Not only this. His intellect, his psychology, his way of thinking and action—all are governed by nature. So, modern science is trying to conquer nature. Indian seers differed. They, instead of conquering nature, wanted to work in harmony with nature.

Indian seers-cum-sociologists tried to build up a society in harmony with nature. So, Indian society, has the following foundations:

1. Matter is lifeless and also not permanent, *Atma*, the soul, which is a part of *Parmatma*, the super-conscious, is permanent. It never dies. So, society was built on the love of *Atma* and not matter.
2. Death means that *Atma*, the soul, leaves the body. This soul, after a time-interval, reappears in another body. Thus, a cycle of birth and death goes on. Modern science is inclined to accept it.
3. The Indian seers tried to make Indian society a living society, a dynamic one in which conscious efforts were made to make man a better man till he achieves the goal. And the goal or aim of life was to achieve salvation from the bondage of birth and death and not the temporary abode in heaven or hell.
4. Man can travel towards the ultimate goal through his good deeds only. He has control over his deeds and not on the results. Results are the resultants of a number of variables, known and unknown, controllable and uncontrollable. Hence, man must insist on good deeds without bothering about their results. Insistence on good acts, without worrying about results, was termed as unattached action (*Nishkam Karma*).
5. On this onward journey towards a goal, it's likely that society should go astray and downfall may start. But this downfall will be short-lived only. When the maximum downfall had taken place, with or without the help of a great man, upward trend will start. Indian seers had hinted that God Himself, in

the form of a great man, takes birth to help man. They had counted more than 24 such incarnations of God meaning thereby that already 24 cycles of ups and downs have taken place. In other religions Prophets have done the same thing.

6. Extreme stands are prohibited in the Indian society. Moderate or a balanced view is always preferred. Here a middle course between attachment and detachment, between fame and love, between *Vidya* (knowledge of soul) and *Dhi* (knowledge of matter), etc. are advocated. Hence, to speak truth is recommended but, at the same time, this truth should not be bitter, it should be sweet. Similarly, in medicine, for health, a balance between three ingredients *Kafa* (phlegm) *Bata* (wind or gas) and *Pitt* (bile), is to be achieved.
7. The Indian seers felt that society should function in accordance with *Dharma* (not religion). And what this *Dharma* is? It has two meanings:

A. *DHARMA* means as per one's nature. Water has a nature to flow, fire has a nature to burn, wind has a nature to blow. Similarly, every man is born with a nature, some basic characteristics, traits, likes and dislikes etc. Indian seers wanted to develop man in accordance with his nature i.e., genes. It was called to follow *Dharma*. In this, two basic postulates were discovered.

(i) *Karma*, i.e., action are in the hands of a person but not their results. Results depend upon a number of factors, known and unknown, visible and invisible. But one thing is certain. Good acts will give good results and bad acts will give bad results. Just as the flowery trees will give flowers, fruit trees will give fruits and thorny tree will give thorns, similarly good deeds will give good results and bad deeds, bad results. The time lag, however, between action and result, may vary, depending upon a number of factors.

(ii) Soul is immortal. After death, soul changes the body but takes along the *Sanskars* of previous life which become nature in the new life. This cycle of birth and death goes on till the ultimate goal of Moksha is achieved.

On the basis of these two cardinal principles, it should not be difficult to conclude that a child is born with some characteristics which are the results of his previous, life's actions. In life, he is bombarded by environment – good, bad or indifferent. Conscious efforts must be made to weed out the bad things and imbibe more and more of good things so that quality of life, in accordance with the basic traits, or nature may slowly improve and take him towards the attainment of salvation, if possible in this life or, in the next life or lives. But the progress must continue.

Indian seers classified, in the broadest sense, human nature in order of gradation, into three categories:

(a) *Satvik* – One that is not at all self-centred and that believes in living for others only.
(b) *Rajsik* – One that is basically self-centreed but also believes in the philosophy of live and let live. It is given to passions.
(c) *Tamsik* – One that is only self-centred and believes in the philosophy of eat, drink and be merry. It does not believe in right or wrong. For it, end justifies the means.

Similarly, they classified human actions into three – *Satvik, Rajsik* and *Tamsik* which follow the aforementioned three basic natures. Indian seers wanted people to move consciously from *Tamsik to Satvik via Rajsik*. Thus, an intergration of nature and action was attempted so that desired results may be achieved.

B. *DHARMA* also means, to observe some fundamental principles of life whose importance have been repeatedly tested in different countries, at different times, by different religious persons. These principles of life, i.e., values, may change in importance as per need of time and place and even healthy additions and subtractions be made. Some of these values are truth, simplicity, love, self-control, non-stealing, non-anger, renunciation of worldly things, non-violence, discipline, patriotism etc. It is the duty of *DHARMA* of every man to imbibe more and more of these vlues – human, social and spiritual – so that his own life may become better and happier, and ultimately he may attain salvation and may have helpful effect on others. These values will certainly improve the quality of society as a whole.

Dharma, in both these senses, has a cyclic effect.

A FEW SUGGESTIONS

On the basis of the above, the following steps for evolving a new indian social order can be recommended:

1. Values

The scholars of three religions – Hindu, Muslim and Christian – opine that all the religions preach almost similar values of life. We must, therfore, find out these common values. For example, Hindus give maximum importance to the values (human, social and spiritual) of purity, non-stealing, knowledge confined to matter, knowledge of soul, truth, self-control, patience, forgiveness, control of *manas*, non-anger, non-violence, fearlessness, discipline, patriotism, renunciation of worldly things.[1] I think Muslim and Christian scholars will not dispute the importance of most of these values. So, after finalising the desirable social values, through modern mass media, the meaning of these values and how to imbibe them more and more in life, be propagted. Let the Indian society be a value-oriented society where materialism takes its proper back seat.

The value of Patriotism, i.e., to develop a sense of belonging to the country, to be proud of its culture, value system and greatmen and to be prepared to lay down even one's life to protect the territorial integrity and culture of the country, should be used as the greatest unifying force. Our experience tells us that at the time of national calamities – an attack from China or Pakistan, for example, generated a tremendous response from all sections of people. People forget their religion, their caste and even their mutual likes and dislikes. The whole nation stood as one man. We should take lesson from this experience and think out national issues which may unite people and force them to act collectively. This flame of patriotism should be kept continuously burning.

Today law and order has been made a casualty by the self-seeking politician. Crime and greater heinous crime has become order of the day. Use of firearms and now electronic devices is increasing. Politicians in office, bureaucrats and criminals have formed a party to rob the people. People ask, was this the freedom for which they had sacrificed a lot? The funniest story is that a law abiding person applies for a licence of a fire arm and gets it for personal safety and not as a status symbol. When violence erupts and he needs his arms most, he is asked to surrender them, for obtaining which he has spent a fortune. On the other hand, persons in possession of illegal arms and ammunitions and those who commit crimes go scot free. So, can a war against criminals, the politicians who patronise crimials and the officers and other people who protect and encourage them, be not waged in the name of patriotism? Mass patriotic awakening can end this anti-national tag-up and enforce law and order.

Wasteful government expenditure for petty personal gains has taken an ugly form. Politicians in office and bureaucrats are specialising in it. The crumbs are thrown to the henchmen and business men. So, a team work to rob the nation of the benefits of freedom and development expenditure and make it bankrupt is in operation. Patriotism demands that the people be awakened and made to oppose politicians, officers and their henchmen who indulge in wasteful expenditure. The loans, both internal and international, can be liquidated and the nation be saved of its hard earned freedom only when such anti-national people are exposed and liquidated. Let it be called a patriotic deed to expose and obstruct such anti-national persons.

Corruption is another mighty evil which is eating away the root of freedom. It is the bounden duty of every patriot to expose and oppose the guilty. Even the tiniest corruption should not be ignored.

2. Samrasta (Integral Humanism)

Great man like Lord Rama, Lord Krishna, Swami Vivekananda, Swami Ramtirth, Rama Krishna Deva, Chaitanya Maha Prabhu, Baba Hari Das, Narayan Guru and others talked about *Samrasta* (Integrated Humanism). To understand it we should be clear about the following:

a. "Diversity" means different things having different nature or families. Diversified things, as such, can be united but they cannot be made equal. This is the Law of Nature.
b. "Inequality" or "Equality" refer to different parts or pieces of one thing. Nature, it appears, does not believe in equality. For example, fertility of land is not the same everywhere. Rainfall in every part of the world or even different parts of

> a country is not the same. Mineral wealth provided to different countries by Mother Nature is not equal. Similarly, all people are not endowed with equal height, colour, intelligence, health, talents, etc.

Similarly, no system can ensure equality. In democracy, each and every person cannot become a Prime Minister or Chief Minister, or M.L.A. Even in a communist country, all people could not become equal, even economically. Mao of China admits that after a bloody revolution and establishment of Dictatorship of the Proletariat, those who came in power became greater equals amongst equal. So, he talks of repeated revolutions. Inequality appears to be in-built in a system.

Lord Buddha saw disparities and consequent sufferings of humanity. He wanted to remove them, through *Karuna* (mercy). He pleaded that the people should have mercy for the needy, the suffering, the unhappy, in grief, in fear, in scarcity and thus help them. *Karuna* or mercy is good but immediately it divides the society into two, one who givew mercy and the other who receives it—the giver and the taker. Obviously, it could not unite the diverse or unequal sections of society. In return, it degenerated a man. It created complexes.

Gandhi almost committed the same mistake when he called "untouchables", *Harijans*. He created a new class. Instead of uniting people or making them equal, he made them class conscious. On the one hand, people were called upon to pity them and help them. Reservations in education and services were made. On the other hand, the scheduled castes became conscious of their number and considered it their right to get patronage. Unity and equality became a farther dream.

Dr. Ambedkar, who was a great scholar and a patriot got swayed by a feeling of revenge. He organised scheduled castes and brought them to fight for their rights. When the calls for rights and duties and of class conflict start, the first casualty is unity and equality.

When we ask our countrymen to have pity on the scheduled castes, scheduled tribes and backward classes; when we talk of reservations for them; when we organise weeks to remove untouchability and we pay similar other lip sympathies, the effect is exactly opposite to that we contemplate. Separatist tendencies, complexes, etc. become more pronounced. A patriot seems to ask:

has anybody seen a mother to have a pity on her invalid child? She loves and the child responds and a new world is created.

India is a multi-religious country. Here Hindus are in a majority and the largest minority is of Muslims. Muslims were taught to organise themselves as a separate identity and fight for their rights. They were taught not to consider this country as their own. They were made to fear Hindus. By implication it meant to be ready to retaliate. This preparedness, this fear complex and this separatist tendency resulted in the division of the country. Not satisfied, the history is being repeated. The appeasement policies pursued by the different political parties seem to have opposite results. Unity is evading us. Communal riots are increasing. We are unable to solve the problem. It confirms the hypotheses that Muslims are being discriminated against, it is in the interest of Muslims to remain united and attack whenever the need be. This mentality is now being increasingly disliked by Hindus, who are, in reaction, getting organised. All this is not providing unity or solving the problem of economic, social and political inequalities. Suspicion, violence, claims for rights etc. act in opposite directions.

So, the need is to the old philosophy of *Samrasta* (Integral Humanism). When milk and water are mixed, they get integrated and it becomes difficult to differentiate between the two. In spite of this intergration they do not become equal. A social reformer should not bother about making all segments of the Indian society equal—economically, socially or politically. Neither nature nor any sytem favours it or can assure it. So, efforts should he made to integrate different sections of society so that they may even lose their individual identity and become a united and healthy society.

How to integrate different sections of the Indian society? *Karuna* (mercy), *Daya* (pity), reservations, demand for rights etc. cannot do it. Experience proves it. It is only the magic of *Mamta*, i.e., love which can integrate the society. So, *Samrasta* (Integral Humanism) means to unite or integrate through *Mamta* (Love). Love alone can help in social, political and economic rejuvenation of each section of the society.

For love, there must be a common ground. A mother loves her children because they are a part of her body and soul. What is the commonness in the different sections of society? Hindus believe in soul and its immortality. Other religions also believe in soul though they do not subscribe to the cycle of birth and death. Modern science appears to be accepting the existence of this soul hesitatingly. So, efforts be made to make this soul the common linkage. Our soul is the tiny part of the super-conscious, i.e., *Parmatma*. So, we are children of the same super-conscious. This concept should generate mutual love and regard. This love will automatically encourage willing sacrifice without drum-beating. This will not only unite but help in speedy removal of deficiencies and weaknesses and grant of equal opportunities to all.

This is the magic of *Samrasta* (Integral Humanism).

3. Family Life

Family is the basic school where the deep rooted impressions are created and the seeds of future life are sown in the child. The family atmosphere, full of respect for elders, sacrifice by elders, discipline, sharing sorrows and happiness together, etc. should be revived in India. This is the most important single unit from where the rays of a good social order may emanate.[2]

4. Ashram Vyavastha

Indian seers turned sociologists, with a view to working in unison with nature, invented a strategy to produce a superman out of an ordinary man who will ulimately achieve *Moksha*, salvation from the bondage of life and death, through *Anand*. This social strategy is popularly known as *Ashram Vyavastha*.

These seers, while trying to produce a superman, wanted to solve many socio-economic problems such as frustration, unhappiness and differences between generations resulting in tensions. For all this, they evolved the scheme of *Ashram Vyavastha*, which admirably succeeded

Meaning

The normal span of life in ancient India, it appears was 100 years. This span, under *Ashram Vyavastha*, was divided into four equal parts, each part extending for 25 years. These parts, on the basis of their characteristics and functions, were called: *Brahamcharya* (student life), *Grahastha* (married life), *Vanprastha* (part time social worker) and *Sanyas* (detachment).

The Brahamcharya Ashram

The first 25 years were devoted to acquiring knowledge, character building and all round development – physical, mental and spiritual. In these 25 years a person was taught three R's and was gradually taught the basic virtues and truths of life such as truth, fearlessness, simplicity, dignity of labour, moral values, patriotism, economic progress and moral progress do not march hand in hand for long, the aim of life is salvation, i.e., eternal happiness (and not temporary pleasures) which comes not through too much attachment to things material but by slow and gradual self-renunciation, self-control of all the senses and service of God through service of His creations. A *Brahamchari* was taught the fundamentals of all these truths and efforts were made by his teachers to sow the seeds of a full life in him. He was also given practical lessons on how to imbibe these virtues. The atmosphere of the school and colleges then known as *Gurukulas*, and exemplary effect of teachers' lives played an important role. The social atmosphere no less contributed in impressing upon the young minds the truth and practicability of these ideas.

The Grahastha Ashram (i.e., the Married and Active Life)

After completion of education adn passing the tests of the *Guru* (i.e., teacher) a student was permitted to enter into the second *Ashram* of life i.e., the *Grahastha*. The span of *Grahastha Ashram* was also of 25 years.

The Hindu saints were well aware of the truth that mere teaching of principles of life did not carry much conviction and that when a person was able to test the validity of these principles in his own life, only then he was convinced and was keen on adopting them. Besides, they also knew that society demanded that the material needs of life should be met and life should continue and not come to an end. So, the young *Brahamcharis*, after the completion of their education and training, were asked to marry, beget and rear up children, have a house and devote all their energies to earning and spending activity. This second leg of life's journey was considered the most important one and normally none was allowed to jump it over. It was said to be the best and most important *Ashram* of life because it was only through this *Ashram* that one discharged one's duty towards the country, society and the family, and through one's own experiences got convinced of the futility of materialism and correctness of the preachings of the Guru (i.e., teacher) and the scriptures.

The Vanprastha Ashram (Social Worker)

During the 25 years of grinding in *Grahastha Ashram*, not only did one gracefully discharge one's duties towards one's country and family but in the process also became aware of the truth of the fundamental principles so arduously taught by the teachers during *Brahamcharya Ashram*. Realising that material pursuit did not give permanent peace and happiness but made one restless and unhappy, running after a mirage, one, by sweet will, started the journey on the third leg of life, i.e., the *Vanprastha Ashram*. Here one started slowly but steadily renouncing material things and devoting more and more time and energy to non-material pursuits. The responsibility of the family was willingly passed on to the younger generation and more and more time was devoted to transcendental meditation and social service. King Dashrath, father of Lord Rama, himself expressed a desire to abdicate throne, the symbol of material power. And this is not the solitary example. It was a common feature prevailing in the Hindu society in antiquity.

When an aging father willingly passed on the leadership of the family to his son, the scope of family tensions automatically ended and instead an atmosphere of mutual love and respect for elders grew.

When a mature, retired and self-satisfied person, on his own, took to social work, which included political work also, the material temptations did not normally sway him, since he had seen the world, had acquired maturity of mind and could dispassionately analyse things. This type of social workers did immense good to society and remained contented themselves. They earned gratitude and respect of society and their advice became law. When such social workers, who were called saints, visited the court of a king, the king used to get up and welcome them. The king, under the compulsion of circumstances and traditions, normally carried out the advice and wishes of such social workers. King Dashrath had to send his two teenage sons, Rama and Lakshmana, with Vishvamitra in spite of the fact that he did not relish the idea.

The Sanyas Ashram

Twenty-five years in *Vanprastha* made a man pretty old and mentally and physically unfit for any arduous work. So, after the age of 75 years, one had to retire even from active social work. But lest time hang heavily, the Indian seers suggested that the persons in *Sanyas* should devote their spare time to transcendental meditation and prayers. They should even leave their hearth and home and start living in comparatively lonely places, away from the noise of cities and habitation, where it might be easier to concentrate on spirit. These elderly persons, on the basis of their experience and knowledge, did educate people through their discourses, writings or any other constructive hobby which they happened to like to follow. These persons were supposed to reside away from their families so that they might not be considered as a liability by their children. Hence, these persons were expected to cut down their wants to the minimum. This kept them physically and mentally fit. And it was the duty of the society to look after these respected persons by providing them the basic necessities of life. However, there was no state compulsion to retire, nor was there any scheme of old age pension. Everything depended on one's sweetwill. The social atmosphere was such as enabled everyone to consider it as one's part of duty to contribute, as per one's resources, to the welfare of these retired persons.

APPENDIX-V

BLUE-PRINT OF GANDHIAN POLITICAL SET-UP

India became independent on August 15, 1947. Soon afterwards a Constituent Assembly was constituted to frame a Constitution for India. This Constituent Assembly consisted of choicest gems of political workers, who had given the very best of their lives to the freedom struggle. It had also the best available constitutional experts, jurists and lawyers. The leaders of industry, commerce, trade, agriculture and noted scholars also found a place in the Assembly. Thus, it had the cream of the country. These people laboured hard and after ransacking all the known constitutions of the world gave India a model constitution. This Constitution came into force on January 26, 1950.

Since the Constituent Assembly was composed of people who were elite and mainly acquainted with the Westminster Model, two things happened. First, Indian Constitution became heavily tilted towards the British system without bothering whether it suits us or not. So, this transplantation resulted in sprouting strange mutation. Secondly, this elite was less bothered about the economic prosperity of the people but more concerned about political freedom. Indian Constitution, therefore, talks more of democratic rights.

During the past forty-one years, the Indian Constitution had to be amended 75 times. In spite of so many changes, people are not satisfied. The demands are daily being raised to change this or that basic structure of the Constitution. These demands are becoming fiercer with everyday that passes. Hence, it seems advisable to give an alternative in the light of the Gandhian goal of *Anand*.

It is the considered opinion of the scholars and confirmed by practical day-to-day experiences that economic life and political life are inter-dependent. One influences the other and in return, gets influenced. Economics touches politics at more than one point because the production and the distribution of wealth are today largely influenced by government, and because the solution of many economic problems must come through political channels. Earlier, due to this close affinity, economics was considered as a branch of politics and was called 'Political Economy', Taxation, Tariff Law, Public Sector, State Aid to agriculture and Industry, Import-Export Policy, etc. clearly show that governmental policies affect economic prosperity. USSR is a living example to demonstrate this point.

Political ideas and institutions are also influenced equally by economic conditions. Rise of feudal government in medieval Europe was because of economic factors. Again, rise of democracy owes not a little to the Industrial Revolution. And rise and seemingly imminent fall of socialist is also due to economic conditions.

It is, therefore, essential that a harmonious relationship should exist between economic and political life. Both should at least try to achieve a common goal. In India, the seers had given the goal of *Anand*. Experience has shown that it appears to be better than the goal of welfare. So, the political effect should also be to help in the achievement of the goal of *Anand*.

The continuity principle requires that efforts be made to base the political life in accordance with our culture, thought process, value system, and way of life and make necessary changes to make it dynamic and up-to-date so that it may successfully meet the demands of the modern times.

Keeping the above two ideas in mind and on the basis of the review of the forty-one years of post-independence period, the following strategy can be ventured.

1. Federation of District States

We have already accepted a federal type of government and artificially created a number of states. Experience has shown that this has not satisfied people. Further, the administrative efficiency is daily deteriorating and politicians are busy to exploit state apparatus for selfish ends. This is eroding morality and encouraging corruption. And in addition, respect for the rule of law is deteriorating and crime is increasing. To set our house in order, it is desirable, on the one hand, to meet the genuine aspiration of people and on the other to decentralise state power to the maximum. Both these ends can be met, to a very great extent, if the number of federating units is increased.

In ancient India, there were Innumerable *Jan-pads* and the size of most of the *Jan-pads* was equal to the present day district. So why each district cannot be made a federating unit now? Of course, where the size of a district is very big, it may be bifurcated further and where the size is too small,more than one district should be clubbed together to form one unit. The viability of a federating unit should be the sole criterion of formation of a state.

(a) Each District state, from administrative point of view, should be divided into cities, Tahsil Towns, Block Headquarters and Focal Villages. These cities, towns, headquarters, focal villages must be made administrative centres for their respective areas. They must house all government and quasi-government essential departments—Administration, Police, Judiciary, Post office, Bank, P.W.D., Tube-well, Irrigation, Electricity, to name a few, on one campus. As far as possible, 'One Window Service' formula should be followed. This administrative set-up will promote real decentralisation of power.

(b) In this scheme of federating District States, the size and composition of the constituencies will have to be changed. Today we have very big constituencies. To stand for elections, one needs lot of money, workers, who include muscle power, and other resources. So, the size of the constituencies should be reduced to manageable size, area-wise and population-wise. To make it more comprehensive, the old idea of demarcating constituencies on the basis of professions and economic interests be given a trial. For example, we must have constituencies of farmers, landless labourers, traders, transporters, industrialists, financial institutions, government servants etc. This will automatically reduce the importance of religion and caste.

2. Presidential Form of Government

We have designed our government on the pattern of England and made it a Parliamentary form of government. Experience has shown that this type of government is not able to deliver the goods. The disease of *Aya Ram* and *Gaya Ram* became so acute that it took no time to reduce a majority government into a minority one. So, 52nd amendment of the Constitution was made in 1985, an Anti-Defection Act was passed (Tenth Schedule) and Articles 102(2) and 191(2) were added. But this did not cure the patient. V.P. Singh's Government, which was a minority government, fell and another minority government of Chandra Shekhar was sworn in. Its life was also short. This malady should be immediately cured. It is, therefore, suggested that we should immediately switch over to the Presidential form of Government.

(a) On the pattern of the centre, District States must also have elected Governors called *State-Pradhans*. This will be in keeping with our national pride and culture. They must be Executive Heads, unaffected by the legislative majority or minority.

(b) It is essential that the qualifications of the President of India and *State-Pradhans* of District States should be specified. For example, they should be healthy, holder of Post Graduate Degree, not below 50 years or above 65 years, no criminal record, no record of changing political parties, etc. These high offices should not be retiring places for rejected persons or career giver for the young. Social service needs maturity and experience.

3. Democracy

Democracy can flourish only when:

(a) There are more than one political party with clear cut different ideologies. Till recently, India had only one party, i.e., Congress. It threw a number of political parties with almost similar ideologies formed by power-hungry and disgruntled members of the Congress. So, socialist parties, Lok Dal, Swatantra Party, Janata Dal, Janata Dal (S) were formed and all are chips of the same block. They have Congress culture, Congress mentality, Congress methodology, etc. Now a new political party in Bharatiya Janata Party is coming up with clear cut differences in ideology. It is a good sign for democracy.

(b) There are responsible legislatures. We did two things. First, given adult franchise to the people. Right to vote requires voter's awareness to his rights. In India, less than 70 per cent voters (now 30%) exercise their right to vote. It also requires voter's rational outlook. Here religious and caste considerations sway the voter. Secondly, we have not prescribed qualifications for a legislator. Membership of a House requires, in modern times, capacity to understand and contribute on the Bills or issues that are before the House. Today bulk of the MLAs and MPs are unable to participate in these debates. So, majority of them has no interest in these proceedings. Often the quorum is not complete. Participation of an average parliamentarian is almost zero. So he freely indulges in non-parliamentary work such as appointments, transfers, promotion, sanction of quotas and permits, interference in police and administrative work, etc. All these activities are injurious for democracy.

(c) There is all pervading spirit of nationalism and patriotism. The Constitution should, therefore, provide:

(i) It will be a crime not to exercise one's right of vote.

(ii) Qualifications of a legislator. He should be a Post-Graduate, between the age group of 45 years to 65 years and should have no criminal record. Criminalisation of politics can be controlled only when no criminal is allowed to contest an election.

(iii) A clause in the Constitution, which will debar a legislator from membership of the House if found interfering in administrative affairs be inserted.

(iv) MP or MLA ship should not enable one to lead a life of luxury. So, none (including Ministers) should be allowed to have big houses, telephones, TV and Radio sets, furniture and other equipment beyond a minimum, Air or even first class tickets for free rides, pensions etc. The Constitution should provide these restrictions. Let not the tribe of new Zamindars and Princes be created. And social service should not be considered an investment to collect huge profits. It should not be a profession either.

(v) It will be ideal if in every constituency a vote is cast to a party and not a person. If the party is elected, it should be free to name any person belonging to any religion or caste subject to his fulfilling the conditions prescribed by the Constitution.

4. Secularism and Socialism

(a) Indian Constitution has provided article after article, to encourage secularism and socialism. The condition of Scheduled Castes. Scheduled Tribes, Backward people has remained almost unchanged in spite of reservations in education and servicc. Of course, a few families of a few privileged classes have pocketed most of the benefits of these constitutional provisions. So, implementation of Mandal Commission recommendations will not make much change except creating a new vote-bank and further dividing the country. Similarly, loud talks of secularism have not benefited Muslims at large except some political leaders of Muslim or some political parties who succeeded in exploiting the religious sentiments of minorities. All this has released tendencies of disintgration. It should be stopped.

It is time that we should remove the provisions of secularism and socialism from our Constitution and in their place add the provision of values—human, social and spritual such as Simplicity, Truth, Non-anger, Self-control, Non-stealing , Patriotism etc. The propagation of values will be in tune with our past and so will easily be accepted by the people. This will help in solving several problems which secularism and socialism have failed to solve.

(b) The concept of Indian culture, in keeping with our national pride, histoical facts and patriotism should be encouraged and given an honourable place in our Constitution. We must accept that Babar and his descendants, howsoever great and noble they might have been, were foreign invaders and forcign rulers. Our national pride and patriotism should forbid us to accept them as national heroes. Even the Islamic countries do not take pride in other countries' great men, thoughts, culture etc. For example, in Iran the death day of the great Muslim Caliph Umar is celebrated like *Id* as a day of redemption. Indonesia, which is a Muslim country, takes pride in giving Sanskritised names to their children and enjoying *Ram's Ramlila*. Every Muslim country takes pride in its own culture. So, why can it not be accepted in

India? One not accepting our heroes, our culture, our thought and value system should be deprived of the citizenship right of India.

This political strategy will assist India to march towards the goal of *Anand* and solving our multiple political problems which have been born in free India and/or assumed present magnitude. Probably, this was the picture of *Rama Rajya* of the Father of the Nation, Mahatma Gandhi.

REFERENCES

1. In the General Elections of May 1991, the percentage fell to 25 per cent to 33 per cent. Add to it rigging which is estimated to be 10 per cent and Booth-Capturing. So, the actual voting is 20 per cent or so.
2. *Dharma* is not religion. It is a duty, justice, well-being of people and a code of conduct covering all these aspects.

Reference Bibliography of Scholarly Writings 1917-1994

AICC Economic Review (Periodical), 1969, Gandhi Centenary Number, *AICC Economic Review*, 21 (6-7) October 2, 58p, special issue

Abraham, Abu, 1978, Gandhiji Stages a Come Back, *Seminar* (Annual Number), 221, January, p79-81

Abraham, A.S., 1981, BJP's Gandhian Socialism : Formula for Ideological Amorphousness, *Times of India*, January 2, p8, col 3-5

Acharlu, K.S., 1969, The Joy of Physical Work, *Integrated Management*, 33, January, p 21-24

Acharya Ramamurti
see Ramamurti, Acharya

Achuthan, R., n.d., *Taking Gandhi to People through Seminars*, 2nd edn, foreword by G. Ramachandran, National Committee for National and International Seminars, New Delhi, 14, 61p

Achuthan, R., ed, 1970, *Relevance of Gandhi to Our Times : As Discussed in the Universities and Other Institutions during Gandhi Centenary Year*, foreword by G. Ramachandran, Committee for National and International Seminars, National Committee for the Gandhi Centenary, New Delhi, 6, 202p, footnotes.

Agarwal
see also Agrawal

Compiled under the supervision of former Director, National Social Science Documentation Centre, ICSSR, Government of India, New Delhi.

Agrawal, S.P.
see Anon, 1974, *Mohandas Karamchand Gandhi*

Agarwal, Shriman Narayan
see Shriman Narayan

Agarwala, Amar Narain, n.d., *Gandhism: Socialistic Approach*, Kitab Mahal, Allahabad 56p.

Agnihotri, S.P., 1971, Gandhian Economic Thought : Retrospect and Prospect, *Agra University Journal of Research* (Letters) 19 (1) January, p11-22

Agrawal
see also Agarwal

Agrawal, A.N.,
see Agarwala, Amar Narain

Ahmad, Fakhruddin Ali, 1969, Vital Role of Small Industries in National Economy, *Kurukshetra* (Annual Number), October, p14-16

Aiyer, N. Chandra Shekhara, n.d., *Gandhi's View of Life*, Bharatiya Vidya Bhawan, Bombay

Alexander, Horace G., et al, 1949 *Social and Political Ideas of Mahatma Gandhi*, Indian Council of World Affairs, New Delhi; Oxford University Press, Bombay, 84p

Ambedkar, Bhimrao Ramji, n.d., *What Congress and Gandhi Have Done to the Untouchables*, Thaker & Co, Bombay, 6, 6, 399p, footnotes

Ambedkar, Bhimrao Ramji, 1937, *The Annihilation of Caste and Reply to Mahatma Gandhi*, Bombay

Ammannayan, K.K., 1970, Gandhian Industrial Policy for Today's India, *Rural India* 33 (1-2) January-February, p32-36

Anadkat, N.K., 1969, Gandhism and Marxism : Are They Rival Ideologies? *M.S. University of Baroda Journal,* 18 (1,2) April-July, p149-151, bibliography, footnotes

Anandi, Krishna Swaroop, 1980, Appropriate Technology : Gandhian Perspective, *Rural India* 43(10-11) October-November, p214-215, bibliography

Anandi, Krishna Swaroop, 1982, Appropriate Technology : Gandhian Perspective, *Sarvodaya* 30 (34) September-October, p73-74, bibliography

Anon = Personal Authorship not established

Anandi, Krishna Swaroop, 1982, Gandhi and the New World Order, *Journal of Gandhian Studies* 9(34), January, p127-134, bibliography

Anandi, Krishna Swaroop, 1983, Trusteeship and Participatory Industrial Democracy, *Sarvodaya* 3 (9-10) March-April, p362-368; 30 (11-12) May-June, p436-443, bibliography, footnotes

Andrews, Charles Freer, 1929, *Mahatma Gandhi's Ideas including Selections from His Writings*, Allen and Unwin, London, 382p

Andrews, Charles Freer, 1940, Economic Philosophy of Gandhi, *Education* (Boston), March, p60

Anjaria, Jashwantrai Jayantilal, 1945, *Essay on Gandhian Economics*, Vora & Co, Bombay, 40p

Anon, n.d., *Gandhi : Papers Read at the Seminar on Gandhi Held under the Auspices of Madras University,* Madras University, Madras, 198p, mimeographed

Anon, n.d., *Gandhian Economics and Congress Policy*, Arthavanijya Gabesana Mandir, Calcutta, 32p, bibliography, Monographs on Indian Economic Problems

Anon, n.d., *Gandhian Thought : Papers Read at the Seminar Held under the Auspices of North Bengal University*, North Bengal University, Rajarammohanpur, Darjeeling, 89p

Anon, n.d., *Gandhian Thought and Contemporary Society: Papers Read at the Seminar Held under the Auspicies of University of Allahabad*, University of Allahabad, Allahabad, 136 p, mimeographed

Anon, n.d. *Unesco Seminar: Gandhian Outlook and Techniques*, Ministry of Education, Government of India, New Delhi

Anon, 1930, Daridranarayana or Gandhian Economics, Sunday Times Office, Bombay, 16p, *My Motherland Series*, 81

Anon, 1938, Economic Guidance of Gandhism : A Way of Tackling Indian's Poverty Problems, *Rural India* 1 (2) December, p 76-77

Anon, 1946, *What Gandhiji has done for India : Being a Collection of Articles on Ghandhiji's Life and Work*, introduction by B. L. Rallia Ram, Ilami Markaz, Lahore, 8,184p

Anon,1961, *Basic Principles of the Gandhian Labour Movement : Trade Union Movement on the Indian Railway : Report on the Seminar, Sabarmati*, National Federation of Indian Railwaymen, New Delhi, 2, 120p

Anon,1962, *Gandhiana : Selective List*, Gandhi Smarak Sangrahalaya

Board, New Delhi, 2, 16 p, mimeographed

Anon, 1967, Economic Swaraj, *Link* 10 (8) October 1, p 13-14, illustrations

Anon, 1968, *Gandhian Literature : A Short Bibliography*, Sri Venkateswara University Press, Tirupati, 37p

Anon, 1969, Bibliograpy of Gandhian Economic Literature, *Commerce* (Supplement) 119 (3052) November 1, p viii

Anon, 1969, *Gandhi 100 Years*, United Africa Press Limited, Nairobi, 200 p, illustrations

Anon, 1969, Gandhian Concept, *Indian Worker* 17 (34) May 26, p 9

Anon, 1969, Gandhian Labour Policy, *Commerce* 119 (3049) October 11, p 693

Anon, 1969, *Gandhian Thought: Papers Read in the Seminar Held under the Auspices of the University of Poona, September 28-29*, University of Poona, Pune, mimeographed

Anon, 1969, Gandhiji and Industrial Relations, *Indian Worker* 18 (3) October 20, p 4

Anon, 1969, Gandhiji and Labour, *Social Action* 19(4) October-December, p 340-342

Anon, 1969, *Gandhiji and Labour: Papers of Seminar on Gandhiji and Labour, New Delhi, 1969*, Indian Institute of Labour Studies, New Delhi, mimeographed

Anon, 1969, Gandhiji and Trade Union Movement, *Indian Worker* 18 (2) October 13, p 71

Anon, 1969, Gandhi's Impact on Economic Thought, *Foreign Trade of India* October, p 9-10

Anon, 1969, *Mahatma Gandhi Centenary Souvenir*, Nairobi Sevadal, Nairobi, 2 + 220p

Anon, 1969, Management Philosophy: The Gandhian Ingredients, *Integrated Management*, 33, January, p 25-30

Anon, 1969, Non-Violent Strategy for Trusteeship, *Sarvodaya* 18 (8) February, p 356-365

Anon, 1969, *Papers of Seminar on Mahatma Gandhi Birth Centenary, Kolhapur, 1969*, Shivaji University, Kolhapur, 4, 128p

Anon, 1969, *Relevance of Gandhi for Our Time: Seminar Papers : All Assam Seminar, Guwahati, December 13-14, 1969*, foreward by Liladhar Barooah, Gandhi Centenary Celebration Committee for the State of Assam, Guwahati 6, p 108

Anon, 1969, *Relevance of Gandhi to Our Time : Programme and Papers of Seminar Held under the Auspices of Shirimati Nathibai*

Damodar Thackersey Women's University, Bombay, September 19-20, 1969, SNDT University, Bombay, 8, 12, 154p, bibliography

Anon, 1969, *Relevance of Gandhian Thought : Papers Read at the Seminar Held under the Auspices of the Bombay University, on October 12, 1969,* Bombay University, Bombay, 2, 49 p, mimeographed

Anon, 1969, *Relevance of Gandhiji for Our Times : Papers Read in the Seminar Held under the Auspices of National Integration Samithi, Sri Venkateshwara University, Tirupati, on October 2, 1969,* SV University, Tirupati, 37 p, mimeograped

Anon, 1969, *Relevance of Gandhism in Modern India : Papers Read at the Seminar Held under the Auspices of Kanpur University, September 21-23, 1969,* Kanpur University, Kanpur, 8, 129 p

Anon, 1969, *Thoughts on Gandhiji,* Khadi and Village Industries Commission, Bombay, 6, 75 p, footnotes

Anon, 1969, Trusteeship in Corporate Management as Mahatma Gandhi Saw It, *Indian Worker* 18 (6) November 10, p 4-6, bibliography

Anon, 1969, Why and Where Gandhi Opposed Industrialism, *Kurukshetra* (Annual Number) October, p 9-11

Anon, 1970, (Book Review), *Illustrated Weekly of India* 91(27) July 5, p53; *Southern Economist* 9(4) June 15, p 23; *Swarajya* 14 (46) May 16, p20
Review of the Book: Rao, V.K.R.V., 1970, *The Gandhian Alternative to Western Socialism*, Bharatiya Vidya Bhavan, Bombay, 83p

Anon, 1970, (Book Review), *Swarajya* 15(16) October 17, p 23-24
Review of the Book: Gandhi, Mohandas Karamchand, 1970, *Gandhiji on Trusteeship Management : An Anthology*

Anon, 1970, (Book Review), *Times of India* (Magazine) July 12, p 8, col 3-5
Review of the Book: Merchant, Vijay, 1969, *Gandhi on Trusteeship Management*, Indian Centre for Encouraging Excellence

Anon, 1970, (Book Review), *United Asia* 21 (1) January-February, p 44-45
Review of the Book : Trivedi, H.N., ed, 1969, *Gandhian Trade Union Movement*, INTUC, 72p

Anon, 1970, *Gandhiji's Economic Thought and Its Relevence at Present : A Seminar*, Gujarat University, viii, 193p

Anon, 1970, Gandhiji's Influence on Trade Union Movement-Labour Management Relations The Worker as Co-Trustee, *Indian Worker* 19 (4) October 26, p 8-10, bibliography, footnotes

Anon, 1970, *Papers of International Seminar on Relevance of Gandhi to Our Time, New Delhi, 1970*, Gandhi Peace Foundation, New Delhi, various pagination, bibliography, footnotes

Anon, 1970, *Relevance of Gandhi to Our Times : Papers Read at the Seminar Held under the Auspices of Marathwada University, Aurangabad, January 20, 1970*, Marathwada University, Aurangabad, 8, 69p

Anon, 1970, *Research on Gandhian Thought : Papers and Proceedings of Round Table on Research Programme on Gandhian Thought, Bombay, 1969*, Khadi and Village Industries Commission, Bombay, 8, 129p, footnotes

Anon, 1971, (Book Review), *Commerce* 123 (3153) October, p9738
Review of the Book : Anon, 1971, *Gandhiji's Economic Thought and Its Relevance at Present*, South Gujarat University, 193p

Anon, 1971, (Book Review), *India Quarterly* 27 (9) October-December, p395-396
Review of the Book : Shriman Narayan, 1970, *Relevance of Gandhian Economics*, Navjivan Publishing House, vii, 256p

Anon, 1971, (Book Review), *Khadi Gramodyog* 17 (8) May, p560-561
Review of the Book : Mathur, J.S., 1971, *Industrial Civilisation and Gandhian Economics*, Pustakayan, Allahabad, 8, 175p

Anon, 1971, (Book Review), *Prabudha Bharat* 76 (11) November, p477
Review of the Book : Shriman Narayan, 1970, *Relevance of Gandhian Economics*, Navjivan Publishing House, Ahmedabad, viii, 256p

Anon, 1971, The Discovery of the Charkha, *Sarvodaya* 20 (10) April, p437-439, reprint

Anon, 1971, *Gandhiji : A Bibliography of Books Available in Maulana Azad Library*, Aligarh Muslim University, Maulana Azad Library, Aligarh, 2, 59p

Anon, 1971, *Gandhiji's Economic Thought and Its Relevance at Present*, South Gujarat University, 193p

Anon, 1972, (Book Review), *India Quarterly* 28 (2) April-June, *p167-168*
Review of the Book : Anon, 1970, *Gandhiji's Economic Thought*

and Its Relevance at Present : A Seminar, Gujarat University, viii, 193p

Anon, 1972, (Book Review), *MS University of Baroda Journal*, 21 (2) July, p103-105
Review of the Book : Shriman Narayan, 1970, *Relevance of Gandhian Economics*, Navjivan Publishing House, Ahmedabad, viii, 256p

Anon, 1974, (Book Review), *Triveni* 43 (1) April-June, p78-79
Review of the Book : Shriman Narayan, 1970, *Relevance of Gandhian Economics*, Navjivan Publishing House, vii, 256p

Anon, 1974, *Mohandas Karamchand Gandhi : A Bibliography*, Orient Longmans, New Delhi, 379p, A Project of Indian Council of Social Science Research (carried out by S.P. Agrawal)

Anon, 1975, (Book Review), *Economic and Political Weekly* 10 (45) November 15, p 1769-1770
Review of the Book : Schumacher, E.F., 1975, *Small is Beautiful : Economics as if People Mattered*, Harper, New York, 289p

Anon, 1975, Gandhian Trusteeship : Some Readings and Reflections, *Indian Labour Journal* 16 (9) September, p 1313-1316

Anon, 1976, (Book Review), *Economic and Political Weekly* 11 (46) November 13, p 1793
Review of the Book : Dhanagre, D.N., 1975, *Agrarian Movements and Gandhian Politics*, Agra University, Agra, 127p

Anon, 1976, (Book Review), *Indian and Foreign Review* 13 (20), August 1, p 24-25; *Times of India* March 14, p 10, col 5-8
Review of the Book : Vepa, Ram K., 1975, *New Technology* : A *Gandhian Concept*, Gandhi Book House, 375p

Anon, 1977, (Book Review), *Commerce* 135 (3464) October 22, p 767; *Southern Economist* 15 (23-24) April 1, p13-14
Review of the Book : Upadhyaya, R.B., 1977, *Social Responsibility of Business and the Trusteeship Theory of Mahatma Gandhi*, Sterling, New Delhi, 385p

Anon, 1977, (Book Review), *Journal of Institute of Economic Research* 12 (2) July, p52-53
Review of the Book : Ram Swarup, 1977, *Gandhian Economics : A Supporting Technology*, ATDA, 32p

Anon, 1977, (Book Review), *Times of India*, (Magazine), October 30, p 10, col 1-3
Review of the Book : Mehta, Vadilal Lallubhai, 1977, *Equality*

through Trusteeship, Tata Mc-Graw Hill

Anon, 1978, (Book Review), *Commerce* 137 (3507), August 26, p 374; *Economic Times* April 16, p 4, col 8; *Yojana* 22 (18) October 1, coverpage 2
Review of the Book : Gandhi, Mohandas Karamchand, 1978, *Mahatma Gandhi on Human Settlements,* comp by S.M. Shah, Navjivan Publishing House, Ahmedabad, 62p

Anon, 1978, (Book Review), *Economic Times*, March 26, p. 4, col 3-6; *Eastern Economist* 70 (1) January 6, p 26-27; *Indian and Foreign Review* 15 (7) January 15, p 23-25; *Indian Economic Journal* 25 (4-5) April-June, p 94-96; *Times of India* (Magazine) April 9, p. 1, col. 1-6; *Yojana* 22 (3) February 16, p37-38
Review of the Book : Charan Singh, 1978, *India's Economic Policy : The Gandhian Blueprint*, Vikas Pub, New Delhi, 127p

Anon, 1978, (Book Review), *Indian Journal of Public Administration* 24 (3) July-September, p 870-872
Review of the Book : Vepa, Ram K., 1975, *New Technology : A Gandhian Concept*, Gandhi Book House, 375p

Anon, 1978 (Book Review), *Southern Economist 17 (21) October 15, p24-25*
Review of the Book : Mehta, Vadilal Lallubhai, 1978, Equality through Trusteeship and Full Employment, Bhartiya Vidya Bhavan, Bombay, 164p

Anon, 1978, Farmers and Workers Make India, *Haryana Labour Journal* 9 (2) April-June, p 5-6

Anon, 1979, Towards a New Social Order, *Gandhi Vigyan* 2 (4) July, p 5-12

Anon, 1980, (Book Review), *Soical Sciences Research Journal* 5 (1-2) March-July, p200-206
Review of the Book : Das, Amritananda, 1979, *Foundations of Gandhian Economics*, Allied, New Delhi, 146p

Anon, 1981, Relevance of Gandhian Economics, *Economic Times* (Supplement) October 4, p 1, col 1-4

Anon, 1982, Gandhiji and Industrial Relations, *Indian Worker* 31 (1) October 4, p. 9-13

Anon, 1983, (Book Review), *Economic and Political Weekly* 18 (42) October 15, p 1794-1795; *Economic Times* (Magazine) April 3, p6, col 1-3; *Financial Express* April 3, p 5, col 5-7
Review of the Book : Radhey Mohan, ed, 1982, *Gandhian Economic System,* Zakir Husain Educational Foundation, New

Delhi

Anon, 1983, (Book Review), *Journal of Sociological Studies,* 2, January, p 175-178; *Socialist Perspective* 10 (4) March, p. 291-293
Review of the Book : Sheo Kumar Lal, ed, 1981, *Gandhiji and Village,* Agricole Pub Academy, New Delhi, 101p

Anon, 1985, Gandhi and Nehru on Economic Development, *Survey* 5 (3-4), p 46-54

Anon, 1986, (Book Review), *Hindustan Times* (Magazine) February 23, p viii, col 3-6; *India Quarterly* 42 (2) April-June, p 209-210; *Indian Express* (Magzine) January 15, p 5, col 1-5; *Patriot* February 2, p 4, col 4-7
Review of the Book : Gangal, Anurag, 1985, *New International Economic Order : A Gandhian Perspective*, Chanakya Pub, Delhi, 160p

Anon, 1986, (Book Review), *Mainstream* 24 (44), July 5, p17-20
Review of the Book : Diwan, Romesh and Lutz, Mark, 1985, *Essays in Gandhian Economics,* Gandhi Peace Foundation, New Delhi, xxv, 243p

Anon, 1986, Discussions on Agriculture-Industry Interrelations, Gandhian Thought, *Southern Economist* 24 (18) January 15, p25-26

Anon, 1986, The Swadeshi Movement, *Sarvodaya* 33 (9-10) March-April, p 355-360

Anon, 1987, (Book Review), *Gandhi Marg* 9 (5) September, p380-383
Review of the Book : Charles, K.J. 1986, *Total Development : Essays towards an Integration of Marxian and Gandhian Perspective,* Vikas Pub, New Delhi, 265p

Anon, 1987, (Book Review), *International Studies* 24 (1) January-March, p 76-77
Review of the Book : Gangal, Anurag, 1985, *New International Economic Order : A Gandhian Perspective,* Chanakya Pub, Delhi, 160p

Anon, 1987, (Book Review), *Times of India* (Sunday Review), April 5, p vi, col 5-8
Review of the Book : Sethi, J.D., ed, 1986, *Trusteeship : The Gandhian Alternative*, Gandhi Peace Foundation, New Delhi

Anon, 1987, (Book Review), *Yojana* 30 (24) January 1, p 32
Review of the Book : Radhey Mohan, 1986, *Gandhian Economic System : A Necessity or Utopia*, Vichar, New Delhi, 156p

Anon, 1988, (Book Review), *Journal of Sociological Studies,* 7,

p 194-195
Review of the Book : Diwan, Romes and Lutz, Mark, 1985, *Essays in Gandhian Economics,* Gandhi Peace Foundation, New Delhi, xxv, 243p

Anon, 1992, (Book Review), *Gandhi Marg* 14 (3) October-December, p 533-535
Review of the Book : Jai Narain, 1992, *Economic Thought of Mahatma Gandhi,* Sehgal Publications, New Delhi, x, 175p

Anon, 1992, Gandhiji and the Indian Economy, *Bulletin (of) Madras Development Seminar Series* 22 (11) November, p 517-523; 22 (12) December, p 549-556, bibliography, tables

Anon, 1993, (Book Review), *Seminar,* 286, June, p 45; *Tribune,* June 25, p 4, col 4-7
Review of the Book : Charles, K.J., 1986, *Total Development : Essays toward an Integration of Marxian and Gandhian Perspectives,* Vikas Pub, New Delhi, xiv, 265p

Appadorai, A., 1969, Democracy, Non-Violence and Social and Economic Equality, *AICC Economic Review* 21 (6-7) October 2, p 25-27

Appadorai, A., 1980, Gandhi and the Settlement of Disputes, *Gandhi Marg* 1 (10) January, p. 634-639, bibliography, footnotes

Argus, *pseud*, 1921, *Gandhism cum Non-Cooperation Exposed*, Shiva Prosad Baruah, Calcutta, 8, 173p

Arora, Krishna, 1970, *Gandhian Approach to Labour Problems,* Agra University, PhD thesis

Arora, V.K., 1981, The Relevance of the Gandhian Socio-Economic Philosophy to Contemporary Reality, *Indian Journal of Political Sciences* 42 (4) October-December, p 65-71, bibliography, footnotes

Arunachalam, K., 1984, Gandhian Way of Management : An Example of Trusteeship Management, *Sarvodaya* 32 (5-6) November-December, p 193-197

Arunachalam, K., 1985, Applied Trusteeship, *Gandhi Marg* 7 (8-9) November-December, p 618-624

Arunachalam, K., 1985, Gandhian Way of Management : An Example of Trusteeship Management, *Sarvodaya* 32 (7-8) January-February, p 282-285

Audholia, B.S. and Tripathi, D., eds, 1959, *Gleanings from Gandhian Thought,* foreword by Jayaprakash Narayan, preface by K.L. Dubey, Satyaratha Publications, Jabalpur, 12, 155p

Bajpai, H.K., 1962, Village Economy and Mahatma Gandhi, *Rural India* 25 (3) March, p 97-99

Bakker, Hans, 1982, The Gandhian Path to Development : Realistic Utopia or Romantic Ideology? *Gandhi Marg* 4 (9) December, p 758-778, footnotes

Banker, Shankarlal, 1969, Gandhiji in the Service of Labour, *Indian Worker* 18 (4), October 27, p 6

Barla, C.S., 1978, Economic Dualism and Relevance of Gandhian Economic Policies, *Rajasthan Economic Journal*, January, p 51-76, bibliography

Barooah, Liladhar, *foreword writer*
see Anon, 1969, *Relevance of Gandhi for Our Time*

Barot, Navinchandra, 1985, Industrial Relations : A Gandhian Way, *Indian Worker* 34 (1) October 7, p 11-16

Barr, F. Mary, 1956, *Bapu : Conversation and Correspondance with Mahatma Gandhi*, 2nd edn, foreword by K.G. Mashruwala, International Book House, Bombay, 14, 237p, illustrations

Barthwal, C.P., 1981, Gandhism Reconsidered in the Context of Uttar Pradesh Hills, *Gandhi Marg* 3 (9) December, p 539-544, footnotes

Basham, A.L., *foreword writer*
see Ray, Sibnarayan, ed, 1971, *Gandhi, India and the World*

Basu, Rumki, 1982, Two Approaches to Economic Development, *Radical Humanist* 46 (11) February, p 43-47

Behari, Bepin
see Bepin Behari

Benjamin, N., 1969, Relevance of Gandhiji's Economic Ideas in the First Half of the Twentieth Century : A Case Study, *Journal of Indian History* 47 (3) December, p 529-534, bibliography, footnotes

Benjamin, N., 1971, Gandhiji and National Planning Committee, *Khadi Gramodyog* 17 (6) March p 417-419, bibliography, footnotes

Bepin Behari, 1963, *Gandhian Economic Philosophy*, Vora & Co. Bombay, 15, 157 p, charts, footnotes

Bepin Behari, 1974, Gandhian Approach to Energy Crisis, *Khadi Gramodyog* 20 (8) May, p 292-296

Bernays, Robert Hamilton, 1931, *Naked Fakir*, Victor Gollancz, London, 351p

Bharathi, K.S., 1991, *The Social Philosophy of Mahatma Gandhi*,

Concept Publishing Company, New Delhi, 159p, bibliography, Gandhian Studies and Peace Research Series, 4

Bharathi, K.S., 1994, *Thoughts of Gandhi and Vinoba: A Comparative Study*, Concept Publishing Company, New Delhi, p, Gandhian Studies and Peace Research Series, 9

Bhargava, Gopal, 1982, Relevance of Gandhian Thought for Building Modern India, *Khadi Gramodyog* 29 (3) December, p 125-127

Bhattacharjea, Ajit, 1973, Trusteeship in Industry, *Indian Worker* 21 (45-46) August 13, p 39

Bhattacharjea, Ajit, 1973, Tursteeship in Industry : A Gandhian Campaign Renewed, *Times of India*, July 30, p 4, col 3-5

Bhattacharya, V.R., 1969, Gandhi as a Practical Economist, *Kurukshetra* 18 (2) November, p 19-20

Bhattacharya, Vivek, 1971, The Spirit of Swadeshi, *Khadi Gramodyog* 18(1) October, p 54-59

Bhattacharya, S.N., 1969, Ethics in Gandhian Economics, *AICC Economic Review* 21(6-7) October, p 37-38

Bhave, Vinoba, *introduction writer*

see Mashruwala, Kishorlal, Ghanshamlal, 1956, *Gandhi and Marx*

Bhole, L.M., 1988, A Gandhian Critique of Planned Development in India, *Gandhi Marg* 9 (10) January, p 611-620

Bist, Narayan Singh, 1984, Gandhian Techniques and Rural Development, *Khadi Gramodyog* 30(11) August, p 433-437

Biswas, S.C., ed, 1968, *Gandhi : Theory and Practice, Social Impact and Contemporary Relevance : Proceedings*, preface by Niharranjan Ray, Indian Institute of Advanced Study, Simla, 16, 635p, Transaction, vol 11

Blanchard, Francis, 1987, Gandhiji Would Have Approved Industrial and Rural Workers Partnership, *Indian Worker* 35(21) February, p 4-5

Bonar, James, 1967, *Philosophy and Political Economy*, 2nd reprint, George Allen and Unwin, London

Bose, Nirmal Kumar, n.d., *Gandhi and the Sarvodaya Idea in Theory and Practice,* Nirmal Kumar Bose, Ranchi, 16p, bibliography

Bose, Nirmal Kumar, 1972, Gandhi and National Planning, *Quest,* 75, March-April, p 39-44, bibliography, footnotes

Bose, Nirmal Kumar, *editor*

see Gandhi, Mohandas Karamchand, 1948, *Selections from Gandhi*

Bose, Pradip, 1983, Against Gandhian Mystique, *Janata* 38(22) August, p23-26

Bose, Rabindra Nath, 1956, *Gandhian Technique and Tradition in Industrial Relation,* foreword by B.C. Roy, All India Institute of Social Welfare and Business Management, Calcutta, 6, 6, 228p

Bose, Rabindra Nath, 1957, *Why the Gandhian Way in Industrial Relations,* Shree Saraswati Press, Calcutta, 16p

Boulding, Kenneth E., 1967, *Human Values and Economic Policy,* University Press, New York

Brahmananda, P.R., 1970, A Theoretical Note on the Economic Foundations of Gandhian Society : The Meaning of Poverty, *Interdiscipline* 7(2) Summer, p167-176

Bright, Jagat Singh, 1945, *Himalayan Blunders of Mahatma Gandhi,* Northern India Publishers, Lahore, 181p

Buch, Maganlal A., 1939, *Rise and Growth of Indian Nationalism : Gandhi and His School,* Maganlal A. Buch, Baroda, 8, 246, 7, 2p, bibliography

Capital (Periodical), 1969, New Light on Gandhian Economics, *Capital* 163(4070) July 10, p47-48, editorial

Capra, Fritijof, 1983, *The Turning Point,* Fontana Paperbacks, London

Catlin, George Edward Gordon., *introduction writer*
see Gangal, S.C., 1960, *Gandhian Way to World Peace*

Chaitanya, Krishna, 1977, *Gandhi's Quest of Being in Becoming,* Gandhi Peace Foundation, New Delhi

Chakrabarti, Mohit, 19 , *Gandhian Humanism,* Concept Publishing Company, New Delhi, p, Gandhian Studies and Peace Research Series-5

Chakrabarti, Mohit, 1993, *Gandhian Spiritualism : A Quest for the Essence of Excellence,* Concept Publishing Company, New Delhi, 184p, bibliography, Gandhian Studies and Peace Research Series-7

Chakravarty, Sukhamoy, 1969, Misgivings about Gandhian Economics, *Janata* 24(37-38) October 5, p 43

Chand,
see under full name of the author, e.g., Tara Chand

Chander, Jag Parvesh
see Jag Parvesh Chander

Chandra Shekhara Aiyer, N.
see Aiyer, N. Chandra Shekhara

Charan Singh, 1977, Charan Sets Middle Path for Janata, *Times of India,* November 7, p 1, col 7-8 +

Charan Singh, 1978, *India's Economic Policy : The Gandhian Blueprint,* Vikas Pub, New Delhi, 127p

Charles, K.J., 1982, Modern Technology and Gandhian Economics, *Khadi Gramodyog* 29(1) October, p 9-14, bibliography, footnotes

Charles, K.J., 1986, *Total Development : Essays towards an Integration of Marxian and Gandhian Perspectives,* Vikash Pub, New Delhi, xiv, 265p

Chatterjee, N.N., 1976, Towards Prosperity on the Gandhian Road, *Yojana* 20(17) October 1, p 9-10

Chatterjee, Saibal, 1993, Mahatma and the Market Place, *Times of India,* October 3, p 17, col 1-8

Chatterji, Rakhahari, 1976, Class Conflict and Nation Building : Gandhi and the Indian Labour Movement, *Indian Journal of Political Science* 37(4) October-December, p 42-57, footnotes

Chaturvedi, H.R. *jt author*
see Shah, Ghanshyam and Chaturvedi, H.R., 1983, *Gandhian Approach to Rural Development*

Chaudhary, Ram Narayan, 1959, *Bapu as I Saw Him*, Navjivan Publishing House, Ahmedabad, 6, 274p, illustrations

Chaudhry, Ram Narayan, *foreword writer*
see Vaswani, K.N., 1955, *Glimpses of Gandhi and Gandhism*

Chauhan, J.B. Singh, 1972, Gandhian Concept to Economic and Labour Problems, *Prajana* 17(2) March, p 95-104, footnotes

Chauhan, J.B. Singh, 1979, Gandhian Concept to Labour Movement, *Indian Worker* 28(1) October, p 9-10

Chauhan, J.B. Singh, 1982, Gandhian Approach to Labour Problems, *Khadi Gramodyog* 28(5) February, p233-238, footnotes

Chawla, Om Dutta, 1970, Man, Machine, Management and Gandhi, *Kurukshetra* 18(8) May, p 2 +

Chhibar, V.P., 1969, Gandhi and Industrialisation, *Janata* 24(37-38), October 5-12, p 32

Clark, Colin, 1969, An Economist's Interview with Mahatma Gandhi, *Hindustan Chamber Review,* October, p 33-35

Cole, G.D.H., 1934, *What Marx Really Meant,* London

Commerce (Periodical), 1969, Gandhiji : Ritual and Reality, *Commerce* 119(3048) October 4, p 631-632, editorial

Commerce (Periodical), 1975, The Economic Relevance of Mahatma Gandhi, *Commerce* 131(3359) October 4, p 547-548,

editorial
Commoner, Barry, 1975, *The Closing Circle*, Alfred A. Knopf, New York
Currell, Melville, *jt author*
see Ostergaard, Geoffery and Currell, Melville, 1971, *Gentle Anarchists*
Dabholkar, Devdatta, 1985, Trusteeship : A Blind Alley or a Break-through? *Gandhi Marg* 7(8-9) November-December, p 587-591
Dada Dharmadhikari
see Dharmadhikari, Dada
Dandavate, M.R., 1957, *Gandhiji's Impact on Socialist Thinking*, Praja Socialist Party, Bombay, 2, 13p
Dandavate, Madhu, 1977, *Marx and Gandhi*, Popular Prakashan, Bombay
Dandekar, V.M., 1978, Gandhian Economic System : A Path to Non-Economic Goals, *Mainstream* 16(29) March 18, p11-14 + ; 16(30) March 25, p 15-19
Dandekar, V.M., 1981, Gandhian Economic System : A Path to Non-Economic Goals, *Economic Times* (Supplement) October 4, p 1, col 1-8 +
Dandekar, V.M. and Rath, N., 1971, *Poverty in India*, Indian School of Political Economy Publications, Bombay
Dange, S.A., 1921, *Gandhi vs Lenin*, Liberty Literature, Bombay, 4, 64p
Dantwala, Mohanlal Lalloobhai, 1945, *Gandhism Reconsidered*, Padma Publications, Bombay, 64p
Dantwala, Mohanlal Lalloobhai, 1985, Trusteeship : Its Value Implications, *Gandhi Marg* 7(8-9) November-December, p504-508
Das, Amritananda, 1970, On the Scientific Reinterpretation of Gandhian Economics, *Interdiscipline* 7(2) Summer, p108-129, bibliography, footnotes
Das, Amritananda, 1979, *Foundations of Gandhian Economics*, Allied, New Delhi, 146p
Das, B.C. and Mishra, G.P., eds, 1979, *Gandhi in Today's India*, Ashish Publishing House, New Delhi
Das Gupta, Sugata, 1969, The Hard Core of Gandhi's Social and Economic Thought, *Voluntary Action* 11(5-6) September-December, p 9-13, bibliography, footnotes
Das Gupta, Sugata, 1979, Restraining Development, *Gandhi Marg*

1(1) April, p 21-25

Datta, Amlan, 1986, Gandhian Economic Perspectives: Technology and Urbanization, *Gandhi Marg* 7(11) February, p 743-755, bibliography, footnotes

Datta, Dhirendra Mohan, 1968, *Philosophy of Mahatma Gandhi*, foreword by A. Campbell Garnett, University of Calcutta, Calcutta, 18, 171p

Datta, Pritish Chandra, 1974, Relevance of Gandhian Thought to the Economic Development of South Asia, *Economic Affairs* 19(3) March, p 114-124

Dave, Rohit, 1969, Gandhian Industrial Relations, *Commerce* 119(3048) October 4, p 637

Dave, Rohit, 1977, Indian Political Parties and Decentralised Economy, *Khadi Gramodyog* 24(1) October, p 27-34

Davidson, W.L., 1942, *Political Thought in England : The Utilitarians from Bentham to Mill*, University Press, London

De Mallac, Guy, 1988, Gandhi's Message for Today : Right and Fair Labour, *Sarvodaya* 34(5) January, p26-30

Deo, Shankarrao, 1969, *Could We Not Agree on Gandhi's Alternative to Capitalism*, Sarvodaya Prachuralaya, Thaujavur, 30, 1p

Deo, Shankarrao, 1969, Trusteeship and Gandhian Economic Order: Adopted from 'Could We Not Agree on Gandhi's Alternative to Capitalism', *Hindustan Chamber Review*, October, p 37-43

Desai, Khandubhai K., *foreword writer*
see Soman, Ramchandra Jaganath, 1957, *Peaceful Industrial Relations*

Desai, M.B., 1969, Gandhiji and Village Economy, *M.S. University of Baroda Journal* 18(1-2) April-July, p 79-83

Desai, Mahadev Haribhai, 1927, *Gandhiji in Indian Villages*, S. Ganesan, Madras, 8, 349p

Desai, Mahadev Haribhai, 1928, *With Gandhiji in Ceylon : A Journal of the Tour, with Authorised Version of All Important Speeches*, S. Ganesan, Madras, 6, 2, 159p, illustrations

Desai, Mahadev Haribhai, 1940, *How Does Gandhiji Live at Sevagram*, P.K. Rajagopal, Srirangam, 30p

Desai, Mahadev Haribhai, 1957, *Story of Bardoli*, Navjivan Publishing House, Ahmedabad, 8, 249p, illustrations, maps

Desai, Morarji, *introduction writer*
see Shriman Narayan, 1968, *Gandhi*

Desai, Nirubhai, 1983, Home-Spun Economics, *Economic Times*,

October 2, p7, col 5-8

Desai, Suresh A., 1981, The Role of Price System in Gandhian Economics, *Gandhi Marg* 2(12) March, p673-685, bibliography, footnotes

Deshpande, Arvind A., 1982, The Gandhian Contrast, *Radical Humanist* 46 (11) February, p49-54

Deshpande, M.S., ed, 1958, *Light of India: The Message of the Mahatma*, foreward by G.V. Mavalankar, Wilco Publishing House, Bombay, 16, 231p

Deshpande, P.Y., *introduction writer*
see Tikekar, Indu B., 1970, *Integral Revolution*

Deshpande, Pandurang Ganesh, comp, 1948, *Gandhiana: A Bibliography of Gandhian Literature*, Navjivan Publishing House, Ahmedabad, 12, 239p, Gujarat Vidyapith Gramthavali, 41

Devdutt, 1981, The BJP and Gandhian Socialism : A Case of Ideology-Transplant, *Gandhi Marg* 3 (4) July, p200-213

Devdutt, 1981, Post Independence Gandhian Rural Technology, *Indian Economic Almanac* 1(4) December, p47-57

Devdutt, 1982, Gandhian Economic Programmes after 1947: Khadi and Village Industries, *Indian Economic Almanac* 2(1) March, p37-43

Devendra Kumar, 1983, Industrialism and Indulgence, *Servodaya* 31(1-2) July-August, p25-28

Devi
see under full name of the author, e.g., Sarla Devi

Dewan, Subhash Chander, 1976, Capital Labour Relationship and Gandhiji, *Indian Worker* 25(1) October 4, p 17-22, bibliography

Dewan, Subhash Chander, 1976, Gandhian Approach to Industrial Relations and the Problems of Labour Strike, *Indian Worker* 24(25) April 5, p 4-5+; 24(26) April 12, p 6, bibliography; *Industrial Relations* 28(3) May-June, p110-117, bibliography, footnotes

Dewan, Subhash Chander, 1977, Gandhiji's Concept of Worker Republic, *Haryana Labour Journal* 8(3), July-September, p 26

Dewan, Subhash Chander, 1979, Gandhian Philosophy of Industrial Relations and Its Impact on Trade Unions : Problems and Prospects, *Indian Worker* 28(1) October, p 11-25, bibliography

Dewan, Subhash Chander, 1981, Gandhiji and Trade Union Movement, *Harayana Labour Journal* 12(3) July-September, p7-10

Dhanagre, D.N., 1975, *Agrarian Movements and Gandhian Politics,* Agra University, Agra, 127p

Dharma Vir, 1967, *Gandhi Bibliography,* foreword by Zakir Hussain, preface by D.S. Kothari, 1 Gandhi Smarak Nidhi, Chandigarh, 24, 575p

Dharmadhikari, Dada, 1985, Gandhi and Trusteeship, *Gandhi Marg* 7(8-9) November-December, p 560-562

Dhawan, Gopi Nath, 1946, *The Political Philosophy of Mahatma Gandhi,* Popular Book Depot, Bombay, 16, 356p

Dhawan, Shiv, 1988, Gandhi and Marx on Socialism, *Gandhi Marg* 10(4) July, p 237-240

Dhebar, Uchhvangrai Navalshanker, 1970, Gandhiji and Labour, *Indian Worker* 19(1) October 5, p 20

Dhebar, Uchhvangrai Navalshankar, 1976, Reviving Rural Economy, *Khadi Gramodyog* 23(2) November, p94-95

Dhiman, O.P., 1972, *Gandhian Philosophy : A Critical and Comprehensive Study,* foreword by R.R. Diwakar, Indian Publications, Ambala Cantt, 207p, bibliography

Dhongade, M.P., *jt author*
see Kasar, D.V. and Dhongade, M.P., 1985, Relevance of Gandhian Thought in India's Planning, *Khadi Gramodyog*

Dikshit, Gopi Nath, 1972, *Gandhi's Challenge to Communism*, S.Chand, New Delhi, 10,185p

Dikshit, J.C., 1978, Gandhiji and AITUC, *Indian Worker* 25(1) October 4, p9-15, bibliography

Diwakar, Ranganath Ramachandra, 1949, *Satyagraha in Action,* Singnet Press, Calcutta, 104p, bibliography, illustrations

Diwakar Ranganath Ramachandra, 1965, *Gandhi: A Practical Philosopher,* Bhartiya Vidya Bhavan, Bombay

Diwakar, Ranganath Ramachandra, 1966, *Is Not Gandhi the Answer?* Bhartiya Vidya Bhavan, Bombay, 8, 53p

Diwakar, Ranganath Ramachandra, 1975, Gandhi: His Rare Insight Real India—Rural India, *Khadi Gramodyog* 22(1) October 1, p31-33

Diwakar, Ranganath Ramachandra, *foreword writer*
see Dhiman, O.P., 1972, *Gandhian Philosophy*; Gandhi, Madan G., 1969, *Gandhi and Marx*; Tendulkar, Dinanath Gopal, 1957, *Gandhi in Champaran*

Diwan, Prabhakar, 1971, Base of Gandhian Economics, *Khadi Gramodyog* 17 (11) August, p 725-728, tables

Diwan, Romesh, 1980, Trusteeship and Decentralization, *Gandhi Marg* 1(10) January, p652-659, bibliography, footnotes

Diwan, Romesh, 1981, Towards an Economics of Human Development and the Gandhian Concept of Swadeshi, *Gandhi Marg* 3(1) April, p5-14, footnotes

Diwan, Romesh, 1985, Income Distribution Theories and Gandhian Economics, *Gandhi Marg* 6(10) January, p707-720

Diwan, Romesh, 1986, Gandhian Economic Principles, *Gandhi Marg* 8(3) January, p177-190

Diwan, Romesh and Gidwani, Sushila, 1979, Element in Gandhian Economics, *Gandhi Marg* (5) August, p248-258

Diwan, Romesh and Lutz, Mark, 1985, *Essays in Gandhian Economics*, Gandhi Peace Foundation, New Delhi, xxv, 243p

Dubey, K.L. *preface writer*
    see Audholia, B.S. and Tripathi, D., eds, 1959, *Gleanings from Gandhian Thought*

Dubhashi, P.R., 1969, Gandhiji and Cooperation, *Indian Cooperative Review* 6(2) January, p 161-170; *Journal of National Academy of Administraton* 14(3-4), p 147-156

Dutt
    see also under full name of the author, e.g., Devdutt

Dutt, R.C., 1974, Gandhism and Planning : Growth and Employment, *Indian and Foreign Review* 11(23) September 15, p20-21

Dutt, T.K., 1965, *Teachings of Mahatma Gandhi*, Gandhian Foundation, Gurudaspur, 4, 128p, Gandhian Literature Series-8

Dwivedi, R.S., 1982, The Gandhian Trusteeship System with Special Reference to Labour Relations, *Indian Journal of Industrial Relations* 17(3) January, p 429-439

Economic Affairs (Periodical), 1977, Gandhian Ideals and the Janata, *Economic Affairs* 22 (9-10) September-October, p 325-326, editorial

Engels, Frederick, *jt author*
    see Marx, Karl and Engels, Frederick, 1951, *Selected Works*

Fakhruddin Ali Ahmad
    see Ahmad, Fakhruddin Ali

Farkya, V.K., 1983, Gandhi and Appropriate Technology, *Gandhi Marg* 5(7) October, p421-422

Fischer, Louis, 1954, *Gandhi: His Life and Message for the World*, New American Library of World Literature, New York, 192p

Fischer, Louis, 1969, The Essential Gandhi, *Hindustan Chamber Review*, October, p51-53

Gadre, Kamla, 1967, Syncretic Approach, *Link* 9(30) March 5, p2-3, letter to the editor

Gadre, Kamla, 1971, *Coming Struggle for Trusteeship,* Trusteeship Forum, New Delhi, 3, 120p

Galbraith, John Kenneth, 1970, *The Affluent Society,* 1st Indian edn, Lalvani Publishing House, Bombay

Gandhi, Arun, 1983, Lessons for a Grandsno, *Economic Times* October 2, p6, col 4-8

Gandhi, Madan G., 1969, *Gandhi and Marx: Study in Ideological Polarities,* foreword by R.R. Diwakar, Vikas Bharati, Chandigarh, 14, 132p

Gandhi, Manubehn Jayiukhlal, 1949, *Bapu: My Mother,* Navjivan Publishing House, Ahmedabad, 4,56p

Gandhi, Mohandàs Karamchand
see also Andrews, Charles Freer, 1929, *Mahatma Gandhi's Ideas including Selections from His Writings*; Jack Homer Alexander, ed, 1958, *Gandhi Reader*

Gandhi, Mohandas Karamchand, 1917, *Speeches and Writings of Mahatma Gandhi*, G. Natesan, Madras

Gandhi, Mohandas Karamchand, 1928, *Satyagraha in South Africa,* S. Ganesan, Madras

Gandhi, Mohandas Karamchand, 1930, *Self-Restraint versus Self-Indulgence,* Navjivan Publishing House, Ahmedabad

Gandhi, Mohandas Karamchand, 1932, *From Yervada Mandir,* Navjivan Publishing House, Ahmedabad

Gandhi, Mohandas Karamchand, 1935, *Satyagraha: Non-Violent Resistance,* Navjivan Publishing House, Ahmedabad

Gandhi, Mohandas Karamchand, 1938, *Cent per Cent Swadeshi,* Navjivan Publishing House, Ahmedabad

Gandhi, Mohandas Karamchand, 1938, *Hind Swaraj or Indian Home Rule,* Navjivan Publishing House, Ahmedabad

Gandhi, Mohandas Karamchand, 1940, *An Autobiography or the Story of My Experiments with Truth*, Navjivan Publishing House, Ahmedabad

Gandhi, Mohandas Karamchand, 1940, Mahatma Gandhi on Cottage Industries vs Large Scale Industries, *Rural India* 3(3) March, p126-128

Gandhi, Mohandas Karamchand, 1941, *Constructive Programme: Its*

Meaning and Place, Navjivan Publishing House, Ahmedabad

Gandhi, Mohandas Karamchand, 1941. *Economics of Khadi,* Navjivan Publishing House, Ahmedabad

Gandhi, Mohandas Karamchand, 1944, *Non-Violence in Peace and War,* Navjivan Publishing House, Ahmedabad, 2 vols

Gandhi, Mohandas Karamchand, 1945, *Teaching of Mahatma Gandhi*, ed by Jag Parvesh Chander, Indian Printing Works

Gandhi, Mohandas Karamchand, 1948, *Delhi Diary,* Navjivan Publishing House, Ahmedabad

Gandhi, Mohandas Karamchand, 1948, *Selections from Gandhi*, ed by Nirmal Kumar Bose, Navjivan Publishing House, Ahmedabad

Gandhi, Mohandas Karamchand, 1953, Gandhian Labour Policy, *Indian Journal of Social Work* 14 (2) September, p 212-215

Gandhi, Mohandas Karamchand, 1955, *Khadi*, Navjivan Publishing House, Ahmedabad

Gandhi, Mohandas Karamchand, 1957, *India of My Dreams,* Navjivan Publishing House, Ahmedabad

Gandhi, Mohandas Karamchand, 1957, *Toward Non-Violent Socialism*, Navjivan Publishing House, Ahmedabad

Gandhi, Mohandas Karamchand, 1958, *All Men Are Brothers*, Columbia University Press, New York

Gandhi, Mohandas Karamchand, 1959, *Ashram Observances in Action*, Navjivan Publishing House, Ahmedabad

Gandhi, Mohandas Karamchand, 1959, *Economic and Industrial Life and Relation,* ed by V.B. Kher, Navjivan Publishing House, Ahmedabad

Gandhi, Mohandas Karamchand, 1959, *Gandhiji's Correspondence with the Government, 1944-47,* foreward and introduction by Pyarelal, Navjivan Publishing House, Ahmedabad, 48, 375 p, footnotes

Gandhi, Mohandas Karamchand, 1959, *Truth is God*, Navjivan Publishing House, Ahmedabad

Gandhi, Mohandas Karamchand, 1961, *Voluntary Poverty,* Navjivan Publishing House, Ahmedabad

Gandhi, Mohandas Karamchand, 1962, *My God*, Navjivan Publishing House, Ahmedabad

Gandhi, Mohandas Karamchand, 1967, *The Gospel of Swadeshi*, Bhartiya Vidya Bhavan, Bombay

Gandhi, Mohandas Karamchand, 1968, *Ethical Religion,* Navjivan Publishing House, Ahmedabad

Gandhi, Mohandas Karamchand, 1969, Bapu Vani, *Andhra Pradesh*, 13 (3-4) January-February, p31-32

Gandhi, Mohandas Karamchand, 1969, Economic Vision of Mahatma Gandhi: Excerpts from His Speeches and Writings , *Commerce* 119 (3048) October 4, p 634-635

Gandhi, Mohandas Karamchand, 1969, Gandhiji on Labour: To Striking Worker, *Social Service Quarterly* 55 (1) July, p 8-16

Gandhi, Mohandas Karamchand, 1969, *Rebuilding Our Villages*, Navjivan Publishing House, Ahmedabad

Gandhi, Mohandas Karamchand, 1969, *Sarvodaya,* Navjivan Publishing House, Ahmedabad

Gandhi, Mohandas Karamchand, 1970, *Capital and Labour*, Bhartiya Vidya Bhavan, Bombay

Gandhi, Mohandas Karamchand, n.d., *Gandhiji on Trusteeship Management: An Anthology*

Gandhi, Mohandas Karamchand, 1971, *Service before Self*, Bhartiya Vidya Bhavan, Bombay

Gandhi, Mohandas Karamchand, 1978, *Mahatma Gandhi on Human Settlements*, comp by S.M. Shah, Navjivan Publishing House, Ahmedabad, 62p

Gandhi, Mohandas Karamchand, *foreword writer*
see Kripalani, Jiwatram Bhagwandas, 1956, *Gandhian Way*; Shriman Narayan, 1944, *Gandhian Plan of Economic Development in India*

Gangal, Anurag, 1985, *New International Economic Order : A Gandhian Perspective*, Chanakya Pub, Delhi, 160p

Gangal, Anurag, 1986, Gandhi and the Third World: Quest for Development, *Gandhi Marg* 8 (2) May, p111-116

Gangal, S.C., 1960, *Gandhian Way to World Peace*, introduction by George E. C. Catlin, Vora & Co, Bombay, 18, 159, 1, 2 p, bibliography

Gangal, S.C., 1993, Gandhiji's Growth Plan Deserves a Try, *Times of India*, February 17, p 8, col 7-8

Gangrade, K.D. and Misra, R.P., 19 , *Conflict Resolution through Non-Violence: Role of the Universities*; Volume I : *Science and Ethics*, Concept Publishing Company, New Delhi, p, Gandhian Studies and Peace Research Series-2

Gangrade, K.D. and Misra R.P., 19 , *Conflict Resolution through Non-Violence: Role of Universities*; Volume II: *Development without Destruction*, Concept Publishing Company, New Delhi,

Gandhian Studies and Peace Research Series-3
Ganguli, B.N., 1970, Dadabhai Naoroji, Gokhale and Gandhi as Exponent of National Economic Thought, *Indian Journal of Social Work* 31 (3) October, p243-262
Ganguli, B.N., 1972, *Gandhiji's Vision of Ideal Social Order*, Andhra Mahila Sabha, Hyderabad, 4, 2, 2, 60 p
Ganguli, B.N., 1973, *Gandhi's Social Philosophy*, Vikas Pub, New Delhi
Garnett, A. Campbell, *foreword writer*
see Datta, Dhirendra Mohan, 1968, *Philosphy of Mahatma Gandhi*
Gautam, Sudhakar, 1977, Decentralisation : Its Relevance Today, *Khadi Gramodyog* 24 (1) October, p 66-73
Ghose, Ranen, 1978, Invoking Gandhian Ideas to Solve Unemployment Problem in India, *Economic Affairs* 23 (1-2), January, p 25-28
Ghose, Sisir Kumar, *editor*
see Visvabharati Quarterly (Periodical), 1969-70, Gandhi Number
Ghosh, Sujit Kumar, 1976, Landscape of Gandhian Economics : Our Planners Paradise, *Modern Review* 140 (1) July, p 37-40
Ghosh, Sujit Kumar, 1977, Gandhian Call of Back to the Village and Planning from below, *Economic Affairs* 22 (9-10) September-October, p 361-367, bibliography, footnotes
Gidwani, Sushila, 1985, Gandhian Trusteeship: A Corporate Management Strategy for Economic Justice, *Gandhi Marg* 7 (8-9) November-December, p 653-663
Gidwani, Sushila, *jt author*
see Diwan, Romesh and Gidwani, Sushila, 1979, Elements in Gandhian Economics, *Gandhi Marg*
Giri, S.B.,. 1969, Gandhian Approach to Trade Unions, *Janata* 24(42-43) November, p 30-31
Gokhale, M.S., 1983, Gandhi's Perspective and Village Industries, *Janata* 38 (22) August, p 5-7
Gopinath Menon, K.
see Menon, K. Gopinath
Goray, N.G., *editor*
see Janata (Periodical), 1969, Gandhi Birth Centenary Number
Goswami, Mathuranath, 1967, The Economic Philosophy of Mahatma Gandhi, *Journal of University of Gauhati* 18 (1), p1-7,

bibliography, footnotes

Gould, James W., 1981, Altruistic World Economics : Gandhi Anticipation of a New International Economic Order, *Gandhi Marg* 3 (1) April, p 23-35, footnotes

Goyal, O.P., 1964, *Studies in Modem Indian Political Thought: Gandhi: An Interpretation,* Kitab Mahal, Allahabad, 2, 4, 100 p, footnotes

Gregg, Richard Bartlett, n.d., *Economics of Khaddar,* Navjivan Publishing. House, Ahmedabad

Gregg, Richard Bartlett, n.d., *A Philosophy of Indian Economic Development*, Navjivan Publishing House, Ahmedabad

Gregg, Richard Bartlett, n.d., *The Power of Non-Violence*, Navjivan Publishing House, Ahmedabad

Gregg, Richard Bartlett, 1930, *Gandhism versus Socialism,* John Day, New York, 30p

Gregg, Richard Bartlett, 1931, *Gandhism and Socialism: A Study and Comparison,* S. Ganesan, Madras, 40 p

Gregg, Richard Bartlett, 1941, *A Dicipline for Non-Violence,* Navjivan Publishing House, Ahmedabad

Gregg, Richard Bartlett, 1957, *Which Way Lies Hope? An Examination of Capitalism, Communism, Socialism and Gandhiji's Programme,* Navjivan Publishing House, Ahmedabad, 8, 219p, bibliography

Guhan, Arun Chadra, 1969, Economic Ideas of Mahatma Gandhi, *Indo-Asian Culture* 18(4) October, p18-24

Guha, Arun Chandra, 1970, Gandhi and Decentralisation, *Indian Worker* 19(8) November 23, p5+; *Khadi Gramodyog* 17(1) October, p27-31

Guha, Arun Chandra, 1970, Trusteeship Idea of Gandhiji, *Indian Worker* 18(15) January, p4+, reprint

Guha, Arun Chandra, 1972, Gandhi and Decentralisation, *Khadi Gramodyog* 18(4) January, p229-233

Guha, Arun Chandra, 1975, Present Economic Crisis and Gandhian Economic Theory, *Khadi Gramodyog* 22(1) October 1, p38-42

Gulati, Hans Raj, 1969, Gandhiji and Labour, *Janata* 24(26) July 20, p3-4

Gupta, K.L., 1980, Industrial Democracy, *Indian Worker* 29(1) October, p19-24, bibliography

Gupta, Nagendranath, 1945, *Gandhi and Gandhism,* foreward by K. Natarajan, Hind Kitabs, Bombay, 4, 12p, Sidelights on the

National Movement in India, 1

Gupta, R.P., 1978, Industrial Discipline and Gandhiji, *Indian Worker* 27 (2-3) October 16, p27-28, bibliography

Gupta, R.P., 1978, Is Gandhian Concept of Workers Participation in Management an Utopia, *Indian Worker* 26(41) July 10, p4-5

Gupta, R.P., 1978, Modern India Industrial Structure and Gandhian Norms of Peace, *Indian Worker* 26(16-17) January 23, p27-29

Gupta, R.P., 1980, Gandhiji's Advice to Capital and Labour, *Indian Worker* 29(1) October 6, p47 +

Gupta, Ram Gopal, 1981, Gandhian Strategy of National Reconstruction, *Rural India* 44(11) November, p257-259

Gupta, Ram Gopal, 1982, Gandhian Strategy of National Reconstruction, *Janata* 36(44) January 3, p13-14

Gupta, Shanti S., 1992, *Integrated Development Plan for India: Goal, Tools and Strategies*, Concept Publishing Company, New Delhi, 274p, bibliography

Gupta, Shanti S., 1994, *Economic Philosophy of Mahatma Gandhi*, Concept Publishing Company, New Delhi, 303 p, bibliography Gandhian Studies and Peace Research Series-10

Gurtoo, D.N., 197, A Reappraisal of Gandhian Thought on Income Distribution, *Interdiscipline* 7(2) Summer, p177-184, bibliography, footnotes

Gurupadaswamy, M.S., 1969, Gandhi and Planning for Rural India, *Kurukshetra* (Annual Number) October, p17-18

Guruswamy, M.P., 1977, Gandhiji's Approach towards Decentralisation, *Khadi Gramodyog* 24(1) October, p 83-88

Guruswamy, M.P., 1984, Gandhian Economics, *Sarvodaya* 32(1-2) July-August, p 33-37

Guruswamy, M.P., 1985, Trusteeship: The Grand Alternative to Capitalism, *Sarvodaya* 33(3-4) September-October, p 105-111

Guruswamy, M.P.,1985, Trusteeship: A Revolutionary Method of Transforming the Present Social Order, *Gandhi Marg* 7(8-9) November-December, p 608-617

Guruswamy, M.P.,1986, Gandhian Approach to Agrarian Reform, *Sarvodaya* 33(11-12) May-June, p 479-484, foootnotes

Handa, Madan L., 1980, The Exiting World Order: A Gandhian Interpretation, *Gandhi Marg* 2(8) November, p421-430, footnotes

Handique, Bhubanchandra, 1967, A Note on Bapuji's Concept of Swadeshi and Industry, *Journal of the University of Gauhati*

18(1), p 93-96

Harijan (Periodical), *Harijan*, all issues

Haryana Labour Journal (Periodical), 1975, Mahatma Gandhi on Workers Life and Living, *Haryana Labour Journal* 6(1) January-March, p 5-6 +

Hathi, Jai Sukhlal, 1969, Seminar on Gandhi and Labour, September 29-30, 1969: Text of Jai Shukhlal Hathi's Address, *Indian Workers* 18(1) October 6, p 50 +

Heilbroner, Robert L., 1969, *Economic Means and Social Ends*, Prentice-Hall, New Jersey

Heilbroner, Robert L., 1976, *Business Civilisation in Decline* Marion Boyars, London

Heilbroner, Robert L., 1983, *The Wordly Philosophers*, Pelican Books

Henderson, Hazel, 1978, *Creating Alternative Futures*, Berkley Publishing Corporation, New York

Heney, Lewis H., 1964, *History of Economic Thought*, 7th edn, Macmillan Company, New York

Herbert , G.S. and Tripathi. D., 1973, Gandhiji on Poverty, *Sarvodaya* 22(8), p 337-341

Hetten, Bjorn and Gordon, Tamm, 1971, The Developement Strategy of Gandhian Economics, *Journal of Indian Authropological Society* 6(1) April, p51-66, bibliography, footnotes

Hindustan Chamber Review (Periodical), 1969, (Special Issue), *Hindustan Chamber Review*, October, 101p, special issue

Hines, Lawrence G., 1973, *Environmental Issues*, Norton and Company, New York

Hira Rai
see Rai, Hira

Hirsch, Fred, 1977, *The Social Limits to Growth*, Routledge and Kegan Paul, London

Huq, A.M., 1981, Economics of Growth and Employment: The Gandhian Approach, *Gandhi Marg* 2(10) January, p572-578

Huq, A.M., 1984, Economics of Income Distribution: A Gandhian Perspective, *Gandhi Marg* 6(6) September, p454-465, bibliography

Huq, A.M., 1986, Investment Criteria in Gandhian Economics, *Gandhi Marg* 8(2) May, p98-106, footnotes, tables

Huq, A.M., 1987, Investment in Human Capital: The Gandhian Perspective, *Gandhi Marg* 9(6) September, p362-369

Huq, A.M., 1988, The Theory of Consumer Behaviour: The Gandhian Model, *Gandhi Marg* 8(6) September, p348-356

Hussain, Zakir
see Zakir Hussain

Huxley, Aldous, 1938, *Ends and Means*, London

Inder Jit, 1987, Current Crises and the Mahatma, *Economic Times* August, p5, col 7-8

India Quarterly (Periodical), 1949, *Social and Political Ideas of Mahatma Gandhi*, Indian Council of World Affairs, New Delhi; Oxford University Press, Bombay, 84p, special issue

Indian Worker (Periodical), 1969, Gandhiji and Labour, *Indian Worker* 18(1) October 6, p2, editiorial

Indo-Asian Culture (Periodical), 1969, Mahatma Gandhi Centenary Number, *Indo-Asian Culture* 18(4) October, 4, 48p, special issue

Interdiscipline (Periodical), 1970, Gandhi and Economics, *Interdiscipline* 7(2) Summer, p103-234, special issue

Iyengar, B.R.I., 1986, Gandhian Approach, *Mainstream* 24(28) March 15, p22-23

Jack, Homer Alexander, ed, 1956, *Gandhi Reader: A Source Book of His Life and Writings*, Indian University Press, Bloomington, 23, 532p, bibliography, footnotes

Jag Parvesh Chander, *editor*
see Gandhi, Mohandas Karamchand, 1945, *Teaching of Mahatma Gandhi*

Jagdish Prassad, 1988, Gandhi's Views on Village Industries, *Gandhi Marg* 10(4) July, p230-236

Jai Narain, 1992, *Economic Thought of Mahatma Gandhi*, Sehgal Publications, New Delhi, x, 175p

Jain, L.C., 1980, Essence and Relevance of Gandhian Economics: A Review Article, *Gandhi Marg* 2(8) November, p421-430, footnotes

Jain, L.C., 1983, Mahalanobis Overrides the Mahatma, *Economic Times*, October 2, p3, col 1-5 +

Janata (Periodical), 1969, Gandhi Birth Centerary Number, ed by N.G. Goray, *Janata* 24(37-38) October 5-12, 47p, illustrations, special issue

Jauhari, B.M., 1985, Relevance of Gandhian Economics to Rural India, *Southern Economist* 24(11) October 1, p19-21, bibliography

Javadekar, A.G., *jt editor*

see M.S. University of Baroda Journal (Periodical), 1969, Gandhi Centenary Number

Jayaprakash Narayan, 1975, *Total Revolution*, Sarva Seva Sangh Prakashan, Varanasi

Jayaprakash Narayan, *foreword writer*
see Audholia, B.S. and Tripathi, D., eds, 1959, *Gleanings from Gandhian Thought*

Jaysukhlal, Manubehn
see Gandhi, Hanubehn Jaysukhalal

Jesudasan, I., 1975, Towards a New Earth: A Gandhian Manifesto, *Gandhi Marg* 19(2-3) April-June, p141-167, bibliography, footnotes

Jesudasan, I., 1986, Sarvodaya: Gandhi's Critique of the Old Ideas of Economics, *Gandhi Marg* 8(1) April, p9-22, footnotes

Jesudasan I. and Kurseoing, S.J., 1969, Gandhian Economics , *Sarvodaya* 19(5-6) November-December, p231-240

Jha, Adiya Prasad, *assist*
see Misra, B.B., ed, 1963, *Select Documents*...

Jha, S.N., 1954, The Concept of Standard of Living in Gandhian Economic Thought, *Rural India* 17(11) December, p419-422

Jha, S.N., 1954, Gandhian Economic Thought, *Rural India* 17(10) November, p377

Jha, S.N, 1955, The Basic Principles of Production in Gandhian Economics Thought, *Rural India* 18(1) January, p13-16

Jha, S.N., 1955, Centralization versus Decentralization in Gandhian Economic Thought, *Rural India* 18(4) April, p133-138

Jha, S.N., 1955, The Concept of Cooperation in Gandhian Economic Thought, *Rural India*, 18(7) July, p253-255

Jha, S.N. 1955, The Concept of Economic Equality in Gandhian Economic Thought, *Rural India* 18(9) September, p331-338

Jha, S.N., 1955, Gandhi's Role as an Ideal, Practical, Social Man in Gandhian Economic Thought, *Rural India* 18(8) August, p291-295

Jha, S.N., 1955, Industrialization vs Self-Sufficiency in Gandhian Economic Thought, *Rural India* 18(3) March, p101-110

Jha, S.N., 1955, Labour-Capital Relations in Gandhian Economic Thought, *Rural India* 18(2) February, p55-59

Jha, S.N., 1955, Man and Machinery in Gandhian Economic Thought, *Rural India* 18(6) September, p213-218

Jha, S.N., 1956, Commercial and Financial Politics in Gandhian

Economic Thought, *Rural India* 19(11) November, p405-408

Jha, S.N., 1956, Economic Bias in Gandhian System of Education, *Rural India* 19(10) October, p382-386

Jha, S.N., 1956, Production by the Masses in Gandhian Economic Thought, *Rural India* 18(5) May, p172-182

Jha, S.N., 1957, The Problem of Birth Control in Gandhian Economic Thought, *Rural India* 20(1) January, p7-8

Jha, S.N., 1961, *Critical Study of Gandhian Economic Thought*, foreword by J.C. Kumarappa, Lakshmi Narain Aggarwal, Agra, 4,4,4,216,2p

Jha, S.N., 1965, Trade Unionism in Gandhian Economic Thought, *Rural India* 19(12) December, p443-446

Jha, Shiva Chandra, 1969, Gandhian Theory of Trade Unionism, *Mainstream* 8(8) October 25, p29-31

Jha, Shiva Chandra, 1979, Gandhi and Industrial Relations, *Mainstream* 17(30) March 24, p7-10

Joshi, P.C, 1969, Distrust of the Rising Forces of Commercial Civilization, *Times of India* (Supplement) October 2, p v, col 1-8

Joshi, P.C., 1988, Gandhi's Economic Approach, *Mainstream* 26(15), p11-15, bibliography

Joshi, R.D., 1969, Wealth and Society: Gandhian Ideology, *Bombay Labour Journal*, 9 December, p19-23, bibliography, footnotes reprint

Journal (of) Maharaja Sayajirao University of Baroda (Periodical) *see* M.S. University of Baroda Journal (Periodical)

Juyal, B.N., 1973, The Role of Religious and Ethical Factors in Development: A Gandhian Point of View, *Religion and Society* 20 (4) December, p42-53

Jyotishi, R.P., 1984, Development of Wardha as a Gandhi District: Why and How, *Gandhi Marg* 5(10) January, p693-702

Kabad, B.K.R., 1978, The Genuine Gandhian Path: Lost Signposts Need to be Rediscovered, *Times of India*, June 20, p6, col 3-5

Kabra, Vijendra, 1969, Mahatma Gandhi: Great T.U. Leader, *Indian Worker* 18(8) November 24, p3

Kalarthi, Mukulbhai, 1960, *Anecdotes from Bapu's Life*, Navjivan Publishing House, Ahmedabad, 47p

Kalelkar, Dattatray Balakrishna, 1960, *Stray Glimpses of Bapu*, 2nd rev ed, Navjivan Publishing House, Ahmedabad, 8, 166p, footnotes

Kalelkar, Dattatray Balakrishna, *foreword writer*

see Prabhu, Ramachandra Krishna and Kalelkar, Rabindra, comps, 1961, *Truth Called Them Differently*

Kalelkar, Kaka

see Kalelkar, Dattatray Bala Krishna

Kalelkar, Rabindra, *jt compilor*

see Prabhu, Ramachandra Krishna and Kalelkar, Rabindra, comps, 1961, *Truth Called Them Differently*

Kalmar, George, 1980, Gandhian Economics: Does It Exist, *Man and Development* 2(2) June, p39-51, footnotes

Kamal Vir, 1981, Gandhian Approach to Planning, *Khadi Gramodyog* 27(5) February, p283-287, footnotes

Kamta Prasad, 1987, Contemporary Relevance of Gandhian Economic Thought, *Gandhi Marg* 8(10) January, p596-607, bibliography

Kanthi, Mahendra S., *jt author*

see Ross, David F. and Kanthi, Mahendra S., 1983, *Gandhian Economics*

Kapil Kumar, 1983, Peasants Perception of Gandhi and His Programme: Oudh, 1920-1922, *Social Scientist* 11(2) February, p16-30, footnotes

Karunakaran, K.P., 1980, Gandhi and the Nation-Building in India, *Gandhi Marg* 2(5) August, p256-270

Karunakaran, K.P., 1988, The Emerging Recognition of Gandhi's Legacy, *Indian Worker* 37(1-2) October 3-10, p11-17

Kasar, D.V. and Dhongade, M.P., 1985, Relevance of Gandhian Thought in India's Planning, *Khadi Gramodyog* 31(6) March, p247-250

Kaul, P.N., 1969, Relevence of Gandhian Approach to Industrialisation, *Journal of National Academy of Administration* 14(3-4), p107-124, bibliography, footnotes

Kedia, Kusum Lata, 1981, Gandhian Concept of Technology and Rural Development, *Khadi Gramodyog* 27(8) May, p381-385

Kennedy, Nancy J., 1956, *Gandhian Economy and Indian Economic Planning*, Fletcher University (USA), PhD thesis

Keynes, John M., 1960, *The General Theory of Employment, Interest and Money*, Macmillan & Co, London

Khamborkar, K.R., 1976, Gandhi and Trade Union Movement, *Indian Worker* 25(4) October 25, p5

Khamborkar, K.R., 1981, Relevance of Gandhian Principles, *Indian Worker* 29(18) February 2, p5 +

Khcr, V.B., *editor*
see Gandhi, Mohandas Karamchand, 1959, *Economic and Industrial Life*

Khullar, M.M., 1969, Relevence of Gandhian Economics, *AICC Economic Review* 21(6-7) October 2, p41-45; *Indian Worker* 18(4) October 27 p4 +

Khurana, V.K., 1983, A Bold Experiment, *Indian Worker* 32(2) October 10, p15-17

Khusro, A.M., 1983, Relevence of Gandhi in Economic Planning: His Thought Permeates Our Planning Process, *Yojana* 27 (19) October, p46

Kothari, D.S., 1977, *Some Thoughts on Science and Religion*, Shri Raj Krishan Jain Charitable Trust, New Delhi

Kothari, D.S., *preface writer*
see Dharma Vir, 1967, *Gandhi Bibliography*

Kothari, V.N., 1969, Political Economy of Mahatma Gandhi, *M.S. University of Baroda Journal* 18(1-2) April, July, p89-100, bibliography, footnotes

Kothari, V.N., *jt editor*
see M.S. University of Baroda Journal (Periodical), 1969, Gandhi Centenary Number

Kripa Shankar, 1988, Relevance of Gandhi to India's Rejuvenation, *Mainstream* 26(29) April, p11-12

Kripalani, Jiwatram Bhagwandas, 1938, *Gandhian Way*, foreword by M.K. Gandhi, Vora and Co, Bombay, 8 + 183p

Kripalani, Jiwatram Bhagwandas, 1938, *Non-Violent Revolution*, Bombay

Kripalani, Jiwatram Bhagwandas, 1956, *Gandhi: A Political Study*, 2nd edn, Akhil Bharat Serva Sewa Sangha, Kashi, 95p

Kripalani, Jiwatram Bhagwandas, 1961, *Gandhian Thought*, Gandhi Smarak Nidhi, New Delhi; Orrient Longmans, Bombay, 14, 2, 281p

Kripalani, Jiwatram Bhagwandas, 1966, *Gandhiji and World Peace and Gandhiji's Economic Ideas*, University of Poona, Pune, 12, 11, 21p, mimeographed, Mahatma Gandhi Lectures, 4th series, 1966

Kripalani, Jiwatram Bhagwandas, 1969, Gandhiji and Organisation, *AICC Economic Reveiw* 21(6-7) October 2, p13-15

Kripalani, Jiwatram Bhagwandas, 1969, Gandhiji's Economic Ideas,

Hindustan Chamber Review, October, p15-21

Kripalani, Jiwatram Bhagwandas, 1969, Swadeshi, *Kurukshetra* (Annual Number) October, p19-22

Kripalani, Jiwatram Bhagwandas, 1970, *Gandhi: His Life and Thought*, Publications Divison, Government of India, New Delhi, 13, 3, 508p, bibliography, footnotes, Builders of Modern India

Kripalani, Jiwatram Bhagwandas, 1981, The Only Remedy: Back to Gandhi, *Gandhi Vigyan* 5(1) October, p28-30

Krishna

see also under full name of the author, e.g., Raj Krishna

Krishna, B., 1969, Gandhiji Wanted Employer Lobour Relations to be Very Different from What They Are Today, *Times of India*, August 24, p8, col 2-7

Krishna Chaitanya

see Chaitanya, Krishna

Krishna Mohan Prasad, 1966, *Gandhian Concept of Sarvodaya*, University of Patna, PhD, thesis

Krishnamurti, J., 1975, *Freedom from the Known*, ed by Mary Lutyens, B.I. Publications, New Delhi

Krishnaswami, P.R., 1969, Gandhiji and the Sewing Machine, *Swarajya* 13(42) April 19, p13-14

Krishnaswami, P.R, 1969, Gandhiji's Concept of Sarvodaya and Cooperation, *Indian Co-operative Review* 6(3) April, p319-29, bibliography, footnotes

Kumar

see under full name of the author, e.g., Kapil Kumar

Kumarappa, Bharatan, 1938, Gandhiji's Way to Peace and Progress, *Rural India* 1(1) November, p23-27

Kumarappa, Bharatan, 1940, *Capitalism, Socialism and Villagism*, Madras

Kumarappa, Joseph Cornelius, n.d., *Peace and Prosperity*, All India Village Industries Association, Wardha

Kumarappa, Joseph Cornelius, n.d., *Present Economic Situation*, All India Village Industries Association, Wardha

Kumarappa, Joseph Cornelius, n.d., *Public Finance and Our Poverty*, Navjivan Publishing House, Ahmedabad

Kumarappa, Joseph Cornelius, 1942, The Gandhian Approach to Planned Economy, *Indian Journal of Social Work*, 2(4) March, p399-412

Kumarappa, Joseph Cornelius, 1942, *Planned Economy: A Gandhian*

Approach, All India Village Industries Association, Wardha, 14p

Kumarappa, Joseph Cornelius, 1945, *Gandhian Economy and the Way to Release It*, C.P. and Berar Students' Congress, Wardha, 18p

Kumarappa, Joseph Cornelius, 1947, *Gandhian Economy and Other Essays*, All India Village Industries Association, Wardha, 47p; 2nd edn, 1949, 3,2,120,6p

Kumarappa, Joseph Cornelius, 1948, *Europe through Gandhian Eye*, All India Village Industries Association, Wardha, 4, 29p

Kumarappa, Joseph Cornelius, 1949, The Gandhian Approach to Economics, *India Quarterly*, p36-52

Kumarappa, Joseph Cornelius,1951, *Gandhian Economic Thought*, Vora & Co., Bombay, 73p, bibliography, Library of Indian Economics series

Kumarappa, Joseph Cornelius, 1952, *Gandhian Way of Life*, All India Village Industries Association, Wardha, 4, 48, 49p

Kumarappa, Joseph Cornelius, 1960, *Why the Village Movement*, Akhil Bharat Sarva Seva Sangh Prakashan, Kashi

Kumarappa, Joseph Cornelius, 1984, *Economy of Permanence*, Sarva Seva Sangh Prakashan, Varanasi, 2 vols

Kumarappa, Joseph Cornelius, *jt editor*
see, Rajagopalachari, Chakravarti and Kumarappa, Joseph Cornelius, eds, 1947, *Nations Voice*

Kumarappa, Joseph Cornelius, *foreword writer*
see Jha, S.N., 1961, *Critical Study of* Gandhian Economic *Thought*

Kupinba, Rao M., 1978, Is Gandhian Economic Theory Relevant Today, *Economic Studies* 19(2) August, p159-161

Kurichiyel, Jose Mathew, 1985, Relevance of Gandhian Economics, *Southern Economist* 23(21-22) March1, p15-16.

Kurseong, S.J., *jt author*
see Jesudasan, I. and Kurseong, S.J., 1969, *Gandhian Economics, Sarvodaya*

Kutty, M.K., 1982, Gandhiji's Conception of a New World Order, *Journal of Gandhian Studies* 9(34) January, p91-100, bibliography

Lal
see under full name of the author, e.g., Sheo Kumar Lal

Lalwani, K.C., 1969, Gandhiji's Contribution to the Economics of Industrial Labour, *Indian Labour Journal* 10(10) October, p1297-1309.

Lenin, *Selected Works of Lenin*, 4 vols.

Lester, Muriel, 1945, *Gandhi: World Citizen*, Kitab Mahal, Allahabad, 201p

Lohia, Rammanohar, 1963, *Marx, Gandhi and Socialism*, Nava Hind Publications, Hyderabad, 8, 58, 550p

Lutyens, Mary, *editor*
see Krishnamurti, J., 1975, *Freedom from the Known*

Lutz, Mark, 1983, Human Nature in Gandhian Economics: The Case of Ahimsa or Social Affection, *Gandhi Marg* 4(12) March, p941-955, bibliography, footnotes

Lutz, Mark, *jt author*
see Diwan, Romesh and Lutz, Mark, 1985, *Essays in Gandhian Economics*

Lutz, Mark A. and Lux, Kenneth, 1979, *The Challenge of Humanistic Economics*, Benjamin/Cummings Publicity Company, California

Lux, Kerneth, *jt anthor*
see Lutz, Mark A. and Lux, Kenneth, 1979, *The Challenge of Humanistic Economics*

M. S. University of Baroda Journal (Periodical), 1969, Gandhi Centenary Number (Combined Humanities and Social Science Number), ed by A.G. Javadekar and V.N. Kothari, *M.S. University of Baroda Journal* 18(1-2) April-July, 4,157p, illustrations, special issue

Mahadev Prasad, 1958, *Social Philosophy of Mahatma Gandhi*, foreword by S. Radhakrishnan, Vishwavidyalaya Prakashan, Gorakhpur, 16,342p, bibliography

Mahadevan, T.K., *jt editor*
see Ramachandra, G. and Mahadevan, T.K., eds, 1967, *Gandhi*; Ramachandran, G. and Mahadevan, T.K., eds, 1970, *Quest for Gandhi*

Mahadevan, T.M.P., ed, 1968, *Relevance of Mahatma Gandhi to the World of Thought : Gandhi Centenary Volume*, foreword by N.D. Sundaravadivelu, University of Madras, Madras, 2,10, 182p

Mahajan, O.P., 1986, Gandhian Economic Theory: Summary of Group Discussions: Rapporteurs Reports of 68th All India Economic Conference, Ahmedabad, December 27-31, 1985, *Indian Economic Journal* 33(4) April-June, p174-180

Mahajani, G.S., *foreword writer*
see Misra, D.K., ed, n.d., *Gandhi and Social Order*

Mainstream (Periodical), 1969, Special Issue on Gandhi Brith Centenary, *Mainstream* 8(5) October 4, 37p special issue

Malkani, N.R., 1972, *Ramblings and Reminiscences of Gandhi*, Navjivan Publishing House, Ahmedabad, 8, 244p

Mallik, Gurdial, 1961, *Gandhi and Tagore*, Navjivan Publishing House, Ahmedabad, 8, 77p, illustrations

Malviya, R.K., 1969, Gandhiji and Labour, *Indian Worker* 18(3) October 20, p6 +

Mao-Tse Tung, *Selected Works of Mao-Tse Tung*, 4 vols

Mapara, Goverdhan, 1969, Mahatma Gandhi's close Association with Labour, *Indian Worker* 18(9) December, p6 +

Marshal, Alfred, 1959, *Principles of Economics*, 8th edn, Macmillan and Co, London

Marx, Karl, *Capital*, Foreign Languages Publishing House, Moscow

Marx, Karl, and Engels Frederick, 1951, *Selected Works*, Foreign Languages Publishing House, Moscow

Mashruwala, Kishorlal Ghanshyamlal, 1941, *Practical Non-Violence*, Navjivan Publishing House, Ahmedabad; 2nd edn, 1947

Mashruwalia, Kishorlal Ghanshyamlal, 1956, *Gandhi and Marx*, Introduction by Vinoba Bhave, Navjivan Publishing House, Ahmedabad, 7, 1, 117p

Mashruwala, Kishorlal Ghanshyamlal, *foreword writer*
, *see* Barr, F. Mary, 1956, *Bapu*

Mathews, P.M., 1969, Gandhiji Wartime Economy Diet, *Modern Review* 124(7) July, p523-524

Mathur, Gautam, 1970, The Framework of Planning for Economic Growth and Social Justice, *Interdiscipline* 7(2) Summer, p130-166, bibliography, figures, footnotes

Mathur, J.S., 1977, Decentralisation: Need for Clear Perspective, *Khadi Gramodyog* 24(1), October, p106-111.

Mathur, J.S., 1982, Gandhiji and New World Order, *Journal of Gandhian Studies* 9(34) January, p116-126, bibliography

Mathur, Jaganath Svarup, 1959, *Essays on Gandhian Economics*, Chaitanya Publishing House, Allahabad, 6, 86p, footnotes

Mathur, Jaganath Svarup, 1969, Gandhiji's Concept of Trusteeship, *Religion and Society* 16(3) September, p26-34, footnotes

Mathur, Jaganath Svarup, 1971, *Industrial Civilization and Gandhian Economics*, Pustakayan, Allahabad, 8, 175p

Mathur, Jaganath Svarup, ed, 1970, *Youth on Gandhi*, foreword by Tara Chand, Pustakayan, Allahabad, 8, 103, 119p

Mathur, Kamal, 1980, Relevance of Gandhian Economics, *Prashasnika* 9(1-2) January-June, p73-78

Mathur, P.C., 1969, Economic Planning in India and the Relevance of Gandhian Thought, *Journal of National Academy of Administration* 4(3-4), p65-88, bibliography, footnotes

Mathur, V.S., 1969, Gandhian Approach to Industrial Relations, *Indian Worker* 18(4) October 27, p7, bibliography

Mauriya, Anil, 1986, The Growth and Apparent Disapperance of Ideology : A Few Tentative Observations, *Janata* (Annual Number) 41(1), p11-12

Mavalankar, G.V., *foreword writer*
see Deshpande, M.S., ed, 1958, *Light of India*

Mazumdar, A.K., 1979, Gandhi's Concept of Decentralisation and Indian Planning, *Journal of Jiwaji University* (Humanities) 1(1) December, p11-13

Meadows, Donella H., et al, 1974, *The Limits to Growth*, Potomac Associates, New York

Mehta, Ashok, 1935, *Socialism and Gandhism*, Congress Socialist Publishing Company, Bombay, 4,25p

Mehta, Behram H., 1942, A Case for Industrilization of India, *Indian Journal of Social Work* 2(4) March, p459-471

Mehta, J.K., 1985, *Gandhian Thought*, Ashish Publishing House, New Delhi

Mehta, Kanti, 1978, Relevence of Gandhi, *Indian Worker* 26(20) February, p7-10

Mehta, Prayag, 1982, Gandhi on Workers Quality of Life, *Indian Worker* 31(1) October 4, p15

Mehta, R.R., 1969, Gandhian Economics and Under-developed Areas, *Yojana* 13(13) July 13, p8

Mehta, Rajendra R., 1970, New Dimension of Gandhian Economics, *Journal of Gujarat Research Society* 32(2) April, p68-72

Mehta, Vadilal Lallubhai, 1977, *Equality through Trusteeship*, Tata Mc-Graw Hill

Mehta, Vadilal Lallubhai, 1978, *Equality through Trusteeship and Full Employment*, Bhartiya Vidya Bhavan, Bombay, 164p

Mehta, Vadilal Lallubhai, 1980, Gandhian Approach: The Only Salution for India, *Economic Times*, April 18, p5, col7-8

Menon, K. Gopinath, 1971, Gandhi and His Economics, *Khadi Gramodyog* 17(12) September, p733-736

Merchant, Vijay, 1969, *Gandhi on Trusteeship Management*, Indian

Centre for Encouraging Execellence

Mishra, G.P., 1977, Gandhian Model of Rural Development: A Retrospect and Prospect, *Economic Affairs*, 22(9-10) September-October, p372-384, bibliography

Mishra, G.P., *jt editor*
see Das, B.C. and Mishra, G.D., eds, 1979, *Gandhi in Today's India*

Mishra, S.N., 1969, A Model of Gandhian Economy, *Indian Economic Journal* 17(1) July-September, p101-11, bibliography, footnotes

Misra, B.B., ed, 1963, *Select Documents on Mahatma Gandhi's Movement in Champaran, 1917-18*, assisted by Aditya Prasatjha Secretariat Press, Patna, 8, 2, 597, 9p, bibliography, maps, tables

Misra, D.K., ed, n.d., *Gandhi and Social Order*, foreword by G.S. Mahajani, Research Publications in Social Sciences, Delhi, 8,128p

Misra, Panchanan, 1985, Indian National Congress: The Gandhian Concept, *National Herald* (Sunday Herald) November 10, p1, col 1-4

Misra, R.P., ed, 19 , Gandhian Model of Development and World Peace, Concept Publishing Company, New Delhi, p, Gandhian Studies and Peace Research Series, 1

Misra, R.P., *jt editor*
see Gangrade, K.D. and Misra, R.P., 19 , *Conflict Resolution through Non-violence*

Mitra, Roma, 1987, Gandhian Philosophy and Its Relevance to Rural Development, *Gandhi Marg* 9(2) May, p88-89, bibliography, footnotes

Mohan
see under full name of the author, e.g., Radhey Mohan

Mohan Rao, U.S., ed, 1968, *The Message of Mahatma Gandhi*, Publications Division, Government of India, New Delhi

Mookerjee, H.C., *foreword writer*
see Sen, Ananth Gopal, 1947, *World Situation and Gandhian Economics*

Morgon, A.E., n.d., *Search for Purpose*, Navjivan Publishing House, Ahmedebad

Mukherjea, D.C., 1969, Dignity of Labour, *Andhra Pradesh* 13(12) October, p12-13

Mukherjee, Chittapriya, 1981, Gandhian Economics: A Gospel of

'Damned Waitlessness', *Khadi Gramodyog* 27(4) January, p275-282, bibliography, footnotes

Mukherjee, Dhurjati, 1974, Gandhi and Rural Development, *Khadi Gramodyog* 21(1) October, p39-42

Mukherjee, Dhurjati, 1977, Efficacy of Gandhian Economic Decentralisation, *Khadi Gramodyog* 24(1) October, p42-48

Mukherjee, Dhurjati, 1978, Equality through Trusteeship, *Khadi Gramodyog* 24 (8) May, p437-439

Mukherjee, Dhurjati, 1982, Planning and Rural Development: Thc Gandhian Perspective, *Gandhi Marg* 4(6) September, p 601-610, bibliography, tables.

Mukherjee, Hiren, 1960, *Gandhi: A Study*, end rev edn, People's Publishing House, New Delhi, 7, 3, 225 p, bibliography, footnotes

Muniandi, K., 1984, Micro Planning: Gandhian Way, *Khadi Gramodyog* 30(10) July, p 393-395

Muniandi, K., 1987, Gandhiji's Contribution to Indian Economy, *Khadi Gramodyog* 33 (9) June, p 369-373.

Muniandi, K., 1988, Economics of Peace and Prosperity, *Khadi Gramodyog* 34 (7) April, p 291-294.

Munjee, Nasser M., 1978, "Gandhian Blueprint" of Charan Singh: Random Thought and Theorising, *Economic Times*, February 25, p5, col 3-84

Murthy
see under full name/surname of the author, e.g., Shantha Murthy, M.C.

Muzumdar, Haridas Thåkordas, 1952, *Mahatma Gandhi: Peaceful Revolutionary*, Charles Scribner's Sons, New York, 16, 127p, Twentieth Century Library

Myrdal, Gunnar, 1957, *Economic Theory and Under-developed Regions*, Gerald Duckworth and Co, London

Nagarajan, N.V., 1986, Mahatma Gandhi and Khadi Movement, *Khadi Gramodyog* 32(11) August, p 495-497

Nageshwar Prasad, 1964, The Doctrine of Trusteeship, *AICC Economic Review* 16(8) September 25, p 9-12, bibliography

Nageshwar Prasad, 1979, Technology and Polity : A Gandhian Approach, *Gandhian Perspective* 2(1) October, p87-98, bibliography.

Nageswara Rao
see Rao, Nageshwar

Nair
see under full name/surname of the author, e.g., Sreekantan Nair, N.

Nair, Pyarelal
see Pyarelal

Namboodripad, Ernakulam Manakkle Sankaran, 1958, *The Mahatma and the Ism*, People's Publishing House, New Delhi, 4, 130 p

Nandwani, S.C., 1980, Gandhi's Concept of Rural Reconstruction in the Context of Present Community Development, *Gandhi Marg* 2(6) September, p 349-356, footnotes.

Nandy, Ashis, 1983, Critic of Conventional Modernity, *Economic Times*, October 2, p. 3, col 1-8 +

Narasimha Reddy, D., 1971, Feasibility of the Gandhian Model of Industrial Relations in the Modern India Industry, *Interdiscipline* 8(1) Spring, p 7-11, bibliography

Narain
see under full name of the author, e.g., Jai Narain

Narayan
see also under full name of the author, e.g., Jayaprakash Narayan

Narayan Rao, J.S., 1982, Gandhian Planning and Poverty, *Gandhi Marg* 4(7) October, p681-686, bibliography, footnotes

Narayan Rao, J.S., 1982, Indian Planning: How Far Is It Based on Gandhian Philosophy? *Southern Economist* (Annual Number) 21(1) May 1, p 25-28, bibliography

Narayana, K.L., 1964, *Gandhi in the Eyes of the World*, K.L. Narayana Research Institute, Tenali, 4,74p, portraits, publication no, 26

Narayanan, K.R., 1979, Relevance of Gandhism Today, *Mainstream* 17(32) April 7, p 14

Narendra Prasad, 1987, Gandhian Economics and Village Industry, *Gandhi Marg* 9(9) December, p 563-567.

Narula, A.L., 1980, Village Reconstruction: Gandhian Approach, *Khadi Gramodyog* 25(5) February, p 205-207.

Natarajan, K., *foreword writer*
see Gupta, Nagendranath, 1945, *Gandhi and Gandhism*

Navin Kumar, 1969, Gandhiji and Labour, *Indian Worker* 17 (42) July 21, p 6 +

Navin Kumar, 1978, Gandhian Labour Ideology, *Yojana* 22(8) May 1, p 17-18

Nehru, Jawaharlal, 1936, *An Autobiography*, London

Nehru, Jawaharlal, 1948, *Nehru on Gandhi:A Selection, Arranged in the Order of Events, from the Writings and Speeches of Jawaharlal Nehru*, John Day Company, New York, 10, 150p

Nehru, Jawaharlal, *foreword writer*
see Tendulkar, Dinanath Gopal, 1960-63, *Mahatma*

Nehru, Jawaharlal, *introduction writer*
see Tendulkar, Dinanath Gopal, et al, eds, 1944, *Gandhi*

O' leary, Basil, 1980, An Approach to Gandhian Economics, *Gandhi Marg* 2 (3) June, p 132-147, bibliography, footnotes

Oommen, T.K., 1981, Gandhi and Village : Towards a Critical Appraisal, *Gandhi Marg* 2 (10) January, p 588-595, footnotes

Ostergaard, Geoffrey and Currell, Melville, 1971, *Gentle Anarchists : Study of the Leaders of the Sarvodaya Movement for Non-Violent Revolution in India*, Oxford University Press, London, 10, 421p, bibliography, tables

Padmanabhan, R., 1975, Gandhiji and the Five Year Plans, *Modem Review* 137 (3) March, p 85

Padmanabhan, R., 1976, Gandhiji's Views on Machinery and Mass Production, *Modem Review* 139 (2) February, p 135-136

Palshikar, Vasant, 1969, Gandhiji's Economic Ideas : Their Present Relevance, *Janata* 24, (37-38) October 5-12, p23-27, bibliography

Panda, G.S., 1975, An Eulogy to Gandhi, *Khadi Gramodyog* 22 (1) October 1, p 78-81, tables

Pandey, B.K., 1987, Contributions of Women in Socio-Economic Development : A Gandhian Approach, *Gandhi Marg* 9 (9) December, p 531-537

Pandey B.P., 1989, Towards a Gandhian Approach to Planning: *Khadi Gramodyog* 35 (4) January, p 177-184

Panditrao, Y.A., 1981, Gandhiji's Economic Ideas, *Economic Times* (Supplement) October 4, p 11, col 1-4

Panditrao, Y.A., 1986, Rural Development : A Gandhian Perspective, *Khadi Gramodyog* 32 (10) July, p 455-462

Panditrao, Y.A., 1987, Rural Development : A Gandhian Perspective, *Journal of Rural Development* 6 (3) May, p 288-301, bibliography

Patel, M.S., 1953, *The Educational Philosophy of Mahatma Gandhi*, Navjivan Publishing House, Ahmedabad, 16, 288p, bibliography

Pateria, A.K., 1984, Industrial Relations and Gandhian Approach, *Gandhi Marg* 6 (3) June, p 150-157, bibliography, footnotes

Pattabhi Sitaramayya, Bhogaraju, 1930, *Currency and Exchange: Eleven Points of Mahatma Gandhi*, Bhogaraju Pattabhi Sitaramayya, Masulipatan, 40p

Pattabhi Sitaramayya, Bhogaraju, 1938, *Socialism, and Gandhism*, Hindustan Publishing Co, Rajahmundry (Andhra), 2, 8, 2, 2, 2, 244p, World Today Series

Pattabhi Sitaramayya, Bhogaraju, 1943-44, *Gandhi and Gandhism : A Study*, Kitabistan, Allahabad, 520p, 2 vols

Pattanayak, Kishen, 1969, The Idea of Trusteeship, *Mankind* 13 (8) October, p 23-26

Pigou; A.C., 1952, *Economics of Welfare*, 4th edn, MacMillan and Co, London

Pillai, A.S., 1985-86, Gandhiji's Approach to Rural Development, *Journal of Gandhian Studies* 13 (51-52) October 1985-January 1986, p 47-56

Pohekar, G.S., *editor and preface writer*
see Rao, U.R., 1971, *Mahatma Gandhi*

Polak, Henry Salomon Leon, et al , 1930, *Mahatma Gandhi*, 7th edn, G. A., Natesan, Madras, 7, 8, 136, 32p

Power, Paul F., ed, 1971, *Meanings of Gandhi*, University Press of Hawaii, Honolulu, 8, 199p

Prabhakar Diwan
see Diwan, Prabhakar

Prabhu, Ramachandra Krishna, comp, 1954, *This Was Bapu*, Navjivan Publishing House, Ahmedabad, 19, 178p

Prabhu, Ramachandra Krishna and Kalelkar, Rabindra, comps, 1961, *Truth Called Them Differently : Tagore Gandhi Controversy*, foreword by Kaka Saheb Kalelkar, Navjivan Publishing House, Ahmedabad, 16, 139p

Pradhan, R.C., 1969, Gandhi : The Trade Unionist, *Janata* 24 (37-38) October 5-12, p 36 +

Prasad
see under full name of the author, e.g., Rajendra Prasad

Productivity (Periodical), 1969-70, Gandhi : The Model of Productivity, *Productivity* 10(3) Winter, p 448-449, editorial

Punekar, S.K., 1969, Gandhian Approach to Industrial Relations, *Indian Worker* 18 (13) December, p 4

Puttaswamy, K., 1970, Gandhian Labour Philosophy, *Indian Worker* 19 (1) October 5, p 23

Pyarelal, 1959, *Gandhian Techniques in the Modern World*, 2nd edn,

Navjivan Publishing House, Ahmedabad, 6, 66p

Pyarelal, 1976, Gandhiji's Concept of Swadeshi, *Kurukshetra* 25(6) December 16, p 4-5

Pyarelal, 1977, Gandhiji's Concept of Swadeshi, *Bombay Civic Journal* 24(6) August, p 6-7

Pyarelal, 1983, A Formula of Trusteeship, *Sarvodaya* 30(11-12) May-June, p 457-458

Pyarelal, *foreword and introduction writer*
see Gandhi, Mohandas Karamchand, 1959, *Gandhiji's Correspondence with the Government, 1944-47*

Radha Raman Singh, 1989, The Growing Relevance of Gandhian Economics, *Gandhi Marg* 10(12) March, p 798-804

Radha Raman Singh, 1984, Relevance of Gandhi's Economic Idea in Indian Planning, *Khadi Gramodyog* 30(6) March, p 239-248, bibliography

Radhakrishnan, Sarvapalli, ed, 1939, *Mahatma Gandhi : Essays and Reflection on His Life and Work, Presented to Him on the Seventieth Birthday, October 2, 1939,* Allen and Unwin , 382p, footnotes

Radhakrishnan, Sarvapalli, ed, 1968, *Mahatma Gandhi : 100 Years*, Gandhi Peace Foundation, New Delhi, 12, 401p, footnotes

Radhakrishnan, Sarvapalli, *foreword writer*
see Mahadev Prasad, 1958, *Social Philosophy of Mahatma Gandhi*

Radharaman Singh
see Radha Raman Singh

Radhey Mohan, 1986, *Gandhian Economic System : A Necessity or Utopia*, Vichar, New Delhi, 156p

Radhey Mohan, ed, 1982, *Gandhian Economic System*, Zakir Husain Educational Foundation, New Delhi

Raghavan, V.P., 1986, Reflection on Gandhian Economics, *Gandhi Marg*, 8 (2) May, p 107-110, footnotes; *Haryana Labour Journal* 17(4) October-December, p9-10

Raghavan, V.P., 1987, Gandhian Alternative for Economic Progress, *Gandhi Marg* 9 (7) October, p430-433

Raghavendra Rao, K., 1985, The Moral Economy of Trusteeshisp, *Gandhi Marg* 7 (8-9) November-December, p495-503

Raghavendra Rao, V., 1985-86, Gandhiji's Approach to Rural Development, *Journal of Gandhian Studies* 13(51-52) October1985-January1986, p22-27

Rai, Hira and Yadava, T.N., 1970, Bibliography on Gandhian Economics, *Interdiscipline* 7 (2) Summer, p 220-222

Raj Krishna, 1969, Some Reflections on Gandhian Economics, *Times of India* (Supplement) October 2, p 1-8 +

Raj Krishna, 1978, Nehru-Gandhi Polarity and Economic Policy, *Mainstream* 16(49), August 5, p8-12 +; *Voluntary Action* 20(9) September, p 4-10 +

Rajagopalachari, Chakravarti and Kumarappa, Joseph Cornelius, eds, 1947, *Nations Voice : Being a Collection of Gandhiji's Speeches in England and Sjt Mahadev Desai's Account of the Sojourn, September to December 1931*, 2nd edn, Navjivan Publishing House, Ahmedabad, 8, 254p

Rajeev, P.V., 1981, Gandhi on Economic Problems, *Economic Times* (Supplement) October 4, p11, col 6-8 +

Rajendra Prasad, 1949, *Satyagraha in Champaran*, 2nd edn, Navjivan Publishing House, Ahmedabad, 12, 224p

Rajendra Prasad, 1962, *Legacy of Gandhiji*, Shiva Lal Agarwala, Agra, 6, 130p, footnotes, portrait

Rajendra Prasad, *foreword writer*
see Shriman Narayan, 1948, *Gandhian Plan Reaffirmed* Shriman Narayan, 1960, *Principles of Gandhian Planning*

Rajkrishna
see Raj Krishna

Rallia Ram, B.L., *introduction writer*
see Anon, 1946, *What Gandhi Has Done for India*

Ram
see under fullname/surmane of the author, e.g., Ram Swarup; Umaram, R.I.

Ram Bhushan Singh, 1981, Gandhi and Development, *Interdiscipline* 3(2) April, p 71-93, bibliography

Ram Bhushan Singh, 1987, Economic Thought of Gandhi and Its Relevance, *Gandhi Marg* 9(8) November, p 477-490

Ram Swarup, n.d., *Gandhism and Communism*, Jyoti Prakashan, New Delhi

Ram Swarup, 1977, *Gandhian Economics : A Supporting Technology*, ATDA, 32p

Rama Shankar Singh, 1987, Poverty, Unemployment and Gandhian Economics, *Gandhi Marg* 9(6) September, p 336-345

Ramachandran, G., 1969, The Core of Gandhian Economics, *AICC Economic Review* 21(6-7) October, p 17-19

Ramachandran, G., *foreword writer*
see Achuthan, n.d., *Taking Gandhi to People through Seminars*; Achuthan, R., 1970, *Relevance of Gandhi to Our Times*

Ramachandran, G. and Mahadevan, T.K., eds., 1967, *Gandhi : His Relevance for Our Times*, 2nd rev edn, Gandhi Peace Foundation New Delhi; Bharatiya Vidya Bhavan, Bombay, 16, 393p, bibliography, footnotes

Ramachandran, G. and Mahadevan, T.K., eds, 1970, *Quest for Gandhi*, Gandhi Peace Foundation, New Delhi; Bhartiya Vidya Bhavan, Bombay, 12, 458p, footnotes

Ramadhar, 1973, Gandhian Doctrine of Trusteeship : A Measure of Social Control, *Indian Worker* 21(50) September 10, p 5 +

Ramamurthi
see under Ramamurti

Ramamurti, Acharya, 1982, Gandhiji and Rural Industries, *Voluntary Action* 25 (1) July-August, p 33-35

Ramamurti, Acharya, 1983, Gandhiji and Rural Industries, *Sarvodaya* 30(9-10) March-April, p 369-374

Ramamurti, Acharya, 1985, Trusteeship : In Agriculture, *Gandhi Marg* 7(8-9) November-December, p 6-2-607

Ramanujan, G., 1969, Gnadhiji and Labour, *Indian Worker* 18(1) October 6, p 7 +

Ramanujan, G., 1969, The Order of Society : Gandhian Trade Union's Role, *Integrated Management*, 38, June, p 21-24

Ramanujan, G., 1979, Gandhian Approach to Trade Union Movements, *Indian Worker* 28 (1) October, p 5-7

Ramashankar Singh
see Rama Shankar Singh

Ramayya, Bhogaraju Pattabhi Sita
see Pattabhi Sitaramayya, Bhogaraju

Rameshwari Verma, P.R.
see Verma, P.R. Rameshwari

Ramjee Singh, 1982, Trusteeship: India's Gift to the World, *Journal of Gandhian Studies* 9(34) January, p 76-90, bibliography

Ramraj, B., 1969, Economic Ideas of Gandhiji, *Chartered Accountant* (Supplement) 18(4) October, p 53-56

Ranga, N.G., 1945, *Four Crore Artisans Hail the Gandhian Plan*, Hind Kitabs, Bombay, 2, 22p

Ranga, N.G., 1969, Gandhism-Negativism-Socialism, *Sarvodaya* 19(1) July, p 19-22

Ranga, N.G. 1969, *Bapu Blesses*, introduction by C. Rajagopalachari, Indian Peasant Institute, Nidubrolu 12, 96p

Rao

see also under full name/surname of the author, e.g., Narayan Rao, J.S.

Rao, H.K., 1983, Gandhian Technique of Trade Unionism, *Economic Times*, October 2, p 6, col 4-8

Rao, Nageshwar, 1981, Gandhian Way to Rural Development, *Khadi Gramodyog* 27(10) July, p 478-481, footnotes

Rao, Nageshwar, 1984, Relevance of Gandhian Thought in the Context of Planning in India, *Khadi Gramodyog* 30(9) June, p 357-363

Rao, Nageshwar, 1985, Organisation of Strikes : Gandhian Way, *Khadi Gramodyog* 31(8) May, p 325-330, bibliography

Rao, Nageshwar, 1985-86, Gandhian Approach to Rural Development, *Journal of Gandhian Studies* 13(51-52) October 1985-January 1986, p 40-46

Rao, S.N., 1983, Gandhi and Class Struggle, *Indian Worker* 32(2) October, 10, p 11-13

Rao, U.R., 1971, *Mahatma Gandhi : The Man and His Mission*, ed with a Preface by G.S. Pohekar, United Asia Publications, Bombay, 4, 4, 112p, bibliography, footnotes, plates

Rao, V.K.R.V., 1970, The Gandhian Alternative to Western Socialism, *India Quarterly* 26(4) October-December, p 331-352, bibliography, footnotes

Rao, V.K.R.V., 1970, *Gandhian Alternative to Western Socialism*, Bhartiya Vidya Bhavan, Bombay, 83p

Rao, V.K.R.V., 1978, Gandhi and Socialism, *Yojana*, 22(4), March 1, p 11-15

Rao, V.K.R.V., 1982, *Indian Socialism*, Concept Publishing Company, New Delhi

Rao, V.K.R.V., 1985, Trusteeship as the Gandhian Instrument for Socialist Change, *Gandhi Marg* 7(8-9) November-December, p 481-494

Rath, N., *jt author*

see Dandekar, V.M. and Rath, N., 1971, *Poverty in India*

Rau, B.R.K. 1965, Gandhian Economic Thought and Indian Development, *AICC Economic Review* 16(18) February 18, p 1316; 16(19) March 10, p 35-39

Rau, B.R.K., 1975, Gandhian Economic Thought, *Khadi Gramodyog*

21(11) August, p 485-492

Rau, B.R.K., 1980, Gandhian Thought to Solve World Problems, *Indian Worker* 29(1) October, p 29-32

Raval, M.N., et al, eds, 1971, *Summary Report of Discussions and Text of Papers Presented at the Seminar Held under the Auspices of South Gujarat University, Surat*, foreword by C.N. Vakil, South Gujarat University, Surat, 10, 193p

Ray, Niharranjan, *preface writer*
see Biswas, S.C., ed, 1968, *Gandhi*

Ray, Sibnarayan, ed, 1970, *Gandhi, India and the World : An International Symposium*, foreword by A.L. Basham, Nachiketa Publications, Bombay 14, 384p

Reddy
see under full name/surname of the author, e.g., Narasimha Reddy, D.

Rieger, Hans Chistopher, 1970, Gandhi and Economics, *Interdiscipline* 7(2) Summer, p 105-107

Righy, Andrew, 1986, Practical Utopianism: A Gandhian Approach to Rural Community Development in India, *Sarvodaya* 33(7-8) January-February, p 329-334, footnotes; 33(9-10) March-April, p 390-396

Rivett, Kenneth, 1959, *Economic Thought of Mahatma Gandhi*, Allied Publishers, Bombay, 4, 32p, footnotes

Robins, Lionel, 1949, *An Essay on the Nature and Significance of Economic Science,* 2nd edn, MacMillan and Co, London

Rolland, Romain, 1963, *Mahatma Gandhi*, Publications Division, Government of India, New Delhi, 130p

Romesh Diwan
see Diwan, Romesh

Ross, David F. and Kanthi, Mahendra S., 1983, *Gandhian Economics*, Prasad Publications, Bangalore

Rothermud, Indira, 1985, 'Satyagrahi Socialism' or Trusteeship of Wealth, *Gandhi Marg* 7(8-9) November-December, p 592-601, bibliography, footnotes

Roy, B.C., *foreword writer*
see Bose, Rabindra Nath, 1956, *Gandhian Technique and Tradition in Industrial Relation*

Roy, Ramashray, 1983, The Gadfly, *Economic Times* October 2, p 3, col 6-8 +

Roy, Ramashray, 1984, *Gandhi Soundings in Political Philosophy*,

Delhi, Chanakya Publications
Roy Burman, B.K., 1988, Gandhian Approach to Nation Building, *Mainstream* 26(25) April 2, p 18-21
Ruskin, John, 1960, *Unto this Last*, George Allen and Unwin Ltd, London
Russel, Bertrand, 1957, *History of Western Philosophy*, George Allen and Unwin Ltd, London
Sachs, Ignacy, 1977, Gandhi and Development, *Seminar,* 219, November, p 16-21, footnotes
Sahasrabudhe, V.G., 1983, The Economic Aspects of Gandhian Philosophy, *Janata* 38(27) October 2, p 5-8
Sahasrabudhey, Sunil, 1983, Gandhi and the Challenge of Modern Science, *Gandhi Marg* 5(6) September, p 330-337
Sahay, B.N., *jt editor*
see Vidyarthi, L.P., et al, eds, 1970, *Gandhi and Social Sciences*
Sahaya, R., 1984, Trusteeship for Harmonious Industrial Relations, *Khadi Gramodyog* 30(12) September, p473-477
Saibaba, V.V.S., 1981, Gandhian Philosophy and the Elimination of Rural Poverty, *Rural India* 44(1) January, p 10-12
Saith, Hira Lal, 1944, *Gandhi : Nationalist or Internationalist*, Indian Printing Works, Lahore, 136p
Samuelson, Paul A., 1980, *Economics*, 11th edn, McGraw Hill, Auckland
Sancheti, D.C., 1962, Rural Reconstruction : The Gandhian Approach, *Rural India* 25(9) October, p327-331, references
Santhanam, K., 1974, Gandhi and Road Reconstruction, *Gandhi Marg* 18(3) July, p 188-191
Santhanam, K., 1974, Gandhism and Communism, *Swarajya* (Annual Number), p31-32
Sarkar, P.C., 1985-86, Gandhi: The Precursor of Development Planning, *Journal of Gandhian Studies* 13(51-52) October1985-January1986, p28-32
Sarkar, P.C., 1985-86, Gandhian Theory of Village Development, *Journal of Gandhian Studies* 13(51-52) October 1985-January 1986, p66-74
Sarla Devi, 1980, Direction of Constructive Work, *Gandhi Marg* 2(3) June, p148-152
Sarma
see also Sharma
Sarma, A.C., 1985, Gandhian Concept of Rural Development, *Khadi*

Gramodyog 31(10) July, p 407-411

Sarma, N.H. Sitarama, 1976, Gandhian Structure of Rural Power, *Khadi Gramodyog* 22(10) July, p 419-426

Saxena, K.S., ed, n.d., *Gandhi Centenary Papers*, Publication Division, Council of Oriental Research, Bhopal, 4 vols

Schumacher, E.F., 1975, *Small is Beautiful : Economics as if People Mattered*, Harper, New York, 289p

Schumacher, E.F., 1978, *A Guide for the Perplexed*, ABACUS edn, Sphere Books Ltd, London

Schumacher, E.F., 1980, *Good Work*, Harper and Row Publishers, New York

Schumpeter, Joseph A., 1961, *History of Economic Analysis*, 4th reprint, George Allen and Unwin Ltd, London

Scitovsky, T., 1976, *The Joyless Economy*, Oxford University Press, Oxford

Seethalakshmi, K.A., 1969, Concept of Trusteeship. *Hindustan Chamber Review*, October, p99-101

Seminar (Periodical), 1963, Gandhism : A Symposium on the Theory and Practice of Non-Violence and Truth, *Seminar*, 46, June, 9,51p, bibliography, Special issue

Sen, Ananth Gopal, 1947, *World Situation and Gandhian Economics*, foreword by H.C. Mookerjee, Book House, Calcutta (2), 4, (2), 2, 2, 82, 21p, bibliography, illustrations

Sen, Mankumar, 1964, *Gandhian Way and the Bhoodan Movement*, Sarva Seva Sangh Prakashan, Varanasi, 72p

Sen, Mankumar, 1981, Planning in Third World Gandhian Innovatives, *Capital* 187 (4670) August 17, p 6-9 +

Sen, Mankumar, 1981, Self-Reliance : Keynote of a Gandhian Economics, *Capital* (Annual Number), p77-81

Sen, P.C., 1968, Gandhiji's Real Economics, *Indian Worker* 17(6) November 11, p 3-4; *Lok Rajya* 24(10) October 1, p 2-6

Sen Gupta, S. and Vinod Narayan Singh, 1986, Gandhian Economics: Its Relevance Today, *Southern Economist* 25(11) October 1, p5-7, bibliography

Sen Gupta, S. and Vinod Narayan Singh, 1987, Gandhian Economics: Its Relevance Today, *Khadi Gramodyog* 33(12) September, p489-494

Sethi, J.D., 1979, Poverty, Alienation and the Gandhian Wayout, *Gandhi Marg* 1(4) July, p 183-197; *Janata* 34(4) February 25, p13-16; 34(7) March 18, p15-16; 34(8) March 25, p16

Sethi, J.D., 1983, Relevance of Gandhi in Economic Planning : No, Not so, Argues Prof Sethi, *Yojana* 27(19) October, p7-11

Sethi, J.D., 1983, Right to Work versus Mainstream Planning, *Economic Times*, October 2, p 4, col 1-8

Sethi, J.D., 1985, Economic Task and Trusteeship, *Gandhi Marg* 7(8-9) November-December, p 625-631

Sethi, J.D., 1985, Gandhian Critique of Modern Economic Theory, *Gandhi Marg* 7(6) September, p 327-329

Sethi, J.D., 1985, Trusteeship and the Crisis in Economic Theory *Gandhi Marg* 7(8-9) November-December, p 540-559

Sethi, J.D., 1986, Gandhian Critique of Modern Economic Theory, *Mainstream* 24(21) January, p 12-14 +

Sethi, J.D., 1986, The Mahatma and the Technocrat, *Sarvodaya* 33(9-10) March-April, p 361-368

Sethi, J.D., 1988, Gandhi on Poverty and Employment, *Mainstream* 27(12) December, p 11-14

Sethi, J.D., ed. 1986, *Trusteeship : The Gandhian Alternative*, Gandhi Peace Foundation, New Delhi

Sethi, J.K., 1978, *Gandhi Today*, Vikas Pub., New Delhi

Shah, C.G., 1963, *Marxism, Gandhism, Stalinism*, Popular Prakshan, Bombay, 30, 360p

Shah, Ghanshyam and Chaturvedi, H.R., 1983, *Gandhian Approach to Rural Development*, Ajanta Book International, Delhi, 140p

Shah, K.K., 1974, Why Gandhiji Pleaded for Planning at Village Level, *Swarajya* (Annual Number), p 33-34

Shah, S.M., *compiler*
see Gandhi, Mohandas Karamchand, 1978, *Mahatma Gandhi on Human Settlements*

Shah, Shantilal, 1969, Gandhian Approach to Labour, *Indian Worker* 18(7) November 17, p 6-7 +

Shankar
see under full name of the author, e.g., Kripa Shankar

Shantha Murthy, M.C., 1987, An Evaluation of A.M Huq's Gandhian Model of the Theory of Consumer Behaviour, *Gandhi Marg* 8(12) March, p 759-764

Sharma
see also Sarma

Sharma, A.K., 1994, *Gandhian Perspective on Population and Development*, Concept Publishing Company, New Delhi, p, Gandhian Studies and Peace Research Series-8

Sharma, Anil Kumar, 1967, Mahatma Gandhi : The Economist, *Journal of University of Gauhati* 18(1), p 131-135

Sharma, Bishan Sarup, 1956, *Gandhi as a Political Thinker,* foreword by Shriman Narayan, Indian Press (Publications), Allahabad, 2, 2, 2, 2, 164 p, bibliography

Sharma Jagadish Saran, 1968, *Mahatma Gandhi: A Descriptive Bibliography*, 2nd edn, S. Chand, Delhi, 38, 650 p

Sharma, P.D., 1978, The Gandhian Model of Development, *Prashasnika* 7(3-4) July-December, p 1-8.

Sharma, S.S., 1969, Gandhian Economics: Some Reflections, *AICC Economic Review* 21 (6-7), October 2, p. 55-58

Sharma, S.S., 1984, Gandhian Heritage in Economic Planning, *Sarvodaya* 31 (9-10) March-April, p 359-366, bibliography, foootnotes

Sharma, Satish, 1988, Inequality and Development: The Gandhian Perspective, *Journal of National Development* 1(1) Summer, p65-83

Sharma, Shashi Prabha, 1992, *Gandhian Holistic Economics*, Concept Publishing Company, New Delhi, 160p, bibliography, Gandhian Studies and Peace Research Series-6

Shastri, P.D., 1984, Gandhi's Theory of Trusteeship: The Way Out, *Gandhi Marg* 6(2) May, p 114-117

Shay, Theodore L., 1955, *Tilak, Gandhi and Arthasastra*, North Western University, PhD thesis

Shenoy, R. Anasuya, 1970, Gandhiji's Ethical Socialism, *Swarajya* 15 (13) September 26, p 11-12.

Sheo Kumar Lal, ed, 1981, *Gandhiji and Village,* Agricole Pub Academy, New Delhi, 101 p

Sheshadri, P., 1969, Gandhian Approach to Co-operation, *Andhra Pradesh* 13(12) October, p 17-19

Shriman Narayan, n.d., *Gandhi Centenary and Our Responsibility*, Government Central Press, Ahmedabad, 44p

Shriman Narayan, 1944, *Gandhian Plan of Economic Development in India*, foreword by Mahatma Gandhi, Padma Publications, Bombay, 8, 115 p, Tables

Shriman Narayan, 1946, *Gandhian Constitution for Free India*, Kitabistan, Allahabad, 136 p

Shriman Narayan, 1948, *Gandhian Plan Reaffirmed*, foreword by Rajendra Prasad, Padma Publications, Bombay, 88p

Shriman Narayan, 1960, *Principles of Gandhian Planning*, foreword by Rajendra Prasad, Kitab Mahal, Allahabad, 8, 342 p, bibliography, footnotes

Shriman Narayan, 1968, *Gandhi: The Man and His Thought*, introduction by Morarji Desai, Publications Division, Government of India, New Delhi, 10, 54 p, Patel Memorial Lecture, 1968

Shriman Narayan, 1968, Gandhian Economic Thought, *Assam Information* 19(9) December, p 7-17, bibliography, footnotes

Shriman Narayan, 1969, Gandhian Economic Thought, *Economic Studies* 9(8) February, p469-480; *Haryana Review* 3(2) April-June, p13-22.

Shriman Narayan, 1969, Patel Memorial Lectures-III: Gandhian Economic Thought, *Indian Workers* 17(14) January 6, p 4-6

Shriman Narayan, 1970, *Gandhian Concept of Decentralised Economy*, Shriman Narayan Agrawal, Ahmedabad, 14p

Shriman Narayan, 1970, Rationale of Decentralised Economy, *Indian Worker* 19(7) November 16, p3-4; *Khadi Gramodyog* 17(1) October, p19-24

Shriman Narayan, 1970, *Relevance of Gandhian Economics*, Navjivan Publishing House, Ahmedabad, vii, 256p

Shriman Narayan, 1973, Gandhiji's Concept of Trusteeship, *Swarajya* 18(16) October 20, p2; 18(18) November 3, p2; 18(19) November 10, p2; 18(20) November 17, p2; 18(21) November 24, p2; 18 (22) December, p2; 18(23) December 8, p2

Shriman Narayan, 1977, Sixth Plan: Time for Gandhian Approach, *Khadi Gramodyog* 23(10) July, p 431-433

Shriman Narayan, *foreword writer*
see Sharma, Bishan Sarup, 1956, *Gandhi as a Political Thinker*

Shukla, Mata Badal, 1983, Gandhi's Views on Rural Industrialisation and Industrial Peace, *Khadi Gramodyog* 30(2) November, p109-112, bibliography, footnotes.

Singh
see also under full name of the author, e.g., Radha Raman Singh

Singh, K.M.P., 1981, Gandhian Concept of Appropriate Technology, *Khadi Gramodyog* 28(3) December, p 153-159, figures

Singh, T.P., 1969, Gandhi on Technology, *Janata* 24 (42-43) November, p 23-27, bibliography, footnotes

Sinha, Chandra Bhusan, *jt author*
see Verma, B.N. and Sinha, Chandra Bhusan, 1987, The Relevance of Gandhian Pattern of Investment Planning, *Gandhi*

Marg

Sinha, M.P., ed, 1970, *Contemporary Relevance of Gandhi*, Nachiketa Publications, Bombay, 18, 110p

Sinha, Ram Vichar, 1986, Fundamental Ingredients of Gandhian Economics: An Appraisal, *Southern Economists* 24(24) April 15, p5-7, bibliography

Sinha, Ram Vichar, 1988, Fundamental Ingredients of Gandhian Economics: An Appraisal, *Khadi Gramodyog* 34(4) January, p171-175

Sinha, Shyam Nandan, 1970, Gandhian Concept of Socialism, *AICC Economic Review* 21(13) February 15, p5-8; March 1, p5-8, bibliography, footnotes

Sinha, Tarakeswari, 1969, Gandhian Economics, *Hindustan Chamber Review* October, p 23-31

Sinha, V.C., 1981, Towards Rural Industrialisation on Gandhian Lines, *Khadi Gramodyog* 27(11) August, p 507-515, footnotes.

Sinha, V.C., 1982, Economic Planning in India: The Gandhian Content, *Khadi Gramodyog* 28(8) May, p375-80

Sinha, V.C., 1982, The Gandhian Content in Economic Planning in India, *Mysore Economic Review* 67(6) June, p15-19 +.

Sinha, V.C., 1982, The New World Order: Gandhiji's Ideas and Their Relevance, *Journal of Gandhian Studies* 9(34) January, p101-105, bibliography

Sinha, V.C., 1983, Gandhian Approach to Balanced Regional Development, *Khadi Gramodyog* 30(3) December, p 121-30, bibliography, tables

Sinha, V.C.,1983, Gandhi's Concept of Bread and Freedom, *Khadi Gramodyog* 29(2) November, p93-97, bibliography

Sinha, V.C., 1983, Industrial Relations : Gandhian Approach, *Khadi Gramodyog* 29(5) February, p 189-193

Sinha, V.C., 1984, Gandhian Thought in Context of Indian Planning, *Khadi Gramodyog* 31(2) November, p 83-89

Sinha, V.C., 1984, Tursteeship and Industrial Relations in India, *Khadi Gramodyog* 30(7) April, p 277-282, bibliography

Sinha, V.C., 1985, Resolving India's Urbanisaton Problems : The Gandhian Way, *Khadi Gramodyog* 31(9) June, p365-373, bibliography, tables

Sinha, V.C., 1985-86, A Gandhian Model of Rural Development, *Journal of Gandhian Studies* 13(51-52) October 1985 - January 1986, p33-39

Sitarama Sarma, N.H.
see Sarma, N.H. Sitarama

Sitaramayya, Bhogaraju Pattabhi
see Pattabhi Sitaramayya, Bhogaraju

Smith, Adam, 1937, *The Wealth of Nations*, Random House, New York

Som Dutt, 1977, The Only Way, *Khadi Gramodyog* 24(1) October, p7-10

Soman, Ramchandra Jaganath, 1957, *Peaceful Industrial Relations : Their Science and Technique*, foreword by Khandubhai K. Desai, Navjivan Publishing House, Ahmedabad, 16, 308p, charts, footnotes, tables

Southern Economist (Periodical), 1977, Return to Gandhian Values, *Southern Economist* 16(8) August 15, p 1-2, editoral

Spratt, Philip, 1939, *Gandhism : An Analysis*, Huxley Press, Madras, 12, 516p, footnotes

Sreckantan Nair, N., 1969, Gandhiji and Industrial Relations in Today's India, *Call* 21(7) Decemebr, p 7-9

Srinivasa, Inguva, 1971, *Gandhi and Development Theory : An Inquiry into the Economic Philosophy of Mahatma Gandhi vis-a-vis Modern Western Theory of Economic Development*, I.S. Publishers, Machilipatnam, 10, 86, 4, 2p, bibliography, tables, footnotes

Srivastava, B.R. *jt editor*
see Vidyarthi, L.P. et al, eds, 1970, *Gandhi and Social Sciences*

Srivastava, C.L., 1987, Gandhian Way : Its Relevance to Our Poverty Eradication Programme, *Southern Economist* 25(20) February, p17-19

Srivastava, Manju, 1986, Economic Philosophy of Gandhiji, *Khadi Gramodyog* 32(8) May, p 375-379, bibliography, footnotes

Srivastava, V.S., 1969, Gandhiji's Approach to Labour Problems, *Indian Worker* 18(9), December 1, p5 +

Stalin, *Selected Works of Stalin*, 13 vols

Stephanian (Periodical), 1948, Mahatma Gandhi Memorial Number, *Stephanian* 40(11) March-April, 8, 75, 20, 32p, illustrations, special issue

Subbarao, M.V., 1985-86, Rural Development through Industrial Decentralisation : A Gandhian Appraoch, *Journal of Gandhian Studies* 13(51-52) October1985-January1986, p57-65

Subedar, Manu, 1936, *Gandhian Economics*, Manu Subedar,

Bombay, 6p

Subedar, Manu, 1939, *Gandhism or Socialiam*, Sanj Vartaman Annual, Bombay, 6p

Subedar, Manu, 1939, Principles of Gandhian Economics, *Rural India* 1(18) June, p499-500

Subhash Chander Dewan
see Dewan, Subhash Chander

Sundaravadivelu, N.D., *foreword writer*
see Mahadevan, T.M.P., ed, 1968, *Relevance of Mahatma Gandhi to the World of Thought*

Sur, A.K., 1977, A Note on Gandhian Economics, *Economics Affairs* 22(9-10) September-October, p 368-371

Suri, Surinder S., 1981, A Gandhian Approach to Employment, *Khadi Gramodyog* 28(2) November, p 119-128

Sury, M.M., 1970, Relevance of Gandhian Economic Thought for Social Transformation, *Political and Economic Review* 1(31) October 7, p 5

Swaminathan, M.S., 1988, Malthus or Mahatma Gandhi : The Choice before Us, *Economic Times*, December 12, p 5, col 3-6

Swarup
see under full name of the author, e.g., Ram Swarup

Tagore, Saumyendra Nath, 1940, *Gandhism and the Labour : Peasant Problem*, Radical Institute, Guwahati, 26p

Tahtinen, Unto,1979, The *Core of Gandhi's Philosophy*, Abhinav Publications, New Delhi

Taimni, I.K., 1974, *Science and Occultism*, Theosophical Publishing House, Madras

Tamm, Gordon, *jt author*
see Hetten, Bjorn and Gordon, Tamm, 1971, The Development Strategy of Gandhian Economics, *Journal of Indian Anthropological Society*

Tara Chand, *foreword writer*
see Mathur, Jaganath Svarup, ed, 1970, *Youth on Gandhi*

Tata, Naval H., 1970, Gandhiji and Labour, *Indian Worker* 19(1) October 5, p 20

Tawney, R.H., 1982, The *Acquisitive Society*, Weatsheaf Book Ltd

Tendulkar, Dinanath Gopal, 1957, *Gandhi in Champaran*, foreword by R.R. Diwakar, Publications Division, Government of India. New Delhi, 8, 4, 115p, illustrations

Tendulkar, Dinanath Gopal, 1960-63, *Mahatma : Life of Mohandas*

Karamchand Gandhi, foreword by Jawaharlal Nehru 2nd rev edn, Publication Division, Government of India, New Delhi, bibliography, 8 vols

Tendulkar, Dinanath Gopal, et al, eds, 1944, *Gandhi : His Life and Work*, introduction by Jawaharlal Nehru, Keshav Bhikaji Dhawale, Bombay, 14, 406p, bibliography, illustrations

Thakar, Vimala, 1970, *Towards Total Transformation*, New Order Publishing, Ahmedabad

Thakar, Vimala, 1984, *Spirituality and Social Action*, Vimala Programs, California, Berkeley

Thanu, L.C., 1980, Gandhiji's Doctrine of Trusteeship, *Indian Review* 75(11) February, p 50-57

Thanu, L.C., 1982, Gandhi and the New World Order, *Indian Review* 77(11) February, p 9-11

Thanu, L.C., 1983, Gandhi and the New World Order, *Sarvodaya* 31(12) July-August, p 21-24

Thanu, L.C.,1984, Relevance of Gandhian Thought of Economic Growth, *Sarvodaya* 31(7-8) January-February, p 289-294, bibliography

Thanu, L.C., 1985, Bread and Freedom : The Gandhian Way, *Sarvodaya* 33(5-6) November-December, p 230-236

Thanu, L.C., 1985, Gandhian Approach to Rural Development, *Sarvodaya* 33(3-4) September-October, p 123-128

Thanu, L.C., 1985-86, Gandhian Approach to Rural Development, *Journal of Gandhian Studies* 13(51-52) October 1985- January 1986, p10-16

Thanu, L.C., 1986, Bread and Freedom : The Gandhian Way, *Sarvodaya* 33(7-8) January-February, p302-306

Thanu, L.C., 1986, Relevance of Gandhian Thought to Economic Growth, *Gandhi Marg* 7(11) February, p780-784; *Sarvodaya* 34(1-2) July-August, p34-39

Thapar, S.D., 1974, Relevance of Gandhi to India's Current Problems, *Voluntary Action* 16(4-5) July-October, p1-4

Thiagarajan, K., 1977, Gandhiji Concept of Trusteeship, *Modem Review* 141(11) January, p50-52

Thiagarajan, K., 1977, Impact of Gandhian Economics on Indian Economic Development, *Khadi Gramodyog* 23(6) March, p270-273

Thiagarajan, K., 1978, Gandhi Blueprint for Social Progress, *Haryana Review* 12(1) January, p15 +

Thimmaiah,. G., 1971, Gandhian Economics Re-examined, *Khadi Gramodyog* 17(11) August, p669-672

Thomson, R.M., 1980, Gandhi at Sevagram : India in a Village, *Gandhi Marg* 2(8) November, p431-452, footnotes

Tikekar, Indu B., 1966, *Philosophy of Sarvodaya*, Banaras University, PhD thesis

Tikekar, Indu B., 1970, *Integral Revolution : An Analytical Study of Gandhian Thought*, introduction by P.Y. Deshpande, Sarva Seva Sangh Prakashan, Varanasi, 18, 2, 266p, bibliography

Tinbergen, J., 1982, A New Life Style and Gandhian Thought, *Journal of Gandhian Studies* 9(34) January, p69-75, bibliography

Tirumalal, T.D., 1975, Gandhiji's Critique on Capitalism, *Swarajya* 20(7) August 16, p9-10

Tripathi, D., *jt author*
see Audholia, B.S. and Tripathi, D., 1959, *Gleanings from Gandhian Thought;* Herbert, G.S. and Tripathi, D., 1973, Gandhiji on Poverty, *Sarvodaya*

Tripathi, K.P., 1969, Gandhian Projection in Labour Movement, *Indian Worker* 18(1) October 6, p8

Tripathi, K.P., 1980, Gandhiji and Labour Movement, *Indian Worker* 29(1) October, p7-8

Tripathi, K.P., 1981, Gandhian Socialism, *Indian Worker* 29(19) February 9, p4-5

Tripathi, S.D., 1966, Economic Philosophy of Gandhi, *Gandhi Marg* 10(4) October, p326-332, bibliography, footnotes

Tripathi, S.D., 1973, Experiments in Trusteeship Management, *Gandhi Marg* 17(4) October, p310-321, bibliography

Tripathi, Satyendra, 1980, The Gandhian Approach to the Rural Energy Crisis : A Case Study, *Gandhi Marg* 2(4) July, p 222-272

Trivedi, H.N., ed, 1969, *Gandhian Trade Union Movement*, INTUC, 72p

Turnbull, Shann, 1985, Trusteeship as Technique for Sustainable Industrialisation, *Gandhi Marg* 7(8-9) November-December, p634-643

Umaram, R.I., 1985-86, Gandhian Approach to Rural Development, *Journal of Gandhian Studies* 13(51-52) October 1985-January 1986, p17-21

Unnithan, T.K.N., 1956, *Gandhi and Free India*, Vora & Co, Bombay, 16, 266p, bibliography

Upadhyay, M.N., 1975, Gandhian Way for Removing Economic

Inequality, *Khadi Gramodyog* 21(5) February, p 233-237, tables

Upadhyaya, R.B., 1977, *Soical Responsibility of Business and the Trusteeship Theory of Mahatma Gandhi*, Sterling, New Delhi, 385p

Upadhyaya, Deendayal, 1979, *The Integral Approach*, Deendayal Research Institute, New Delhi

Uppal, J.S., 1957, Economic Thought of Mahatma Gandhi, *Rural India* 20(10) November, p395-398

Vakil, C.N., *foreword writer*
see Raval, M.N., et al, eds, 1971, *Summay Report of Discussions and Text of Papers Presented at the Seminar...*

Varadaraja Rao, Vijayendra Kasturi Ranga
see Rao, V.K.R.V.

Varma
see also Verma

Varma, Ravindra, 1985, Gandhi's Theory of Trusteeshsip : An Eassy in Understanding, *Gandhi Marg* 7(8-9) November-December, p509-539, bibliography, footnotes

Varma, Vishwanath Prasad, 1959, *Political Philosophy of Mahatma Gandhi and Sarvodaya*, Lakshmi Narain Agarwal, Agra, 4, 2, 4, 308, 3p, bibliography, footnotes

Vasudevan, K., 1969, *Gandhian Economics*, Bharatiya Vidya Bhawan, Bombay, 14, 57p, footnotes

Vaswani, K.N., 1955, *Glimpses of Gandhi and Gandhism*, foreword by Ram Narayan Chaudhry, K.N. Vaswani, New Delhi, 84p

Vaswani, K.N., 1979, Relevance of Gandhian Economics Today, *Khadi Gramodyog* 25(4) January, p185-196, footnotes

Vaswani, K.N., 1980, The Challenges of Poverty in India : Gandhi's Answer, *Khadi Gramodyog* 26(7) April, p289-294, footnotes

Vepa, Ram K., 1975, *New Technology : A Gandhian Concept*, Gandhi Book House, 375p

Vepa, Ram K., 1977, Development of Backward Economy Relevance of Gandhian Technology, *Indian Journal of Public Administration* 23(3) July-September, p579-594

Verma
see also Varma

Verma, B.N. and Sinha, Chandra Bhusan, 1987, The Relevance of Gandhian Pattern of Investment Planning, *Gandhi Marg* 8(12) March, p 752-758, bibliography, footnotes

Verma, P.R. Rameshwari, 1978, Gandhian Economic Thought

General Exposition, *Vishleshan* 4(1) March, p 25-38, footnotes

Vezhavendan, K., 1970, Gandhiji and Labour, *Indian Worker* 19(1) October 5, p 21-22

Vidyarthi, L.P., et al, eds, 1970, *Gandhi and Social Sciences : Papers of the Seminar on Gandhi's Contribution to Social Sciences, Ranchi, 1970*, Bookline, New Delhi, 16, 296p, footnotes

Vinoba
see Bhave, Vinoba

Vinod Narayan Singh, *jt author*
see Sen Gupta, S. and Vinod Narayan Singh, Gandhian Economics : Its Relevance Today, *Southern Economust; Khadi Gramodyog*

Vir
see under full name of the author, e.g., Kamal Vir

Visvabharati Quarterly (Periodical), 1969-70, Gandhi Number, ed by Sisir Kumar Ghose, *Visvabharati Quarterly*, 35, May 1969-April 1970, 2, 250p, illustrations, special issue

Vyas, Madan, 1966, *Economic Philosophy of Mahatma Gandhi and Its Application to Economic Planning in India*, Vikram University, PhD, thesis

Vyas, Madan, 1969, *Economic Philosophy of Mahatma Gandhi*, Popular Prakashan, Bombay

Vyas, Narendra, 1981, Towards a Saner Civilisation, *Economic Times* (Supplement) October 4, p 11, col 1-5 +

Waiz, Thomas, 1986, Organizational Behaviour and Non-violent Management : A Gandhian Analysis, *Gandhi Marg* 7(11) February, p 756-767

Wellock, Wilfred, n.d., *India's Social Revolution Led by Mahatma Gandhi and Now Vinoba Bhave*, Wilfred Wellock, Preston, 32p

Wilber, Ken, ed, 1982, *The Holographic Paradigm and Other Paradoxes*, Shambhala Publications, London

Yadava, T.N., *jt author*
see Rai, Hira and Yadav, T.N., 1970, Biblography on Gandhian Economics, *Interdiscipline*

Yojana (Periodical), 1976, The Relevance of the Mahatma, *Yojana* 20(17) October 1, p3, editorial

Yojana (Periodical), 1977, Returning to Gandhi, *Yojana* 21(15) September 1, p3-4, editorial

Young India (Periodical), 1923, *Young India, 1919-22*, Ganesan, Madras

Young India (Periodical), 1927, *Young India, 1924-26*, Ganesan, Madras

Young India (Periodical), 1935, *Young India, 1927-28*, Ganesan, Madras

Zakir Hussani, *foreword writer*
see Dharma Vir, 1967, *Gandhi Bibliography*

Index